Praise for *Haunted Homeland* . . .

"In the new book *Haunted Homeland* by Michael Norman, you'll read about ghost sightings around the United States. . . . Norman writes of malevolent specters, bells from the underworld, poltergeists with mean streaks, and dozens of other terrifying tales. A few years ago in Mississippi, there stood a mansion that wasn't very old but was very haunted. The family that lived there heard agonizing moans and snarling dogs, and the youngest son once complained about a 'bogeyman' near his closet. After the house burned down under suspicious circumstances, one former owner was contacted by a spirit who made a chilling demand. In North Carolina, workers found bits of bone and cloth in an unmarked grave. Did those earthly remains belong to the spirit who pulled the bedclothes from the bed of the newest owners of a nearby mansion? Or could it be the ghost who followed the female owner from her old apartment to her new home? So you say that none of this scares you. It's only a bunch of stories, right? Just a bunch of overactive imaginations, huh? Well, then—if you dare—read the story of the Texas ghost steer with an eerie brand on his backside. Check out the story of the Maryland family who allowed a psychic to perform a séance. Settle in with the Oklahoma tale of the woman who was haunted by the guilt-inducing ghost of the man she loved and murdered. Ah, there's nothing like a dim light, a cold night, and a good ghost story. These are perfect."
—*Herald Standard* (Uniontown, PA)

"Michael Norman has got stories that will turn a trick-or-treater ghostly white. His are the real deal ghosts, goblins, and ghouls—or so some believe—that don't wear costumes or come out annually for a sugar buzz. They are there creaking floors, walking through doors, and doing what they dang well please whenever they want for as long as they want."
—*Pioneer Press* (St. Paul, MN)

"*Haunted Homeland* is a nightstand book, something to read a couple of short bits from before closing one's eyes."
—"The Agony Column," *trashotron.com*

HAUNTED HOMELAND

HAUNTED AMERICA BOOKS
FROM TOM DOHERTY ASSOCIATES

Haunted America
Historic Haunted America
Haunted Heritage
Haunted Homeland

HAUNTED HOMELAND

Michael Norman

TOR®

A TOM DOHERTY ASSOCIATES BOOK
NEW YORK

HAUNTED HOMELAND

The author gratefully acknowledges permission to quote excerpts from the following material:

Dixon, S. C. "Something Cold at the Foot of the Stairs," *Emporia Journal*, n.d. Used by permission of the author.

Hayes, Joe. *La Llorona: The Weeping Woman*, El Paso: Texas, Cinco Puntos Press, 1987. Used by permission of Cinco Puntos Press.

Helm, Mike, *Oregon's Ghosts and Monsters,* Eugene, Oregon: Rainy Day Press, 1983. Used by permission of Rainy Day Press.

A Tor Book
Published by Tom Doherty Associates, LLC
175 Fifth Avenue
New York, NY 10010

www.tor.com

Tor® is a registered trademark of Tom Doherty Associates, LLC.

ISBN-13: 978-0-7653-4105-1
ISBN-10: 0-7653-4105-0

First Edition: September 2006
First Mass Market Edition: October 2007

Printed in the United States of America

0 9 8 7 6 5 4 3 2 1

This book is dedicated to
my son James Norman,
and his wife, Samah Fahmy,
with love and gratitude from Dad.

Contents

CONTENTS   xi

CANADA

Acknowledgments

COUNTLESS INDIVIDUALS, ORGANIZATIONS, and institutions have provided assistance as I compiled the stories you will find in this book. Many of them must remain anonymous at their own request, but others are listed below:

Alaska Department of Natural Resources, Division of Parks and Outdoor Recreation; Cherie P. Barnett, Surratts-Clinton Library, Clinton, Maryland; W. Ritchie Benedict, Calgary, Alberta, Canada; Brodhead, Wisconsin, Chamber of Commerce; Brother Timothy Arthur, O.F.M., Santa Barbara, California; California State Military Museum, Fort Hunter Liggett, California; Carmel Mission, California; Chalmer Davee Library, University of Wisconsin–River Falls; City of Sitka, Alaska, Convention and Visitors Bureau; Chris Cowman, Washington, D.C.; City of Corpus Christi, Texas; S. C. Dixon, Emporia, Kansas; Cliff Ensor, correspondence with the author, May 1998, January 2001; Columbia University Libraries, New York; Scottie Dayton, Madison, Wisconsin; Department of Natural Resources, State of Maryland; Diocese of Corpus Christi, Texas; East Troy Area Chamber of Commerce, East Troy, Wisconsin; Rita Ann Freeman, Green Bay, Wisconsin; Roswitha Heuer, Kewaunee, Wisconsin; Ron Heuer, Kewaunee, Wisconsin; Federal Writers Project (Illinois) Collection, Illinois State Historical Society; Diane B. Feheley, Maryland Forest and Parks Service; Franklin College, Franklin, Indiana; Virginia Gregory, Gulfport, Mississippi; Mary Hammen, Wilmington (Illinois) Public Library; Jean Hillaire, Fort Hunter Liggett, Jolon, California; Historic Hotels of America, Washington, D.C.; Hotel Boscobel, Boscobel, Wisconsin; Idaho State University, Pocatello; Indiana University Folklore Archives, various materials, Bloomington, Indiana; Innu Nation, Canada; Iowa State University, Ames; Patty Ostberg, Minnesota State Capitol, St. Paul, Minnesota;

Karsten Inn, Kewaunee, Wisconsin; Kentuckiana Digital Library, Transylvania University; Dr. Charles Lauterbach, Boise State University, Boise, Idaho; LeClair Grier Lambert, St. Paul, Minnesota; Heather Lynch, Office of Communications and Marketing, Maryland Department of Natural Resources; Lynda Majarian, University of Vermont, Communications Department; Bruce Micnski, Lake County (Michigan) Historical Society; Minnesota History Center, St. Paul, Minnesota; Minnesota State Legislature, Office of Public Information; Kathleen Mortensen, Boise State University, Boise, Idaho; Murray State University, Kentucky; Museum of North Idaho, Coeur d'Alene; Muskogee (Oklahoma) Public Library; National Park Service; National Register of Historic Places; National Trust for Historic Preservation, Washington, D.C.; North Idaho College; Old South Mountain Inn, Boonsboro, Maryland; Penn State University–Mont Alto; Point Lookout State Park, Maryland; Al Preston, Ranger, South Mountain Recreation Area, Maryland; San Diego Historical Society; Thomas Schuller, Kewaunee Historical Society, Kewaunee, Wisconsin; *Seattle Press Times*, January 10, 1892; Richard Senate, Ventura, California; Michael Speiker, Minnesota State Capitol, St. Paul; Stagecoach Inn Museum, Newbury Park, California; Surratt House Museum, Clinton, Maryland; Suzi Taylor, King City, California; Mary Frances Tipton, University of Montevallo, Alabama; Transylvania University Archives, Lexington, Kentucky; Jennifer Ulrich, Columbia University Archives; University of Montevallo (Alabama) Undergraduate Bulletin; Joseph Varno; Marla Vizdal, Archives Specialist, Western Illinois University, Macomb, Illinois; Greg Walker, Spring Hill College, Mobile, Alabama; Washington County Free Library, Hagerstown, Maryland; Wayland Baptist University, Plainview, Texas; Western Illinois University Archives, Macomb, Illinois; Olive Wollesen, Lockwood, California; WPA Historical Survey of The Monterey Peninsula Archives; Holly Yingling, Penn State University–Mont Alto; James A. Zimmerman, University of Wisconsin–River Falls.

A special note of thanks should go to my agent, Mark E. Lefebvre, for his encouragement and enthusiasm for this project, and to Brian Thomsen, Deborah Brown, and Ed Chapman. To all of you, my sincere gratitude.

Numerous individuals and organizations provided information. I have endeavored to acknowledge their contributions above, but should I have missed someone, I apologize, and will include that information in future editions as it is brought to my attention.

Michael Norman
September 2006

Author's Note

The names of some individuals in this book have been changed either at their own request or to ensure their privacy. Those names are marked with an asterisk.

Some events portrayed in this book have been dramatized or modified for the purposes of clarity or continuity.

The author makes no claim or stipulation as to the authenticity of the stories included in this book.

The ownership of some buildings and properties mentioned in this book may have changed since publication. Please be respectful of individuals' privacy.

HAUNTED
HOMELAND

UNITED STATES

1
The Lady in Blue

When the footpads quail
at the night bird's wail,
and black dogs bay
at the moon.
Then is the specters' holiday—
then is the ghosts' high noon.

—William S. Gilbert

BY THE SIDE of my bed, not farther away than I could have touched her with my outstretched hand, stood a beautiful woman. She was dressed in a pale blue silk dress, with a satin sash of the same color tied around a tapering narrow waist, and falling in great lengths down over the unnaturally large hips, almost to the bottom of the wide expansive crinoline skirt.

The extremely décolleté corsage exhibited a lovely neck and snowy, finely chiseled shoulders, while the arms were covered with very full bishop sleeves, with narrow bands at the wrists.

On her black hair, so black that it seemed almost blue, and which hung down in corkscrew curls on both sides of a most beautiful face, was resting a silver band in the shape of a tiara or crown. Her black eyes were so large and piercing, that they seemed almost like two burning coals, but as she closed them for a moment, as with a painful movement, there came over the face an expression of despair, sorrow, and suffering so intense, as I have never seen depicted on human face, save in the wonderful painting of the Mater Dolorosa in the Royal Museum at Madrid.

In her left hand the lady in blue held a silver candlestick, in which was a burning wax candle. With the right she made several quick, imperious motions, as if pointing over her shoulder to the door of the room.

She then turned. And with her right hand around the flame of the candle, as if sheltering it from the draft, the magnificent Juno-like form slowly glided over the polished floor to the door, which opened as in obedience to her silent command, and half closed again behind her.

THUS BEGINS ONE of the earliest poignant descriptions of Sitka, Alaska's, legendary Lady in Blue, a Russian princess who is said to have haunted the city's long-vanished Baranof Castle, which once dominated that city's spectacular waterfront. Dating from 1838 and built on the remains of an earlier structure, the Castle was both the home and seat of authority for the Governor General of The Russian American Company until the 1867 sale of Alaska to the United States for $7.2 million, a purchase derided as Seward's Folly. The Castle was the site of the actual transfer of Alaskan possession from Russia to the United States on October 18, 1867, a date still commemorated as Alaska Day.

Hardly resembling the stone and plaster fortifications of the Old World, the Castle was actually a four-square, rambling, three-story wood-framed mansion surrounded by a stockade fence with guard towers at the corners. A cupola crowned the complex. Inside, however, were beautifully appointed meeting and dining rooms, bedrooms for the governor's family and guests, and other public areas. Though the Castle may have lacked the impressiveness of a Bavarian palace, it more than made up for it through its location atop a sixty-foot-high rocky promontory with an expansive view of Sitka Sound and its scores of islets. The Castle fell into disuse after the United States government took control of the territory. It burned to the ground in 1898 just as renovation work was beginning.

SITKA, ON THE southeast coast of Alaska along the famed Inland Passage, retains much of the rugged allure and the rich natural resources that first brought Russians to its shores two centuries ago. What they found was a rocky landscape surrounded by splendid, nearly inaccessible mountains and endless pine forests. They also discovered that the Tlingit people had occupied the region for millennia, harvesting their livelihoods from the forests and seas. They called their community Shee Atika, or "people of Shee." (Sitka is a contraction of the original Tlingit.)

The Russians arrived in 1799 under the command of Alexander Baranof, manager of the Russian American Company and eponym of Baranof Island upon which Sitka is situated. The Tlingits did not submit gracefully to the newly arrived Russians and several fierce battles between the two were fought over the next several years. The Russians finally prevailed and in 1804 renamed the settlement New Archangel.

A building boom replaced the earlier clan houses on Castle Hill with Russian-built fortresses. The settlement prospered for the seventy years Russians controlled the region; Los Angeles and San Francisco were mere outposts when Sitka became known as the "Paris of the Pacific" to whalers and fur traders. In the 1840s Sitka and the surrounding region had grown to over 2,000 inhabitants and boasted, among other attractions, a Russian Orthodox cathedral and a scientific weather station.

The Imperial Russian flag was taken down for good in 1867 when representatives of the United States and Russia signed documents at Baranof Castle transferring ownership of Alaska to the federal government. The Russian influence gradually waned as the U. S. began its stewardship of the region. Sitka lost its status as the center of Alaskan government and commerce as Juneau, Fairbanks, and Anchorage were developed over the ensuing century. Alaska was granted statehood in 1959.

Today, Sitka retains vestiges of its Native, Russian, and American histories; over thirty locations there are either national historic places or landmarks.

Built in 1914, the Alaska Native Brotherhood Hall is the community center of the traditional Tlingit village. The Sitka National Historical Park preserves and interprets the site of a Tlingit Indian Fort and the final battle fought between the Russians and the Natives in 1804. The Tlingit Cultural Center teaches Native culture to both Tlingit and non-Tlingit.

The Russian period is represented by numerous legacies including Castle Hill, the site of recent archaeological excavations; a Russian military block house; an original 1835 log cache building; and a collection of exquisite Russian art and church treasures at a reconstructed St. Michael's Cathedral on the site of the original Orthodox Church. During the summer, Sitka women in authentic Russian and Ukrainian costumes perform traditional dances at the Harrigan Centennial Hall.

More recent additions to Sitka include a Raptor Center dedicated to pioneering efforts to protect Alaska's native birds of prey; a whale park dedicated in 1995, and Japonski Island, a World War II-era military installation now operated by a collection of local, state, and federal agencies.

Baranof Castle was actually a latecomer to the most commanding site on Sitka Sound. The hill has long been the central landmark in the region, and one of the most famous in Alaska. Archaeological evidence suggests that the Tlingit lived on the Hill at least as long ago as A.D. 1,000. In excavations during the late 1990s, researchers found an astonishing two tons—300,000 pieces—of artifacts which are still being catalogued at the University of Alaska Museum, Fairbanks.

During the later half of the nineteenth century, the Castle fell victim to the elements. A few events were held there over the years, but for the most part it became a ruin. The federal government tried to rescue it in 1893, and completed some remodeling that enabled it to become the seat of the Sitka District Court. But on March 17, 1894, a suspicious fire broke out near the judge's chambers. The wood framing had become so dried out that the Castle burned like a tinderbox. Firefighters could only focus their attention on saving several nearby structures. Suspicions arose that an arsonist had wanted to destroy court records relating to financial irregularities that a judge had been examining earlier that day, but no charges were ever brought in the case.

JUST WHEN THE ghost of Baranof Castle first gained credence is difficult to determine. Author Eliza Scidmore described a trip she took to the Sitka region in her 1885 book, *Alaska, Its Southern Coast and the Sitkan Archipelago*. She visited Baranof Castle, then little more than a shambles, and listed the ghost among its "attractions," although she thought the story had been "concocted . . . to keep sailors and marauders away at night and to entertain the occasional tourist." She did describe the legend as it was repeated to her:

> The signal officer has rescued two rooms on the ground floor for his use, but otherwise the only tenant of the castle is the ghost of a beautiful Russian whose sad story is closely modeled on that of *The Bride of Lammermoor*. She haunts the drawing room, its northwest chamber, where she was murdered, and paces the governor's cabinet, where the swish of her ghostly wedding gown chills every listener's blood. Twice a year she walks unceasingly and wrings her jeweled hands.

The poet Henry E. Haydon used *The Song of Hiawatha* as his model when he composed a saga of the doomed princess and her lover in an 1891 book.

In December 1888, *Alaskan Magazine* carried a brief letter from a Sitka resident describing his experience at the decaying Castle only the month before:

> Last Saturday, November 24, I paid my first visit to Baranoff (sic) Castle. As usual, the weather was rather rainy and dismal. I first went into the ballroom and, with my back to the door, was looking at the decorations in the window left there from the last ball. Suddenly, a sound of something in motion attracted my attention; turning, I heard a noise as if of a man with heavy shoes ascending the first flight of stairs. I immediately went to the foot of the stairway and continued to hear the noise, this time as if it were on the second flight, and still on it seemed to go upward until it reached the roof, when it ceased. I then went upstairs and searched every room, but could find nothing in the shape of a human being. Subsequently I continued my search to the very top of the building and still could find no one.
>
> I do not believe in ghosts, but I cannot imagine what caused the noise. Someone might suggest 'rats'; if this be

the case, the rodent in question must have weighed about one-hundred-and-fifty pounds. I believe that on the occasion of the ball of the Boys in Blue, the man on watch heard noises during the night, but what I heard was in the afternoon, about two o'clock.

The editor noted that the author of the letter was "well and favorably known here, with veracity that is unquestioned . . ."

Author and historian Clarence Andrews devotes a single paragraph and a footnote to the legend in his 1922 tome *The Story of Sitka*.

"There is a legend of a beautiful princess whose ghost haunted the Castle for many years. The story has been told by many at different times and is one of the romantic tales that cluster around the old metropolis of the fur trading days. Her lover was sent away or killed through the influence of an *ober offitzer* (under officer) who sought her hand in marriage. Eliza Ruhamah Scidmore, who wrote so delightfully of Sitka in her journeys in Alaska in 1883, says that, 'By tradition the Lady in Black (sic) was the daughter of one of the old governors. On her wedding night she disappeared from the ballroom in the midst of the festivities, and after a long search was found dead in one of the small drawing rooms.' "

Andrews then adds an intriguing footnote, a portion of which points to some similarities with what he claimed were actual historical events:

"There is a strange fact which gives some color to the story. In the Russian American Company's Archives now on file in the State Department, Washington, D.C., under the date of September 23, 1833, a letter from St. Petersburg refers to a report of Baron Wrangell of November 30, 1831, which reported the death of under officer Paul Bulkof, and implicating one Colonel Borusof. Unfortunately, the records of 1831 are missing and so the report cannot be had. Baron Wrangel's daughter, Mary, died during his stay in Sitka."

However, another writer and authority on the Sitka ghost, Richard A. Pierce, maintained that Wrangel's daughter died in infancy and that Andrews's source for the report on the death of Bulkof was never identified.

Although writer Pierce and others believe the story is all or mostly fictional, it has gained a status as one of Southeast Alaska's premier ghost stories, and certainly one that will not be put to bed easily. Further, with evidence suggesting that the ground on which Baranof Castle stood has been the site of human settlement for millennia, the likelihood of at least one ghost prowling the site is not too far-fetched.

THE GHOST OF Baranof Castle was forever enshrined in the Alaskan imagination by John W. Arctander, a now largely forgotten turn-of-the-twentieth-century writer and novelist of such books as *The Apostle of Alaska* and *Guilty?* But it was *The Lady in Blue: A Sitka Romance,* published in 1911, that gave the fullest telling of the legendary lady.

Although writer Pierce lacerated Arctander's version of history in a lengthy critique—". . . there are so many holes in Arctander's tale that it must be dismissed as almost entirely fiction"—most of what is recited about the lady in blue seems to come from Arctander's work.

Arctander's tale is told in the first person by an unnamed narrator. He is at dinner one evening at the home of a married couple of his acquaintance. The story appears to take place somewhere in the "lower 48," though the location is unnamed. The couple quizzes the narrator (Arctander?) about his Alaskan adventures. When he talks about his visit to Sitka, and its dramatic beauty, the couple exclaims upon the coincidence and then gives him a manuscript purportedly written by the woman's father, a U.S. Army chaplain named Cramer who was assigned to accompany Army troops when they were sent to Sitka in 1867 to participate in the ceremonies turning over control of Alaska. The narrator settles down to read the chaplain's memoirs.

They purport to tell of the chaplain's experiences in the settlement. Among the events he recounts is an evening he spent at Baranof Castle as the guest of the Russian governor. When the other guests continue dancing into the night, Chaplain Cramer wishes to retire for the evening and asks to be excused from the festivities. He is shown to his chambers by an elderly

Russian priest who mentions in passing that this is "Princess Olga Feodorovna's bedchamber." The priest mysteriously mentions that the "castle is haunted," but does not to go into detail. He wishes to ensure the army chaplain a restful sleep. Cramer tells him he doesn't believe in ghosts anyway.

The visiting clergyman awakens some hours later to find at his bedside the lovely wisp in a silk dress. He watches her for several moments until she turns and drifts from the room. Rather than staying put, he goes after her:

Although it seemed impossible for me to make the slightest move while she was standing near my bed, now—that she had disappeared behind the door—I felt an irresistible impulse take possession of me to follow her out in the hall, and, if possible, fathom the mystery.

I jumped out of bed, and ran to the door as quickly as I could, for fear that she would disappear without my knowing whither.

Reaching the door I was surprised to find it closed, but it readily responded to my eager grasp, and letting my eyes flash first in one direction and then in another, I felt my heart beat faster upon discovering the lady in blue gliding silently along the corridor in the direction of the great salon, from which were wafted toward the place where I stood, the measures of a stately minuet. She was still shading the flame of the candle with her hand.

Then suddenly I lost sight of her and of the candle, which had been glittering like a distant star in the dark hallway.

I hastened my steps and was soon rewarded. Only a short distance and an open door showed a staircase leading upward. From six or seven steps up her candle threw just enough light to show the stairs.

I ran up the steps, determined that she should not escape me.

As I reached the landing, I observed her by the window on the opposite side of a large glass cupola, peering out into the dark night, shading her eyes with her beautiful and transparent hand.

Oh, the sadness and sorrow in that face!

I was about to speak, to comfort her, to remind her of the great Master, who always had a kind word or a tender look for a sorrow as deep and as seemingly inconsolable as hers, to ask her to turn to the cross for her comfort and her consolation, when I heard coming from down below, from out of the darkness of the night, in the deep basso tones of the Russian sentry stationed on the bastion in front of the castle, these words: "One o'clock and all is well."

As if these words of human voice had awakened the lady in blue from out of a trance, I observed a sudden tremor in the hand shading her eyes.

An awful, unearthly cry of anguish resounded in my ears.

The candlestick fell to the floor with a crash and all was—darkness.

Determined to do what I could to assist the sad-eyed, sorrowing lady, I crept cautiously across the tiles over to the place where I had seen her stand but a moment before, and groped around in the dark. My hands touched the panes of the window, against which she had leaned, but she had vanished with the flickering flame.

I spoke, trying to make my voice as tender as possible, offering her comfort and help in her trouble, but there was no response—only my voice seemed rusty and unnatural. From the panes of the cupola my words of comfort came back, as if they had struck a stone wall, harsh and unfeeling. They sounded in my own ears like a hollow mockery.

I have always had the impression, that even in the dark, I could perceive the presence of a human being. I now experienced the opposite, a feeling of utter solitude, of lonesomeness—of being left utterly alone.

I was satisfied that the apparition, whether human or spirit, had gone out of my conscious existence.

My next thought was how to get back to my room. Cautiously feeling my way in the utter darkness, I finally succeeded in locating the landing and after descending what seemed to me a great many steps, I found myself in the corridor leading to my chamber.

They were now dancing a gay polka in the dancing hall, and its strains seemed to chase me in the opposite direction toward the door of my bed chamber, which I fortunately found standing open, the candles in the candelabra on the mantel still burning dimly.

After spending a restless night in his room, Cramer seeks out the priest, who takes one look at the chaplain and recognizes that he's seen the castle ghost.

"I read it in (your) face," the Orthodox priest says. "It is pale, as if the color of the ghost was reflected in it. There is disquietude in (your) eyes. The little father is not so sure any longer, that there are no ghosts."

The chaplain—nicknamed Little Father by the Russian—agrees that after his experience the night before he is no longer sure that ghosts do not exist.

The priest quizzes Chaplain Cramer:

"She had a candle?"
"Yes."
"She protected it with her hand from the draft?"
"Yes."
"She ascended the stairs?"
"Yes."
"She shaded her eyes and peered out into the night toward the South, where the one hundred and thirty forest-clad little isles of Sitka lie sleeping?"
"Yes, she did."
"She dropped the candle, did she not, and shrieked, and was gone?"
"Just so!—But how can you know, father?"
"You are not the only one who has seen the 'Lady in Blue of Baranof Castle,' little father. That is the explanation. You did see a real ghost last night, as sure as there is a God in Israel."

THE PRIEST THEN tells the story of Princess Olga Feodorovna.

———

THE BEAUTIFUL YOUNG woman was the niece of the elderly Count Adolphus Etholen, who had been sent by Tsar Nicholas I in 1840 to be governor of Sitka and of The Russian American Company. He brought his much younger wife and his orphaned niece, the Princess Olga. The priest described her as "one of the richest and most beautiful heiresses in the Tsar's dominion." She was "dark as the raven's glossy wing, or as a starless night."

Soon after young Olga's arrival, every single man—and some not so single—in the Russian delegation fell instantly under her spell. It is said men fought duels in the hopes she would favor the victor with "a look from her black eagle eyes."

But Princess Olga was as personally reserved as her beauty was impossible to turn away from. Yet, she favored no one soldier, sailor, or diplomat.

Until, that is, Victor Gregorovitch Schupkin landed in Sitka.

Described by the priest as "a young nobleman of fine bearing and appearance and a midshipman in the Tsar's navy," Victor Gregorovitch and the princess saw one another across the floor at an officer's club reception. It was to be a momentous occasion for them both. He was smitten, of course, as was every other eligible young man there. But he saw something more in the princess's eyes, something that told him she found him to be her favorite among all those present. He was correct, for that very night she took aside her beloved old nurse and whispered giddily she had found the man with whom she wanted to spend all her days.

In the days and weeks that followed, Princess Olga and midshipman Victor Gregorovitch only met in secret to share their devotion to one another. It is said they rendezvoused at a lovers' lane, near the Indian River outside Sitka, which was still in existence a century after these events.

Governor Etholen evidently did not object to the match.

But soon there came a man who would despoil all that was sweet and romantic about this loving courtship.

His name was Prince Ivan Sergovitch Peploff, a much older Russian nobleman. A man who the young princess and her lover wished had never been born.

Prince Ivan Sergovitch had squandered three fortunes in his debauched lifestyle of carousing, gambling, and drinking before escaping to Sitka. The prince had lost his properties and even his family. His wife had been driven to suicide.

So he had come to Alaska partly to start over again, but also for a far more sinister reason. The prince and Governor Etholen had been close friends in St. Petersburg during the 1820s. In fact, he had met Princess Olga in the same city before she left for Alaska with her uncle.

The prince made it known that he and the governor shared many daring escapades during their youth in St. Petersburg. Adventures that included, it was whispered among the Sitka Russians, memberships in a secret revolutionary society dedicated to the overthrow of the Russian monarchy. Further, Governor Etholen may have been the trigger man in the assassination of a prominent general, acting on the society's behalf. No one knew that the governor had such a dark secret, especially one that would have landed him in jail or worse should it have been revealed.

But Prince Ivan knew, of course, and made the most of it.

He made himself a persistent presence at Baranof Castle. He told everyone he met what old and great friends the governor and he were and of how he looked forward to spending many hours with the governor reliving their youthful exploits. And perhaps reminding him of the debt he owed for silence.

Even though he was more than twice her age, the prince also rekindled his desire for Princess Olga. When in time Prince Ivan made it known that he wanted the princess's hand in marriage, the governor could not easily object, even though he knew his niece and the midshipman were very nearly betrothed.

The governor took Princess Olga aside and demanded that she marry his old "friend." She refused. He then ordered her to stop seeing Victor Gregorovitch. He banned the young navy man from the Castle and sought on any occasion possible to belittle him in front of his peers.

The lovers continued to meet in secret, but their trysts became known to the governor and he determined that unless the couple was split *permanently* a marriage to Prince Ivan would not be possible.

Thus a plan was hatched. A Russian sailing ship was to set out on a mission to force Natives south along the Alaskan coast to surrender to the Tsar's rule. A naval superior acting at the governor's behest sent Victor Gregorovitch to the ship captain with a "secret" communication. Once aboard, however, the midshipman was locked below deck and the ship sailed, all according to the governor's wicked strategy.

If Governor Etholen thought this would move Princess Olga to give up and marry Prince Ivan, he was to be greatly disappointed.

She said she would never marry the old prince and cried that she would rather die alone than live without Victor Gregorovitch. Weeks and then months went by. No word ever came back to her from her lover, yet she still refused her uncle's protestations.

Prince Ivan grew restless. He knew that at his age he might not have many more years. He threatened to reveal the governor's secret unless his niece once and for all agreed to the marriage.

The governor went to the local bishop and asked him to approach Princess Olga. He made it clear that unless his niece married Prince Ivan he would be forced to resign and quite possibly be imprisoned, their family name ruined for all time. She would have to leave Sitka in shame.

She acquiesced to protect her uncle, but only on one condition. The marriage would take place on the governor's coming birthday, March 18, 1844, *if* she had not heard from Victor or had received no word from the ship on which he sailed.

It is said that the young princess and her nurse went ceaselessly each night to the cupola high atop Baranof Castle to watch for her beloved. They lit the signal lantern used to guide ships through the perilous Sound.

Still no word came, and so on the chosen date Princess Olga Feodorovna, attired in a blue silk wedding dress, and the delighted Prince Ivan Sergovitch Peploff were wed at St. Michael's Cathedral.

Afterward, the revelry commenced at the Castle. Princess Olga sat pale and subdued, barely speaking to her guests. Her aged groom chatted amiably with his good and dear comrade the governor.

Then signal cannon boomed, indicating the presence of an incoming ship. The beacon was lighted in the Castle's cupola; a bonfire on Signal Island acted as a second guiding light.

Toasts were made and drunk, including a grand one by a tight-lipped governor who wished the couple happy wedded bliss. Suddenly the door to the ballroom swung open and the princess's nurse stuck her head in. She motioned feverishly to her young charge, as the chaplain's manuscript explained:

The bride noticed, made an excuse of sudden illness, and flew more than walked to the door leading to the corridor.

Outside the door:

"He is here?"

"Yes, child; he is waiting in the hall outside your chamber door."

It was a matter of a few seconds only.

"Olga!"

"Victor!"

Their lips met in a long, passionate kiss.

"Hush!"

There was the noise of a step on the landing. Her right hand fumbled for the poniard suspended at his left side. She has unsheathed it! The next moment it has penetrated her heart, and a warm stream of blood strikes him in the face. As she falls dead in his loving arms a look of joy comes into his eyes. The poniard is in his hand! Now it is buried in his own heart!

As his life blood gushes forth, he sinks to the floor with his precious burden in his arms.

Separated in life. United in death.

The chaplain wrote that the governor permitted the couple to be buried together, but not in consecrated ground. They were interred in a plot not far from the lovers' lane where they spent so many blissful hours.

ARCTANDER'S ANONYMOUS NARRATOR concludes:

"How strange! It was on the eighteenth day of March, 1894, just fifty years to the day from the wedding—from the death of the beautiful Russian princess—that Baranof Castle burned to the ground. No one at Sitka can explain how the fire started, but all who had an opportunity to know, agree that it was first observed in the glass cupola on the roof."

"Strange indeed!"

Strange it may be, but is it true?
Doubtful.

Writer-historian Richard Pierce found all sorts of problems with the Castle ghost when he looked into its origins in the late 1960s.

Among them, he said, were these:

- There was no "Chaplain Cramer" with the troops assigned to take control of Sitka in 1867, though there was a Chaplain Raynor;
- Neither Governor Etholen nor his wife had a niece named Princess Olga Feodorovna;
- The governor's actual birthday was not March 18 but January 9;
- There is no record of a Prince Ivan Peploff ever having lived in Sitka;
- Russian brides usually wore white and not blue;
- The Castle burned on March 17, not March 18; and
- The fire appears to have started near a judge's chambers and not high above in the cupola.

Pierce notes there have been many renderings and even more variations over the years, including one in which the *daughter* of the Russian governor falls in love with an American *sailor*. But Pierce points out that no American ship visited Sitka until 1867.

Still another telling from the pages of the *Alaska News* in 1896 sets the tale in the 1830s when a Baron Wrangel held the position of governor general. In this version, the young sailor returns to find his love has wed just a half hour earlier and, incensed, stabs her in the heart. He escapes, but filled with remorse at what he has done, he then throws himself into the sea. "Ever after her spirit was seen on the anniversary of her wedding night, her slender svelte-like form robed in heavy brocade, pressing her hands on the wound in her heart, the tears streaming from her eyes," the newspaper said. "Sometimes before a heavy storm she would make her appearance in the little tower (cupola) at the top of the castle once used as a lighthouse. There she would burn a light until dawn for the spirit of her lover at sea," it concludes.

CASTLE HILL IS quiet now. It is a designated Alaskan state historic site and a National Historic Landmark. A walkway guides visitors to its peak. They are treated to panoramic vistas of downtown Sitka and the waterfront. Archaeologists have found remains of at least four early Russian-American buildings and, of course, vestiges of the Tlingit Indian presence for the thousand years before the coming of the Europeans.

Somewhere in that great expanse of history there may well have been a young man and a young woman in love, and yet who were torn apart by time and circumstance. Quite often even the most incredible legends have a serving of truth about them.

So if you should happen to be atop Castle Hill at twilight listen carefully for the approach of footsteps, and don't be surprised if you turn to see a willowy, raven-haired beauty in a blue silk wedding gown holding a flickering candle in her pale and delicate hand.

2

Along the Spectral Trail

When we turn to the tales told by modern percipients (of ghosts) . . . we find them hardly distinguishable from those of a century before.

—R. C. Finucane, *Ghosts: Appearances of the Dead and Cultural Transformation*

BETWEEN THE CONCRETE landscapes of Los Angeles and the urban eccentricities of San Francisco is a California of dramatic coastlines, rugged mountains, expansive farmland, and close-knit communities. In this region, where recorded history reaches back hundreds of years to the Spanish supremacy, and Native Americans have lived for millennia, times past are dotted across the countryside in a landscape that has remained essentially unchanged in thousands of years. Countless vestiges remain of those ancient Native American settlements, striking Spanish missions, rustic frontier outposts, and deserted ghost towns rarely visited. But with all that instantly recognizable history are spectral tales that add an authentic sense of mystery to this still-rugged land.

The Late Pierre Duvon

The hulking mountain man with the flowing black beard showed up at the Conejo Valley hotel sometime in the latter half of 1889. He scribbled his name in the register, grabbed a room key from the desk clerk, threw his saddlebags over his shoulder, and clambered up the steps to his second floor room. He was dressed no differently than the scores of other hard-bitten cowboys, drifters, and human flotsam that passed through that rugged territory near Thousand Oaks in the old days. Folks who saw him probably didn't pay much attention to his comings or goings. No reason to.

The fact of the matter is that this man of indeterminate age and whose name might have been the elegant-sounding Pierre Duvon has become much better known in death than he ever was in life.

On the night he is said to have checked into what was known as the Grand Union Hotel, Pierre Duvon checked *out* of this physical realm. Permanently. He was shot dead by a person or persons unknown.

And it is his ghost that is said to haunt the famed Stagecoach Inn Museum complex in Newbury Park.

Of course with any event a century and more old it's hard to know where the truth runs out and hearsay takes over. But there does seem to be something to Pierre's untimely demise and his subsequent resurrection as cowboy entity-in-residence to warrant a second look and perhaps a visit to a place where Old California is as close as the pungent odor of worn leather hanging in the Inn's nearby carriage house.

NEWSPAPER ACCOUNTS FROM April 1970 called the historic Stagecoach Inn the "grand old gal" of Ventura County when the hotel, converted into a museum just five years earlier, burned to the ground in a fire of undetermined origin. Also destroyed were priceless early California artifacts housed inside the complex. All that was left, according to one account, were "two smoke-blackened chimneys and a pile of smoldering rubble."

A little more than a year later Conejo Valley preservationists announced that they would rebuild the inn with state and local funding, along with the insurance settlement from the devastating fire. The rebuilt inn and museum opened on July 4, 1976. A second floor was finished four years later.

The original inn was built from native redwood nearly a century before by pioneer Santa Barbara businessman James Hammell at a then-impressive sum of $7,200. The Grand Union Hotel was designed in what was called the Monterey style with a wraparound porch on the main level and a similarly designed porch on the second floor. The numerous rooms were for the accommodation of tourists and of stagecoach passengers moving between Los Angeles and Santa Barbara. Hammell tried to lure tourists to the scenic Conejo Valley through advertising in various newspapers, including Ventura's *The Signal*, which boasted "shooting, fishing, and bathing . . ." for hotel guests.

Named at various times the Grand Union Hotel, the elegant El Hotel Grande, and finally the more prosaic Stagecoach Inn, the hostelry was bought by Englishman Cecil Haigh in 1885. Over the ensuing decades, the building also served as a tea room, restaurant, the local post office, and as an elite gift shop. Movie cowboy Hoot Gibson even filmed an early Hollywood epic on its premises. The hotel was still owned by Haigh's descendants when it was faced with obliteration after the state said it was in the way for a planned expansion of the Ventura Freeway–Ventu Park Road interchange. A local historical society successfully lobbied the state to designate the hotel a California landmark in 1965. Haigh's grandson turned over the building and some land to the park district, which in turn leased the property back to the historical society to operate as a museum and cultural landmark. The old inn was moved to the current location in 1966 and operated as a museum for five years until the 1970 fire. Today, the complex in Newbury Park includes the reconstructed Stagecoach Inn, a blacksmith shop and carriage house, replicas of early Native American, Mexican, and Euro-American settlers' homes, and Timber School, a re-created Conejo Valley elementary school from the 1880s.

But what of Pierre, the legendary spectre whose alleged murder has sparked some paranormal interest at today's Stagecoach Inn? Is there anything more than conjecture and guesswork connected to his ramblings?

Noted California ghost researcher Richard Senate has had at least one experience there that indicates perhaps there is something to the legend.

Senate, who has written extensively about Ventura County hauntings, took a group of students in his "ghost hunting" class to the Inn. As Senate and his students began exploring the second floor, Senate has written that he had an unusual reaction:

"When I walked into the 'haunted room,' I sensed something, a vibration or somber feeling. I had experienced nothing like it elsewhere in the building. I asked if this was the infamous room where Pierre is believed to have been murdered. I had never been to the place before and there was no indication that this room and not any of the others was the haunted chamber. When I asked, the docent shook her head and said no. But I knew my feelings were not in error. A check with the head of the museum proved my impression had been correct. Others in our group also felt a disturbance in the room. Several of my students felt a cold spot near the stairs."

Senate wasn't surprised. He'd known about famed psychic Sybil Leek's visit to the Stagecoach Inn years before and her identification of the suspected ghost. Senate quoted the former museum director's remembrance of Leek's visit:

"She reported that there was nothing on the first floor, but that there was a strong disturbance on the second floor. She had received a message from a Pierre Duvon, a mountain man who had come to the Inn for a night's stay in 1885, but had been murdered there while asleep. She described him as a bearded, stocky man, about thirty-five years old. She questioned me, but I knew of no corroborating evidence."

No corroborating evidence. A key problem with verifying the *living* antecedent of a spectral visitor. But perhaps that issue waned with two follow-up events.

The late, former museum director, Cyril W. Anderson, said that following Sybil Leek's published comments, he had a visitor who brought him a pistol holster and chaps that, the stranger claimed, he'd gotten from his father along with the story that the rustic items belonged to a man who'd been murdered at the inn. But again there was no way to authenticate that assertion.

During the 1960s struggle to save the inn, Anderson recalled for Senate that a workman reported a bizarre incident. He had been supervising the placing of rollers under the structure in preparation for its move away from the new freeway construction. Suddenly, a two by four sailed out of a second floor window and "damned near brained me," the workman told Anderson. He ran up to the second floor to see who'd be so malicious but, as he'd suspected, found the building empty.

The other issue here, of course, is that the present Stage-coach Inn is a *replica* of the original construction and is in a different location. Can it be that the ghost of Messr. Duvon did not disappear with his original resting place? Possibly. Disregarding the thought that perhaps he *prefers* more modern surroundings to hang about, Duvon's ghost may simply be adding to the lore that hauntings occur in *space* and not in *time* nor in any particular *physical* place. Perhaps he simply likes it there, in Newbury Park.

There is one more slender bit of evidence that Pierre Duvon might be more than speculative history. When the original inn burned in 1970, photographers captured several pictures of the devastating blaze. In one of the photographs, there appears to be the figure of a bearded man standing in the flames. Pierre Duvon? Perhaps. Visitors can decide for themselves. The photograph hangs in the museum.

The Angel's Adobe

Californians know Father Junipero Serra as the famed Franciscan missionary and founder of Catholic missions in the western wilderness along the seven-hundred-mile El Camino Real from San Diego to Sonoma. From the time he left Spain in 1750 at the age of thirty-six, until his death in 1784, Father Junipero made it his life's work to convert the Native Americans to Christianity and to establish Spain's claim to California by building mission churches, many of which are in use even to this day. Although he had chronic asthma and a painful leg lesion that hobbled him all his life, Father Junipero walked and rode hundreds of miles up and down the Pacific coast, often with Gaspar de Portola, from San Diego to Monterey. He died on August 29, 1784, and is buried at the Mission San Carlos in Carmel.

According to historian Charles Skinner, during one of Father Junipero's journeys near the village of Monterey, the priest and his long-time friend and fellow Franciscan, Padre Francisco Palou, found themselves deep in the wilderness when night overtook them. With no decent shelter in sight, their faith that providence would provide for them proved to be correct in a most uncanny way, and in a manner that perhaps helped Father Junipero strengthen his religious convictions so as to overcome the certain loneliness and despair that must have come with his great, self-imposed task. This is the story Skinner related about Father Junipero's strange night:

"Well, brother," said Father Junipero, looking at his traveling companion as the sun dipped beneath the horizon, "we can go no farther tonight. God will not let us come to harm. We have a loaf of bread for supper and a cloak for a bed. The stars are coming out and the snakes are going in. We shall sleep in peace."

"Let us say our prayers, for I am weary from the day's journey," Father Palou replied.

The two knelt on the hillside and offered up their thanks and their petitions, asking that heaven shelter them through the dark hours with its loving kindness and bless their work of spreading the gospel.

As they arose from their knees, Father Junipero caught a twinkle of light a half mile ahead. He gave a little cry of surprise.

"It must be white men," he said, noting it was not the red light from an Indian fire. "Yet who would have thought of finding our people in the wilderness?"

Palou held back, his face pale.

"It is not our people," he said warily. "There is no house or cabin all the way from San Juan to Monterey. It is surely the Devil who seeks us, far from our churches. He tempts us with a hope of shelter when there is none."

Father Junipero was less apprehensive.

"Be of better faith. We will go forward. Surely a house may have been built here since we last crossed this country."

"If your faith is strong I will follow," Father Palou agreed, "though I shall keep tight hold on my crucifix, and constantly repeat the Virgin Mother's name."

A walk of a few minutes brought them to the light. It was shining, white and calm, from the window of a small, neat adobe house, all set about with flowers. The door stood open. The sturdy figure of a man was dark against the luminous interior as he peered into the night. When the travelers had come in sight he showed no surprise; on the contrary, he stepped from the doorway with a grave courtesy and motioned them to enter.

"Good friends," he began, "you are worn from your journey and hungry. Be pleased to become our guests. You are welcome here."

With hearty thanks for this unexpected hospitality the missionaries walked into the plain but clean and sweet-smelling room. It was simply furnished and everything was distinct in a soft yet brilliant light of candles. A saintly faced, lovely lady greeted them and motioned them to places at a table where a supper of bread, herbs, and wine had been prepared. A gentle, sunny-haired boy held his mother's hand, leaned his rosy cheek against her, and smiled at them.

The solemn, yet kindly man who had made them welcome—he with the brown face and hands, the simple dress and honest way of an artisan—served the food and drink, and all spoke of the work on which the fathers were traveling. It seemed to them as if on earth there could be no other home like this, so sweet and gracious were their hosts, so low and musical their voices, so pure the air and feeling of the place. When the supper was ended they would have begged to rest on straw outside the house; but before they had put this request into words an inner door had been thrown open and they were ushered into a white chamber holding two beds, warmly though daintily covered. With pleasant good nights the family withdrew, leaving the missionaries to their rest.

"We spoke truly when we said we should sleep in peace," Father Palou said thoughtfully.

Father Junipero nodded.

"It is as if God had turned our steps here. Brother Francisco, there is such a peace in my soul as I have never felt before. It is well with the world, for heaven is kind to men."

Tired though they were, they prayed long and earnestly before they slept. In the morning, before day had broken, they awoke without a call, were bidden to another simple meal, and presently resumed their journey, after many thanks to the man, the woman, and the child for their goodness. They solemnly invoked the blessing of God on all three, and bowed low and stood awhile in silence when the family asked to bestow a blessing on the travelers—silent because they were strangely moved and thrilled.

They had been on their way not many minutes when they encountered a mule driver, who looked at them curiously.

"Good day to your reverences," he said. "You look as happy and well fed and freshened with sleep as if you had breakfasted with his excellency the governor and had lain on goose feathers all night."

"We have fared notably," said Padre Palou. "We stopped at the house yonder, and so kind a family can be found nowhere else."

"At what house did you say?" asked the stranger. "There is no house for miles and miles. Even the Indians come into this part of the land but seldom."

"It is plain that you, like us, have not been here for some time," Junipero replied. "The house we have just left is there by those trees—or—that is—Why! Look, brother! It is gone."

The dawn was whitening, and the morning sun threw down one long beam on the place where that house had been; a silver mist seemed to swirl about the site, now as devoid of human habitation as might be found anywhere in the wilderness.

Father Junipero Serra commanded that they all kneel.

"A miracle has been done," he said. "The cottage must have been built by angels, and they who served us were Joseph, Mary, and Jesus. God smiles upon our work. From this hour we dedicate ourselves to it with new vigor and a firmer faith."

FATHER JUNIPERO SERRA'S final resting place is the Mission San Carlos de Borromeo de Rio Carmelo at Carmel—the Carmel Mission. After decades of falling into ruin, the Mission was restored in the 1930s and later raised to the status of an independent parish. It is now a Minor Basilica of the Roman Catholic Church. Father Junipero was beatified by Pope John Paul II, who, in 1987, had visited the Carmel Mission as part of his United States tour.

As one might imagine, interesting stories can be found swirling about such an ancient edifice. One such tale is of the mysterious event witnessed by Christiano Machado, who in the 1880s was the caretaker of the Mission ruins, and whose son Antonio Machado lived for many years in Carmel.

Antonio recalled that his family lived at that time in an adobe house near a pear orchard, about a hundred yards away from the Mission proper. For some time Christiano had told his family that he'd seen an odd light every morning between two and three A.M. in the ruins of the Indian adobes adjacent to the Mission.

And then one evening near the midnight hour, Machado left his home for a brief inspection of the property, as was his routine. But at the ruined gateway into the Mission yard, he came upon a white horse walking slowly toward him. As it passed by, Christiano saw upon the horse's back a rider clad in white, sitting erect and staring directly ahead. The startled caretaker could not see the man's face. Strangest of all, a light shimmered on the horse's forehead directly between its eyes. Neither horse nor rider took any notice of Machado standing but a few feet away. He watched them disappear down the road toward Monterey.

When Machado was out again a few hours later, he waited for the mysterious light to return to the ruins as it had done on all those nights before. It did not. At daybreak, Machado returned to the adobe ruins. He found a deep hole had been dug in their midst. He believed, as did others who heard his story, that in the ruins had been buried treasure, and that the stranger on the white horse had been seeking it. The light Machado had seen in those early morning hours had been the light on the horse as its master searched the Mission grounds. On this night, the mysterious horseman had succeeded in his quest and ridden away, never to return.

Maria Madariaga

The two most famous trees in Pebble Beach are cypresses along Pescadero Point on the famed Seventeen-Mile Drive, south of Monterey. The Witch Tree and the nearby Ghost Tree are bone white landmarks visited and photographed by thousands of tourists each year.

Less well-known, and never photographed as far as can be determined, is a phantom lady in lace who startles drivers as they navigate the scenic highway on especially foggy nights.

The vaporous figure seems to glide along the highway's center stripe with an infrequency that causes some to question whether her "presence" isn't simply a product of a particularly dense wisp of fog.

Yet in this case it is not so simple, for the murky lady has a possible identity.

Maria del Carmen Garcia Barreto Madariaga was once the fortunate owner of the land where the ghost reportedly flits about.

The story goes that Maria and her husband Fabian Barreto moved to Rancho Pescadero shortly after he was granted the land by the Spanish governor. Sadly, Fabian died less than a year later. His widow stayed even though she preferred the lively Monterey society to the splendid yet lonely surroundings along the coast. Monterey, of course, was California's first capital city during the time of the Spanish influence. Yet she added to her ranch holdings by purchasing what was known as Rancho Canada Honda—Deep Canyon—and then marrying Juan Madariaga in 1844. Wife and new husband remained on the ranch.

By 1846 Maria had found a small house in Monterey from which she could immerse herself in the city's social milieu. She sold the four-thousand-acre Pescadero property for five hundred dollars—just twelve cents an acre. When the new owner died soon thereafter, however, his widow sold it to a New Jersey investor for over four *thousand* dollars. The investor—a man named Gore—traded the property for land on the Eastern seaboard.

Maria was apparently deeply disturbed at this turn of events. Sometime in 1860 she sold her Deep Canyon property—and *resold* the Pescadero land even though she legally had no entitlement to do so—to land baron David Jacks, once the most prominent property-owner in the region. Jacks took possession, put fences around the property, and went to court to force Gore and later his heirs to give up their claims. Only when the last of the Gore family was killed in the 1906 San Francisco earthquake was the Jacks family able to settle the legal claims.

Maria lived her life in the house on the small lot in Monterey she named Casa Madariaga. Yet she was said to have never fully recovered from the real estate entanglements in which she found herself. Thus, if you should see that strange lady gliding silently along Pescadero Point merely understand that she is still regretful over the way in which her fortunes vanished. And perhaps marveling at the untold millions of dollars that have changed hands as her old rancheros were developed over the past century.

Monterey's historic Casa Madariaga—Maria del Carmen Garcia Barreto Madariaga's old home—is on Abrego Street between Church and Webster.

The Headless Horsewoman of Fort Hunter Liggett

"I saw her!" said the young soldier. "She was riding a big horse. It was like a cape or cloth of some kind was floating back from her shoulders. She did not have a head."

Olive Wollesen quizzed him further. Had he heard a horse? Seen hoof prints?

"Yes," he solemnly replied.

What Ms. Wollesen discovered in her interview with the startled young man is what other soldiers have sometimes reported within the central California coast's Fort Hunter Liggett, a sprawling, 165-thousand-acre military installation southeast of Monterey along the foothills of the Santa Lucia Mountains. That, along with unexplained shadows at the old Mission San Antonio de Padua and legendary buried treasure, there is a mysterious woman who sometimes rides along the crest of a mountain overlooking the guard towers. Her name may be Cleora . . . and she still hasn't found her missing head.

FORT HUNTER LIGGETT is some twenty-five miles southwest of King City, between Morro Bay and Monterey. The installation originated in 1941 when the government bought much of the land from publisher William Randolph Hearst. Opened as Camp Hunter Liggett Military Reservation, the base was named for World War I General Hunter Liggett. The fort now operates as an army reserve command training center. Both active and reserve soldiers are quartered there.

The reservation is rich in history. The Hokan people settled the region some ten thousand years ago, ancestors of the modern-era Salinan Indians. Spanish missionaries led by Father Junipero Serra established a mission along the San Antonio River. By the mid-1800s, the California gold rush and statehood led to extensive European-American settlement with thriving gold and other mineral mining. Nearby Jolon, California—a ghost town today—was a bustling city serving a wide geographic region.

It is little wonder that mysterious historical revenants may continue to occupy certain corners of the fort since several significant structures there are on the National Register of Historic Places. The oldest is the so-called Painted Cave—*La Cueva Pintada*—filled with detailed pictographs created by ancient peoples. Mission San Antonio De Padua is an eighty-five acre preserve dating from 1771. Although the mission closed in the 1950s, restoration of the original buildings was a major undertaking by base soldiers. Milpitas House, known today as "The Hacienda," was built by Hearst in the late 1920s as the headquarters for his ranch holdings. The house and ranchland were sold to the government for use at the newly commissioned Camp Hunter Liggett.

The legendary bandit Tiburcio Vasquez, sometimes called the "Robin Hood" of Old California, plied his trade robbing stagecoaches on the old route between King City and Jolon. Indians often hid him from posses because he had stolen horses and cattle which he gave to the Native peoples. Women were attracted to him because of his plentiful supply of (stolen) money. But in the end it was his mistress who betrayed him to the authorities in San Jose. A posse swarmed the house and when Vasquez tried to make his escape out a window he was captured. Later tried and convicted, Vasquez was hanged at San Jose in 1875.

THE STORY OF Cleora, the headless horsewoman, is one of the more persistent ghost stories at the army base, yet most of the specifics can't be traced back much earlier than to the 1960s. Author Olive Wollesen found that the legend may be much older: "An Indian man and his wife lived in the neighborhood of Jolon (in the late 1800s), and they were happy. As time went on, the husband discovered one night that his wife was unfaithful. He was beside himself with grief and anger. He was in a towering rage. He slew his unhappy wife, took her body to the nearby cemetery, and buried her there—except that he first cut off her head. He carried her head away from the cemetery. . . . Through the years from time to time she rises at night from the grave and rides forth searching for her head. Sometimes she walks," Wollesen has written.

She said that although the legend is quite old, reported incidents began about 1969.

"Certainly for many years from time to time soldiers have said they saw a woman in flowing garments riding a horse—and she had no head," Wollesen said. "The accounts are true, but the legend is not from old time among the Indians, for it originated among the soldiers in what was then Camp Hunter Liggett's Military Reservation, now a Fort. The whole thing is weird. . . ."

What exactly did the soldiers see?

Hunter Liggett base newspaper reporters Ron Stewart and Ric Young compiled a comprehensive log of the various encounters during their time on the base.

A private in the transportation company told the reporters that he "saw it while at the ammo supply point. . . . It was a female, I'm sure of that. And there was nothing from here up," he said, gesturing to his neck.

Another private, also at the ammunition supply point, saw the headless figure and shouted for her to halt. He cried out again, but the figure kept moving forward. Finally he raised his gun to fire but the apparition vanished.

Stewart and Young wrote that occasionally the ghost grew bold and seemed to want some human contact with the soldiers.

"A guard was on duty in a small shack with a large glass window overlooking the Gabilan impact area where the (Combat Development Experimentation Command) was conducting an experiment," the pair noted. "He heard a knock on the door.

" 'I thought it was the duty officer or the sergeant of the guard coming for the nightly check,' the guard said. 'I asked who it was but received no answer. I called again but still no answer, and all the time the knocking continued.'

"Thinking it was probably a tree branch or a bush bumping against the door, the guard went outside to check. Finding there were no trees or bushes near the shack, he assumed his mind was playing tricks on him, and went back inside where he took a final look out the large window. Peering in through the glass was the figure of a woman wearing a long cape or overcoat and flowing clothes, but with no head.

" 'I screamed and aroused the guard at the bottom of the hill and he called the duty officer. (He) arrived soon after to check the situation out. I swore that I was telling the truth, although the officer found nothing.' "

A Franciscan brother at Mission San Antonio said several military policemen came to him troubled after seeing a ghost. A guard at the ammunition dump radioed in that he'd seen a headless woman riding nearby. Two jeeps of MPs roared out to catch the intruder. They spotted her on horseback and gave chase, but she disappeared into the night. The Franciscan said the horsewoman might have been the same ghost reportedly seen riding by the old mission. One of the graves that may be the site of her remains is near the old San Antonio mission.

Some believe the ghost is nothing more than eerie hearsay dreamed up by bored soldiers or the descendants of the Native Americans who once farmed the region. Some who claimed to have witnessed the strange ride were willing to go on the record when reporters checked into the sightings, while other long-time residents remained tight-lipped. The only certain conclusion is that the truth behind stories of the headless horsewoman remains as elusive as she.

3

Watch Out Below

Everybody said so. Far be it from me to assert that
what everybody says must be true.
Everybody is, often, as likely to be wrong as right.

—Charles Dickens, *The Haunted Man*

THE AMERICAN WEST is crisscrossed with thousands of abandoned mines and many more thousands of miles of deserted mine tunnels. Countless of these excavations eventually yielded unimaginable wealth for the absentee owners hauling out millions of tons of coal, silver, lead, gold, and other minerals on the backs of the anonymous workers who toiled deep inside the earth. Most mining operations, however, ended in disappointment when the sought-after riches proved to be nonexistent or too inconsequential to extract.

Regardless of the eventual outcome of a particular operation, there was and is one constant in mining—accidental death is the most dogged of companions. A mistimed explosive charge, fatal toxic fumes, or a sudden shift in the timber supports snuffed out the lives of countless miners.

Sometimes death came so quickly that stories spread of those miners' spirits remaining a good long while where in life they once labored. It was as if they didn't quite realize their time on and under the earth was through.

Was there a mine that did not have at least one catastrophic mishap? One that did not have certain eerie legends associated with ghostly miners? It's little wonder that miners are among the most superstitious of all working people.

No Man Aboard

Colorado may have more ghosts per mining claim than any other state west of the Mississippi River.

The nearly abandoned town of Rosita, in Custer County, boasted the ghost of a notorious killer and claim jumper, Colonel Graham. With his old saber rattling, the former Army officer strutted back and forth across the bridge where he'd been shot and killed by angry townsfolk.

Mad Jack Strong accidentally blew up himself and his burro with an ill-timed explosive at Brown Gulch, near Silver Plume. Later, prospectors swore they heard his pickax *chinking* at the rock and his burro *whinnying* dolefully over his dismantled condition. Their pale, luminous forms hovered for years near the old silver claims.

The cemetery at the Silver Cliff mining camps is famous for its dim, dancing blue lights that some claim to be the lights from the helmets of dead miners. Others say it's a form of phosphorescence or swamp gas or the onlookers' imaginations.

Then there is the bloody saga of the Mamie R—a legendary silver mine reputedly situated on Raven Hill, in Cripple Creek.

The year was 1894 and three men had already met sudden death at or near the mine. A worker died when a cable snapped, sending a heavy mining bucket careening down a shaft, delivering a crushing blow directly atop the unsuspecting victim. Another miner died in an unforeseen detonation. The third casualty was a man named Garson, the proprietor of the mine's boarding house. He died within a few days of contracting what was known on the Western frontier as mountain fever, perhaps today's Rocky Mountain Spotted Fever.

Named to replace Garson on November 15, 1894, was an E. D. Blake. He would serve double duty, as had Garson, as the boarding house "boss" and as a miner.

Nine days later, on Thanksgiving night, 1894, Blake, a foreman curiously nicknamed Fatty Root, and two other men were assigned to work up top. Although no one was scheduled inside the mine that night, one of the men was standing by the main hoist used to lower and raise men and materials into and out of the mine.

Everything had been routine until the signal bell abruptly rang out in three quick successive rings, followed by a pause, and then one sharper ring. That was the indicator of *man aboard, hoist away*. A steam-powered engine operated the hoist itself. Although none of the men had been told about any miners working the diggings that night, they didn't want to take the chance of leaving someone below. As soon as adequate steam pressure had been built, the hoist man started the bucket back up the shaft.

All four men were then doubly startled when the bell rang once again, the sign for the bucket to stop. It then rang out twice more, the indication that it should be lowered.

Suddenly a cacophony of bell signals rang out, according to one account.

Fatty Root and E. D. Blake ignored the contradictory signals and hauled the bucket up.

Nothing was inside.

Root and Blake jumped in the bucket and ordered that they be lowered to the deepest tunnel. Once down there, they looked all around the workings but found no one in evidence, as they had been certain was the case.

Back on top, the hoist engineer insisted no one else had been brought up while Root and Blake were below investigating.

Several days later, another miner, working at the three-hundred-seventy-five-foot level, emerged from the mine telling his foreman that he thought someone had been killed in his section. He explained that he had planted explosive charges to widen an especially narrow tunnel. He'd just set the shots when someone walked by him directly into the path of the explosives. He yelled out to the man, but the stranger ignored the warning.

The miner shook his head as he told the story. No one should have been down there. What was especially odd is that he didn't recognize the fellow; he assumed it was someone new to the crew.

When the smoke had sufficiently cleared and the debris settled, a work party went back down to that level.

What they encountered down there would stay with them for the rest of their days.

A pale figure with crimson rivulets of blood streaming from

several gashes in his head staggered toward them from the darkness just beyond their lanterns' beam. The bright red fluid stood in harsh contrast to the thick coating of dust over his work clothes and exposed skin.

That wasn't the half of it.

He was missing an arm, or rather the arm itself he had casually propped against his one good shoulder. The shredded flesh dangling from his empty shoulder socket made it abundantly clear that until quite recently his arm had been firmly attached.

The unfamiliar miner walked toward the bucket. He said not a word. The men yelled at him but got no reply. They poked and prodded, but their fingers and arms went through this apparition—for that is what they were certain it was—as if they were jabbing at thin air. The shift boss was along and he threw a drill at the . . . thing . . . but that, too, sailed right on through.

The ghost climbed aboard the bucket, tugged four times on the signal bell and rode the swaying contraption up and out of sight.

The rescue party finally got up the nerve to call the bucket back down. When they finally reached the surface the hoist man swore on his mother's grave that he'd never been signaled to haul anyone else up.

A month later Christmas Eve rolled around. Fatty, E. D., and their two cronies were passing the time on top.

The signal bell clanged to life.

"Who do you suppose is down there?" Fatty wondered.

"Not anybody I know of," the hoist man shot back.

Nevertheless, he started the steam engine that sent the bucket on its journey up the shaft.

E. D. Blake remembered what they saw as the container cleared the opening:

"The blood curdled in our veins. I hope to be spared ever seeing such a sight again. Old, dead Garson himself got out of the bucket, him with his yellow pinched face and staring eyes just as he looked the night I saw him die of mountain fever. Then out came that one-armed man with blood spattered over his features and the shattered stump of an arm. Between them, they lifted out the body of another poor fellow lashed to a plank and laid it on the platform. Then the one-armed man reached down in the bucket and brought out his arm. He laid it on top of the body that was lashed to the plank, and the two raised the whole horrible thing to their shoulders and walked out into the night. For a minute, no one spoke and then we all rushed to the door. As true as I live we saw the two dead men, ghosts, or whatever they were, walk over the edge of the dump, and disappear in the darkness."

That was not to be the end of tragedies at the Mamie R.

Fatty Root drew the task of taking the bucket dumper's place on Christmas Day. His job was to empty the tailings into wagons and take the loads to the mine dump. Even though it was Christmas, it had been a long day of work. Near midnight, Fatty must have grown tired or careless, or perhaps he was just in the wrong place at the wrong time. No one ever really found out. A bucket of water had just been hoisted down and the bucket was moving toward the top when the winding spool slipped out of its frame and the rope came off the coils. One of the loops caught Fatty around his ample neck, slicing off his head "as clean as if it had been done with a razor sharp Bowie knife," one witness claimed.

The story is that the Mamie R was shut down forever about a month later with the company taking a big financial loss.

THERE IS A caveat to the haunting of the Mamie R.

The Colorado Division of Mines has complete records back to 1896. Before then, mining documentation is limited or non-existent. One investigator found no evidence that the Mamie R ever existed on Cripple Creek's Raven Hill. There was the Jack Pot Mine, the Ingham Mine, the Julie E and the Elkton Mine, but the Mamie R?

It has proven to be an elusive quarry, and just as hard to pin down as those innumerable bloody ghosts hitching rides in rusty mining buckets.

Oops

Sometimes an entity is not the thing you think it is.

Take the case of the presumed Wild Woman of the Rockies, a widely reported ghost of an emigrant's daughter prowling the

Cameron Pass district of Colorado, northwest of the headwaters of Colorado's Cache de la Poudre River.

At least that was the story geologist W. C. Hart and two colleagues heard when they explored the territory in the early 1880s.

The public records of the Hart expedition are unclear about their precise location, but the men were collecting geological samples as they camped near lava beds, not too far distant from an extinct volcano. They wrote that gnarled trees and great boulders scarred the countryside. That is not remarkable in the mountains of Colorado. Earth tremors sometimes rattle the area northwest of Denver; a ten-second quake jolted Fort Collins in September 1903. An early written history of Larimer County, in which most of the Cache de la Poudre River is located, bragged that the county "prides itself upon having as interesting examples of ancient volcanic disturbances as can be found in the entire Rocky Mountain region."

What was barren wilderness in 1882, visitors now consider some of the most spectacular surroundings in the lower forty-eight states. The Cache de la Poudre River, a federally designated Wild and Scenic River, rises in Rocky Mountain National Park along the Continental Divide, and flows east for nearly one hundred miles, entering the high plains near Fort Collins. It meets the South Platte River outside Greeley. The river's name is French for "hiding place of the powder." The origin of the name goes back to 1836, when a band of fur traders under the command of French Canadian Antoine Janis became trapped by a snowstorm near what is today called Bingham Hill. He ordered that their heavy packs be emptied of everything that could be spared, including several hundred pounds of gunpowder (*poudre*). The hiding places (*cache*) were near the then–unnamed river.

Geologist Hart wasn't thinking about all this, however, when he set off for the area in August 1882. He had been warned away by locals who swore that the emigrant girl's ghost often showed up unannounced in wilderness camps. She was an outcast. Her own father declared that she had loved too unwisely—and too well. He had sent the girl away from her own mountain community to live on her own in the wilderness.

Mountain guide Joe Shepier was leading geologist Hart's expedition through the territory. Shepier had often seen the ghost, he revealed, and promised his companions that they, too, would doubtlessly observe the strange apparition before returning to civilization. Shepier said the girl's habit was to quickly flit in and out of mountaineers' camps, carrying off food and furniture before the startled men could take any action. Shepier didn't explain why a ghost girl would need food and furniture.

Thus it was at suppertime on August 12, 1882, that Shepier quietly whispered to his companions that he had caught sight of the ghost girl of Cameron Pass approaching camp. Sure enough, a waiflike young woman was swiftly moving their way. She stopped some fifteen-hundred feet distant, near a table rock on which they'd placed a haunch of venison. She hurriedly grabbed the meat, turned, and trotted back the way she came.

W. C. Hart evidently had skills beyond the identification of rocks for he quickly took charge, picked up his rifle, and ran off in pursuit of the "ghost," shouting back over his shoulder for his men to follow. The "lively race," as one observer noted, led directly toward the lava beds. Over jagged rocks and downed timber, the hunters followed the hunted. Neither was willing to give up. Somewhere along the trail, she dropped the meat she'd been carrying. Just when she seemed to be cornered she darted into a cave opening. The pursuers followed her in. Just inside the entrance, the men made a grim discovery. The girl's body lay crumpled on the hard-packed earth, her body still warm. Their conclusion was that "the fright and exertion had killed her."

She appeared to be an attractive, albeit filthy young woman in her mid-twenties with long, tangled hair and a deeply sunburned face. She was dressed in rough animal skins yet wore no shoes. Hart ordered that a grave be dug and that the nameless woman be accorded a decent and proper burial.

The men explored the girl's cavern lair. Bones and scraps of meat covered the ground. Some evidence of fire pits led to the conclusion that the girl had cooked the food; although eating utensils lay neatly piled in a corner, there was no indication that they'd ever been used. Some dried meat, apparently for winter subsistence, hung from pegs wedged into small crevices. Otherwise, it looked like she lived on a diet of roots and leaves.

Thus it was that the spirit of Cameron Pass was unmasked. The strange and anonymous wild girl who had plagued mining camps and settlers was no more. She obviously looked more illusory than real so it is no wonder that even the sturdiest of men fled at her sudden approach.

Yet, one is tempted to speculate: Did this Wild Woman ever then return as an authentic ghost? No one ventured an answer to that question. It's no wonder. If the sight of a strange girl wearing animal skins could send grown men into paroxysms of fear, imagine what effect a *real* ghost would have.

What Am I Bid? . . .

A Denver journalist once had up for sale a family heirloom clock with a most peculiar history.

Helen was an editorial assistant at a Denver newspaper. The timepiece went back for at least five generations in her family. When her great-great-grandfather died, the clock stopped at the precise hour and minute of his death. It eventually came into the hands of Helen's great-uncle. When he died, the clock again stopped at the hour and minute of his death.

The clock resumed its timekeeping for the next owner, Helen's grandfather. If by now one assumes that it stopped at the hour and minute of *his* death one would be correct.

Helen's father took possession of the eerie timepiece. He determined that enough was enough. He stopped the mechanism and put it in storage well out of sight.

Helen came into the clock's ownership when her father passed away—without, it is presumed, the clock noting the event—and put it up for sale. The identity of its final owner remains a mystery.

Hare Today, Gone Tomorrow

A favorite illusion of many magicians is to vanish from one location and then to appear just as suddenly at another. Sometimes the performer creates the deception using doves, white mice—or often rabbits. In one bizarre incident on Pueblo, Colorado's, south side, it seems that rabbits *all by themselves* might have learned how to perform this trick.

The year was 1961. The befuddled homemaker who provided the details understandably chose to remain anonymous. After all, who would want to admit to being outmaneuvered by a hare?

Simply put, her two pet rabbits had wanderlust . . . and a seeming ability to unlock and relock their own cage doors. At least that's what she claimed in the story she told.

The lady had a two-level rabbit "apartment" hutch in her backyard. Each level consisted of three pens. On the second storey level a black buck rabbit resided in the far left pen, a white doe in the middle pen; the flat on the far right was unoccupied.

The trouble began one morning when the pet owner found the white doe in pen number one on the far left, formerly occupied by the black buck—he was now in pen number three, formerly unoccupied. The middle pen was empty. The puzzled owner scratched her head and put her hares back in place.

The same thing happened again the next night, and the next, and the next, and the next. Her husband, children, and neighbors all denied responsibility.

Exasperated by the endless maneuverings of her haunted rabbits, she assigned her burly husband to hide in the garage the next night and keep watch over her rabbit lair. The couple made sure the cages were secured and the rabbits all in their right quarters before he took up his post. The night rolled on. Nothing untoward happened. No one came into the yard, nor did he take his eyes off the cages.

Along toward dawn, the sentinel husband grew tired and decided to give it up for the night and go to bed. He walked back to the cages to make one last check. The rabbits had changed pens.

The word is that the young housewife in the story divorced her husband, remarried, and moved to another city, doubtlessly tired of her hare-raising experience.

4

Souls in Torment

Requiescant in pace

—The Mass in Latin

THEY APPEAR SWATHED in all manner of clothing—nuns' habits and flowing capes, long, formal gowns or mud-spattered wedding finery; though the colors lean toward dingy gray, drab black or faded white, a few seem partial to mint green or sunburst yellow.

Though they sometimes mingle with the living—asking about a ride home, on occasion—more often than not they shy away from direct human interaction, preferring rather solitary strolls along darkened lanes.

They are the wandering, female apparitions along the world's roadways, distaff revenants that linger somewhere between here and there and yet forever remain just beyond the reach of the here and now. There is likely no country on earth without its woman in black—or gray, or white, or yellow, or green—confronting the unwary motorist or casual pedestrian in a most disturbing manner.

Along the A4 outside Bath, England, it happened early one morning to truck driver Laurie Newman. His headlights caught the form of someone darkly clad scurrying along the roadside. Newman thought it might be a nun and slowed down to offer his assistance. Much to his dismay, however, the mysterious walker leaped onto the running board and pressed its face against the window. Newman saw a fleshless skull inside the habit-like hood drawn close.

A somber gray lady lurking along Britain's A677 highway near Samlesbury Hall, Lancashire, startled a bus driver in the 1970s. He thought she was a prospective passenger. She wasn't.

In the German city of Darmstadt resides one black-clad lady, the ghost of the late Marianna, wife of the long dead Grand Duke Ferdinand. She is a portent of death in her funereal dress and long veil, especially for the Hesse family.

Several experts maintain that green ladies prefer Scotland to any other country, but for what reason there is no explanation. The Burnett family of Crathes and the Campbell clan at Dunstaffnage Castle had jade-hued ladies appear on the eve of family deaths.

The United States has not been without its rambling lady ghosts. The infamous Ocean Born Mary prowls the streets of Henniker, New Hampshire, still looking for a golden treasure buried by her second husband, the notorious Captain Pedro.

Resurrection Mary is a celebrated woman in white in southeast Chicago who disturbs late night drivers along Archer Avenue should they pull over to offer her a lift. After a few blocks and perhaps a minute or two of listless conversation, she asks to be let out. But before her gallant escort can pull over, she's gone. Her vanishing act always occurs near Resurrection Cemetery, where the *real Mary* was buried several generations ago.

Noted historian Louis C. Jones spent decades studying variations of women in black in New York State. He termed many of these female apparitions Hitchhiking Hatties and maintained they were the most widely told ghost story in America with, as he wrote, "antecedents and descendants, variants and analogues."

Whether they are simply wandering a city's streets, or asking passersby for a short ride, these vaporous vamps in variegated hues all have one thing in common—they can shock the hell out of the unwary, as the good citizens in several Illinois cities discovered.

Annie

Mount Vernon is an historic, yet thriving city of some seventeen thousand souls, nestled in far south-central Illinois, about ninety minutes east of St. Louis. Today it is best known for its remarkable preservation efforts, as home to the largest industry in the southern half of Illinois, and for being the first All-American-City in the state. The famed beauty of the eighteen-thousand-acre vacation destination Rend Lake lies just beyond its southern city limits.

Few in the city know, however, that Mount Vernon gained something of a reputation in its early days as the setting of several of the most persistent and odd encounters between a number of its citizens and a strange woman known variously in city history as Black Annie, the Lady of Sorrow, or Cyclone Annie. By which name she was recognized in Mount Vernon seems to depend upon the teller of the story and the period of the city's long history during which she made her unexpected appearances.

The earliest mention of something akin to a phantom lady came in 1866, the first year after the Civil War, when a witch lady showed up at dairy farms around the community to worry farmers and their cattle herds. After several weeks, enough was enough and the townspeople supposedly drove the witch out of the region. One history of the city contends the episode constituted the state's first dairy war, but that through the mob's forthright action, a milk shortage was averted.

Who or what was the unexplained visitor? A ghost? No one seems to have known for certain, although it was thought that she might have been a quite mad maiden from a neighboring town who had some sort of grievance against the rural farm folk she hounded.

Twenty-two years would pass until the lady, or her younger sister, made another appearance in Mount Vernon. She would always be remembered on that occasion as Cyclone Annie for the date of her visit was a horrific one for the community. On February 9, 1888, the city was struck by a tornado that leveled the business district, claimed over fifty lives, and injured hundreds more.

Dressed in a long, black dress with a matching opaque veil covering her face, this Annie flitted about the town's ruins, especially the grounds of the old East Side School which had been obliterated, taking several children's lives with it. One writer said, "She tripped across the ruins emitting mournful sounds as of a soul in torment."

"Yes, I remember Cyclone Annie well," recalled the late Uncle Elisha Rogers, a Mount Vernon cobbler who was ninety-three when he talked about Annie in an interview years after the tornado.

"I saw her the very night following the storm. She was standing at what is now the southeast corner of the public square. It was about 7:00 P.M. My horse was hitched in front of my shoe repair shop about fifty feet south of the corner. I mounted and rode north. She flittered out into the road yelling and screaming and so frightened my horse that I could hardly keep on his back. When I looked again she was gone. I sure did see her though."

By all accounts she frightened the daylights out of nearly everyone who saw her. Though Uncle Elisha claims she disappeared in an instant, most other observers thought she was a bereaved mother who lost her family in the tornado.

The corner of Fourteenth and Broadway in Mount Vernon attracted the next Annie scare. In that year of 1918 she was known widely simply as Black Annie. As twilight fell on several nights during the summer of that year, Annie chased after unsuspecting buggy drivers, horsemen, or young couples out for an evening stroll, again alarming nearly everyone who came in contact with her. Such was this Annie's antics that an armed posse patrolled the streets for weeks on end, but had little success in catching her. Writer Thomas H. Wells said that as a young boy if his mother asked him to go to the store at dusk, he would run as fast as he could so that the lady in black wouldn't catch him. Although some believed the ghost to be a man dressed in women's clothing, a plausible explanation was never proffered for this peculiar Annie sighting.

The final—so far—appearance of Annie or her kin might have occurred in a bizarre incident from the mid 1930s. As was common in those years before air conditioning, families in southern Illinois slept with their windows open on hot, humid summer nights. During the summer of 1936, authorities were alerted by scores of homeowners that someone was throwing sleeping powder on them through ground-level bedroom windows in an effort to leave the unsuspecting sleepers unconscious. In some cases, the distressed victims claimed the phantom prowler then climbed through the open windows and tried to drag them away.

Of course a local physician, Dr. Clarence Hamilton, assured residents that "there is no powder known to medical science which when thrown into the air will produce sleep, 'voilà.'" The attempt to kidnap people out of their homes may have put this case beyond the ability of even the beefiest of Annies, but no one knows for certain, as the nighttime assaults were never solved.

The only good that came out of the ordeal, according to one observer, was that husbands got to sleep nearer the cooler breezes coming through the screenless windows.

The appearances of Annie were also excellent tools for parents to discipline misbehaving youth. For decades Mount Vernon mothers and fathers warned their offspring to behave or they'd be put out onto the street for old Annie to snatch.

ANNIE WAS NOT the only reputed ghostly manifestation in old Mt. Vernon. A small body of water known as the Brick Hill Pond on the north side of Mt. Vernon, near the former Southern Railway tracks, achieved some notoriety in the early twentieth century as the site of four drownings and subsequent stories of ghostly cries.

The pond was actually a deep pit created by excavating clay used in the manufacturing of bricks. The fill pond, as it was termed, was reputedly seventy-five feet deep. On the north side of the pond stood a brick urn and several brick ovens that had been used years before in the baking of clay paving bricks.

After the brick plant was abandoned in 1911, superstition and fear quickly surrounded the desolate pond. At least four young boys reportedly drowned there, each one not knowing how deep and how cold the pond really was. The eerie cries of the boys could be heard by those daring enough to venture close.

For most Mt. Vernonians, however, it was not necessary to post KEEP OUT signs at the Brick Hill Pond.

The Peeper

In Lebanon, Illinois, some ninety miles northwest of Mt. Vernon, a strange lady of another ilk worried the good citizens of that city.

Today, Lebanon is a fairly typical small city coping with creeping suburbanization from St. Louis, Missouri, a scant twenty miles to the west. The city celebrated its bicentennial in 2004, but archaeological evidence found at nearby Emerald Mound suggests that the Mississippian Indian culture settled the region over a thousand years ago. McKendree College was founded there in 1828. It's the oldest college in Illinois. Even Charles Dickens stayed in Lebanon while visiting Looking Glass Prairie in 1842. He was a guest in the whimsically named Mermaid Inn, now partially restored and open for short visits.

But all of that would have been of scant interest to the city's residents in 1921 who were startled by a woman clad head to toe in black peering through their windows of an evening.

"I would sure like to have known who or what she was looking for at the time she was wandering upon the streets of Lebanon and looking into our windows," one man said shortly after the incidents ceased.

But neither this man nor anyone else had a chance to ask her any questions. When anyone got close enough to try and get a glimpse of her, she would vanish into the darkness or quickly dart across the street. Oddly enough, it was her persistent window peeping that finally got the populace riled up enough to do something about her. But it took four weeks of peeking to get the authorities to act.

The problem was that the entire Lebanon police force at the time consisted of a day marshal and a night watchman. They'd heard rumors and whisperings about this mysterious lady's odd behavior for some time. What spurred them to action, however, was the woman's penchant for following young women out for an evening's stroll. The women were frightened by the lady in black's sudden appearance and pestered the marshal until he agreed to organize a formal search.

According to later reports, on the third night of the hunt, the marshal and his deputy watchman spotted the woman skulking along about a block distant. They darted after her, but by the time they got to where they'd last seen her, no trace remained of their quarry. The search continued for several nights, but the two policemen never again saw the elusive woman in black.

Who or what might have been Lebanon's female stalker remains forever a mystery.

Not with My Daughter

Is it possible that one or more of the ladies in black which menaced the streets of Lebanon and Mt. Vernon also showed up in Carlyle, thirty miles east of Lebanon and about the same distance northwest of Mt. Vernon?

The city's history can be traced to about 1820 when the Vincennes, Indiana-to-St. Louis road was opened. The route had been known as Goshen Trace earlier, and there has been speculation that it actually had been in use for centuries as an Indian trail. A convenient ford across the Kaskaskia River at the site of present-day Carlyle was used for travelers on the newer Vincennes-St. Louis road.

The river, which once flowed freely through Carlyle, was tamed in the 1960s when a dam was built northeast of town creating Carlyle Lake, and a hoped-for residential and economic boom that never quite materialized.

Local Carlyle historians were careful to note that their mysterious figure back in the early 1930s was someone dressed in black female garb, alluding to the fact that folks were never sure about the sex of their peculiar prowler.

Some things *are* known about her, and we will use the feminine pronoun for a lack of evidence to the contrary. She was always heavily veiled and especially slow moving until members of several specific families came along. Then she would step along quickly behind them, always far enough to stay in the shadows, until they reached their destination.

People suspected that the supposed woman may have actually been a man because the figure was never seen on the better lighted roadways in town, but always on distant streets with dim lighting.

Members of the families targeted by the woman in black

were particularly distressed and many of them spent the entire time of her tenure in Carlyle never venturing out after dark, especially those on the outskirts of town.

Speculation soon arose about who the person might be. Some claimed it was the ghost of a woman who had been financially wronged and set about to avenge the misdeed. But a few others noted that after the woman who was subject to the speculation passed away, the lady in black vanished as well.

One of the more interesting theories, however, is that the figure was actually a mother dressed in strange and somber black garb to frighten away her teenage daughter's prospective suitors. The woman was a bit deranged, insisting that her daughter and friends never go out after nightfall. But there didn't seem to be any reason for her to be against such a seemingly normal teenage routine. Neither is it known if the daughter acquiesced to her mother's request.

FOR A SHORT time, Lebanon thought they had a lady in yellow as well.

Her routine was similar to the lady in black's routines, only the yellow lady confined her strolls to the south part of town. The sheriff and several deputies hastened to one particular street when they got a call that the lady in yellow had just been spotted going down a particular passageway. But when the posse arrived, the woman was gone. They found only a pile of bright yellow clothes. As one observer wryly noted, "After the finding of the clothing in the alley, the idea of the ghost was given up."

Beware the Sausagemaker

Sometimes Midwestern family life belies dark secrets best concealed from public scrutiny, as individuals discover much to their chagrin.

Mrs. Christine Feldt approached the doorstep of her apartment building at 149 Clybourn Avenue in Chicago. This late December night was bitter. A stiff wind plunged in off Lake Michigan and so it was perfectly reasonable that the couple scurrying toward her on the sidewalk had caps pulled low over their foreheads and heavy fur coats cinched tightly about their waists.

The young woman nodded a cursory greeting. Neither one acknowledged her as they passed under a streetlamp. Christine caught a quick look at their faces and instinctively drew back. These were people she knew. Knew quite well. The couple was Adolph and Louise Luetgert; he was one of the city's better known meat processors, while she was fairly prominent in second tier social circles.

But that didn't cause Christine Feldt to suddenly scream and crumble to the sidewalk in a dead faint.

No, her fright came because of what *else* she knew about them.

Although Louise Luetgert seemed, at that moment, to be passing Christine on the street, she was in fact *quite dead*. And had been for the better part of a year.

Mrs. Luetgert's few mortal remains—a cupful of bones and some inexpensive jewelry—had been discovered the previous May in and around a vat of toxic chemicals at her husband's sausage-making works.

Christine also knew that on this very cold December evening of 1897—though the late Louise's husband seemed for the entire world to be at her side there on Clybourn Avenue—Adolph Luetgert in truth sat in the county jail accused of her premeditated murder, one of the grisliest in early Chicago history. He had already escaped a conviction for her murder in a trial earlier in 1897, which had ended in a mistrial; a jury deadlocked nine to three for conviction. Luetgert was now on the eve of facing his second capital murder prosecution.

Christine Feldt also knew quite well how all of this had come about.

She had been Adolph's lover. He had promised her great wealth if, as she later testified against him in court, "anything happened to Louise."

The illicit affair between Christine and Adolph had begun sometime before his wife's most opportune passing. Later news reports even coyly hinted at the couple's making love "while his wife was living." The sausagemaker admitted giving his young paramour $4,000 in cash shortly before he was arrested for his wife's slaying.

But all of that was in the past. On this night a police officer discovered Christine regaining consciousness on the street where she lived and escorted her to her door. She recounted the strange event to the cop and it soon was on the tongues of thousands of Chicagoans. Newspaper accounts of the uncanny encounter breathlessly insisted it was just another chapter, the latest twist, in a bizarre case of illicit sex, failed business, and a horrific killing. Now added to the mix was a case of a dead woman walking.

ADOLPH LUETGERT WAS a fifty-two-year-old German immigrant who had arrived in the United States following the Civil War. After landing in New York City, he set off for the Mississippi River town of Quincy, Illinois, where he labored about six months for acquaintances of an older brother already in the States. He testified at his murder trial that he had $125 when he left Europe for America, and but three cents in his pocket at the time he left Quincy for Chicago in about 1867.

In the five years after his arrival in Chicago, Luetgert worked for several small tanning factories, saving his money all the while, so that in 1872 he started wholesale liquor businesses at "A" and Dominick Streets, and later near Clybourn and Webster Avenues, both in Chicago.

Luetgert married Caroline Rabker in 1872. She gave birth to two boys, only one of whom, Arnold, survived childhood. Caroline herself died five years later, in November 1877. Luetgert sold his liquor business in 1879 and moved to North and Clybourn Avenues where he opened a sausage-making business in the same building where he established his residence.

Meanwhile, in January 1878, two months after his first wife's death, he married Louise Bicknese. For a time he moved his family to a sixty-acre farm near Elgin in an effort to regain his health which, he said, had been ruined by the hard work necessitated at the sausage factory and the "constant care it entailed upon him."

The country life came to an end in a very short time. His wife did not take to the rural isolation, especially after an inmate from the old Elgin asylum escaped and ended up chasing Mrs. Luetgert around the property. She insisted upon returning to Chicago, to which Adolph acquiesced.

Back in the city, Luetgert dragged his small family through a veritable parade of homes. He bought property at North and Sheffield Avenues that would combine a residence on the upper floors and his sausage-making business on the lower levels. The family stayed there until 1891 when he bought another home, this one on Howe Street. Louise Luetgert found the smoke of the sausage-making disagreeable when she entertained friends. They moved to several locations before settling into a home on Hermitage Avenue in 1894, not far from another sausage plant Adolph built at Diversey and Hermitage Avenues.

Adolph Luetgert was from all indications a hardworking businessman, albeit with limited good fortune and modest financial sensibilities—he consistently underestimated the costs associated with his various enterprises and fell prey to constant borrowing to raise needed capital. The economic panic of 1893 had a particularly deleterious effect on him; he later told the court at his murder trial: "I had built my factory for running a business too large for the capital I had. I couldn't run it, as it ought to be run—in such capacity—to cover all expenses. The expenses were such that they would almost run away with the profit because I didn't have quite capital enough."

Once he developed the Hermitage Avenue factory, he said, "I did not have a cent (left) . . . and relied on borrowed capital."

The Luetgert marriage was not a happy one. Testimony at his trial portrayed Adolph as a volatile husband consumed with business dealings which were aggravated by his mounting financial woes. He was portrayed as a man who struck out physically at his wife (though he denied it under oath) and once watched passively as his son jumped upon and then broke a mahogany table in the family parlor. Adolph had egged on his son to perform the stunt.

Louise in turn appears to have been a woman with social aspirations who couldn't understand why all of her husband's hard work had not paid off in a lifestyle which would lift them above their struggle to stay ahead of creditors and bank foreclosure. She was preoccupied with the idea that their failing businesses would make them the subject of ridicule by their friends and relatives.

Adolph and Louise's relationship seems to have started its final unraveling in late April 1897, only two weeks before her disappearance, according to the trial testimony. He'd made plans to sell a portion of the sausage business to outside investors, anticipating an economic windfall. When the deal collapsed, he fell to paying off loan interest with even more loans until the prospect that he'd lose both his factory and his home forced him to reveal to his wife even more depressing details of their deteriorating financial condition.

"I did not tell her before because she was all glorious over the prospect of my good business and (having) so much money," Luetgert testified. "I had promised to give her $50,000 after the deal went through, and we were to move into a nicer neighborhood. She kept on asking me about the business until I finally had to tell her."

Louise did not take the news well. In fact, Adolph testified, she told him that she planned to go away and that he would not see her again. He pleaded with her that he would continue to make a good living for his family. But she feared losing their livelihood. He tried to joke away her concerns, but his insouciance added to her ire.

A FEW DAYS before her disappearance and alleged murder, Louise Luetgert took unambiguous steps to leave her husband. She hired an express company to move several trunks and wrapped bundles to her sister's home on Lincoln Avenue. She told the deliveryman the packages contained clothing and that she was moving out of her house, though there is no indication that she lived long enough to actually have left her husband.

While Louise made her plans, evidence at trial pointed to Adolph making his plans to murder her, knowing there would be nothing left in his life if his business failed and his wife abandoned him. He didn't hide his bitterness. A house painter named Frank Handel testified that Adolph talked to him at a tavern near the sausage factory about what could be done if you were unhappily married. Handel replied that if it were he, he would get a divorce or move away. But Luetgert said, according to Handel, ". . . they (women) are all beasts, and if he had a woman like that, he would take her and throw her where there would not be enough left for the sun to shine on. . . ."

Meanwhile, at his sausage factory, Adolph was undertaking unusual preparations to "clean" his factory by manufacturing a potent, potash-based soap, even though he had never made his own cleaning solutions before. He mixed the solution in the basement of the factory in a wooden vat nearly twelve feet tall. The prosecution argued that the 348 pounds of potash he ordered for the concoction, along with other ingredients like tallow, mutton, suet, lye, fat, and other factory bone waste, would have made 6,700 pounds of soap, far too much for cleaning purposes. A barrel of soap weighing 175 pounds could be purchased for one dollar in 1897, while a similar amount of Luetgert's potash soap cost well over eight dollars in ingredients alone.

LOUISE LUETGERT VANISHED from sight late on Saturday night, May 1, 1897. The circumstances of her disappearance are as mysterious today as they were a century ago and the method used for her probable demise as dreadful as one could imagine.

Adolph testified that on that Saturday afternoon, and later at the evening meal, he and his wife argued again about their family's future and that of his business. A deal to sell part of his business collapsed earlier in the week and he failed to negotiate loans to pay a long-standing $5,000 debt. Louise was fearful that not only would the business be taken over by the loan guarantors, but that the family would lose their home, possessions, and life savings.

Luetgert's testimony was quite blunt concerning his wife's fears:

"My wife asked me what I was going to get for all my hard work since I came to this country. I felt bad, but I told her I could work again, as I used to, and that I could carry my dinner basket as I did years ago. I told her not to worry. She knew I was willing to work, but she said that people would laugh at us if we had to begin over again. I told her to let them laugh, that we would go to some other town. She said she wouldn't stay in Chicago, where everybody would be pointing fingers at us."

Luetgert tried to laugh off his wife's concerns, but his own recollection of her distress did not help his defense.

"She was very much worried and sad," he said. "She told me I had been working hard for thirty years and was ruined. She cried and said she wished she and the children were with the other children in Waldheim Cemetery."

THE SIGNIFICANCE OF the potash mixture—as he prepared it, such a combination easily could have dissolved human bone and tissue—played a key role in the prosecution's case against Luetgert. They argued that Luetgert murdered his wife late Saturday night or early Sunday morning and then used the chemical solution to liquefy the corpse.

Here is what is alleged to have been the chain of events on those two days in early May:

At their evening meal on Saturday, the couple's argument about their financial troubles culminated in Adolph's revelation that since he could not raise the money to pay off the loans, the Cook County sheriff might take charge of his home and business property and sell it at auction. Louise wept at that prospect.

"If the sheriff comes then you won't see me again," Louise told her husband.

Also at suppertime, the couple's son Louis asked to attend a circus with friends, to which his parents agreed. He was gone until later in the evening.

A live-in servant girl, Mary Siemering, had sprained her ankle and was restricted to her room. Adolph said he went to a nearby store to purchase liniment for her injury, which he said he brought back and gave to her.

(He denied under oath that he'd also had an affair with young Mary.)

Adolph maintained that he departed for his factory sometime after eight forty-five Saturday night—later confirmed by his factory's night watchman and another employee—to do some work and tend to the preparation of the potash soapmaking. He sent the watchman, Frank Bialk, on an errand to get a bottle of medicine at a nearby drugstore. Bialk spent the rest of the night in the factory's engine-room. Another factory worker, William Charles, was helping Luetgert with the potash mixture. The two men also spent some time drinking in a neighborhood saloon.

A few hours later, Luetgert returned to his house, ostensibly to get tea, which was typically prepared by young Mary Siemering and taken to him each night at the factory. But with her injuries she had been unable to attend to the errand.

"My wife was sitting in the kitchen when I got home," he insisted.

He testified that his wife was reading a German language newspaper under a bracket gaslight, which was her usual custom in the evenings. After making his own tea, he said he bid his wife good night, grabbed up his lantern, and left by the front door.

"I have not seen her (Louise) since," Luetgert maintained.

He said he met his son coming in the door after returning from the circus. The child went straight to bed. Adolph said he then returned to his factory, alone.

However, Diedrich Bicknese, Louise's brother, told the court that little Louis contradicted his father's testimony. Louis told him that his mother and father "went downstairs" together after they saw him to bed the night of May 1.

Luetgert claimed that later that night music from a neighboring dance hall was still playing when he came home. He said he felt ill and didn't go to sleep right away. He said he got up Sunday morning at about five-thirty and went back to the factory. The soap mixture was too rich and he had to add water to thin it out. He then had breakfast alone sometime between six and seven A.M.

He did not notice his wife's absence. He thought she might have been out somewhere, and besides he "had to doctor a sick horse at the barn" Sunday afternoon. The couple did not sleep in the same room.

"Mary told me that my wife was not at home, so I thought she might be over to the store," Luetgert testified. "After breakfast I went back to the factory. I went home to dinner and Mary Siemering told me that my wife had not returned. I talked to the girl about my wife, but made up my mind she was somewhere in the neighborhood. Mary told me that she had found the front door open and asked me if I left it open. I told her I had not. I knew she had not been at the store, because I had asked one of (my) boys about it. Mary also told me that my wife had not occupied her bed that night."

The prosecution's argument was that Luetgert used some means to entice his wife to accompany him to the sausage factory between the hours of ten and eleven Saturday night, killed her in an undetermined manner, removed her clothes, and then secreted the body in one of his factory's meat curing smokehouses. He kept it there until he could take it unobserved to the solution of caustic potash. The smokehouse and the vat were in basement rooms not far away from one another.

Very early Sunday morning, he dumped his wife's remains in the potash solution and turned up the steam pressure to bring the liquid to a boil. Most of the unfortunate Louise's remains were dissolved. Later, he scooped out a few remaining small bones, her false teeth, several rings, and, together with the clothing he had removed from the body, burned it all in the factory furnace.

But he didn't clean up thoroughly enough.

Police later found bone fragments, rings, and a false human tooth in their search of the furnace and vat rooms. Medical witnesses for the prosecution identified the bones as human, and the rings had Louise's initials on them. Burned matches, an unusual quantity of sawdust, and ashes, with prints of human feet, were found in the furnace room as well.

CHRISTINE FELDT'S ROLE in the actual murder is unclear at best. Luetgert evidently had known her for nearly thirty years by the time of the trial. She was a widow whose husband had also been a friend of Luetgert's. She, too, was a German immigrant. Her approximately fifteen letters to Luetgert while he was in jail awaiting trial, and the court testimony about their relationship prior to his wife's murder substantiated the prosecution's claims that the couple had made plans "should anything happen to Louise."

He denied that they were romantically involved, but admitted to "a warm friendship for her . . ."

The warmth of their friendship did not extend to her protecting him against the charges. She testified against him at both trials. At the first, she said he told her "after I get the factory troubles arranged, I'll settle with her (Louise)." But at the second trial, her memory changed. She swore he told her that "after I get my troubles with the factory settled, I'll make up my mind what I'll do with her."

Although Christine was clearly Luetgert's mistress and confidante, her testimony was a major factor in his conviction. There are indications she may have tried to extort money from him and had designs on acquiring his home and at least part of his failing business.

MEANWHILE, LOUISE REMAINED missing. Her disappearance had been reported to the police, but not by her husband. A friend had gone to authorities with concerns about her well-being. Adolph claimed that the police were not competent to conduct a search for his wife and refused for the most part to cooperate with them. Searches for her were conducted as far afield as Wheaton, Kankakee, and Elgin. One person claimed to have seen her at the train station in Monmouth, Illinois. The informant said he recognized the woman after noticing a poster seeking information about Louise's whereabouts. That report was never substantiated.

Her husband became a suspect almost immediately. Searches of the Luetgert factory and home had turned up little in the way of evidence until May 15 when those rings, later identified as belonging to Louise, were discovered in the potash vat. A more thorough sweep of the basement rooms located bone fragments and dentures. Several medical doctors at trial identified the bones as human and the dentures as similar to those worn by Louise Luetgert.

Adolph Luetgert was arrested on May 17, 1897, nearly two and a half weeks after his wife's disappearance, and was arraigned on May 18. A Chicago grand jury on June 6, 1897, charged him with first degree murder.

His trial began on August 23 and dragged on for sixty-one days until Judge Tuthill dismissed the jury on October 21 when they couldn't agree on a unanimous verdict—they deadlocked nine to three for conviction.

Luetgert was retried in a proceeding that stretched from November 26, 1897, to February 9, 1898, when the jury returned with a guilty verdict. He was sentenced to life imprisonment.

THE VISITS BY the departed Louise Luetgert to Christine Feldt began almost immediately after the murder, increased in intensity over the coming months, and were so disturbing that she at last persuaded Captain Schuettler, of the Sheffield Avenue Police Station, to station cops at her door each night so that they might "keep out the haunting faces." Even the doors and windows to her apartment were barricaded to keep Louise's wan visage at bay.

INTERESTINGLY, SCHUETTLER WAS one of the cops who investigated the murder. During the trial, Christine claimed both Schuettler and an Inspector Schaack threatened to "ruin her reputation" if she did not cooperate by testifying against Luetgert.

The ghost of Louise Luetgert visited Christine both in and outside her home on Clybourn Avenue. The frightened woman tried to speak to the ghost during each visit. She never got a reply. As the second trial went on, Christine claimed that Louise's ghost came each and every night so that rarely did she sleep very long. And when she did manage to fall asleep, the nightmares came, the dreadful dreams in which Adolph himself made appearances, imploring her to remain by his side during the ordeal. No one could explain how he was able to accomplish the feat of being in two places at the same time.

Captain Schuettler assigned two patrolmen to accompany Christine Feldt home after trial each day. None of the officers reported seeing any apparitions.

However, the insistent haunting took its toll.

Mrs. Feldt was in a pitiable condition, the press reported, expressing the fear that she might lose her reason.

That would have been a prospect that might have pleased Adolph Luetgert, the malevolent sausagemaker she spurned.

Restless Haven

"There are some mighty strange things going on out there. The folks are easily scared."

Thus with striking understatement did Will County Deputy Sheriff Chester Moberly sum up his investigation of a peculiar case of poltergeist commotion in the community once known as Rest Haven, a few miles south of Wilmington, in northeast Illinois.

Literally hundreds of onlookers, newspaper reporters, and photographers spent days tramping around the yard and through the home of the James Mikulecky family, which also included their teenage granddaughter, Susan Wall. And all because various household appliances, homely objects—and food!—somehow took flight at various times and lurched about the family homestead.

The events began unfolding in early August 1957 in the small village then known as a summer retreat for residents of Chicago, about fifty miles away. There were some 300 homes—cottages to the locals—at the time. The Kankakee River is close by so people there and in nearby Wilmington referred to the places as "cottages by the river."

An Associated Press article on August 18 ratcheted up the excitement level by describing "newspapermen and photographers joining hundreds of curious visitors in an effort to spot (a ghost)." It all centered at the Mikulecky home. James and his wife were both described as being in their 60s, and their granddaughter, Susan Wall, as fifteen.

The couple said that for over a week objects had been hurtling through the air in their home, including various kitchen food items that had struck young Susan. Worse still, the family poltergeist had followed them to two other residences to which they had fled, including the home of Mrs. Mae Vlasek directly across the street. Some neighbors were hardly consoling—one woman called Mrs. Mikulecky a witch, which she understandably denied.

A reporter for the local Wilmington newspaper seems to have broken the story with her firsthand account of watching in amazement as items buzzed around her head. "Soap and a soap dish (flew) from the bathroom wall, a stuffed kitten twice jumped mysteriously from atop a television set to the floor, and magazines propelled themselves off an end table," the reporter said.

At the height of the bombardment, hundreds of people from Rest Haven, Wilmington, and elsewhere thronged the Mikulecky home's yard and nearby streets hoping to catch a glimpse of the ghost. Two dozen journalists and photographers prowled closer to the house trying to unravel the mystery. Although they asked, reporters were denied access inside the Mikuleckys' cottage. The turmoil had left Mrs. Mikulecky in tears, according to the newspaper report.

THE OFFICIAL RECORD about the Mikulecky cottage following the supposed poltergeist incident is nearly nonexistent, with one fascinating footnote: a mysterious fire leveled the home of Susan Wall's father, directly across the street from one of the homes to which the Mikuleckys and Susan Wall had fled.

The fire call came at 12:55 A.M. on Monday, August 26, 1957, nearly three weeks after the first reported poltergeist incident. One account said "the fire had a good start before the (fire) department was called." Firefighters were on the scene for two hours. No one was injured or killed in the fire. The house was a complete loss.

The cause of the fire was initially listed as undetermined.

Could it have had something to do with the pesky Mikulecky poltergeist?

Apparently the poltergeist theory was brought to the fire department's attention.

"Firemen at the scene ... discounted the idea that any ghostly apparitions were connected with the blaze," one newspaper account reported.

Firefighter Bill Kurth said the fire may have been caused by faulty wiring. Wilmington officials turned the investigation over to the state fire marshal's office.

After that, the case, and the families, receded from public view. Even a poltergeist can grow tired of crowds.

5

The Beckoners

> Are we not spirits, that are shaped into a body, into
> an appearance, and that fade away again into air and
> invisibility? Oh, Heaven it is mysterious, it is awful
> to consider that we not only carry a future ghost
> within us, but are, in very deed, ghosts!
>
> —Thomas Carlyle, *Sartor Resartus:*
> *Natural Supernaturalism*

A VICTORIAN-ERA LIBRARY, a rural churchyard and a formerly secluded roadway do not seem to have much in common, yet they
are three among Indiana's more interesting haunted sites. Not
that the state needs any more. It may be among the most haunted
in the Midwest. In earlier volumes, we've found other suspect
library presences—DePauw University's in Greencastle, for
instance—eerie graveyards such as Stepp Cemetery in the
Morgan-Monroe State Forest, phantom soldiers on their way to
the Battle of Tippecanoe, the remarkable Hannah House in Indianapolis, and other Indiana ghost stories. But for the moment,
consider these three to be just the tip of the spectral iceberg.

The Willard's Lady in Gray

"On a cold winter morning in 1937, a janitor grabbed his
flashlight and headed down into the pitch black basement
of the Willard Library to stoke the coal furnace. But
then . . . he was stopped in his tracks by the ghostly vision of a woman dressed in grey, from the veil covering
her face down to her shoes. Since then, a number of
Willard staff members have reported seeing the shadow

'lady in grey' or witnessing weird happenings among the shelves."
—James Pritchard, Associated Press, October 31, 1999

What is it that haunts the 120-year-old library in Evansville, Indiana?

Housed in a grand Victorian Gothic building, the oldest public library building in Indiana certainly looks the role of the premier haunted library in all the United States. Some call it a "living, breathing haunted house." So prominent is the ghost of Willard Library that the local newspaper installed perhaps the only "ghost cameras" in any public building anywhere. Several of the library's rooms are outfitted with stationary video cameras that can be accessed via the Internet. The picture changes every few seconds, allowing viewers the opportunity to participate in a sort of stop-motion, ghost-hunting expedition through the library.

That janitor back in 1937 never did get the coal shoveled. He was so astounded at the sudden appearance of this pale lady who seemed to glow in the dark that he hastily scooped up his flashlight and ran out of the building, never to return, according to the story.

Named after local philanthropist Willard Carpenter, the Willard library is near downtown Evansville. It was placed on the National Register of Historic Places in 1972.

According to the library history, the Willard's lady in gray appearances and near-appearances have been plentiful over the years:

• Margaret M. Maier worked at the library for over forty years, from her high school graduation in 1937 until 1980. The children's room—one of the locations of a ghost camera—was renamed in her honor. She claimed the lady in gray followed her home one night when the children's room was undergoing renovation. Miss Maier and her sister felt an unseen presence in their home and several times were enveloped in a sudden chill. The strong scent of perfume also attended the lady's visit to the Maiers.

• The same pungent odor of perfume abruptly swept over two members of a local genealogy group working on cemetery records in the library's research room. Experts say ghost sightings are sometimes accompanied by the scent of flowers or of perfume.

- Bettye Elaine Miller, a long-time Willard employee, was the head librarian from 1972 to 1975. Her work often required staying after hours. One evening at her desk, she heard water running from somewhere on the second floor. She rushed up the stairs to discover a faucet in a bathroom had been turned on. Sometime later, another librarian using that same bathroom saw a faucet slowly turn on all by itself.

- The apparition of the gray lady appears and vanishes so quickly that it's been difficult to affix an identity to her, yet so many librarians and patrons report seeing her that there seems little doubt among believers that a ghost does, indeed, live at the library.

But who, in fact, might this persistent, ethereal library patron be?

The prime candidate seems to be Louise Carpenter, the embittered daughter of the library's benefactor, Willard Carpenter. Louise unsuccessfully sued the library's board of trustees at the time of its construction. She claimed her father was "of unsound mind and was unduly influenced in establishing the library." There isn't any explanation of what she meant by this ambiguous accusation. The supposition is that she has returned to the library that she objected to in life and will stay in residence until the property is returned to the living descendants of Willard Carpenter.

The Evansville Courier & Press worked with the library to install the ghost cameras. They became so successful and so widely viewed that what began as a temporary Halloween "promotion" has now turned into a permanent attempt to capture on video a visit by the lady in gray at: www.libraryghost.com.

The original camera was in the Willard's research room because many of the fleeting sightings had occurred there. A second was installed high on a bookshelf in the children's room. Another camera is in the basement not far from where the janitor had the first recorded encounter with the ghost seventy years ago. This last camera can be moved right and left by remote control for a more sweeping view of the area.

An editor at the newspaper told an Associated Press reporter the cameras have been very popular with Internet users. There have been enough unusual incidents to make him something of a believer. One of the bookshelf-mounted cameras was found one morning inexplicably turned in the opposite direction from the day before. Employees denied touching it.

"I think something is out there, to paraphrase *The X-Files*," the editor said. "We stand ready and willing to believe."

Several hundred thousand hits have been recorded at the Web site. Viewers are invited to share their comments and share any pictures in which they think they detect the ghost. Some of the ghost images are fuzzy and easily dismissed as optical illusions or distortions. Others, however, are more difficult to write off.

The children's room seems to be one of the more popular sites, based on these responses from ghost cam enthusiasts:

A viewer from Amsterdam enclosed a picture in which a child is staring intently through a doorway, beyond which there seems to be a hazy figure. "The child is clearly looking at (the figure) with anxiety or fright," the woman, named Andrea, wrote. "When I zoomed in, the spirit was holding a book, as if she was reading to the child. I thought this was a parent but colors were missing. Interesting is that she is also wearing clothing from around that time. . . ."

In another image, a figure appears to be crouching in that same doorway.

A hooded figure peers over a bookshelf in another captured picture forwarded by a viewer.

The research room also has its share of possible sightings:

The faint likeness of a woman appears to be sitting at the end of one of the tables. The Internet viewer of this image said: "I saw the gray lady. I was (looking at the site) with my brother . . . and spotted her. It was (on screen) when it refreshed twice, then she was gone."

Another ghost cam user circled a hazy, yet distinct object that does indeed appear to be a candle. She said: "I am not sure what this is, but on the first table, second chair to the left I think I see the faint image of a candle . . . or something. I don't know if my mind is just playing tricks or what."

A viewer circled in blue what may possibly be a seated figure bending over the table holding something in its hand. "I saw this Friday, October 25, 2002, 6:55:39 P.M. It (seems) to me that there's something sitting at the table holding a writing instrument. . . ." she wrote to the library website.

Another viewer circled what seems to be a person in almost the same area, yet on a different day. "I was looking on your ghost cam . . . and I think I have caught a sighting of the lady in gray. I have circled her in green. It looks as if she is bending over looking at the books on the shelf in the back of the research room," a viewer named Samantha wrote.

The ghost is not a technophobe. One captured image appears to show a faint head peering from behind a computer terminal.

Although Louise Carpenter objected to the library's construction, her ghost might be more accepting. A digitally enhanced image from the ghost cam seems to show the ghost returning a book to its proper shelf.

Since there is little chance the library property will revert to Carpenter heirs, the lady in gray, if it is indeed Louise Carpenter, may be doomed to wander among the bookshelves for decades to come.

Old Graybeard

What was it in rural Benton, Indiana, a century ago that stirred so much national curiosity that a major Philadelphia newspaper included the event in an assortment of ghost stories from around the world?

It came to be known as "the ghost in the churchyard," and for folks in that now-vanished Pike County community, the puzzle was never solved. This is the way the haunting unfolded, according to the reports:

A farmer named John W. French and his wife were first to see the apparition on a bright, moonlit summer night. Returning to their farm home after visiting with some neighbors, the couple was in their horse-drawn buggy as they drew abreast of the neighborhood's old, moss-covered church with its adjoining cemetery. The Frenches' mare, Belle, suddenly snorted and reared back. John French couldn't see what caused her sudden terror. As a precaution he reached for a shotgun that lay on the floor of the buggy. Robbers had been known to frequent the area.

But roving criminals were not to be his trouble.

"John, look over there!" his wife cried out. She was pointing down the road.

At the edge of the cemetery several yards ahead was the looming figure of a tall old man clad from head to toe in some sort of white garment. A scraggly gray beard hung down to his chest. In his right hand he held a club, and with his left he beckoned the couple to come forward. The farmer was too distressed to do anything but try and regain control of his prancing and snorting horse. He saw the figure gliding toward him seemingly without effort. Its feet did not touch the ground.

"John, for the love of God get us out of here," Mrs. French shrieked. "We shall be killed if we do not!"

She implored her husband to turn the trap around and head back to their neighbors' house.

As the strange old man advanced on the couple, he slowly raised the club to shoulder level much as a soldier might raise a rifle before firing. After what seemed an eternity to Mrs. French, her husband got Belle under control and whipped her hard as the buggy spun around and headed back in the direction from where they'd come.

The couple nearly collapsed from exhaustion as they recounted their harrowing tale to their skeptical neighbors.

That might have been the end of the affair, and the dismissal of their story as an invention or hallucination, had it not been for one Milton Moon, a Benton man renowned for his wisdom and fearlessness. He was the next one to see this nocturnal phantom.

Mr. Moon found himself in much the same position as John French and his wife, but his report was taken far more seriously. Indeed Moon's experience led to several "delegations" of local people scouring the cemetery and surrounding woods in hopes that they might be able to identify the spectre, if indeed that is what it was.

In the end, the people of Benton agreed that the Frenches and Milton Moon had seen the revenant of an old hermit who once lived not far from the church. He was known for paying a daily visit to visit the grave of his late wife. He also had something of a reputation as a miser—rumors were that he had a stash of gold buried somewhere on his property.

One night a decade earlier several robbers set upon him as he returned home from the graveyard, demanding to know where he had hidden his money. He refused to tell them and the thugs slit his throat. He was buried in the church cemetery, in a plot next to his wife's.

The dead hermit's wraith and the fear it instilled in that isolated community eventually faded away with the passing of years . . . and of memories.

The Devil's Hollow

Teenagers and Hollywood filmmakers have long shared a fascination with gruesome murders on lonely lovers' lanes. They are among the most widely known of horror story lines. Whether haunted by recently escaped homicidal maniacs, or by towering, grim spectres wielding bloody hatchets, a town's favorite trysting place has proven to be a nearly universal symbol of naughty behavior rewarded with swift and awful retribution.

While most people assume that such locations exist only in the fervid imaginations of those selfsame teens and screenwriters, in truth this fragment of urban lore is often based on real places with forbidding reputations. They have elements of the ghost story and of teenage anxieties.

Such is the case near Fort Wayne, Indiana, where the forbiddingly-named Devil's Hollow has captured the imagination of locals for many decades. Located in Aboite Township, in the southwest corner of Allen County, what is now renamed Devil's Hollow Road extends southward from Liberty Mills Road, northeast of Interstate 24. It is a winding road that remained gravel-covered until recent years. In years past, dense stands of trees and heavy brush grew within a few feet of the road, keeping it gloomy on even the sunniest of days. Some of the wealthiest families in Fort Wayne had homes in the area.

The Hollow was notorious for many mysterious events, according to research now at the Indiana University Folklore Archives.

"Originally Devil's Hollow was much larger than at present and only had a dirt path leading through it instead of a road. There were many Indians in this area . . . and when white settlers attempted to settle here, they were massacred. These murdered settlers supposedly put a type of curse on Devil's Hollow which was to set the stage for the strange events that would occur in the future," a researcher and writer noted in an informal account of the legends.

"I have been to Devil's Hollow many times walking or visiting friends, yet every time I approach it, I feel a sensation of uniqueness and a slight fear because of the surroundings," the writer added.

She said that the region always seems to have a hazy cast in the air.

While some of the stories are similar in nature to other "lovers' lane" lore around the nation, what sets Devil's Hollow apart to some extent is that a real event may have instigated at least some of the beliefs.

One college student said that he ignored most of the stories until he had his own alarming experience.

"I've lived in Devil's Hollow all my life and I've heard all the stories but they never bothered me too much," he said. "I . . . didn't get too shook up . . . I knew it was just a . . . fake. But now the story that bothers me is the one about the escaped convict with the hook arm. He was supposed to be hiding in Devil's Hollow because it's so heavily wooded. He'd attack kids who were parking there. One couple heard scratching on their car, so they spun out and when they cleared the area, they looked outside the car and saw the guy's hook stuck to the handle of the door.

"Now, the reason this story is strange to me is because there was an escaped convict . . . hiding in Devil's Hollow, but he didn't have that hook arm. One of our hounds started to bark and broke loose then, so (my brother) and I went out to look for him. We finally got him back. We were coming up our drive . . . and we found somebody's truck parked about a third of the way up. Then this guy jumped us from nowhere and held us at gunpoint. He told us if we made any noise he'd blow our brains out, so he got in the truck and took off. We called the cops after he left and they finally chased him down with a helicopter. . . ."

THE TWO MOST prominent tales associated with Devil's Hollow Road—and lovers' lanes in general—are those of the man with the hook and another that's sometimes called the "hanging boyfriend."

A twenty-three-year-old nurse said she knew about the legends of Devil's Hollow from an early age:

"One was supposed to be about a man who escaped from prison and was somewhere in the area. He had a hook arm that everybody was supposed to be able to identify him by. Devil's Hollow (was) a great place for parking and it just happened that two teenagers were parked there the night he escaped. They heard on the radio that the escaped convict was supposed to be in the area. They didn't think too much of it, and jokingly locked the doors. After awhile, the girl thought she heard a scratching noise on the side of the car. They turned around and looked outside and thought they saw the image of a man. The boy and girl got really scared and took off as fast as they could. When they got back to the girl's house, they got out and found the man's hook hanging from the door handle."

The same woman said she also knew the legend of the hanging boyfriend:

"A couple was riding around down there and ran out of gas. There aren't any gas stations around, but the guy got out to walk anyway. He told his girlfriend to stay put and lock the doors. If she heard any noises she was to get down on the car floor so no one would see her or bother her. She followed his instructions and locked the doors after him. After some time she heard a weird scratching across the roof and got very scared. She did get down on the floor but she began to think that the noise was just a branch and that she was being really stupid. . . . She finally got out to stretch her legs and looked up. Her boyfriend had been hung by his feet somehow, and the noise she'd heard was his hands scraping across the top of the car."

Many stories about horrifying lovers' lanes contain a variation of a menacing old man in a decrepit mansion. Devil's Hollow was no exception, except that in this case there was an element of truth.

An old wagon-wheel arch leading to a rutted driveway once marked the entrance to the estate of a wealthy Fort Wayne man. He was eccentric and is said to have once tried to begin a wildlife preserve on his land. In one of the stories, a group of local teens decided to harass him after they'd consumed a vast quantity of beer.

"They all got in a car and parked it outside his drive with the wagon wheel arch," according to the folklorist who tracked down the story. "Some of them decided to stay with the car so they could get away fast if they had to. The others went back down the lane. After awhile, the boys in the car heard dogs barking and then gunshots. They took off, leaving the others stranded in the woods. After they'd sobered up, they realized what they had done and went back to pick them up, but they were gone and were never seen again."

Adding to the mystery was the fact that the drive was eventually plowed up and the wagon-wheel archway taken down. In reality, the old man who lived on the property died and his estate was sold. A new addition was planned and the old driveway was plowed under to make way for a different entrance to the property.

Fort Wayne's Devil's Hollow Road may be a modern thoroughfare today, but its status as an authentic lovers' lane with all the attendant legends remains unchanged.

6
Old Deg

There is something beyond the grave; death does not end all, and the pale ghost escapes from the vanquished pyre.

—Anonymous

S. C. DIXON MIGHT have known something was not quite right when he went to work in the old photography studio. The year was 1974. Dixon had hired on with the elderly woman who had bought the business from the founder decades before. She was now getting ready to sell it herself. Dixon was an eager young man who found the selling price of less than five thousand dollars a real bargain for a college student like himself who was anxious to be his own boss.

Maybe it was a good buy because the premises came with more than cameras, photo chemicals, and a steady clientele.

Also in residence was the ghost of its first owner.

"She would make these little allusions to 'Deg,'" Dixon says today, referring to the first photographer/owner, D. D. Degler, who founded the studio in the 1920s. "She'd gone to work for him in 1931 and worked there until I bought it. She stayed on for several months after I bought it to help me get acclimated to the business, to help me learn what I needed to know. But if we were downstairs in the darkroom and heard a crash from somewhere or smelled pipe smoke, she'd say, 'Oh, it's probably Deg checking us out.'"

Sudden noises.

Tobacco smoke.

A long-dead business owner curious about the new man in "his" store.

It all became part of an extraordinary fifteen years for S. C. Dixon, a time spent fending off an odious spirit that never accepted the studio's third and, as it turned out, final proprietor.

THE GRANADA PHOTO Studio occupied the north wing of the Fox Granada Theater building, in the 800 block of Commercial Street, in downtown Emporia, Kansas. Built in 1929 during the golden age of movie palaces, the plush, Spanish Renaissance-design Fox Granada is undergoing extensive renovation and is scheduled to reopen in a few years. During the heyday of its operation, the theater featured films and live vaudeville entertainment. Ginger Rogers danced on its stage. Old posters backstage boast that it was the finest theater "this side of Kansas City." The Granada had two wings extending out from the main theater center itself that housed various businesses over the years. The Degler Photo Studio was one of the original tenants. It opened in 1928, a full year before the movie house itself welcomed its first audience, and remained in continuous operation until S.C. Dixon closed it down in 1989.

"I was the last original tenant in the building," Dixon remembers. "It was up for tax sale. A (movie) theater company from Kansas City purchased it, came down once, and never came back."

Dixon said in the last months of his operation the heat didn't work and the electricity was "tentative at best." When a twenty pound piece of concrete fell from the ceiling—Deg's doings?—and missed Dixon by a few feet, he decided that the time had come to leave. That and the city's confusion over unpaid taxes and building ownership.

"I hadn't paid rent for the last six months I was there because there was no owner to pay it to. The city served me with a notice for nonpayment of taxes. It was very comical. I went to a city meeting and they asked why I hadn't paid taxes. I said that I didn't own the building and I didn't have any idea as to who did."

Though the Kansas City company had earlier paid back taxes they never actually claimed the title to the building, Dixon said.

The grand old theater was scheduled to be razed when government agencies and an Emporia historic preservation group, the Granada Theater Alliance, combined to save the building. Through grants and fund-raising, the group hopes to return the theater to its golden age with film showings, community theater performances, meeting rooms, and a new home for the Emporia Arts Council. A coffee shop has already taken up residence in Dixon's old photo studio quarters.

THE GRANADA PHOTO STUDIO, S. C. Dixon's livelihood for fifteen years, was a fairly typical small town photography business with the customary specializations in high school graduation pictures, weddings, anniversaries, and family reunions.

Dixon is a straightforward small-town businessman who continues in the photography business, although in another downtown Emporia locale. He does not, as he notes, "see dead people." But those years in the old Degler studio bring back some unpleasant memories.

"I always had the feeling that whatever this was . . . that it was resentful. That was my overwhelming sensation. I'm a pretty straight-laced guy. I had noticed so many things happening long before I ever mentioned the fact to anyone. When I started talking to my friends or my employees or to my family, I did it in a fairly joking manner. Then I found out that almost everyone who spent any time in that studio with me, whether it was a friend or an employee, had been noticing the same things all along. That smell of pipe tobacco, and most predominant of all the feeling of being watched, the sense that someone else was in the room, but never seeing anyone. But I'd put a condition on that. When you're in a darkroom for extended periods of time it's not uncommon for one to see shadowy movements in your eyes. So I'd say I didn't see anything that I could pinpoint."

Though Dixon didn't *see* anything that he could identify as a ghost, the almost palpable sense of dread grew inexorably more pronounced over the years.

"It seemed like the skeptics never stayed skeptical very long. I got to the point near the end that hardly anything could convince me to go into that darkroom after two or three in the afternoon. It was just so incredibly uncomfortable, extremely oppressive. This presence, Degler, if indeed that's who it was, simply never accepted me as a photographer or as an interloper on any level. It was almost a malevolent feeling. Not just being uncomfortable but knowing that somebody wanted me out of there. I was more than happy to oblige."

DIXON'S DECADE AND a half in the Emporia photography studio business is a study in perseverance, not only in surviving with a small-town commercial enterprise but also in combating the manifestation of a force that seemed to be waging as much of a psychological war against him as a physical battle.

This is the story S. C. Dixon tells:

In the autumn of 1975, he was finishing his first year as owner of The Granada Studio. He'd left college short of a degree to buy the business from Mrs. Udene Burnell, the woman who'd taken over after the death of D. D. Degler. Dixon had no way of knowing then that he would be the final owner.

Degler was an "old-timey" fellow, Dixon says, who had something of the showman about him, which you had to have to survive as a traveling photographer on the Great Plains. At one time he owned seven portrait studios around Kansas, including his original one in Emporia. Degler was an inveterate promoter, as illustrated in this story Dixon heard from Mrs. Burnell about the difficulties of staying in business during the rationing of World War II:

"He knew how to actually mix the chemicals to make a film emulsion," Dixon says. "So he got his hands on some plate glass, which was also being rationed at the time. He painted the glass with the emulsion, let it dry, and then created the photograph. He had a built-in sales tool because he would tell the people that if they wanted more enlargements they needed to get them now because he had to scrape the glass clean and repaint it for the next portrait. During the war they were doing a hell of a business," primarily because of Degler's keen "buy it now before it's gone" marketing skills.

"At one time there were four people working simultaneously in the darkroom," Dixon says of the original studio years. "Mrs. Burnell said they'd work until two or three in the morning or, and I loved the expression she used, until the last dog was hung." He has no idea where that expression came from.

Since Degler's portrait studio was open a full year before the movie house, Dixon thinks it possible that he had some say in the construction of his main floor portrait studio and the darkroom below it.

"The darkroom was dark as a tomb," Dixon says. "He had state-of-the-art equipment, but it had to be assembled down there in the darkroom. He had a huge print dryer with gas lines run into it for power. It was a big drum that turned. The prints were laid on the drum and then covered with fabric. This thing was gargantuan, no way to ever get it out of there, and to my knowledge it may still be down there."

Degler developed smoking-related health problems in the 1950s and sold the Granada business to Mrs. Burnell. He had sold his other portrait photography studios in the late 1940s and early 1950s.

By the time S.C. Dixon bought the business in 1974, the fortunes of the old-fashioned portrait photographer had begun to wane. The huge old view cameras were virtual dinosaurs. Smaller, faster formats like 35mm had made location shooting more desirable by both photographers and customers. Wedding portraits were being made in churches, rarely in the studio, and much of the old equipment had been relegated to the status of quaint artifacts of a bygone era.

"The most recent technology she had was a five-by-seven plate camera," Dixon recalls. "It even had the hood the photographer put over his head. The image was on a glass negative that you saw upside down and backward. She was still making a living. But she made a lot of her income from copying and restoration work."

Early on in the business, Dixon met another young photographer who seemed to share his excitement for photography. His name was Charles Evans.

"Charles was full of energy and ideas, and what he lacked in acumen he more than made up for with enthusiasm," Dixon says. "Like me, he loved to work in the darkroom where the true magic of photography is found. He would spend hours there with the gloomy red safelight watching images appear on blank white sheets of photographic paper."

As it turned out, Charles Evans was one of the first skeptics Dixon ran into who had his doubts shattered in a disturbing episode.

But in the meanwhile, their friendship led to the men consolidating their resources and becoming partners in the Granada Studio.

They decided to alternate their time in the darkroom so as to fairly divide their labors. Dixon would take one day, Evans the next, and so forth. They also installed equipment to process color print film as well as the more traditional black-and-white.

The darkroom was located in the deep basement below the street-level studio showroom. A steep set of steps led down to a corridor that ended at the "little bunker sort of affair" that was the darkroom, Dixon says. The basement had twelve-foot ceilings.

"Imagine an old concrete dungeon reborn," he adds. "The dripping walls and chemical-stained floor, ancient electrical outlets corroded by condensation—and there in the middle, two state-of-the-art high-tech enlargers, illuminated by the eerie green from Evans's newest safelight."

Evans was quick to catch on to Dixon's reluctance to work in the darkroom after four or so in the afternoon.

"He frequently asked me why my aversion to the place was strong enough that I would sacrifice the quiet early morning hours before opening rather than finishing things up during the evening and nighttime hours, as was his habit," Dixon says.

Dixon admitted after a time that working in the darkroom after midafternoon made him a bit "uncomfortable" alone in the semidark.

"I told Charles that I had experienced several previous encounters with a certain foreboding, a presence that I had taken to calling 'Deg.' I thought there was something odd down there, something vaguely out of sync. Blood didn't drip from the ceiling, nor had I seen ectoplasm heads floating in midair, but there was still that oddness."

The problem was that Dixon had a difficult time giving voice to his admittedly illogical fears.

"I stammered a good deal trying to come up with a reasonable adult explanation. That old darkroom was completely light-tight with not a breath of moving air. The dominant odor was acetic acid and musty stone, concrete and mortar, yet one would often catch the faint yet definite, unmistakable smell of pipe tobacco."

Dixon did not smoke pipe tobacco, nor did Evans, nor did their employees.

The darkroom air was always cool summer and winter, but sometimes what Dixon called a narrow column of frigid air would suddenly envelop him.

"That cold spot seemed to have an unnerving propensity to move about from one side of the darkroom to the other," Dixon says. "I told Charles to pay attention the next time he walked down that long, concrete stairway, to notice that the air would gradually become cooler, of course, but notice also that there was almost always something cold at the foot of the stairs. A deep chill waiting as if to meet the person intruding into the dark. . . ."

Another darkroom oddity was that it acted almost as an echo chamber for any sounds coming from upstairs. The ceiling of the darkroom was the floor of the gallery part of the photo studio. Dixon says the floor was concrete and steel over a foot thick in places. Yet the softest of footsteps from above could be clearly heard.

"The darkroom was very compact. It reverberated like a drum with every sound from upstairs. If I was down there and had an employee working part time, I'd find that even with the water running in the darkroom it was very easy to hear people walking around up there. Sometimes if I was alone and had to work down there, I'd have to lock up because a buzzer didn't work. But I could always tell when someone walked up to the street door. If they stood there or if they knocked, you knew because you could hear with amazing clarity."

Dixon could tolerate acoustic high fidelity, but it was the other qualities in his basement lair that troubled him the most.

"The most altogether disconcerting aspect of working alone in the darkroom was the grisly feeling of being watched. I called it a 'presence' because that is exactly what it was, a presence of someone or some thing there in the darkness with me while I worked."

Dixon says there was a kind of "tide" about the thing's appearances, a certain ebb and flow.

"Its nadir was during the morning, increasing during the afternoon, and reaching a pinnacle toward evening and into the night," he says. Rarely did Dixon work in the darkroom later than early afternoon. Evenings were off limits.

"I had noticed that the later the hour, the greater the sensation of uneasiness would become," he says. Dixon found the limitations difficult to handle. He was reestablishing a waning studio portrait enterprise and wanted to spend as much time as possible on developing a reputation for quality print finishing.

The presence seemed to manifest itself most frequently whenever Dixon himself chose to be in the darkroom. He soon connected it to something Udene Burnell had told him when she sold the business.

"During the studio's boom days in the 1930s and again during World War II," Dixon says, "the evening and night had been prime time for Degler and his staff to play catch-up on the day's accumulation of work."

Dixon's partner, Charles Evans, did not understand Dixon's reluctance to work late hours in the darkroom. He wasn't being bothered. Yet.

"Almost daily he would chide me good naturedly about 'the ghost,'" Dixon says. "Why, he'd ask, did I believe that something in the darkness was out to get me?"

But Dixon didn't think the entity was necessarily out to get him. He thought that whatever or whoever it was might be content to watch him or perhaps work alongside him.

"Or perhaps it was oblivious to my being there as I had been initially unaware of it," Dixon reasons. "Or maybe it was still there simply doing in death what the flesh and blood had enjoyed so in life."

The malicious feelings Dixon encountered increased as he and Evans made every new change in the business or remodeled the studio environs. Udene Burnell had done little to modernize the facilities. Dixon said his dislike of the darkroom "had matured into a genuine dread if I were required to complete a project during the prime time period."

Evans continued to enjoy his work without any interruptions from unseen dreadful things. Meanwhile Dixon, who had once found photography work so enjoyable, found it becoming "nearly intolerable."

Charles Evans's "day of reckoning" came on an October afternoon, Dixon wrote later:

It was a sunny, crisp lazy Sunday. Charles and his teenage daughter, Mary Ann, decided to get a head start on the upcoming week's work by processing a roll of film, washing and drying it, then proofing each negative. Charles was drying the film with a handheld dryer. Since Mary Ann loved to help during the actual printing process, Charles decided that this would be a good time to send her up the street to the local grocery store for some chips and sodas. By the time she had walked there and back the film would be dry enough to safely slip into the negative carrier.

For the drying process he had turned on the darkroom's only incandescent bulb. Deciding that now would be a good time to acclimate his eyes to the upcoming gloom, he turned off the "white" bulb and switched on both red and green safelights. He gave Mary Ann the studio key and told her to take her time but be sure to lock the door behind her to ensure that he wouldn't be interrupted. He told me he remembered quite distinctly the sound of her footsteps outside the building and the turning of the key in the lock. Charles turned on the water to the print washing drum and began cutting the dry negatives into work-strips of six. He said he remembered catching the faint aroma of pipe tobacco at the same time he noticed a stiff draft of "coolish" air.

He had just exposed the first sheet of photo paper and had slipped it into the developer tray when he clearly heard footsteps above him. He thought it was odd. He had not heard the lock or the sound of the door opening. He was concentrating on the print and assumed that Mary Ann must have realized, halfway to the store, that she didn't have enough money with her. . . . The footsteps paused at the top of the stairs. The bottom door was ajar so he yelled through to her,

"Come on down, it's all right, I have the safelights on."

No answer. After a pause of a few seconds he heard her feet on the rough concrete steps, coming down very slowly. Even in the darkness he had never known Mary Ann to take the stairs slower than two steps at a time. The lower door creaked slightly on its rusted hinges and he heard her round the corner and come down the narrow hallway to the opening of the printing room and stop. Not glancing up from his work he asked, "Forget something?"

When she didn't answer he assumed that she had not been able to hear him over the sound of the running water.

"Come here," he said again, "and bring me the blue-tipped tongs, honey."

Again no answer.

At that point, he told me later, he could feel the hair on the back of his neck start to rise. He turned and stared. . . . Nothing. Shadows and darkness. He stood there for some time, seconds or perhaps minutes, his concept of time having escaped him. Still, he didn't feel the impact of what was happening until, still staring at the empty doorway, he heard footsteps approaching from the street, heard the outside door lock turn, feet moving across the floor above and then skipping—two at a time—down the stairs toward him.

"Daddy, it's me!" his daughter called out.

When she walked into the room, Mary Ann saw her father was standing with a pair of dripping acid tongs in his hand, as though still expecting someone to hand him the pair he had asked for earlier. He had a look of total astonishment on his face. The image he'd been working on had "come up" on the photo paper, but had over-developed, leaving only an image of total blackness with a crisp white edge.

Evans felt a strange mixture of panic and exhaustion. He turned off the darkroom water, grabbed his daughter by the shoulders, and rushed her up the staircase to the brightness of the studio. He didn't tell her what happened, but simply turned off the lights and moved swiftly out the door into the calming sunlight of a pleasant October afternoon.

It was more than two weeks before Evans told his partner about the disconcerting episode. And that only came after Dixon pointed out to him that he was falling behind in his darkroom work.

"I never knew of a single occasion when he entered the old basement again after twelve noon. The joking stopped. He never mentioned that day to me again," Dixon says.

Months later, Evans and his family moved away from town, although financial difficulties he was facing may have had as much to do with his leaving as did his run-in with the traces of D. D. Degler.

DESPITE CHARLES EVANS'S departure and a self-imposed schedule that kept him *out* of the darkroom from early afternoon on, S. C. Dixon stayed open in the old Granada Studio until 1989. The foreclosure on the theater complex was the ostensible reason for his leaving, but there was one final episode with "Old Deg" that proved to be decisive in his decision to relocate his business.

The matter involved the makeshift electric buzzer that had been installed on the front door. Two pieces of copper metal would touch when the door opened, completing an electrical circuit that would loudly signal whenever anyone walked in. In that way if the shop owner or an employee needed to work in the darkroom they didn't have to lock the door. The problem was that it rarely, if ever, worked.

"I had tinkered with it time and time again trying to make it work. I never had any luck with it, so I'd put a sign on the counter saying I was in the darkroom and I'd be right up," Dixon says. "The only way that the buzzer could be tripped was when the front door opened and the two pieces of copper touched each other."

Dixon discovered on a snowy winter afternoon that something else could trip it. But what it was he doesn't know, or prefers not to think about. And it came about because, despite his aversion to working afternoon and evening hours in the basement darkroom, he had to do exactly that.

On this day, because of the lateness of the hour and the faulty buzzer, Dixon securely bolted the front door.

"I absolutely had some project I had to get done, so I . . . went down there and tried to immerse myself in my work. But I was bothered to a dramatic degree and was hurrying because I wanted out of there. Finally, I finished my work. I'm going up those long, steep concrete stairs and I remembered I'd forgotten something down there that I needed. I went back down and I was about parallel with a little side room when that buzzer went off. I will not deny that I screamed like a little girl and jumped about four feet in the air."

Dixon had never, ever heard the buzzer ring except for an occasional short beep. This time it was "ringing like a fire bell."

He had no trouble scrambling back up the stairs and into the shop within a few seconds. Of course he found no one in the shop. The door was tightly secured.

"I left. That was actually one of the last times I went down to the basement."

Dixon spoke with friends familiar with electricity and electrical devices and they said the door had to have been opened to make that kind of connection. Electricity follows set laws and rules and someone opened the door, they told him.

"Obviously the front door was locked, locked up tight. That's what was so disconcerting about it. That was the last straw for me."

THOUGH DIXON HAS been gone from the Granada for nearly two decades, the stories about the haunted photography studio will not die. Nearly every year, Dixon is reminded anew of his personal familiarity with the ghost of Mr. Degler.

Just one year after restoration work on the Granada had gotten underway, the local newspaper sent a reporter and a photographer to meet Dixon at the old studio. The newspaper was publishing a story about the ghost and wanted to talk with Dixon in the remains of the darkroom. Perhaps against his better judgment, Dixon agreed to meet the newspaper men there one afternoon.

"I kind of knew the photographer. He was a young guy, very skeptical, and thought the whole thing was silly," Dixon says.

The photographer came loaded down with several floodlights, but since the electricity had been turned off in the basement, he had to run long extension cords from the main floor down the staircase. He unpacked his gear and had everything set up for the interview and photos.

"I kind of expected something spooky to happen," he laughed, glancing at Dixon.

At that moment, the two big floodlights exploded, first one and then the other.

"We were standing in total darkness. I said, 'Good job pal! Now you're going to have to deal with the poltergeist in the dark,'" Dixon recalls.

The sudden explosion freaked out the photographer, Dixon says.

"The way we finally got out was that he kept pushing the flash button on his camera so it was like walking out under a strobe light. It was funny at the time, funny because there were several of us down there. But, I'll tell you what—if it had been just me alone down there, it wouldn't have been funny at all."

BEV BEERS IS the co-owner and manager of The Granada Coffee Company, a specialty coffee shop that now occupies the north wing of the Granada complex, the space once taken up by S. C. Dixon's photography studio. A chocolate shop is open in the Fox Granada's south wing.

Beers says she firmly believes that old Degler is still around, but her experiences with him have been nothing but positive. She considers him a "guiding spirit" in her business there.

"The only thing I can figure out is that S. C. was a photographer and maybe Deg saw him as a kind of competition, but we're not," Beers says. "We've had a friendly and warm embrace from it."

She does *not* advertise the presence of a poltergeist in her coffee shop.

"I don't talk about it much. People look at me a little funny. But whether you believe in these things or not, once it happens to you there is no longer any doubt in your mind."

The Granada Coffee Company opened in late 2002, and from the very beginning Beers and her partner had "a sense that something was here." And that *something* was a bit of a trickster.

Beers says, for instance, that struggling in the early months to establish their business, only she and her partner were the full-time help. To minimize their workload, and because they're in a small space, the couple were intent on making sure there was a specific place for every utensil they used. Once they were done with the implement, they put it back in its right space. But even with that zealous commitment to organization, they'd find that items had moved to some new location all the time, or even vanished. For a time.

"We had a tool that we used to clean the espresso machine. One day it just disappeared. We couldn't find it anywhere in the shop. The next day it was right back where it belonged," Beers says.

The couple worked long, long hours to establish their small business. Their great love of the old theater building in which they're located is obvious in the photographs of the Granada in its heyday that they've hung on the walls. Visitors have a grand time looking at them, especially senior citizens who visit each afternoon and regale the owners and employees with stories of their own movie-going youth at the Granada.

Bev Beers thinks Deg has embraced the coffee shop owners because of their interest in conserving the building. She believes he has shown directly and irrefutably on several occasions just how much he cares.

At the end of long days when Beers and her partner were still the shop's sole employees, she would wearily count out the day's cash receipts. When she got tired or confused, perhaps losing track of the totals or becoming frustrated in some other way, she would find that a sense of calm would suddenly settle over her. The answer she was struggling for, or a clear solution, would soon be there. "And it certainly didn't come from me," she laughs.

"That happened on almost on a daily basis," she says. "There's really no way to describe it.

"I think we were pure of heart in starting this business. We really had no clue about what we were doing. I taught school for sixteen years and my partner worked as an assistant to film set decorators. Perhaps because of that we were being embraced by Deg."

One winter afternoon shortly before Christmas, and not long after the shop opened, Beers felt that embrace. She found herself alone in the shop. No one was about on the cold, snow-swept streets. The shop has several big, fluffy chairs by the front windows. She gave in to the quiet winter scene outside and dropped into one of the chairs to relax and enjoy the snowfall.

Now she had grown used to dramatic temperature plunges in the shop, that was just part of having Deg around, but they'd always go right back up. Deg was passing by, she figured. But this time when she sat down in the chair, the air turned much, much colder. And it stayed that way.

"I knew he was sitting in the other chair," she says.

The air didn't get warmer until she got up and went back to work.

However, Deg may still see S. C. Dixon as competition. Both Dixon and Bev Beers say that when he comes around for coffee, something odd or unusual always happens sometime later that day. Nothing bad or evil, but "there are issues" that Degler may still have with Dixon, Beers sighs. While he is always welcome, she did have to take him out onto the sidewalk to explain why she was nervous to have him there. She didn't want Deg to overhear.

BEFORE BEV BEERS and her partner opened their coffee shop, the new owners of the Fox Granada Theater approached Dixon about moving back in once the restoration was complete. His photo studio is only a few blocks down the street.

He declined the invitation.

Probably a wise move.

7

Gone with the Mist

Ah! Age is drear and death is cold.

—William Cullen Bryant, *A Dream*

MARYLAND IS A state of remarkable contrasts. While the broad Chesapeake Bay slices through its eastern region like a crescent moon, its northwestern counties rise grandly into the craggy Cumberland Mountains. The suburban lifestyles of Silver Spring or Bethesda have little in common with the waterman's traditional existence up and down the Delmarva Peninsula. Standing atop Maryland's highest point—thirty-three-hundred-foot Backbone Mountain in the corner of Garrett County—an ambitious hiker might think he's a thousand miles from Greater Baltimore rather than a mere two hundred.

However, not just geographic differences mark the uniqueness of the Old Line State. Maryland's resident ghosts and haunted places seem to diverge in a similarly interesting manner, reflecting in odd ways perhaps the state's historical and geographical significance as a volatile border region between Eastern sophistication, Western bluster, and Southern gentility.

In exploring an assortment of tales from supernatural Maryland, we may well find:

- a stone house in Cockeysville, near Baltimore, with the ghost of a beautiful young woman whose debilitating struggle with depression ended with her suicide by hanging;
- the very old college on the Eastern Shore that might naturally be suspected of having at least one ghost—and correctly so;
- something unexpected suddenly blocking our paths in the region around primordial South Mountain, near Hagerstown—a fiendish black dog or else the wraith of a lovelorn phantom soldier;
- at Point Lookout State Park, at the far end of St. Mary's County, where the Chesapeake Bay and Potomac River course into one, the heartbreaking story of the four thousand Confederate prisoners of war who expired there; we'd then discover that more than a few of those long dead may not lie moldering in their graves; and
- a mirror rumored to have once hung in the home of a notorious Lincoln assassination conspirator that proved disturbingly noisy for the unsuspecting antique hunters who bought it.

In Susannah's Room

Since he was a youngster and may have had the customary uncertainties associated with childhood, Clif Ensor's claim that "something was watching me in *that house*" might be rejected out of hand, coming as it does nearly seven decades removed from the events of which he spoke. A skeptic might say that his memory created complex explanations for the creaks and groans commonplace in old houses. On the other hand, perhaps he listened too intently as chilling stories told to him before bedtime conjured up nightmarish, albeit unseen, images of slippery fiends under his bed or of discreetly moving shadows deep in his bedroom closet.

Yes, that is what one *might* suspect if one did not know what happened there long *after* Clif Ensor moved out. When you hear about that, the man becomes nearly prescient in his own personal early haunt-warning system.

That house to which Clif Ensor referred in later years became known as the Simonson House in the small town of Cockeysville, Maryland, a few miles north of Baltimore on State Highway 145. Clif was born there in 1926 and lived in the mansion until he was about eleven years old.

However, its history went back nearly two hundred years before Clif Ensor thought something concealed watched over his youthful amusements.

Built in the early 1700s as the centerpiece of a long vanished plantation, the stately house was positioned in the middle of expansive grounds reached by a winding driveway shaded by a sweep of ancient oaks. One writer said of his own twentieth-century visit there that it gave him the "feeling that the years have melted away and you've been transported to another time."

Only a few outbuildings remained by the time Clif Ensor explored the dwelling and grounds. In a tangle of weeds and vines near the main house was a decaying crypt that held the mortal remains of slaves who died at the plantation in the time before the Civil War. The most unpleasant building on the estate was the original barn, little used as the farmland gave way to development and quite near collapse during the estate's final decades.

The ghost story of the Simonson House really begins in that barn, for it was in the hayloft that young Susannah Plowden took her life nearly two centuries ago.

Who was Susannah Plowden? In a surviving oil painting of the young woman, she is strikingly good-looking, with fiery red hair and clad in a flowing white dress with blue sashes. Her beauty was not enough to save her from a sad life. She apparently lived at the plantation with her uncle and his family. For reasons not known, he banished Susannah's husband of only a few days, one of the plantation's overseers, and forbade Susannah from leaving her room. She grew increasingly despondent until the night in 1857 when she slipped out of the house, climbed the ladder to the hayloft, and hanged herself.

It is her ghost that many believe walks the musty corridors of the Simonson Plantation house.

ALTHOUGH CLIF ENSOR was one of the first people to sense that all was not well in the Simonson house, the circumstances of his family living there began in a quite ordinary manner. His father had graduated from the Baltimore Medical College in 1900 (later the University of Maryland–Baltimore) and taken a position as the country doctor around Cockeysville. He would spend his fifty-three-year career attending to the health needs of the people there. He was really a farmer at heart, according to his son, and even operated a local dairy delivery service.

Dr. Ensor bought the stone plantation house and attendant farmland in the early 1920s when he fell in love with the charm and rich history of the old place. Much of the interior remained intact at that time. Century-old beams supported the lower level's interior ceilings, a staircase off the living room led to twin hallways on the second floor, along which several bedrooms were located; each bedroom incorporated its own fireplace, antique canopy beds, and old steamer trunks.

It was in this house that Clif Ensor, from an early age, understood that his family's historic home was somehow . . . different.

"I would be petrified to be alone," Ensor remembered. "I was afraid to go in one of the bedrooms upstairs, which I later found out was Susannah Plowden's. That was my older brother's bedroom. He always complained of it being cold."

Neither did Clif venture to the old barn where Susannah hanged herself. He was just too plain scared.

Not until much later, however, did Ensor learn *how* different the house truly was, and of how his nervousness in Susannah's bedroom was shared by others.

MR. AND MRS. Gordon Simonson bought the house in the 1950s. Their name was attached to it for the rest of its existence. He was an official at the Greater Baltimore Medical Center; his wife was a physician there. Like the Ensor family, the Simonsons' attraction stemmed in part from the historic nature of the property. However, it wasn't long until the couple had gathered enough anecdotal evidence to suggest they'd bought into a piece of history where not only they might touch the past, but where the past might touch them . . . and walk near them . . . and sometimes even be photographed, according to accounts they gave to reporters over the years.

In one eerie incident, Mrs. Simonson stood on the main staircase off the living room as her husband took a photograph of her. When the film was processed, the faint image of a man appeared to be looking out of a room near the staircase. The Simonsons were home alone at the time.

Houseguests found themselves unexpectedly keeping company with *the other side*, especially if they stayed in the unfortunate Susannah's bedroom. The Simonsons sometimes tried vainly to persuade their overnight guests that the incidents were the product of bad dreams.

A friend of the Simonsons, a surgeon in a Korean War MASH unit, stayed in Susannah's room. He later confided to the Simonsons that during the night a blonde woman dressed in a long white gown with blue sashes had pulled the bed blankets up over his head.

On another occasion, another family friend suddenly awoke to come face to face with the same specter. Only this time, the vapory young woman was crying. When she discovered that she was being watched, she quickly backed out of the room.

The Simonsons' curiosity about the afterlife in their rambling mansion led them to hire a psychic to conduct a séance. Their goal was to find out more about the haunted nature of the place.

They got more than they bargained for.

After the medium went into a deep trance, she grew increasingly agitated. In a high-pitched scream, she yelled:

"Oliver! Oliver!"

The Simonsons hastily stopped the séance. From their research into the house's early history, they knew that name to have been the first name of the overseer who married Susannah Plowden and was then inexplicably driven from the property.

Their discovery of his name had been purely by chance. Off the attic was a well-hidden room that the Simonsons believed may have held escaped slaves. As they rummaged around its dusty contents, they discovered a diary, Susannah Plowden's diary with a final entry on a day in 1857. She detailed the heartbreaking conditions that led to her unrelenting emotional decline—a reluctantly agreed-upon marriage, her new husband's subsequent kidnapping and banishment from the plantation, her forced seclusion in her own small bedroom, and finally, her plan for suicide.

The Simonsons showed the diary to a couple in the area who happened to be descendants of the Plowden family. The man and his wife, in turn, ushered the Simonsons into their own living room.

"That is Susannah Plowden," the woman told Mrs. Simonson, gesturing toward a portrait of a handsome young red-haired woman in a white dress with a saucy blue sash around the waist.

It was a near perfect match for the woman the Simonsons' houseguests described for them.

DR. SIMONSON HARDLY needed to be told by others that her house was atypical. Two reporters for a Baltimore medical newsletter described several episodes of odd activity during their visit with the Simonsons while researching a story about the house.

"During the tour, the doctor's favorite cats followed her into every room, playfully jumping on beds and getting underfoot," Lisa Grandi and Jim Bova later wrote. "When she entered Susannah's room, (the cats) did not, nor have they ever, entered the room. Neither did the caretaker's dog, which used to snarl and show its teeth when in the room's proximity."

Reporter Bova ventured alone into Susannah's room and turned off the lights. When he came out, he said he'd felt a stream of air blowing across the back of his hands. Dr. Simonson said that was quite a common experience. Further, she claimed a refrigeration engineer was stumped when he probed for the source of that draft.

That ill wind blowing through Susannah's room may have been but one example of more poltergeist activity in the Cockeysville house than actual ghost sightings.

For instance, two kitchen cabinets were alleged to have wrenched free of their wall mounts and hurtled to the floor, nearly striking a maid's feet.

Photographs and paintings traveled about without human intervention. A particularly disquieting episode that took place in Susannah's old room involved an unidentified portrait of a woman who was not Susannah. The Simonsons regularly found it lying face down in various parts of the room. After uncountable instances of this annoying behavior, Mr. Simonson attached toggle bolts through the picture frame and into the plasterwork. Within minutes of returning to the living room, a crash from the bedroom brought the couple running. As they opened the door, the painting fell to the floor from its resting place against the door. Something had torn it free from the wall—bolts and all—and tossed it across the room.

The Simonsons said any painting or photograph of a young woman usually fell victim to unfortunate accidents—being either stripped off a wall or, in some rare instances, torn to shreds.

Is it possible that Oliver was driven from the old plantation when he was caught with another woman? Could that be why Susannah hated the sight of another woman's face?

CLIF ENSOR HAD good reason to remember his first, earliest experiences with his judgment that ghosts might walk the earth—or at least that portion of the earth on which he resided.

For over a decade, Ensor also owned one of the most famous haunted houses in Miami, Florida—Villa Paula, a distinctive ten-room mansion on North Miami Avenue built in the mid-1920s by the first Cuban consul there, Don Domingo Milord. He had named the home after his wife, Paula, who, sadly, died in a bedroom of the house following surgery to amputate her leg.

Ensor bought the house in 1974. It had gone through several owners over the years before being turned into low-income housing. He spent thousands of dollars remodeling the house to its original grandeur, repainting the interior, scraping and refinishing the flooring, installing glass chandeliers, and decorating the interior with his own nineteenth-century Empire-style cherry and oak furniture highlighted with whorls and intricately carved scrollwork.

His distinctive interior designs perfectly complemented the grand dwelling. The ten rooms had ceilings eighteen feet high. Tuscan columns inside set off exquisitely painted tiles installed in the 1920s by consul Milord himself. The white stucco exterior covered up yellow bricks imported from Cuba. Ionic columns graced either side of the front entrance.

The architecture was not the only thing out of the ordinary at Villa Paula.

Although rumors had circulated for years that the house was haunted, Clif Ensor spoke most freely about Paula, the resident ghost, presumed to have been Don Domingo's one-legged wife.

She was quite well behaved, he maintained; she allowed her presence to be discovered most often during séances held by the psychics Ensor invited to his home.

Ensor documented the other incidents he thought Paula instigated:

- A steady rapping at the front door didn't mean someone had come to call. An iron gate leading to the front door from the sidewalk was kept locked, yet the knocking persisted. Ensor would usually look out to see if anyone was there and, of course, there wasn't.
- Paula Milord was a dedicated pianist. Ensor's bedroom was in the room she used to practice piano. If he forgot to shut the door upon leaving, it would slam shut afterward. An elderly neighbor who had known Paula claimed that when she played the piano she always insisted that the door be closed to enhance her concentration. In that same bedroom, Ensor might discover his bedcovers turned over.
- Aberrant smells permeated the house: pungent Cuban cigar smoke even though Ensor did not smoke and the scent of roses in a dining room when none was blooming.
- Ensor told reporters that he never saw a clearly defined ghost, yet on at least two occasions, he caught sight out of the corner of his eye of something skittering away. In a hallway, Ensor said he got a quick, fleeting look at a begowned figure with jet-black hair pulled back into a tight bun. Paula? Ensor had little doubt.

Unlike the Simonson House, with but a single ghost haunting its precincts, Villa Paula had at least five ghosts, according to one psychic Ensor consulted. They included: a corpulent feminine ghost in a red dress; an elderly man in a top hat and tails; a desperately unhappy Hispanic woman, perhaps a member of the household staff, mourning for the child she lost in an abortion decades ago; a garden ghost looking for a precious medallion she lost on the grounds; and the one that Ensor thought might have been Paula Milord: a piano-playing, coffee-grinding, rose-loving spirit.

CLIF ENSOR MOVED away from Cockeysville, Maryland and the Simonson House when he was eleven years old. He sold Villa Paula in the 1980s. Two houses, two sets of ghosts, two disparate settings, yet connected forever in the mind of one man who somehow survived two *more* hauntings than most other people ever have.

What Stirs on South Mountain?

Is it possible that an unsolved and long forgotten death—and one that quite possibly was a homicide—has given rise to at least one of the many supernatural legends near western Maryland's craggy South Mountain?

The curious connections between the documented death of one George Kirk at South Mountain sometime in 1813 and a celebrated South Mountain legend that recounts the chronicle of William the reluctant soldier bear some striking resemblances.

The soldier purportedly fell in love with the daughter of the owners of a local wayside inn back in the early 1840s. He subsequently deserted his company to hide in the mountains hoping his comrades might move on without him. For as long as anyone can remember, the puzzling lights along the mountainside have been labeled the "Saxon's fires," for the campfires built by this soldier named William, a young Michigan militiaman with wavy, dark-blonde Saxon hair and penetrating blue eyes. William and the other troops were passing through the region in 1841 on the way to the Seminole Wars, a long and bloody conflict between the United States and Florida's Seminole Indians.

His story must be consigned to legend since there are no known records about William or his bride.

However, the earlier puzzling death of Pennsylvanian George Kirk was connected to the same inn that William's love worked at, located now, as it was two hundred years ago, above Turner's Gap on the old National Road near Boonsboro. Today it is a restaurant known as the Old South Mountain Inn. It has also been known as the South Mountain House or simply the Mountain House.

Not a great deal is known about George Kirk. Records from Washington County, Pennsylvania, indicate that he and his wife immigrated to the United States from Ireland in the early 1800s. The couple eventually gave birth to five children and, by 1811, the family lived on Main Street in Canonsburg, Pennsylvania, a hamlet some seventeen miles southwest of Pittsburgh on the Chartiers River, according to a Washington County history.

But sometime in 1813—and it isn't clear on what dates the following events took place nor the specific circumstances—George Kirk set off with two other Canonsburg men, a Dr. McFarland and a Dr. George McCook, for a trip back east, in this case to western Maryland, a few hundred miles away. The journey may have been undertaken to sell some horses.

On one of their first days out, the men stayed the night at the Old South Mountain Inn, the same establishment at the center of the young soldier William's fateful love affair.

However, George Kirk met a far different fate.

Early the next morning, McCook and McFarland discovered their companion missing from his room. The proprietors claimed that Kirk had gotten up during the night and left the inn. A search of the lodging and of the surrounding area turned up no traces of the man.

McCook and McFarland returned to Canonsburg to tell Kirk's family the awful news. A few weeks later, and for reasons not at all apparent, John McFarland, Dr. McFarland's father, traveled to the South Mountain Inn where he launched his own investigation. Within days, he found George Kirk's badly decomposed body in the mountains not far from the inn. Whether by accident or by design, the circumstances of the Pennsylvania man's death were never resolved. Little more seems to have been written about the case.

Is George Kirk's ghost among those that haunt South Mountain, and particularly the neighborhood around the historic Old

South Mountain Inn? Moreover, could it also be that the renowned Saxon's Fire mystery lights originated with George Kirk's death and not with an elusive soldier named William?

FEW AREAS IN Maryland have so many entrenched stories of ghostly activity as the region encompassing South Mountain, a daunting quartzite ridge in the eastern Appalachians between Hagerstown to the northwest and Frederick to the southeast. The romance of the Saxon soldier is only one of the oft-told tales from the region. Other chronicles of the unknown include the headless *Drear Phantom,* a sort of screaming banshee; and one slavering, dreadful black dog. They've all stalked the wind gaps, shaded hollows, and dense forests of that mountainous region since well before the Revolutionary War, according to local traditions. Some of the mystery is almost certainly tied to the mountain's sheer immensity and near impenetrable forests, a difficult barrier to westward settlement in the early decades of eighteenth century North America. Not until 1755 did British General Edward Braddock and a young surveyor by the name of George Washington lay out a road through a South Mountain pass. Even today, the 10,000 acres along the Appalachian Trail that make up South Mountain State Park preserve many of its formidable characteristics.

THE CENTRAL LANDMARK in both the George Kirk death and the legacy of soldier William is the Old South Mountain Inn, which through various name changes and functions over the past three centuries has served alternately as a stagecoach stop, a Confederate general's headquarters, a private home, a tavern, and as a restaurant. The original 1732 stone section of the inn was one of the earliest coach stops on the original National Road. Several presidents and prominent politicians, including Henry Clay and Daniel Webster, frequented the inn. In 1859, the inn reputedly was captured and briefly held by John Brown and his followers prior to their raid on Harpers Ferry. During the Civil War, the inn served as the headquarters for Confederate Major General Daniel Harvey Hill during the Battle of South Mountain, September 14, 1862.

Madeleine Vinton Dahlgren bought the inn in 1876. She was the widow of Rear Admiral John A. Dahlgren, the commander of the South Atlantic Blockading Squadron during the Civil War and the creator of the first organized research and development program in U.S. naval history. Admiral Dahlgren is best known today as the "father of American naval ordnance."

Madeleine Dahlgren was a wealthy woman in her own right who became a widely published author of travel and historical narratives, including a whimsical collection of South Mountain folklore that she'd gathered in many of her visits to communities in the region. Historians may write off her research, but it is reasonably representative of the widespread beliefs of that region a century ago.

She transformed the inn into what she called the South Mountain House, all the while maintaining the original building's historical integrity. Mrs. Dahlgren is buried at the nearby native stone Dahlgren Chapel, which she had erected.

In 1925, the South Mountain House was sold again to new owners who converted it back to one of its original purposes, as a country tavern. By the early 1970s, the inn's owners served dinners as well as drinks. The unique Old South Mountain Inn continues to offer visiting diners select American cuisine.

MADELEINE DAHLGREN WAS one of the first to suggest the origins of the soldier ghost. An overnight guest had told her the story at the South Mountain House. He claimed to have learned it as a boy from a man who'd been in the army with William the soldier. This is what he told her:

In the early nineteenth century, South Mountain was an unbroken wilderness with only a narrow, dirt roadway over which to travel. A tough band of Michigan army recruits marching off to fight in the Seminole Wars arrived at the old inn looking for hot meals and a night's rest. After stacking their weapons in the barroom, most of the men got right down to the business of putting away all the beer and whiskey they could hold.

One young soldier was not like his buddies. He sat morosely by the great open stone hearth in the kitchen, letting its warmth seep deep into his weary bones. He was William, a young man barely out of his teens with a solid build, bright blue eyes, light brown hair—sometimes called Saxon hair in that era—and a shy manner befitting his isolated childhood in the wilderness that had been the Michigan Territory until 1837, a scant five years earlier.

Around the kitchen bustled Saidee, the innkeeper's daughter, as she prepared heaping suppers for the hungry soldiers. Coffee boiled over from the pot hanging above the flames in the open hearth; bacon and eggs sizzled in an iron skillet; fresh, whole chickens roasted on a spit above the hot coals. Maryland biscuits of freshly ground flour and lard baked on the griddle.

The young soldier seemed oblivious to satiating his appetite even after long days afoot. He could not take his eyes off Saidee.

William was not sophisticated in the ways of courtship yet he somehow knew he was in love. The raven-haired beauty with the flashing black eyes was the girl for him.

Young Saidee was far more adept at conversation than the quiet young man who sat silently staring at her. She'd been working nearly all her life at the inn with all manner of blunt-talking wayfarers. However, this boy was different from all the other roughnecks who'd passed through her father's door. She, too, felt an attraction.

"What's the matter?" she suddenly asked of him. "I rather reckon you be tired."

"Saidee, I wish I'd got to die for you!" he stammered mournfully, mindful that in just a few hours time he'd be marching away with his company.

Saidee plopped down on the stool next to the young soldier.

"*Die* for me, mister! Well, ain't I worth *living* for?"

"Living for!" the soldier cried out. "A thousand lives if I had them; but I can give you only one."

That was as good a proposal as Saidee had ever heard and so their plans were laid.

William would secretly leave his company and find a lair high on the mountainside from which he could keep watch. His company would search for him; that much they both knew would surely happen once they realized he was gone. For her part, Saidee agreed that she would take him food every day and described where she would leave it: on a rocky ledge near a waterfall. Each night she would watch for smoke from a small campfire William would build signaling to her that he was safe.

During the day she'd secretly shadow the soldiers' movements as they conducted the anticipated search and warn her young beau with a screech like that of a wildcat should they come too near his hideaway.

William made his escape just before dawn. A few hours later, his mates discovered him missing. Saidee insisted that he probably lost his way while out for an early morning walk. They searched for him the rest of that day and then into another and another. At last, they concluded that their young comrade had met with some misfortune. Once the soldiers entirely departed the region, William emerged from his hiding place and with Saidee as his bride built their cabin where they lived ever after.

THE STORY—OR LEGEND as it may be—did not stop with this happy conclusion. Out of it grew the strange lights someone christened *the Saxon's fire*.

According to Madeleine Dahlgren,

"It is thought by some that now and again the wraiths of these two repeat their cunning devices. At midnight, the soldier's distant fire may be seen lighted, or the stealthy step of the winsome Saidee is heard. She makes known her approach by giving the peculiar cry of the wildcat, in order to frighten away the curious."

On the western slope of South Mountain, the old National Road cut through a canyon. Alongside the road is a stream that legend has it was the site of William's late night campfires. Travelers passing through the gorge sometimes think they see a fleeting glimpse of a uniformed soldier at a place where the stream spills over a rocky outcrop. He is there sitting quietly by a small campfire stirring its dying embers. He looks up with expectant eyes at the approach of the traveler and then, disappointed not to see his beloved Saidee, fades away into the canyon mist.

A lovelorn soldier's nightly vigil . . . the premature death of an Irish-American far from his home and family . . . both on the surface seemingly distinct events, yet each linked to the re-mote countryside that is so much a part of the South Mountain mystique.

SOLDIERS ARE A significant element of another South Mountain ghost tale.

While visiting South Mountain House many decades ago, two men witnessed what they claimed to be a reenactment of the Civil War's Battle of South Mountain, three days before the famous and much deadlier Battle of Antietam near Sharpsburg. Twenty-three-thousand men died on a single day at Antietam, the bloodiest twenty-four hours in American military history.

The South Mountain encounter, while lesser known to the general public, is significant because it derailed, at least tem-porarily, Confederate General Robert E. Lee's plan to carry the war into the North. After some success at South Mountain, he was able to regroup his forces and march on to Sharpsburg and the disaster awaiting him at Antietam Creek. He then re-treated into Virginia. The war dragged on for several more years.

The battle at South Mountain took place at Fox's Gap, Crampton's Gap, and at Turner's Gap, the latter just below the Old South Mountain Inn.

The two men came to South Mountain House years after the Civil War, when the inn was again hosting overnight guests. Near midnight, one of them decided to climb up to a small ob-servation deck on the rooftop. In the dim moonlight, he no-ticed what looked like wisps of smoke arising from the direction of a barn some distance to the east. He'd tromped around that area with other guests earlier in the day. He awoke his friend so that he could verify that smoke was coming from that direction. Together they climbed back to the roof. Not only did both men see the smoke, but also by now, the air was heavy with a distinct sulfurous odor, similar to that produced by gunpowder. They also noticed other gray wisps of smoke arising from a field next to the barn.

The men roused a member of the house staff and told him what they'd seen. They feared the barn and field were on fire. Though they volunteered to go with the employee, he said he'd go by himself to investigate. The men waited on the veranda. The worker soon returned looking puzzled and not at all pleased with being awakened in the middle of the night and sent out on what he proceeded to call a wasted errand. He said he'd found nothing to confirm the men's suspicions even though he'd gone on well past the barn. Nothing untoward stirred below the inn, nor was there any sign of a fire, recent or otherwise. He scowled one final time at the surprised guests and went off to bed.

Somewhat embarrassed by the findings, yet perplexed because of the clarity of what they'd seen, the men went back up to the observatory.

The nearly full moon had risen higher, giving the entire countryside an eerie glow. The smoky haze was still in evidence, as was the strong sulfurous stench. Yet something more had been added—the smoke was coalescing into swiftly moving figures, lunging and charging across the earth—two vaporous columns of men moving against one another as if in bloody battle. As the columns met head on, a thunderous crash followed immediately by a booming explosion rang out shaking the very foundation of the old inn. That was definitely *not* their imagination because irritated voices quickly arose from the inn's rooms as sleeping guests stumbled from their rooms to look for the source of the disturbance.

All they found were two very frightened men huddled together on the roof, unable to describe for a very long time what they'd just witnessed—the apparent ghostly reenactment of the skirmish at Turner's Gap in the Battle of South Mountain.

THAT WAS NOT to be the last encounter with phantom soldiers on South Mountain.

The Appalachian Trail is a two-thousand-mile-long footpath that extends down the eastern seaboard from Maine to Georgia. It traverses a forty-mile-long section on the ridge of South Mountain and passes not far from the Old South Mountain Inn.

It was on this trail, long after the two men saw the ghostly Civil War reenactment, that hikers camping in the fields below the inn encountered their own phantom army. They'd gone to sleep at dusk, but were rousted a few hours later by yelling, screaming, and by the clanging of metal. A curious stench clung to the air.

As they peered from their tent, the pair saw luminous uniformed figures moving in ragged formation less than a hundred yards away. The clash of metal against metal—saber against saber—was followed by a series of quick muffled explosions as the soldier specters moved forward. Then, as suddenly as they seemed to have appeared, the figures, the smoke, the stench, the noise were all consumed by the night.

AMONG THE CROWD of supernatural beings supposedly inhabiting South Mountain are those every bit as unpleasant as the earlier revenants that surface out of unrequited love or ghastly slaughter-producing soldiers who then linger on the battlefield long after their deaths.

One authority describes the dank and dismal *Drear Phantom* as a hideous thing, "darkling, headless, and dragging in his fleshless grasp a clanging chain . . ." as it slowly advances upon its quarry.

The thing prefers to roam about on cold December nights in a thick wood from whence it shuffles across the former National Pike, today Alternate State Highway 40, until it disappears into the rocky crags nearby.

The origins of the *Drear* are a bit obscure, though author Madeleine Dahlgren believed the ghost was that of a farmer who committed a dishonest act.

It seems a farmer and the neighbor with whom he was feuding over property lines spent a good deal of time with lawyers trying to come to some agreement, but to no avail. Late one night, and with the aid of his son, the offended farmer solved the problem by moving the cornerstones marking the property boundaries to a more favorable location. His thought was to have the properties resurveyed, thus ensuring he would win the case.

Sadly, for the farmer it did not work out quite that way. He died just days after his deceitful nighttime maneuver, well before the property could be resurveyed.

Stay dead he did not do. His ghost came back that very night to accost his own son.

"Come on!" the dead man shrieked at his offspring, who, as might be suspected, was cowering in the corner of his bedroom. The young man was so frightened by his father's apparition that he fell into a faint and died of heart failure.

After those twin misfortunes, the farmer was condemned to wander the open countryside bearing in his arms the great stone boundary marker from his field. The rock glowed red-hot and threw off sparks in all directions. He was damned to carry it until he could repent for his misdeed.

The years passed. Still he roamed. All who met the specter farmer gave him the widest berth possible. No one dared utter a word to him or glance in his direction for fear of being plucked into his ghostly vortex.

And they never, ever, ever answered his plaintive query: "Where shall I put it?"

But that all changed when a jovial and somewhat inebriated young fellow out for a late night stroll happened upon the farmer.

"Where shall I put it?" the passerby snickered, co-opting the ghost's celebrated question of all he chanced upon.

"*Indeed*," replied the ghost, "where *shall* I put it?"

"Fool!" shot back the young man. "Put it back from where you got it."

Ah-ha! That simple solution had apparently escaped the farmer, who was a bit slow in his mental capacities. The stone he held suddenly cooled, its crimson glow snapping off just as surely as if a light switch had been thrown. The phantom high-tailed it for the very field in which the stone had rested years before. He put it back in the corner from which he had taken it and disappeared down the National Highway and forever more from South Mountain's nighttime landscape.

The moral of the story, if there were one, would be the necessity of restitution.

"This spook would have been a public pest until Doomsday, unless he had made his crooked line straight," writer Madeleine Dahlgren suggested.

THE MOST PECULIAR creature in the South Mountain region would have to be the *snarly yow*, a mysterious black dog that had its beginnings as far back as the mid-nineteenth century, yet turned up as recently as the late twentieth century.

Just what is this beast? Is it of normal or paranormal origins? Or, no origins at all save for those that began with some impressive imaginations?

The enormous *dog-fiend*, as others term it, followed a nightly routine that never wavered, in an unnamed canyon on the western slope of the mountain, according to those who claim firsthand knowledge. It always drank from the same stream alongside the National Road, not far from William the phantom soldier's lair. The beast might clamber onto the highway as startled drivers slammed on their brakes. It glared at the unwary travelers before wandering off into a wooded cleft quite near an old summer home known as Glendale, just below a point given the name of The Pinnacle. Even though it had some of the outward characteristics of a canine, this dog was many times larger than its domesticated cousin. That led many to wonder if it wasn't some sort of unknown mammal whose habitation had not been explored, nor its species identified by science.

However, the one peculiarity that argued against such a proposition is that *no physical traces of the beast were ever discovered*. Some of the stories about the giant dog are, to say the least, quite astonishing:

- A sharp-eyed mountain man said he saw the dog slinking out of a small corral. He claimed that the dog turned from coal black to white and many shades in between.
- Repeated rifle shots at the beast seemed to have little effect. A hunter who was the surest shot around was coming home one evening when the nasty critter leaped into his path a few paces ahead. He raised his rifle to his shoulder, took a steady aim, and pulled the trigger. The bullet went right through the creature. Shot after shot after shot rang out, but all with similar desultory results. The animal crouched right where it was. That was enough for the so-called marksman. He threw down his rifle and scampered back down the trail in the direction

from which he'd come, never daring to look back to see what had become of his obviously supernatural adversary.
• An elderly South Mountaineer had a similar confrontation, but this time the only weapon available was the old man's wooden cane. The giant dog was ensconced in its favorite gorge when it leaped out. The fellow tried to defend himself by chucking his walking stick in the dog's direction. No good. A cane can't clobber that which is not flesh and bones.

Was it this same spectral illusion that confronted a young farmer returning home from Boonsboro, or something else indeed?

This married father of several children lived with his family in a snug little cabin a short distance from the legendary hound's lair. He often went on foot into Boonsboro to buy farm tools and family provisions. Thus, it was on this particular drizzly night at about ten o'clock that he encountered the four-legged specter standing stock still in the middle of the way, its yellow eyes staring balefully back at him. As the farmer moved first to one side and then to another in order to get around, he found the dog mirrored his every step, blocking his way. Now, this fellow was quite strong after years of frontier home-steading and unafraid of most things—man, or beast. He decided to take the direct approach. He leapt upon the dog, beating at it with his broad fists. To his alarm, his powerful fists pummeled the air and not the animal's damp fur. At the same time, the dog grew even taller and ever longer until the thing came to stretch across the road. The nasty fiend glared back with narrowed eyes; deep, guttural snarls rolled out through a devilishly wide and slavering mouth.

This night was not to be the farmer's last. Just as quickly as the dog had appeared in the road, it gave out one mighty growl, then bounded silently into the undergrowth and disappeared from sight.

"MY NERVOUS SYSTEM was racked to its center!" complained another gentleman who chanced upon the dog slinking down a mountain trail toward him. He looked up at the creature and suddenly had the dreadful sensation that the entire rocky mountainside was sliding down upon him, the four-legged snarly yow and all. Yet the fellow and his nervous system escaped intact.

MOST HORSES SENSED this slippery dog beast's presence well before it showed its infamous nasty disposition.

Take the case of a character nicknamed "Samson" for his legendary feats of strength. His broad back and bulging biceps were the envy of many a lesser man.

One night Samson was drinking at a local saloon when his rowdiness attracted the attention of the night constable. He quickly dispatched the lawman with a swift right hook.

The altercation sobered up the strongman. He jumped on his horse for the ride home that, as it happened, passed through the snarly yow's canyon habitat. No sooner had he started through the passage than he heard a growl coming from the underbrush and his horse reared. The giant dog leaped onto the trail directly in the path of horse and rider. No amount of spurring or slapping at the horse's neck could get it to move on. On a final mighty buck, Samson fell to the ground, breaking his collarbone and knocking him unconscious in the process.

STILL SOME HORSES must have been more fearless than Samson's nag.

"Big Joe" was another mountain man, yet he had no problem with his horse on the night he confronted the yow. The sighting was somewhat different from earlier encounters. Joe was astride his horse going through the canyon when the dog jumped from a thicket. Then it did the oddest thing ever reported of it—instead of confronting horse and rider, it took off down the road. Dirt and dust flew in the air as the dog scrambled through the loose gravel. Joe dug his heels into the horse's flanks and gave chase. It was no match. The dog was not to be overtaken and soon vanished into the night.

A WOMAN WHOSE physical stamina was the equal to that of Big Joe or Samson saw the dog one winter's night as she and her husband passed by the stream in their one-horse sleigh.

She saw the beast dog standing stock still on the riverbank. She later said it appeared to be brownish in color rather than its traditional black. Her husband was holding the reins and didn't notice the dog. However, his old mare did. She snorted and stomped in the harness until the man had her under control and with several sharp cracks of his whip goaded her ahead. The cautious wife did not point out the storied beast hiding in the shadows because she feared her husband would want to prove his courageousness and go after it.

BANSHEE STORIES ARE an ancient part of the Gaelic tradition. Those screaming harbingers of death have moved from the British Isles comfortably around the world during the past few centuries; there are countless variations in North America alone.

The region around Maryland's mountainous western reaches is no different. Here the wailing phantom is renowned as the White Woman, yet her actions and the impact that she has on those who claim to see her are the same as for any ancient spirit chanced upon by modern man.

Writer Madeleine Dahlgren said that from what she could gather in the South Mountain region, "The White Woman can neither be confronted by primer or prayer-book, for she is an *accepted fact.*"

SOMETIMES THE IDENTITY of the banshee was not a mystery at all, as when a young mother died shortly after childbirth. The surviving infant was given over to her grandmother for care. That very night the baby's mother reappeared in the guise of the White Woman. Grandmother knew in her heart the consequence of the visit—the newborn was dead within a fortnight.

A SINGLE, UNANTICIPATED appearance by the White Woman can be worrisome even if nothing untoward immediately occurs. Such was the case with Dave's wife. She and her little son were bustling down a country lane shortly after dusk. They were late getting home after visiting some distant neighbors. As they crossed a hilltop, the four-year-old stopped in his tracks and pointed out across a field.

"What's that, Mama?"

His mother looked off in the distance. Sure enough, there was the White Woman. In an instant, it vanished.

She didn't hear any wailing in the few seconds the banshee was visible, yet the child's mother worried for many years to come that perhaps one of her children or her husband would take sick and die.

SOMETIMES THE OTHER sightings of the mystery woman are very, very strange.

She's been seen . . .

. . . waiting in a mountain glade, a kerchief tied about her head;

. . . standing at the bedside of a man named Otho who, neighbors understood, became quite depressed over her frequent visits, which is abundantly understandable; or

. . . lurking about in the selfsame canyon as the legendary snarly yow.

DESPITE ALL THIS, some folks maintained she was an agreeable sort of ghost, affable and kindhearted.

However, that's not what a young woman named Annie would have told you.

Annie lived with her old granny and widower father in a rustic hut quite near the old National Road. They raised a few hogs for food each year but otherwise depended on some scraggly crops that they planted and harvested in the hard soil. The cabin wasn't much to look at, inside or out. A grapevine curled around a crude pole, framing the front door. Rough shutters that closed over the windows were all that kept out severe weather. The only cheery note was a patch of sunflowers near the front stoop.

Annie was a simple mountain girl whose shadow had never fallen across the doorway of a nearby mountain schoolroom. She was not known for anything approaching an imagination.

What happened in front of her was about all she thought she needed to know.

That's why what occurred on a particular late summer afternoon was so strange. Annie sat on the cabin stoop staring vacantly down the pike. Suddenly there arose out of the dusty road the form of what she immediately took to be the White Woman. She was swathed in a cloak of heavy fabric, a ratty hood pulled tight about her head to hide her face, errant strands of worn cloth dragging along the ground behind her. She walked slowly, but deliberately, toward Annie and the cabin door.

The poor child fainted dead away.

She awoke to her granny splashing water on her face. Hot tears mingled with Granny's well water as she cried that she had fainted just as the terrible banshee glided right up to her. A cold, damp wind had enveloped her as she felt the ghost pass through her body and on into the house.

Forty-eight hours later Annie's father, Granny's son, Ike, was dead.

"It would be quite useless to try and dispossess the minds of these people of the firm belief that the White Woman came to announce this death," wrote Dahlgren of this episode, "or was not in some uncanny way responsible for this calamity."

To add to the mystery of young Annie, her granny's cabin burned to the ground a few weeks later. The two women survived but moved far away from western Maryland.

ALL WAS NOT grim death and ruin in the White Woman saga. Sometimes a widespread belief in the ghost was used to good advantage by those in need of some backup.

Zittlestown is a village on the western slope of South Mountain below Turner's Gap. In the last century and before, this insular German community displayed strange superstitious behavior, including a belief by its young people in the legend of the White Woman.

That credence in the appearance of the mysterious woman played right into the hands of one middle-aged lady who had had quite enough of some young boys who liked to whoop it up way past midnight. She decided that the only way to quiet them down was to scare the living daylights out of them. So one night, when the rapscallions were particularly noisy, she got out of bed, threw a white sheet over her head, and marched out of the house. She found the gang at the corner of her yard and with despondent cries of "Ohhh! Ohhh!" chased after the panicky youngsters until they had all dispersed for the safety of their homes. For many days and weeks afterward, the resourceful homemaker would laugh uproariously as she told her lady friends about how she brought peace to the neighborhood—with a little help from the White Woman.

Now You See Him . . .

The four men, good friends all, were exhausted from a long night of beach fishing in Point Lookout State Park. They'd been within eyesight of the celebrated Old Point Lookout Lighthouse, one of the crown jewels in this exquisitely beautiful natural and historical preserve in southern Maryland.

The dawn broke with a thick fog rolling across the long stretches of beach and then draping itself like a musty cloak about the distinctive stands of loblolly pine; a light mist drifting down from the colorless leaden sky added to the gloom. The fishermen dumped their gear in the car and pulled out of the parking lot, headed up State Highway Five, the only route northward off the peninsula. They'd gone only a short distance when they all caught sight of a man shambling along the highway. Without looking back at the sound of the approaching car behind him, the stranger suddenly and inexplicably turned and started across the highway. The squealing tires from the sudden braking ricocheted across the quiet landscape. The driver yanked the wheel hard to the left to avoid the impact that he knew surely would come. He failed and the car slid sideways into the man.

Once the car came to a halt alongside the ditch, the anxious fishermen piled out and ran back up the roadway, looking feverishly in the ditch along the way.

There was no blood, no torn clothing fragments.

There was *no body*.

The man had vanished just as if he'd never been there at all. Perhaps he never was.

IF THERE WERE a category for the most haunted state park in North America, the thousand and sixty-four acres of Point Lookout State Park would surely contend for the title. Situated as it is at the very end of the stunningly panoramic Maryland peninsula in lower St. Mary's County where the Potomac River meets the Chesapeake Bay, Point Lookout has a century-old reputation for the extraordinary number of incidents in which visitors and park workers say they've encountered telling signs of the supernatural.

The parkland's four centuries of settled history make it effortless to assume that more than fishermen, tourists, campers, and hikers prowl its historic confines.

The peninsula's strategic location between the bay and the Potomac attracted the attention first of British settlers and soldiers. As early as 1612, Captain John Smith explored the area. King Charles I later deeded the land to George Calvert, the Lord of Baltimore. Calvert's youngest son, Leonard, the first governor of Maryland, built a manor house on the peninsula in 1634, the first of three homes he built there. Point Lookout itself was home to one of Leonard's mansions, St. Michael's Manor; that locale today is located across from a Confederate memorial.

During the American Revolutionary War and later in the War of 1812, British troops conducted frequent raids on peninsula settlements and fortifications. The very tip of the peninsula was a prime vantage point from which American military observers could keep track of British ships moving into Chesapeake Bay or trying to slip up the Potomac River.

When peace finally descended on the region, the federal government erected Point Lookout Lighthouse in 1830. Lightkeepers lived in a simple wooden and masonry house for the first fifty years. More rooms were added to the building to accommodate a second lightkeeper since the keepers and their families shared the duties of manually keeping the light ablaze and sounding the foghorn. After the U.S. Navy took control of the light's operation in 1965, they subsequently built an off-shore automatic beacon, effectively ending Point Lookout's one-hundred-and-thirty-five-year history of assisting mariners navigating the treacherous shoals. The lighthouse was occupied until 1981; it's still open to visitors.

Although the park's paranormal history includes many stories about the lighthouse, there is a far better reason that ghosts remain on this isolated strip of land. The district that now encompasses the park has a prominent historic notoriety as one of the federal government's Civil War prisoner of war camps.

The road from the Calverts' grand colonial estate to infamous prison camp began innocuously enough. The homes and lands had passed out of the Calvert family's hands to new owners who converted the property into a bayside resort for wealthy Washingtonians in the years preceding the Civil War. However, by the early 1860s and the outbreak of the war, the resort lost its appeal and began experiencing financial predicaments so that, in 1862, when the federal government needed a facility to care for wounded Union soldiers, it leased the old resort. An addition named the Hammond General Hospital opened on August 17, 1862. But within half a year, the government also found itself lacking secure facilities for the growing number of Confederate prisoners taken in battle. Camp Hoffman was established adjacent to the hospital to house ten thousand Rebel soldiers, most of them from Maryland. By June 1864, however, over twenty-thousand prisoners were crammed into the camp at any given time and forced to live in squalid conditions. Simple canvas shelters called Sibley tents were the prisoners' only protection from the elements. A wooden stockade built along the shoreline held the men during the daylight hours.

By the war's end in April 1865, over fifty thousand men had passed through Camp Hoffman. An inexact number—estimated by some historians at between three thousand and eight thousand men—died of disease, starvation, or ill-treatment. The government hastily tore down the camp structures so that within eighteen months of the Civil War's end virtually nothing remained to remind visitors of the horrific conditions in which Southern soldiers had been imprisoned. Later, there was an unsuccessful attempt to build a home on the site for disabled Union Army and Navy veterans.

The federal government and the State of Maryland erected monuments over the ensuing years to honor the memory of the deceased prisoners on Point Lookout, but it wasn't until the mid 1960s that Maryland bought the land to establish Point Lookout State Park. Today the park includes a Civil War Museum, nature center, boating, swimming, overnight cabins and myriad other activities. In October of each year, special nighttime programs describe the numerous ghostly legends associated with the park.

THE VANISHING WALKER the four fishermen encountered is but one of the many uncanny experiences visitors have reported to park authorities. What's more, the identity of this frequent visitor might be known—some experts claim he's the captain of a steamboat that went down off Point Lookout over a century ago.

A former park superintendent described in an interview with a reporter what he's heard from park visitors.

"One night a man walked up on shore and the person who was talking to him could see the man's features very clearly. When the figure supposedly vanished, the shaken tourist reported what had happened to the park rangers," the former park manager told the reporter.

At other times, a casual conversation a visitor might engage in with another sightseer turns truly bizarre when the stranger with whom the conversation is being held disappears.

Sudden changes in the weather seem to trigger the most number of purportedly supernatural activities.

Park Ranger Donnie Hammett told reporter Dorcas Coleman of *The Maryland Natural Resource* magazine that he, too, saw a disappearing man on a park roadway:

"On several occasions, I have witnessed a man running across the road through Point Lookout. (My) sightings always took place during the day, on the same section of road, and the man always crossed the road just after my truck had passed, causing me to view him in my rearview mirror. The (ghost) was always crossing in the same direction. Other rangers have experienced the same phenomenon while passing other vehicles at different times of the day and different times of the year.

"The first time I saw the man I immediately returned to the crossing site. The man was running, using long strides. He first appeared at the edge of the road adjacent to one of the Point Lookout camping areas. He crossed the road and dashed into the woods on the other side, leaving park property. My first thought was that he was a trespasser fleeing the area. I . . . was unable to find any type of path on either side of the road or any evidence of human or animal crossing. I did not get a good enough look at the intruder to identify him or describe his attire."

Hammett then carefully analyzed the ghost's behavior.

"The site of the man's crossing is very near but not in the original Confederate soldier cemetery . . . used to bury prisoners who had died of smallpox at the nearby smallpox hospital where sick Confederates were held. Had the man been making the same trek during the Civil War, he would have been running in a route taking him directly away from the smallpox hospital.

"Reportedly, Confederate prisoners would trick their Union guards into sending them to the hospital and then would attempt an escape through the same woods from which I had seen the man flee. Could the figure have been the spirit of a Confederate prisoner who escaped from the smallpox hospital, only to die in the nearby woods, having himself been infected with the deadly disease? . . ." Hammett speculates.

An unhappy, wandering Confederate ghost would not be such a surprising apparition at Point Lookout. The Confederate dead were removed from their original resting places long ago and moved to another cemetery farther north on Highway 5. The U.S. government manages that cemetery. Near the shoreline, visitors can still see earthen depressions where the original cemetery dead were buried.

PERIPATETIC SPIRITS MIGHT abound around those old Point Lookout cemeteries, given another experience Ranger Hammett had on a warm March afternoon in the late 1970s, when he was new on the job, and later recounted to a reporter:

"At about 4:30 P.M., I was on the Potomac River beachfront gathering and recording weather data when I noticed an elderly woman standing about forty yards from me. She caught my attention because she was strangely shuffling along, looking toward her feet. She appeared to be desperately looking for something she had lost in the grass.

"After I had watched her for about five minutes, I walked over to offer my assistance. My first thought was that perhaps she had lost her keys. She seemed very distant and our conversation was very brief. I only remember three points she made: she did not need my assistance, she lived up the beach 'a ways,' and she asked if I knew where the gravestones were that used to be where we were standing.

"I remember that for some reason I felt I was imposing on the woman and, not wanting to be an imposition, I left to walk three hundred yards east to the Chesapeake Bay shore to record more data. About five minutes later, while I was walking back to my truck, that I had left parked near the river, I noticed that the woman had disappeared. It was then that I realized the adjacent parking lot was empty. Furthermore, from my vantage point since our conversation, I would have had to have seen any cars entering or leaving the area. None had. I did not conduct a search for the woman even though I often wish I had done so.

"A few hours later, I asked then park manager Gerry Sword if he knew anything about a graveyard near the Potomac River picnic area. He wanted to know why I was asking, so I told him about my odd encounter with the old woman. After Mr. Sword heard my story, he told me that there had once been a graveyard somewhere near where the mysterious lady had been wandering. It was the Taylor family graveyard. Its exact location is no longer known but its former existence is well documented."

A tombstone belonging to one of the Taylors buried there—Elizabeth Taylor—was stolen and later discovered in a local hotel by a park ranger.

An old woman carrying out some genealogy research perhaps on early family members? A lonely ghost seeking her final, elusive resting place? Which was it? A perplexing question for which there was no persuasive answer.

FORMER PARK BOSS Sword came upon more than mysterious characters on park roads during his tenure at Point Lookout. Odd, flickering lights, disembodied voices hanging in the air, and other flitting specters perturbed him over the years.

He told a reporter "most of the experiences seem to center around hearing voices, one woman heard a baby crying in the woods, but they could not find the child when they went to investigate, although it had sounded close by."

On one occasion, a memory from the Civil War era at Point Lookout may have slipped into the present. "Fire if they get too close to you," an incorporeal voice called out near the area where prisoners were marched from the steamboat dock to the prison entrance.

Other unexpected and unexplained voices might interrupt a tourist's solitude if he ventures too near the site of the old Hammond Hospital, used for the sick and wounded detainees at Camp Hoffman.

THE OLD TWENTY-ROOM lighthouse is the axis for many of the park's stranger stories.

Ranger Sword lived in the lighthouse for a time. He has said that he, too, heard voices coming from various rooms and even outside in the front and back yards. As often as not, when he dashed about trying to find the source, he would come back disappointed . . . but for one occasion. While he sat in the kitchen, Sword intermittently heard what sounded like someone snoring. He traced it to a wall area behind the kitchen cabinetry, but could not figure out what caused it.

Sword also reported seeing shadowy figures amble in and out of the lighthouse.

Then there was the candles incident. A good supply of them is a necessity for people who live on that lower peninsula. Electric outages are frequent. If the power lines are interrupted in any way, there aren't other means to bring electricity to the farthest reaches of the narrow peninsula, including the lighthouse.

Sword was dealing with one of those periodic blackouts when he lighted three candles and put them in the living room's candelabrum. Soon after going back into the kitchen,

Sword heard a noise coming from the living room. What he found puzzled him, and later, those to whom he told the story. The candelabrum still contained the three burning candles—it had not fallen, as he might have first feared. Yet he must have thought his eyes were deceiving him. Though he had been gone for only minutes, just one of the candles had burned about an inch, which is what he considered would have been normal. Nonetheless, one of other two candles had burned down nearly *four inches* while the third one had remaining just *an inch*-long stub. A big chunk of that candle lay on the floor, its wick showing signs of having been lighted. Sword's conclusion was that the candle somehow broke in two and the new piece by some means relighted. Seems to be impossible, yet the ranger could not come up with any other explanation.

ANOTHER FORMER RESIDENT of the lighthouse had several encounters with elusive revenants, according to what she later reported.

Most of her experiences seem to indicate that whatever ghosts dwell within are cheery souls. She heard happy voices coming from several unoccupied rooms and once caught snatches of an unidentifiable but jolly song floating down from the top of a staircase. Two transparent figures she glimpsed floating through the basement didn't even bother her.

The lighthouse ghosts are compassionate sentinels as well, if another of her experiences is any indication. The woman abruptly awoke one night and, in that twilight time between wakefulness and slumber, she saw six lights hovering in the bedroom. A quick look out the window proved that they were not reflections from any artificial illumination such as boat or car lights. But she jolted fully awake when she caught the unmistakable odor of smoke. She dashed down the stairs. An electrical cord on the space heater was smoldering. Quickly putting out the small blaze, she saw scorching on the wiring and the electrical socket. She stayed out of harm's way—along with the old lighthouse itself—through the inexplicable appearance of those six lights.

Mirror, Mirror on the Wall . . .

Imagine, if you will, poking through the remarkable bric-a-brac at an out-of-the-way antique shop in Washington, D.C. You and your spouse happen upon an intriguing old mirror. You think it would look simply perfect hanging in your bedroom. It's in nice condition but for a few barely perceptible hairline fissures at the corners of the glass. The heavy gilded frame is a tad corroded and the old cardboard backing needs replacing, but otherwise the bargain price makes the purchase irresistible. You pack it up, take it home, and hang it on the wall.

And then the troubles begin.

Somewhere in the middle of the first night, you are both jolted out of a sound sleep by a quick succession of raps that seem to be coming from the direction of the mirror. Your dutiful husband climbs out of bed, creeps over to that lovely old mirror and carefully lifts it up and away from the wall so that he can look underneath, perhaps expecting to see . . . what?

Though the room is gloomy, there is enough light to make it clear that nothing is lurking behind the mirror. Moreover, what could possibly be hidden back there? Maybe it's a mouse inside the wall. You, too, tread softly over and stand next to your husband. Just for your own self-assurance. You look over at him and he shrugs his shoulders, arranges the mirror carefully back in place against the wall, and goes back to bed.

Thankfully, all is quiet for the rest of that night.

But not the next.

The exasperating knocking returns and, once more, your husband is the sleuth trying to deduce what in the devil is causing the sleep-depriving disturbance. But this time you hear his sharp intake of breath as he makes his way across the floor. He whispers to you that a dark shadow seemed to pass as a reflection across the glass, yet it is indistinct enough for him not to be entirely certain of what he saw, given the early morning hour and his own edginess at being unable to solve such a simple puzzle.

The next morning, you decide that a sound sleep trumps interior decorating. You move the mirror to the dining room.

That night, however, you're awakened not by the knocks but

by your cat squalling from the dining room. You both jump out of bed and head for the source of the commotion.

No sooner do you push open the dining room door than you detect the same sort of rhythmic tapping coming from behind the mirror. The cat normally sleeps in a box on a small porch off the dining room. It's out there yowling for what seems to be its very life. You reach through the small window overlooking the porch. It's summer so the screenless window is open. You reach out, grab the cat, and start to pull it inside, but it will have nothing to do with your deft maneuver. The cat lets out a shriek and springs back out through the window. It leaps off the porch. You see it scampering for the street.

That's when you decide enough is enough. The mirror must go. You take it down off the wall intending to put it out with the trash—let it be someone else's problem—but first you want to take a closer look at it. Your husband peels away some of the pasteboard covering against the back. In fading script, you see a name:

Mary Surratt.

You think back to your American history class. You remember. Could it be *that* Mary Surratt? The middle-aged woman hanged as a co-conspirator in the assassination of President Abraham Lincoln?

Mary Surratt—the first woman executed by the United States government?

Could this be the link to the nightly disturbances? Did the mirror somehow embody the *spirit* of the dead woman?

Disturbing questions indeed.

The idea of haunted furnishings is not new. Entire books have been written on the subject. Perhaps this mirror was a reflection *in more ways than one* of its notorious former owner.

However, a haunted mirror is not the only oddity Mrs. Surratt might have left behind; there are other ghostly legacies connected to her homes that involve, inevitably, her still controversial role in the events leading up to Lincoln's assassination nearly a century and a half ago.

ANYONE WITH EVEN a modicum of knowledge about the assassination of President Abraham Lincoln knows something about Mary Elizabeth Jenkins Surratt.

Born in 1823 on a Prince George's County, Maryland, farm that is now a part of Andrews Air Force Base, young Mary Jenkins received more education than was normally the case for girls in that era. At the age of twelve, she was sent by her parents to a girls' school operated by St. Mary's Catholic Church across the Potomac River in Alexandria, Virginia, where she reportedly converted to Catholicism.

Not much else is known about her until her marriage at the age of seventeen to John Harrison Surratt, of the District of Columbia. The couple spent their early married years on property he had inherited near Oxon Hill, Maryland. Their three children—Isaac, Anna, and John, Jr.—were all born there. A calamitous fire in 1852 forced the family to move several miles to the southeast, where they bought nearly three hundred acres of farmland near the intersection of the old New Cut and the Marlboro-Piscataway roads, known today as Maryland routes 223 and 381. Mary's new home was but a short distance from her birthplace.

John Surratt got to work straightaway clearing the land for farming. He cannily recognized that there were business opportunities to be had at those busy frontier crossroads. At a cost of six hundred dollars, he built a sizeable two-story wood-frame house for his family. To augment his meager farming income, Surratt began serving food and liquor to neighbors and travelers; a short time later, he started renting out sleeping rooms on the second floor at twenty-five cents a night. He added a blacksmith shop and a livery stable across the road. The intersection soon acquired the name Surrattsville for obvious reasons. The government approved a post office in the Surratt Hotel; John Surratt was the first postmaster. Later, new election districts drawn up for that section of Maryland included the Ninth, or Surratt's, District with the Surratt Hotel as the designated polling site. District number nine retains the name Surratt's District to this day.

More ominously, Surratt's Hotel became a haven for Southern sympathizers and secessionist activities in the late 1850s. As did most of his neighbors in that section of Maryland, John Harrison Surratt owned slaves—at least seven in the years immediately preceding the war—and thus was a vocal opponent of federal interference in slaveholding. When the Civil War erupted following the assault on Fort Sumter, and as an avowed secessionist, Surratt used the hotel as a key Maryland waystation and safe house for Confederate espionage agents.

However, Surratt's wife Mary Elizabeth's certain route to the gallows really began a year or so into the war when, on the night of August 25, 1862, her husband of twenty-two years collapsed and died. Medical historians generally attribute John Surratt's sudden death either to a heart attack or to a cerebral hemorrhage. Whatever the cause, he left his widow deeply in debt and unable to keep up with the bills. Further, the Surratt slaves had escaped with slavery's elimination in the District of Columbia. The Surratts' oldest son Isaac had already left home to join a Texas cavalry unit, so their other son, John, returned home from college to help his mother with the farm and businesses. However, his sympathies were so clearly with the South that the federal government took away the hotel's postal designation. Most historians believe John, Jr. was a Confederate spy. Mary and her young daughter Anna did the brunt of the farmwork and business upkeep.

Mary was able to retain most of the Maryland property for nearly two years by selling off some of the farmland; unfortunately, the men who purchased the acreage fell behind in their payments. Various other sums owed by neighbors went uncollected. The devastating war meant money was scarce for everyone, especially in tumultuous border states like Maryland.

Mary Surratt decided that her only recourse was to move away from the isolated, debt-laden country property. What made her move possible had been a decision by her husband some nine years earlier to swap some of his farmland for a house at 541 H Street in Washington, which he then had rented out. In October 1864, Mary Surratt and her daughter Anna moved to the city and opened a boardinghouse at the H Street address. Mary then rented out the farm to one John Lloyd, a former Washington police officer and, fatefully, the man who less than a year later would provide the damning evidence that put the hangman's noose around Mary Elizabeth Surratt's neck.

The Surratts' Washington boardinghouse was respectable by all outward appearances. Looks were deceiving. John Surratt's earlier success as a Confederate spy and courier drew the attention of Dr. Samuel Mudd and the handsome actor John

Wilkes Booth, who were plotting an outlandish intrigue to kidnap President Lincoln and hold him as a bargaining tool to release Confederate prisoners in the waning months of the war. Mudd recruited John Surratt Jr. into the affair. As the mastermind of the plot, Booth used the boardinghouse to meet with his henchmen. Although nothing came of the kidnap scheme, their discussions turned to a far more heinous conspiracy, nothing less than the assassination of President Lincoln and members of his cabinet. Although historians sometimes disagree on the degree of complicity in the plots by Mrs. Surratt and Dr. Mudd, Booth indisputably spent a good deal of time at the boardinghouse and knew well the family members. Later investigations found that the conspirators used the Surratts' country home as a hiding place for the guns, ammunition, and other supplies they figured the assassins would need during their escape.

The plot culminated on the evening of April 14, 1865, when Booth shot President Lincoln in the back of the head at a Ford's Theatre performance of the British comedy "Our American Cousin." The president died of his wounds the next day. Near simultaneous attempts to assassinate Vice-President Andrew Johnson and Secretary of State William H. Seward failed, though Seward was wounded.

Booth fled to the rural Surratt tavern/farmhouse with co-conspirator David Herold. They drank whiskey with the renter and ex-policeman John Lloyd. Booth had broken his leg as he leaped to the theatre's stage from Lincoln's private box. The whiskey doubtlessly quelled the pain until the bone could be set. Booth and Herold collected the rifles, ammunition, and field glasses hidden earlier in the farmhouse.

The pair got to Dr. Samuel Mudd's house early on Saturday, April 15. He set Booth's leg as best he could and then made crutches for him before sending the men to an upstairs bedroom to sleep. They left Sunday morning and moved continuously around the countryside for over a week, hiding by day and trying to elude capture by the federal troops and investigators who were on the men's trail.

Early on April 26 soldiers cornered Booth and Herold in a tobacco barn near Port Royal, Virginia. Herold surrendered, but Booth refused. The barn was set on fire. As Booth limped to the door, he was shot once in the neck. Soldiers dragged him out the door, but the only man who knew every assassination detail died before he could get medical treatment.

The net cast by federal investigators caught up others involved in the conspiracy, including Mary Surratt, arrested on the night of April 17, 1865, at her Washington boardinghouse. Authorities were actually looking for her son, John Surratt, Jr., but he had been in New York City on Confederate business and escaped to Canada when word of the assassination reached him.

Based on the testimony of her tenant John Lloyd, Mrs. Surratt was convicted by a military commission of conspiracy in the assassination plot. She was sentenced to death by hanging. Lloyd told the court that she had personally delivered the field glasses to him earlier on April 14. She asked him to hide the glasses and carbines until Booth and Herold came by to collect them after the assassination.

Mary Elizabeth Jenkins Surratt went to the gallows on July 7, 1865, at a District of Columbia penitentiary, now the site of tennis courts at Fort McNair in southwest Washington. Hanged alongside her were coconspirators Lewis Powell, George Atzerodt, and David Herold.

Paradoxically, the United States Supreme Court ruled less than a year later that military courts had no jurisdiction in civilian matters if civilian courts were functioning. The civilian courts were operating at the time of Mrs. Surratt's trial. Further, when John Surratt was returned from Canada two years later to stand trial for conspiracy in the assassination, a federal court was unable to convict him although the government presented nearly the same evidence and the same witnesses. If his mother's trial had been delayed or if there had been a more thorough appeal of her conviction, she would likely not have been found guilty.

THE LINCOLN ASSASSINATION conspiracy continues to reverberate in the American consciousness, not only among historians as to the degree of guilt or innocence of Mary Surratt, Samuel Mudd, and the others, but in the tales, legends, and even ghost stories associated with the Surratt Tavern.

The haunted mirror is but one of them. Is there any truth to this story?

In the original account, the niece of the woman who supposedly bought the mirror mistakenly wrote that Mrs. Surratt's middle name was Eugenia (actually her confirmation name) and that the mirror was salvaged from "a very old house on H Street—a house which had been demolished many years before."

However, an historian with the Surratt Society, a group that focuses on the history and circumstances surrounding the Lincoln assassination, mildly disputed these facts.

He wrote about the mirror:

"Now we know that Mrs. Surratt's middle name was really Elizabeth and that the boardinghouse was not torn down as the article says, but doesn't this make a terrific story? Should we pick apart a good ghost yarn on just a few little technical points?

"Or was there something more to the story? Was there really a mirror that once belonged to Mrs. Surratt that surfaced in an antique shop? We'll probably never know.

"Like most folk stories, enough time has passed so that the truth of the matter (whatever it was) is certainly lost and the only thing that remains is the story. I, for one, vote that we accept this precisely for what it is—a good story. . . ."

OTHER GHOST STORIES are far more specific to the Surratt House Museum, in Clinton, Maryland, and operated by the Maryland Department of Parks and Recreation.

Surrattsville became Clinton in the nineteenth century to disassociate it from the notoriety of the family forever connected to the Lincoln assassination. The old house and tavern remained in various private hands until 1965 when the Maryland-National Capital Park and Planning Commission took it over. The Commission had fully restored the property by 1976. Today the Surratt House is open to the public as an authentic depiction of life on a typical mid-1800s Maryland plantation home.

Nevertheless, with the known history of the place comes another, more shadowy history.

Unofficial history, like the stories of a woman, strikingly similar to surviving paintings of Mrs. Surratt, and a lanky man in a black waistcoat suddenly appearing in odd places and in extraordinary manners that make it unlikely they are *living* beings.

The man—whom some presume to be Mrs. Surratt's tenant John Lloyd—looks out of place in his old-fashioned clothes as he climbs the few steps onto the wide front porch and walks in through the door. Trouble is the house is closed to the public at those times and no one ought to be around.

The heavy scent of cigar smoke and an occasional step across the upstairs floorboards or down the main floor hallway add to the suspicion that John Lloyd's heavy-booted spirit remains a distinct presence. At least one observer theorizes that Lloyd's ghost may haunt his old residence because it was his testimony that doomed Mrs. Surratt to the gallows. If he indeed lied about her involvement, as some historians conjecture, perhaps his ghost seeks to atone for the sin.

Not to be outdone by her malevolent tenant, however, Mrs. Surratt herself appeared as long ago as the 1940s, when the house was still privately owned. A witness said a woman who bore an uncanny resemblance to Mrs. Surratt was standing on the staircase leading to second floor bedrooms. Perhaps her ghost—if that's who it was—knows what other historians since her execution have postulated, that she was wrongly convicted and still seeks the justice denied her in life.

Perhaps the oddest anecdote was related to writer Trish Gallagher: A costumed docent had finished showing a group through one of the bedrooms and moved on to the next. She had the intuition that someone had lagged behind, so she walked back into the bedroom she'd just left. A small girl, in what the guide later described as Victorian clothing, smoothed out the bedspread and then glanced under the bed as if she'd lost something. The docent assumed she was the daughter of someone on the tour and started back to find her parents. When she got to the hallway, she realized there hadn't been any children on the tour. She looked back through the doorway, but now the room was quiet and empty.

The little girl might also be the source of a childish whimper or occasional crying some visitors report near the house's front parlor.

IT IS SAID that history is all around us. We mistakenly assume the phrase means merely the *physical* residue of times gone by. The careful visitor to historic sites understands that the people *from* history, those who *lived* the history we study, are from time to time quite nearby and eager to make their attendance known.

8

Bleak Roads

> Individual ghosts of the dead are understandable,
> once we accept the spirit theory of human survival,
> but what shall be said of ghosts of bygone scenes, of
> buildings that no longer exist, of battles fought in
> the past, or some every-day scene involving ancient
> costumes and long-forgotten settings?
>
> —William O. Stevens, *Unbidden Guests*

The Bog People

THE VISITOR FROM Cambridge, Massachusetts, made his way along the dark and narrow lane on Inishbofin, a wild and desolate land mass off the west coast of Ireland. Bits of moonlight glancing through the scudding clouds helped direct the man's way through the boggy and barren landscape. It was after two o'clock in the morning when he'd left the old man's cottage near an abandoned lighthouse. He'd taken the same pathway several times during his winter-long stay on the island while he researched a novel. The man he'd been visiting was a story-teller and bearer of Irish traditions. The visitor wanted to learn all he could from him.

But this walk back was to be different.

Remarkably different.

On this cold night, Larry Millman's literary explorations into Gaelic lore would result in his own intimations of im-mortality, his own encounters with an ethereal landscape he'd only heard about from elderly Canadian Inuit shamans or sto-rykeepers like the recluse he'd visited several times here in Inishbofin.

Millman, who lives in Cambridge, Massachusetts, is a world-renowned explorer and writer who also happens to have a doctorate in English literature. He has traveled to the re-motest regions of the globe and then written about his adven-tures in nine books and countless magazine articles. He even has a mountain named after him in East Greenland.

Millman's original idea in moving to Inishbofin (Gaelic for "island of the white cow") during that bleak winter was to find a story for a novel set on the island.

"But I found it too depressing. It's an island of old bache-lors," Millman says now. "That one old man who was a superb storyteller lived off by himself about a mile and a half from the nearest other person. He was a bit of a curmudgeon, but I'd wander over to see him after I'd had my dinner and he'd tell me stories and I'd record them."

It would typically be well after midnight before Millman packed up and left for his own rented lodgings some distance away.

Down the lonely bog road on which he now found himself.

As he trod his way carefully along, Millman saw approach-ing him at a short distance a young couple. They appeared to be holding hands. The occasional, filtered moonlight didn't provide many detailed features of the unexpected walkers, ex-cept that they were clad in dark clothing that looked a bit . . . out of date.

"There were only about 200 people there on the island and I would have known anyone who had been courting. And the Irish don't tend to hold hands, gestures of affection tend to be very private," he says, adding that it was also quite unusual for him to meet anyone else on the road at any time of day. Or night.

He thought perhaps the couple had gotten off the ferry from the mainland earlier that day or the day before and he'd just not seen them around the small island.

The couple was now only a few feet away, walking directly toward him. Millman raised his hand in greetings.

But what he saw next nearly petrified him. The couple's faces looked like melted wax, as if they'd been exposed to some horrifying heat which had then caused all their features— eyes, noses, mouths—to dissolve in a formless, fleshy mass.

Later, Millman compared the faces to those painted by noted twentieth-century Irish artist Francis Bacon. Bacon was famed for work in which he would take a brush to his nearly finished paintings and distort the faces of his subjects so that they took on an unsettling, almost Halloween-mask appearance.

Staring at liquefied faces was terrifying enough to Millman, but what he noticed next was even more disquieting. The dark figures drawing nearer to him seemed to be floating a few inches above the ground.

The couple didn't acknowledge Millman as they brushed past.

Millman turned to watch them walk away. But there was no one there.

"Between the time I saw them coming toward me and when I turned there was no sound whatsoever," he adds. "It was very quiet."

ALTHOUGH HE WAS poised to be freaked out, as he says, he thought there had to be a natural explanation for the couple's alarming appearance . . . and disappearance.

"I thought maybe they'd slipped behind a rock, that maybe they didn't want me to see them and so they were off hiding. There were very few rocks along there, and I looked behind each one. They weren't there."

Millman turned around and made his way back to the old man's house. Fortunately, he was still awake.

"I told him the story and asked if anything like that had happened to him living way back there the way he did. He nodded and said that about two years earlier a Danish folklorist visited him and had almost the same experience. The only difference was that there was a smell when he saw the couple. He didn't identify it immediately as the smell of the grave, only that it was bad."

But that wasn't the end of the explanation. The old man admitted that he probably knew who they were.

About fifty years before, a young island couple in their late teens had been seeing one another. It was a secret courtship because their families despised one another. They had kept their assignations to the more isolated parts of the island, including the lighthouse near which the old man now lived.

The boy had been a fisherman, but on one trip out to sea he had fallen overboard and drowned. His body washed up on Inishbofin nearly a week later.

The funeral drew nearly the entire island population, including, of course, his secret love. At the gravesite, the distraught girl could contain herself no longer and threw herself onto the coffin, but she slipped on the muddy soil and hit her head as she fell. She lapsed into a coma and died a few days later.

The parish priest considered her death a suicide, and thus her remains were entombed in a smaller, obscure cemetery reserved for unbaptized babies and suicides.

"Those were the spirits of that young couple, walking over the same ground in death as they had when courting one another in life," Millman speculates sadly.

That encounter with the supernatural had a lasting effect on Millman, especially given its eerie locale.

"If it had happened in Cambridge, near Harvard Square, I might not have thought much about it. But it was in a place that has a truly haunting quality in and of itself. It's such a remote, barren island. It was late winter, on a remote road through a bog where there were no real landmarks of any kind. It's such an austere landscape that that adds to one's fears."

Millman did go back several more times to visit the old storyteller, but afterward, on his way back home, he always took the much longer, more roundabout route. He didn't want to stumble upon any more dead, albeit ambulatory, lovers.

An Icelandic Snake Story

If Larry Millman thought that his real-life brushes against eternity would begin and end in Ireland, he was to be proven wrong several years later.

It all began near the end of a semester teaching American literature at the University of Iceland. He found that the pull of home is irresistible, even for ghosts.

"At the end of the term, I decided to celebrate my release from the classroom by hitchhiking around the Westfords," he recalled. The Westfords are in the far northwest region of Iceland, a dramatic landscape famed for its long, mountainous peninsulas, exceptionally strong winds, and barely maintained roads.

One morning Millman found himself ambling along a particularly dreadful stretch of gravel road filled with ruts and potholes. He heard the crunching sound of tires on gravel signaling an approaching car. A battered old Volvo pulled up alongside him. Staring up at him from behind the wheel was a gaunt-looking fellow with hair sticking out "like lengths of a thirteen-amp fuse wire," Millman says.

"You are going to Patreksfjordur?" the driver asked.

"No, Latraborg," Millman replied.

"Ah, Latraborg. Its bird cliffs are spectacular. A bit smelly, but spectacular. I will take you there," the stranger offered.

Millman tossed his rucksack into the backseat and climbed in the front.

The man didn't say a word for quite some time. He appeared to be brooding over something.

"He didn't pay the slightest attention to me," Millman remembers.

At length the pensive driver turned to Millman.

"I will tell you about my own travels," he suddenly offered.

This is what he told Millman on that long ago Icelandic morning:

A couple of years earlier he had sailed to Caracas, Venezuela, as a deckhand on a Danish freighter. Christmas Day found him in a squalid little Caracas bar trying to make up his mind about whether or not to hang around South America for the winter. His drinking partner was a Venezuelan prospector, who made up his mind for him.

"Diamonds," the prospector whispered. "Diamonds as big as your eyeballs, señor. You will get them in the district of El Mundo Perdido."

By New Year's Day, the visiting Icelander had given up the sea and was headed to El Mundo Perdido district with a few packhorses and a half-breed guide named Jorge.

The journey took nearly two weeks.

At the River Corigyama he hacked a clearing in the bush and set up his camp. Then, day after sweltering day, he proceeded to jab his pick into the hard earth. He found no diamonds.

But he did stumble on a bushmaster, the massive and deadly poisonous snake native to South America. Or rather it found him.

Wherever the man went, around the camp or to the river, the snake seemed to watch him with its tiny, pellet-sized eyes. But always it managed to elude the blade of his machete.

"It is no ordinary snake, señor, but a shape-shifter, or maybe it's a demon," whimpered the guide, Jorge, hastily crossing himself.

Then one morning the man stooped over to pick up his hat. The bushmaster was coiled inside. The snake's fangs sank into his thigh just above his knee with excruciating pain. Jorge flung him over one of the packhorses and hauled him to a hospital at Santa Elena, near Venezuela's border with Guyana. The snake's poison had infected his entire leg.

"If your bone is black," the hospital's German doctor pronounced after examining the sailor-turned-failed prospector, "the leg will have to come off."

He drilled into the leg bone. The bone fragments that came back were black.

"Tomorrow I will amputate," the doctor said.

But the next day there were several emergencies that kept the doctor busy.

On the following day, however, the doctor prepped for the amputation by again drilling into the man's leg. This time the fragments came back white.

"You are a lucky man," the doctor said, nodding his head. "For today I would have taken your leg off and added it to my collection. I have nine legs already. Yours would have been my tenth. . . ."

LARRY MILLMAN WAITED for the man to finish his story, but he again fell silent. An apparently happy ending to the story.

"He didn't say another word until we reached Latraborg," Millman says. "I thanked him for the lift—and the story, too—and started to get out of the car. But then his fingers gripped my arm."

"Wait," the man said. "You must hear the rest."

Once his leg healed he flew back home to Iceland. One day he was gathering driftwood along the shore of his family's holding at Patreksfjordur. Suddenly he saw a great black snake coiled up on the beach as if ready to strike at the first creature unlucky enough to happen by.

"IT WAS A bushmaster," the man whispered to Millman. "The *same* bushmaster."

"There are no snakes in Iceland," Millman said skeptically as he got out of the car.

"You are wrong, my friend," the stranger replied. "There is at least one snake. The snake from El Mundo Perdido. I see it everywhere now."

With that the man put the old Volvo in gear and drove off, a cloud of dust marking the car's disappearance into the distance.

Several days passed. Millman was hitchhiking between Latraborg and Patreksfjordur when he again heard a telltale crunching noise and the sputtering of a car engine from behind him down the gravel road. Within a few minutes, the same old battered Volvo pulled to a stop beside him. But instead of the pallid driver Millman had expected, the car was being driven by another man entirely, and one with a decidedly healthier complexion.

"Hop in." The man smiled, opening the front door for Millman. He gave his thanks and climbed in.

As the car pulled away, Millman said that he'd ridden in it, or one that was very nearly identical, only a few days before.

"It must have been another one," the driver said, looking carefully at Millman. "This wreck is unfortunately mine. I inherited it from my brother after he died several years ago."

Millman was uneasy.

"Your brother?" Millman asked.

"A freak accident," the man replied, pausing momentarily. Millman waited for the rest.

"He seems to have been bitten by some kind of poisonous snake. Doctors amputated his leg, but it was too late," he continued. "That was in South America. Poor fellow."

"Yes, poor fellow," Millman muttered. "Please stop the car."

"You'd like to enjoy the view?" the man asked somewhat puzzled as he rolled to a stop.

"No," Millman said. "I'd just like to walk the rest of the way, stretch my legs, that sort of thing. Breathe a little bit of fresh air. Thanks for the lift."

Millman grabbed his rucksack, hopped out, and started walking as fast as he could. In the opposite direction.

WHAT ARE WE to make of Larry Millman's Icelandic snake story, as he calls it? The cadaverous-looking first driver was quite real, Millman says, with nothing of the grave about him. He thought the story a bit strange, but there was certainly nothing about the experience that gave him pause, wondering if he was talking with a dead man. The man's brother was equally lively.

Could someone—these two brothers perhaps—have been creating their own ghost story for the visiting professor interested in folklore and the supernatural?

Millman isn't certain about that probability, but what he does know is that it all "actually happened" to him. And that is enough to have shifted his personal understanding of the supernatural from musty legend to modern possibility.

The Cottage

"I wish to heaven I could hear a *little* from your *precious* poltergeist," Martin Ames* said skeptically, staring at his host sitting across the table from him. He sounded every bit the sensible lawyer.

"You may be gratified," replied Harlan Jacobs,* satisfied

*Martin Ames and Harlan Jacobs are pseudonyms.

that he had done his level best to apprise Ames of what mysteries might lie ahead of them that evening.

Jacobs, a Columbia University professor, had just finished recounting for his weekend guest the series of most peculiar and inexplicable outbreaks of household disturbances he and his wife Helen had been living with all summer long in their picturesque cottage on Cape Cod. By now, in late September, the mysterious footfalls, a phantom plague of vanishing moths, the crashing noise of a nonexistent piano, incessant clacking from the walls, ceilings, and floors, and unseen objects clattering about on the floor had taken a toll on the quiet couple's psyche.

Most upsetting of all was that in all the months they had lived in their snug summer place, not one of the unpleasantries had been satisfactorily explained.

"I should certainly like to know" what caused the disturbances, Jacobs said later in a written account of the experience, "but I gravely doubt whether I ever shall. I have done all I could to find out, but absolutely to no avail. I do not believe in ghosts, though I am of course aware that we have no final evidence against them. But something strange was loose in that house, and I wish I could discover what it was."

Now that Martin Ames was down for the weekend with his wife and daughter—he, as Jacobs's lawyer, to help draw up a particularly complicated contract; they to enjoy a brief holiday by the sea—Jacobs thought it best to describe for his friend what he and his family might encounter.

He spoke to Ames in confidence while the women were elsewhere.

"It's because I don't want Sarah and Dorothy to have a scare," Jacobs said to his friend. "They may not hear a single sound in the house, but all the same there is a good chance that they may. So let's tell them a little about it in advance. We may save them from a fright."

Ames, however, made it clear he did not agree with Jacobs's approach. Not only should they *not* tell the women such nonsense, Ames argued, but they need not worry because such things were clearly impossible! His derision extended to his keen anticipation of "seeing" the "ghost," as Jacobs told Ames he had taken to collectively naming the various manifestations.

JACOBS RELUCTANTLY ACQUIESCED. Thus Mrs. Ames and her daughter knew nothing of the weird behaviors in the cottage.

A pleasant dinner followed with not a mention of ghosts or mysterious noises. Helen Jacobs, Sarah Ames, and her daughter decided to take in a play at the local community theater while the men began their work on details of the contract that had brought them together for the weekend.

Lawyer Ames found that sometimes one may regret what one wishes for.

"I was reading off a long list to (Martin) when all of a sudden came a crisp little click in the wall right behind his head," Jacobs said.

Ames looked up from his work.

"Your friend the Universal Click?" Ames asked. Jacobs's name for this particular annoyance came from the sound it made and from its habit of occurring nearly everywhere in the house.

"Yes," Jacobs replied.

Ames was nonplussed.

"Some little snap in the drying wood, no doubt," he offered. "Has it rained here lately?"

"The wood *is* very snappy in these parts, but the weather is immaterial," Jacobs rejoined.

With Ames's summary dismissal of his concerns, Jacobs had made up his mind to ignore—for that evening anyway—any repeats of the disturbances with which he and Helen had been plagued. Let Ames discover the peculiarities for himself. Thus, Jacobs made no move to investigate the sound. For his part, Ames merely stared at the wallboard as if waiting for some entity to present itself.

The men fell back to work. Jacobs went on reading from a list of figures that were to be part of the contract language; Ames jotted down the information.

A few minutes later, both men were unexpectedly jarred from their writing tablets.

"It was the familiar footfalls directly over our heads," Jacobs recalled of the sudden interruption.

Ames leapt to his feet.

"What on earth is that?" he barked.

"Only the ghost." Jacobs smiled.

"Ghost your grandmother! There's a man upstairs or I'm a ghost myself. Come on!"

Ames scampered up the staircase. Jacobs fell in close behind.

"I will say . . . that he made a thorough hunt," Jacobs said of their search. "He ransacked rooms and attic, he pried and prodded into closets. He tiptoed on the railing of an upper balcony and scanned the roof with a flashlight. He tramped the floor to see how it would sound, and he made me tramp it while he went downstairs to listen. He left no stones unturned or any mattress either. But he had to give up."

They did not resume contract work that night, nor did they tell Helen Jacobs or Sarah and Dorothy Ames of what had transpired earlier in the evening.

But that was not to be the end of the Ames family's encounter with whatever or whoever it was that Harlan and Helen Jacobs shared their home with that long ago Cape Cod summer.

"HARLAN JACOBS" WAS actually the pseudonym used by a highly respected professor at New York City's Columbia University when he wrote a detailed recollection of what he entitled "Four Months in a Haunted House" in the November 1934 *Harper's Magazine*. The candid account put his peculiar experience in the national spotlight, though he was understandably reluctant to share his true identity and the precise location of the cottage. His university colleagues might not have been able to put up with someone so intimately familiar with the paranormal.

Though the magazine never revealed the author's true identity, that there actually was a Professor Jacobs is incontrovertible. Even before he published the account in *Harper's*, the Columbia academic known as Jacobs personally passed on the tale to noted New York historian and folklorist Louis C. Jones, a graduate student of Jacobs in the 1930s. Jones later wrote about the haunting. He said the professor was "a very kind but practical, hard-headed scholar who vouched for the truth of every word of his article. Knowing him, his word was beyond question. Furthermore, he is not a believer in the supernatural in general, nor in ghosts in particular."

Jones himself was later the founder and executive director of the New York State Historical Association and a prolific chronicler of ghostlore, particularly in his two popular collections, *Things That Go Bump in the Night* and *Spooks of the Valley*.

Jacobs's account, Jones wrote, was "the meticulous report from a man we can believe. . . . Personally, I have no explanation for . . . these cases, but I think even the most realistically minded can accept them at face value."

THE METICULOUSNESS JONES attributed to his professor did not extend to real estate agreements. Perhaps Harlan and Helen Jacobs ought to have paid more attention to the details of their rental contract. Though the house was nine years old, they were the first persons to occupy it, to have spent, as Harlan wrote, "a day or a night in it."

Their purpose in secluding themselves that summer on Cape Cod was to work on a book on which they were collaborating. The quiet of the Cape in the early 1930s provided an ideal retreat from the hectic schedules they both maintained in New York City. Not much is known about the location of their Cape Cod quarters other than the sketchy details Jacobs provided in his published history of the events. He didn't indicate whether or not he learned why the house had been so long unoccupied.

We do know the cottage was a typical-enough oceanside vacation dwelling: the upper floor consisting of two large bedrooms, front and rear, separated by a wide hallway; downstairs was the living room, kitchen, and dining area. An attached garage was used to store Jacobs's research books and files.

What transpired during those four months is a classic occurrence of what experts in paranormal activities would describe as a poltergeist, from the German *polter*, to make a noise by knocking, and *Geist*, or ghost. It is a particularly invasive haunting in which the entity creates chaos by throwing objects about, hiding household items, and generally making an awful nuisance of itself. Oddly, given the experiences of the Jacobses, the poltergeist most frequently is found in households with adolescents, thus causing skeptics to presume it is the child who is behind the turmoil. Aside from Dorothy Ames, who came on the scene long after the disturbances began, there were no other children reported to have been in the home.

This is the story of the Jacobs haunting that summer in a small cottage on Cape Cod.

ONCE THEY'D MOVED in, the Jacobses didn't have long to wait before they discovered that their summer would be out of the ordinary.

On their first night, Helen had gone to sleep in the front bedroom while her husband continued to work at a desk in the rear bedroom. The night was warm, so both bedroom doors were ajar. Harlan could see his wife while he worked.

She stirred and sat up in bed.

"Was it you who made that tapping noise?" Helen called out.

Harlan said it might have been and rocked his desk a bit. As it did not sit quite square on the floor, the legs knocked a bit against the floor.

"No, that's not the sound at all," Helen said. "What I heard was a tapping that seemed to come from the brick wall in front of the door downstairs. It was like somebody tapping on the bricks with a cane."

Oddly, Harlan hadn't heard it. He suggested that it might have been a dream, but his wife insisted that it had been loud enough to awaken her and that it had continued even when she was wide awake.

Although the couple tried to put the incident that evening out of their minds, it turned out to be the first of at least a half-dozen similar episodes that summer, and not the only one in which some of those present did *not* hear or see what the others did.

On night two in their cottage, Harlan would find his own introduction to their "haunted house."

It came as the couple sat in the living room reviewing their work of the day.

"About ten o'clock the taps came, on the brick wall just outside the door—or about ten feet from where I sat," Jacobs said. About a dozen taps took place, each separated by a second or two of silence.

"That's what I heard last night," Helen exclaimed.

Her husband grabbed a flashlight and rushed to the door. But just as he reached it, the tapping suddenly stopped. He ran outside anyway, but a careful search failed to turn up any evident source.

"There was absolutely nothing to explain the noise we had heard," Jacobs remembered. "Yet it seemed impossible that any man or beast could have made off in the instant between the last tap and the first flash of my light."

Nearly fifty times in all during the Jacobses stay that summer the tapping came round, and just about always at ten o'clock at night.

"We found no cause whatever. Over and over we scrutinized the sidewalk in the daylight, brick by brick. A dozen nights I took my station by the door as the hour of ten drew near; but if the tapping came it ceased the moment I sprang out, and left no vestige of a cause behind it. A dozen other times I lay in wait for it, in some bushes just outside the cottage, but on those nights it never honored my vigil."

JACOBS WAS EVER the diligent academic and scrupulously catalogued the baffling events, the "marvels" as he termed them, according to their complexity and frequency.

There were, for instance, "minor" marvels that took place on countless days or nights yet fell into only one of three categories: "universal clicks" similar to their first two nights, falling objects, and sourceless footfalls.

BUT IT WAS during the couple's second week on Cape Cod that Harlan had an experience that left him as perplexed as his wife had been on that first night.

"I had not fallen asleep," he recalled, "because it takes me at least half an hour to doze off. . . . Barely had I put my head upon the pillow when I heard a sound as of a box of matches falling from the (chest of drawers) and striking flat on the floor."

Jacobs thought it must have been a box of wooden safety matches of the sort used to light the fireplace in the downstairs living room.

He crawled out of bed and snapped on the light.

"There was nothing to see. Not a thing had fallen."

On the two successive nights, further falling objects disturbed him as he tried to fall asleep.

The first was the rustling of a large sheet of paper as it seemed to be propelled across the bedroom floor by some sort of unfelt breeze. Jacobs, who thought it might be sheets from a newspaper, heard it quite distinctly but again saw nothing amiss when he flicked the light switch.

"I was hardly surprised to find no sort of paper in my room, or anywhere on the whole upper floor, which I searched at once," he said.

On the third night, a noise of an entirely different sort greeted him within minutes of his retiring.

"Something like a rolling pin or a length of broom handle seemed to fall flat on the floor from a vertical position, and then to roll across the room, *ker-lump*, *ker-lump*, *ker-lump*, until it clattered against the wall and came to rest," the puzzled professor recalled.

A close examination of the room, once he'd got the lights back on, found no object capable of producing such a sound.

IF THE PAST is but prologue, then the rolling pins, rustling paper, and dropped matches turned out to be but an intimation of even more bizarre behaviors to come.

Quite literally hundreds of times over the summer, according to Jacobs, the couple, either separately or together, heard what they came to call those "universal clicks."

Jacobs likened it to the *click-click* of the old-fashioned remote unit used to control slide projectors.

The noxious clicking pervaded the cottage.

"We heard it at any hour of the day or night, in every room of the house, and literally in every wall and partition . . . both of which were the thickness of a single strong board. It came from any point in any wall. There can hardly have been a single square foot of board in any wall or partition that did not yield the sound sooner or later."

The couple pored over the floorboards, ceilings, and corners for signs of insects or insect damage. They found none. It was later suggested to Jacobs that certain wood-boring pests such as termites, or the anobiid, powderpost, house longhorn, and death-watch beetles, can produce sounds that might mimic the kind of click Jacobs heard. Termites, for instance, can be detected from five to six feet away.

Jacobs was unconvinced.

"We have never encountered the (insects) elsewhere . . . there was not a sign of (their) presence on the outside of the boards when we went over them, time after time, with all but microscopic scrutiny."

Several individuals suggested in correspondence to *Harper's Magazine* after Jacobs's story was published that they could identify the particular insect sound Jacobs heard. But, according to the publication's editors at the time, "they all describe the sound as very different from the 'universal click,' which our author heard so often."

However, entomologists assert that certain anobiid beetles, for instance, do feed on seasoned wood and will produce a *ticking* sound in their burrows inside furniture, flooring, or old walls. They have been given the name "death-watch" beetles by the superstitious, who claimed that the ticking or clicking portended death.

AMONG THE MORE frequently cited disturbances in purportedly haunted houses is the steady *galumphing* of footsteps on floorboards. The Jacobses' cottage boasted a veritable parade of footfalls—nearly four-dozen separate episodes averaging a dozen steps each time, according to Jacobs's records. They began in the couple's third week on the Cape and continued on and off for the entire four months they were there.

"Sometimes we would hear them three or four times in a given day or night, though sometimes a whole week would pass without our hearing them at all," Jacobs remembered. "They were very audible. . . . No one need imagine I am speaking of any muffled sound in some far corner of the cottage or in some obscure corner of our own brains. I am speaking of a steady *tramp, tramp, tramp* as of a person with good leather heels walking on the floor of the room right over our heads, or almost as often on the floor downstairs when we happened to be on the upper story."

Jacobs said it was impossible to mistake the footsteps for

anything but "the natural gait of a grown man," a steady stride across the floors with no faltering steps or abrupt stops and starts. Yet their source remained unexplained.

When the lawyer Martin Ames heard the footsteps on that September weekend he spent at the cottage with his family, his insistence that it was indeed a man walking about overhead mirrored Harlan and Helen's experiences and would seem to confirm that the couple was not imagining the insistent pacing.

An incident involving a young neighbor woman acquaintance of the Jacobses underscores the mysterious footsteps' ability to disrupt even the most tranquil of days. And made it clear to them a living person's footsteps and those of their unseen guest were indeed quite identical.

The woman in question, whom Jacobs called "Mary Smith" in his story so as to protect her identity, became such a good friend that she would often walk right into the Jacobses' cottage without knocking—doors were rarely locked on Cape Cod during that era. If the couple was busy, or no one was home, she would make herself comfortable in the kitchen or living room with a book or one of her many knitting projects.

One afternoon when Helen Jacobs was home alone working on a research task she heard someone walk through the front door and then wander around the first floor.

Helen thought it might be Mary and called down to her. When she didn't get an answer, she walked downstairs to see who it might be. It was quite clear no one was on hand.

The couple were getting used to their "ghost" by this time so, according to Harlan, "she merely muttered something about the old ghost at his usual tricks and went back up to her work."

The footfalls started up again as before, round and round the first floor, until Helen quietly stole down the steps hoping to catch whoever had come in. But as with the first time, only silence and the proverbial thin air greeted her search around the cottage.

She returned to her room once more, and once more the "thing" started walking around. Again Helen tiptoed downstairs and again the footfalls ceased.

When it happened a fourth time, Helen vowed to simply ignore the intrusion and stayed in her upstairs workroom.

"Very busy up there?" came a suddenly loud voice from below.

It was Miss Smith come to visit.

Could she have been the culprit? Absolutely not, said Harlan Jacobs.

Mary Smith was on Cape Cod for only part of that summer, and the Jacobses' mysterious footfalls preceded and followed her stay. Neither had they told her about their experiences, "for fear of scaring her out of her wits," Harlan said.

Further, he had been walking behind the young woman for about a hundred yards on her way to the cottage that day, and arrived home only moments after she walked in.

"All the footsteps we heard in that house are still the same mystery to us now as on the first night I heard them and rushed upstairs with a (fireplace) poker in my hand," Jacobs noted. "It is not for lack of effort to find out a reason for them. We lost many an hour from work in the endeavor, and we turned the cottage inside out. But we ended just where we began, without a shadow of an explanation."

THE JACOBSES' "WEIRDEST" experience, using their word for it, came about one evening when Harlan, who had been working in the living room with Helen, went looking for a reference book in the cottage's garage, which he had converted into a kind of library/storage space for their research material. Harlan needed to verify a certain date.

"As I opened the door . . . I switched on the light. Instantly there flew out into the room a fearsome swarm of big brown moths. . . . There could hardly have been less than two hundred of the creatures . . . flying about like mad hornets. They hit me all over the face and even in the eyes," Jacobs said.

He quickly looked up the needed information and fled back into the house.

He told Helen she wouldn't believe what he'd just run into.

"It's a plague of Egypt in the shape of brown moths," he said. "There must be hundreds of them. Can you imagine how they could have got in?"

Helen couldn't. Neither could her husband. The garage door

had been closed all summer. The walls and ceiling were Sheetrock; the floor concrete.

She suggested that perhaps one or two had earlier laid eggs in their books and papers and then hatched, giving birth to the multitudinous descendants he'd seen.

But then in the excitement Harlan forgot the date.

"Come and see the pests for yourself," Harlan said as he led Helen back through the door.

He snapped on the lights. Nothing. Not a moth in sight.

"I do not think I have ever had such a surprise in my life," he remembered of that moment. "Five minutes earlier the room had been alive with the creatures, and now the last one of them was gone. Yet there was no way for them to get out through the concrete and iron, not even any crevice where they could have hidden."

"It's the ghost," the couple exclaimed nearly together, unable for the rest of the summer to come up with any better explanation.

But they were not done with the phantom moths.

Later that same night, Helen went to bed earlier than her husband. As he climbed into bed, he saw a light come on in his wife's bedroom across the hallway.

He called out to ask if there was a problem.

"Nothing important," she replied. "Just one of your brown moths flapping in my face and waking me up. I had to turn on the light and kill him."

Though he was puzzled, Jacobs turned off his light. His wife did the same in her room. A few minutes later he saw Helen's light snap back on.

"Another moth?" Jacobs called out.

"What?" his wife yawned.

"Did you have another moth?" he asked again.

"No. I was asleep," she said.

"But you turned on the light again," he argued.

"No! I haven't had had the light on. I was fast asleep."

Jacobs walked into his wife's room, picked up the bedside lamp, shook it, jiggled the wiring and "in every way I could devise" tried to make the lamp come on of its own accord. He could not. Yet the light *had* come on, of that he was entirely certain, and there was no earthly reason for his wife to have misled her husband about being awake.

No sleep for them that night. Harlan and Helen Jacobs stayed up until dawn trying to make sense of their increasingly curious surroundings.

INTERESTINGLY, THE COUPLE'S experiences with moths correspond in some of their particulars to several ancient superstitions and folk beliefs. The European Death's Head Sphinx Moth, for instance, has symbolized mortality for centuries due to the plain outline of a skull on its back. Salvador Dali incorporated one in his painting "The Life Of A Fireman." In Eastern Europe, the undead were thought to return as moths or butterflies, while Islamic Sufism holds that a moth that immolates itself in a flame is in fact the soul losing itself in the divine fire.

Even in some parts of the United States the moth has come to denote wickedness or impending death. If one appears in the room of a newborn child then the infant will die, according to one folk belief. Italian-Americans at the turn of the last century thought a moth landing in a house meant someone there would soon die.

Nevertheless, Carlos Castaneda's *Tales of Power* prominently features a moth as a guardian spirit.

There is no evidence that either Harlan or Helen died premature deaths, or that a friend or relative fell prey to the moth curse.

THE INVASION OF those disappearing moths was matched in its improbability by an event in midsummer so peculiar and so puzzling that the Jacobses characterized it as the Great Piano Smash.

"In the living room one night we heard a crash from the garage which was enough to deafen our ears and to set the whole house quivering," Jacobs wrote in his account of the summer residency. "It was just as if a grand piano had suddenly lost its legs and crashed to the floor."

There was no furniture in the house, and certainly none in

the garage, that would come close to making such a racket. The couple jumped from their chairs and raced to the garage. They were through the door within seconds of hearing the noise, Harlan said.

Everything was orderly inside the garage. Not a book, box, or shelf was out of place. Nothing had fallen. A subsequent meticulous search of the house and yard failed to turn up any physical basis for the commotion.

The Jacobses heard the same thunderous crashes on two other occasions in August, about ten days apart. Again there was no discernible cause for either one.

MARTIN AMES AND his family might have observed another Grand Piano Smash in September at the time of their visit, but oddly—even by the standards of that curious summer— neither of the Jacobs noticed the commotion that fourth time. The caveat "might have been" is fitting because Harlan himself noted that he was not entirely persuaded it indeed took lace.

The incident happened later on the same night the Ameses arrived at the Jacobses' cottage, and after the earlier episodes. During the course of his conversation with Ames, Jacobs had revealed details of some of the other oddities in the house, including the Grand Piano Smash.

Both families went to bed immediately after Helen, Sarah, and Dorothy returned from the community theater. Nothing at all had been said to them about the earlier events, according to Harlan. Because the cottage was quite compact, Martin, Sarah, and Dorothy Ames stayed together in the front bedroom, which had been Helen's bedroom. Mother and father shared the large bed while Dorothy slept on a cot nearest the wall. Meanwhile, Helen moved into Harlan's room, while he camped on the couch downstairs.

"Helen went to sleep almost at once, but I lay awake for the best part of two hours," Harlan said. "Shortly after I went to bed I heard our visitors above get up and walk around a little, and I heard also their muffled voices. Thereafter all was silent for the night."

Harlan did not get up to inquire about his guests' activities, nor did Helen as far as he knew.

It wasn't until the next morning that the reason for the Ameses' nocturnal pacing became apparent.

"What was that awful crash last night?" Martin Ames asked his host at breakfast.

"Crash? What crash?" Martin responded.

"That fearful crash just after we went to bed. It sounded like the ceiling falling in the garage," Ames explained.

Harlan and Helen exchanged anxious glances.

"Did you hear a crash?" Harlan asked his wife.

"Not a sound," she confirmed.

"Neither did I . . . tell us what you heard?" Harlan prodded.

And then Martin Ames described precisely a raucous Grand Piano Crash in all its particulars.

"I could not have described the noise more truthfully," Jacobs recalled.

So alarmed had the Ameses been that the entire family huddled together all night in the single large bed.

However, Harlan was not satisfied it had in fact taken place, particularly since he and Helen had heard nothing at all.

"I thought he might have possibly conspired with his wife and daughter to give me back a bit of my own coin," Harlan said. "He was not that kind of man, to be sure, and certainly he had not been in that kind of mood the night before. Still, I had my suspicion, and it may be I shall never be sure of the truth."

Both Sarah and Dorothy confirmed Mr. Ames's description of the event. Later, Harlan went upstairs alone. He looked through the room in which the Ameses had stayed. While the cot had definitely been slept upon, there were also three distinct impressions on the pillows in the large bed, leaving the inescapable conclusion that the Ameses had indeed slept in the one bed.

THE HAUNTED SUMMER on Cape Cod ended shortly after the Ames family's visit. There is no indication that the professor and his wife returned to the cottage. Neither could they find anything in the history of the house or its location that could explain the events the Jacobses and Ameses witnessed. Not even a local legend surfaced about the neighborhood in which the house had been built. That the Jacobses were the first tenants is the only oddity they were able to come up with.

Professor Jacobs told very few close friends what had happened; he did not talk of it around the Cape Cod colony "well knowing how the owner of the house would feel." That person lived in the vicinity.

Those of Jacobs's friends he did tell usually pointed to mice or the natural creakiness of wooden homes as possible obvious causes for the troubles. The cottage did creak and groan as many homes do, he maintained, but those sounds were entirely dissimilar from those the couple could *not* explain. He discovered several mice inside, but they were trapped and disposed of.

There was some frustration at not being taken seriously by those around them, but the Jacobses weathered the doubt.

"When we hear about creaking boards and scampering mice," he said, "we merely have to do our best at managing a weary smile."

In his *Harper's Magazine* account Jacobs sought to head off possible criticism that he and his wife may have been overly naive, closet spiritualists, or ready advocates of the supernatural.

"We have never known any other such experience, nor ever expected to know one. There is nothing at all unusual about either of us; least of all is there anything 'psychic.' We are very plain citizens, of later middle age; and if we enjoy repute for anything among our friends, it is probably for ordinary common sense. The fact that we stayed in the house all summer may be evidence to that effect," he wrote in *Harper's*.

Louis Jones, the New York historian and friend of the Jacobses, seconded the veracity of the report as one written by "a man we can believe."

Jones added that he himself did not recount in his own books "the stories of the Jacobses . . . because I wish to claim that either the house was haunted or that poltergeists were responsible. Rather, the stories serve to show the kind of experience people in our time occasionally go through. . . ."

The inevitable question in a case like this is, why? Why would someone choose to remain in a home seemingly haunted by a somewhat malevolent spirit? Jacobs's answer is characteristic of myriad others who face the same quandary.

"Well, it was a nuisance on occasion," Jacobs said, "and I cannot say we were not scared at times, especially in the beginning. But it is one thing to hear of all these visitations at a sitting, and quite another to have them creep gradually into your daily life over a period of weeks. They came upon us slowly, and in general the simpler things came first. We just got used to them and to their apparent harmlessness. By the time we began to talk about a ghost we were ready to cease from trembling at his uncanny ways; and by the close of the summer he was such an old familiar in our home that we had almost come to have a sort of love for him."

A love for him. A love for a *ghost*?

Sounds somewhat peculiar coming from a distinguished university professor, yet arranging the details of a haunting in such a tidy, chronological order presents the reader with the sense that the nasty behaviors of the entities must have intensified to such a degree that all but the foolhardy or stout-of-heart could not have endured such mounting terror. Quite the opposite is frequently the situation as days, weeks, or even months might go by without a performance by poltergeist or spirit. Thus it is that any fear brought on by such unexpected, unexplained, and possibly supernatural activity under one's own roof is tempered by countless hours of longed-for calm.

And in the end all that is left is a variation of Harlan Jacobs's own words about the matter: "To this day I have no better notion of what our 'ghost' was than of what lies on the other side of the moon."

IF PROFESSOR JACOBS was reluctant to offer any explanation other than his own observations, not so the readers of *Harper's Magazine*, who wrote in with their own experiences, explanations, and suggestions.

One letter writer told *Harper's* about a "large brownstone house in Washington" in which the correspondent's family heard pounding footsteps and their own Grand Piano Crash "repeated so many times as to be monotonous." When the writer's father and her husband took off to search for the crash's source, "a sound would come from the first floor as though a large tray of silver had been dropped, or as though a large picture had fallen, with a tremendous crashing of glass."

Another writer, who had passed a creepy night in a New England village house, suggested the formation of an "I've Been Haunted Association" for all those with experiences similar to his own or that of Professor Jacobs. "I look back on that night as the weirdest of my life . . . though I have learned not to tell other people about it," he wrote to the *Harper's* editors.

An electrician was convinced a thorough examination of the wiring would provide the answers. A furnace manufacturer offered the explanation that the professor and his wife were obviously suffering the effects of carbon monoxide poisoning. However, there was no furnace or stove in the cottage.

A psychiatrist explored several possible answers and then arrived at what he felt was the correct diagnosis: hallucinations. This in spite of the fact that at least five different people heard or otherwise experienced that summer's events. How to explain?

The good doctor offered the following lengthy if somewhat astonishing take on that puzzling aspect to the case:

"We know that the brain is composed of nerve cells which generate a form of energy in many ways similar to that of electrical energy, and that these cells are also sensible to stimulation by the same energy. We know that electrical energy can under certain circumstances be broadcast because we daily experience it in our radios. (*Note: this is 1935.*) It is not beyond the realm of conjecture that this nervous energy might under proper circumstances also be broadcast. Such a phenomenon is spoken of as telepathy. In my opinion the existence of telepathy has never been scientifically established. We must, however, admit its possibility. . . . Therefore, it seems to me that either your wife or yourself, without your conscious knowledge, was stimulated by certain peculiarities of your surroundings which caused the subconscious to generate hallucinations . . . and that the one mind, generating this, broadcast them by telepathic means to others."

LOUIS JONES MAY have let his old teacher off too easily in the matter, and didn't have much skepticism, yet he couldn't figure out what else to say.

"Personally, I have no explanation for . . . these cases, but I think even the most realistically minded can accept them at face value," Jones wrote.

Most readers of the *Harper's Magazine* account in the fall of 1934 seemed to agree. According to the periodical's editors, most of the letters they received after the publication of Jacobs's article came from readers who wanted to know the precise location of the cottage—not out of idle curiosity, but so they could go to the Cape and rent an actual haunted house all to themselves.

IN THE END, Harlan and Helen Jacobs might have been sorry that he hadn't seen the advertisement for Metropolitan Life Insurance Company on the page opposite the *Harper's* editor's commentary about his article a few months earlier. The marketing copy extols the virtues of regular home inspections—for efficient heating, adequate ventilation, correct light, and so forth. An illustration of a woman encouraging her husband to get up and out of an easy chair for a look around includes the caption, "Come along. You and I are going to inspect this house from top to bottom."

The Jacobses could have added another inspection guideline for homeowners—assess the potential for unexpected poltergeist activity.

For Mercy's Sake

Behind the town, a thin sickle of pale moonlight shimmered high overhead against the twilight. To eastward, the Marblehead Neck was already wrapped in the swiftly descending night. Far across the bay, a ship hove into sight, half lost in the darkness, slowly coming around the point from the sea, slipping as silently as any ghost ship into the harbor. An hour later found her halfway up the sheltering water and with the wind all but gone. A faint splash as her anchor slipped into the tide and she lay still, with limp, hanging sails.

On shore a few scattered lights marked the houses of the town, while on the strange vessel one lantern faintly illuminated the deck. A high-pooped, bluff-bowed, Spanish galleon, she presented an unfamiliar picture in the harbor of this little fishing settlement.

With those words begins one portrayal of a ghost story as old as Marblehead, Massachusetts itself, a tale once as traditional in that town as its narrow, twisting streets, granite cliffs, and weather-beaten cottages. To some, the story has always been simply the screaming woman of Marblehead, while others attached the lady's lair more specifically to the shore of Oakum Bay, a lowland between old Franklin and Pickett Streets, between Codner's Cove and the grandly named Great Harbor. In truth, the legendary story has been placed at various Marblehead landfalls: Codner's Cove, Oakum Bay, Great Harbor, and Little Harbor.

With its murky origins in the last years of the seventeenth century, it is also possibly the longest-told ghost story in the United States, if not the most authenticated.

The year is thought to have been about 1690, when the small colonial coastal fishing village of Marblehead included fewer than one thousand residents, most of whom were engaged in one way or another with gaining their livelihoods from the sea. A more recent Marblehead pundit said of that era: "Our ancestors came not here for religion. Their main end was to catch fish." Tough fishermen from the Channel Islands and Cornwall had settled Marblehead (harbor) sixty years before as a Salem, Mass., "plantation." They were a largely illiterate population, but as enduring and resilient as the toppled rocks that formed the great "Neck" sheltering them.

It was a dangerous time. Superstitions and a belief in all things supernatural were as ingrained in the souls of Marbleheadians as was their dependence on the sea and its anticipated blessings. Odd, irascible behavior was looked upon with suspicion. The witchcraft hysteria which swept through Salem and other colonial outposts did not escape Marblehead. A woman of the town called "Mammy Red" met eternity in the hands of the Salem hangman because the Puritans declared that she "knew how to turn an enemy's butter to blue wool."

The very real presence of evil meant that few in Marblehead ventured forth at night for fear they would meet a corpse carrying its own coffin, or chance upon Satan himself ensconced atop his own splendid coach gleefully whipping the team of four snorting, black stallions up Brimblecom Hill.

But as disturbing to one's aspiration for eternal salvation as those relentless encounters with witchcraft and the forces of darkness might have been, far more lethal and immediate danger lurked just off the eastern horizon—the fiendish buccaneers who, in that era, preyed upon treasure-laden Spanish ships up and down the Atlantic seaboard.

Ships in need of repair had sailed into Marblehead's sheltered harbors from the earliest days of colonial America. At low tide, with the ship temporarily aground, ships' hulls were scraped and caulked. Thus it was that Oakum Bay—an old section of Little Harbor—was so named for oakum, the untwisted hemp rope used by sailors as calking material.

In those years the able-bodied men of Marblehead were too poor to own their own ships, so for weeks and sometimes months on end they would crew aboard fishing vessels plying the Grand Banks. The men would leave wives, children, and aging parents behind to confront alone whatever hardships might befall them on those arduous ocean voyages a century before American independence. The city was most vulnerable during those times when a few old men and women, destitute widows, sailors' wives and their children were the only defense the struggling village had against the sea-borne marauders. Whenever a strange ship was spied heading into the harbor, the villagers prayed that whoever commanded the ship would not fancy a quick foray to Market Square to see what amusements might be found there. Fearsome men, such as the Eastern Seaboard's infamous brigand Peter Quelch, or the Boston pirate cutthroat Ned Low, had been known to lay waste to both ships *and* towns that did not provide them with adequate diversions.

Thus it was that on that one particular night in 1690 as the furtive vessel stole toward Marblehead its populace was alerted to the ship's presence so that they could remain barricaded behind locked doors and thus out of harm's way. But on this night, too, they also remained unaware of a horror that would soon transpire. The ship was a galleon recently wrested from its Spanish masters by pirates who were now in control. They'd slaughtered the captain and his crew. The few passengers had been dumped overboard far out at sea, save for one beautiful English lady whom the blackguards thought might provide some feminine distraction after so many weeks at sea.

But it was not to be that simple. An argument soon broke out between the captain and his first mate as to which man ought to claim the prize. There was only one way to settle such a dispute in the pirate's code of conduct. That match between the two men, and its awful aftermath, explain in this further retelling derived from a Boston newspaper account how there came to be a screeching ghost of Marblehead.

AS THE GALLEON lay hove over, the door leading into the ship's after-cabin opened. A squat, heavily-built man with flaming red hair and a pockmarked face advanced into the dim moonlight. Ned Crotch stopped and stood with folded arms. A moment later a tall, lean figure stepped suddenly from the shadows beside the rail.

He was something of a dandy, affecting velvet breeches somewhat the worse for wear and a shirt of fine, white linen, open nearly to his waist. His restless hand left the hilt of his thin sword and caressed a bit of black moustache.

"Ah, Mr. Crotch!" Captain De Longe exclaimed to his red-haired lieutenant. "I see that you are prompt. I suppose you've come as you said you would to divide the booty once we could come to anchor in some sheltered harbor?"

His burly companion nodded.

"Certainly," he agreed. "When Ned Crotch says a word he means it. It's not the cargo as interests me, rich though it may be. Nor do I think you are so greedy yourself, De Longe, for a share. Best let the crew fight over it. It's the wench that I'm after. We're both agreed to that. There's but one of her and two of us."

"Suppose we let the lady decide the question for herself," De Longe offered.

Crotch erupted.

"No! Damn you to hell," he swore, hitching his broad cutlass forward. "That trick's too thin. Think I'll be fool enough to agree to that? You with your fancy clothes and fine airs. What chance do I have?"

"Remember, Crotch," De Longe rasped, "I'm captain here. Go bring the girl!"

"Very well. I'll get the wench and we'll settle the matter once and for all!"

He disappeared within the cabin and shortly returned, dragging a reluctant figure behind him. She was an English girl, quite a lovely young woman with auburn hair flowing over her shoulders. Sadly her tresses were in need of a substantial brushing. Clinging to her willowy frame was a long dress, dirty and torn, obvious confirmation of the abuse she had endured. The rich, thin brocade which once hemmed the dress's neckline lay in bedraggled strands down her bosom.

She stood trembling with her arms wrapped about her, glaring from one ruthless pirate to the other. Her pale face was lined with terror and sorrow, dark circles stood under her eyes, and she started at every sound.

"The captain here says that you must make a choice between us," Ned Crotch sneered. "What say you, girl?"

"Oh, no, I cannot!" cried the girl. "Please! I don't want to make a choice. For the love of God just let me go!"

"See!" cried Crotch triumphantly. "For all your finery, you stand no higher than me. There's only one way to settle this. I'll fight you for the wench."

"So be it, then," De Longe consented. "I'll order more lanterns on deck."

"Not here," Crotch argued. "Ashore, alone, just us two and the girl. I'll not trust you here. It would be too easy for some man of yours to slip a knife between my shoulderblades while I was, er, busy."

A boat was lowered, the captain took his place. Crotch swung the girl crying and struggling down to him. Following, he took the oars and pulled away for the dark outline of the shore. After some time he swung into Oakum Cove and beached the boat. De Longe got out and gallantly helped the terrified English girl ashore, while Crotch, knee-deep in the water, placed his shoulder beneath the stern and heaved the craft up onto the gritty shoreline.

There was no formality about the duel. Each man rolled up his sleeves, kicked off his boots, and bared his weapon: for De Longe, a slender, Spanish rapier against Crotch's heavy cutlass.

With only the radiance of the stars and the faint reflection of moonlight on the sea to light them, steel slid along steel and the fight was joined.

The girl stood with clenched fists, fascinated by the swift movements of the pair yet at the same time repelled by knowing that her future lay in the fortunes of one of these vicious buccaneers.

Suddenly, De Longe cursed and leaped back; his sword had snapped in half. Crotch showed no mercy. He cut the captain down with a lunge that stretched him silent on the sand, a broad crimson stream puddling next to the body.

Casting aside his reddened blade, Crotch advanced toward the dim feminine shape. He laughed in anticipation of collecting his prize. She half turned as though to run, then suddenly stooped, picked up something from the sand, and stood facing her foe.

Crotch reached out and roughly drew her to him.

"I've won, do ya' hear? I've won!" he cried, panting. "You're mine! Only mine!"

"Please," the girl wept, "stay away from me!"

And then with a vengeance born of desperation she plunged De Longe's broken rapier into Crotch's shoulder.

The pirate victor screamed and staggered backward against the pain, reaching up to yank the blade from its fleshy scabbard.

His passion changed to terrible rage and his strong hands closed about the girl's thin, pale throat. Slowly and with evident delight he lifted her slowly off the ground and swung her about like a straw doll.

"For mercy's sake!" she screamed into the silent night. "Lord save me—oh Lord Jesus save me . . . !"

A terrible gurgle issued from deep within her throat. Presently it grew fainter, weaker, and finally died away like the receding waves upon the dusky shore.

Early light found the sails of the galleon but a speck upon the eastern horizon, yet a sign of the ship's visit remained in the cove—Crotch had hastily buried the hapless girl's remains under a mound of sand just above the high tide mark.

There were some who heard those terrible cries that night, old people and the women and children whose men were away fishing in the Grand Banks. Yet despite the bloodcurdling cries, none dared venture out of their cottages.

The years passed and the mound beside the sea disappeared, but the legend grew and flourished. On the night of the anniversary of the brutal murder, the English girl's piteous cries could still be heard, beseeching the miserable Ned Crotch for mercy at this, her dying place.

Hell's Bells

Excitement mixed with not a little fear led residents of a stately manor on old Springfield Street in the South End of Boston to finally call police in a bizarre case of mischievous poltergeist commotion. It seems word of the weird events trickled out so that sometimes-unruly crowds gathered each day in hopes of hearing what some took to calling "hell's bells."

On several days in June 1869, the house near Shawmut Avenue was plagued with a "furious tintinnabulation," as one observer called it, arising from the continual pealing of the bells used to summon household staff. As in many mansions of the past, the home had its various rooms wired to bells usually located in the servants' quarters. Each room's bell had a particular tone or buzzed a specific number of times so that its ringing would bring a servant scurrying to answer the summons in that particular area of the house. In this case, ten bells lined the wall in a basement corridor.

But what happened here was not typical of the behavior one usually associated with nineteenth-century Boston gentry.

Singly, or in pairs, trios, or quartets—indeed sometimes all ten at once—the bells resounded with maddening regularity and always, always, without a human hand within reach of the rooms' bell wire. Some witnesses said that the ringing was accompanied by other "unaccountable and supernatural" noises. On several occasions, the head of the household claimed that he saw specters "flitting around the premises."

To try and alleviate the infernal noise, workers disconnected the wiring from the bells. The ringing continued on as ever. Even the wires—hanging loose from the bells—vibrated as the disengaged bells chimed away. Several especially strong men tried to hold still the wires and bells but their efforts were to no avail.

The house was adjacent to a grammar school where the teachers and students spent days trying to figure out what plagued the house next door. A skeptic of the entire affair said the academics' speculation was a "detriment to their studies."

Boston police eventually had to be called to disperse the restless crowds that gathered on a daily basis to hear these supposed bells from hell.

Father Chuck's Poltergeist

"I cannot account for it all."

With those plain words, the Reverend Charles F. Donoghue told reporters about the maelstrom of flying household objects that afflicted the parish house at the Church of the Sacred Heart in South Hanover. The case from the early twentieth century was never resolved.

Father Donoghue said furniture was thrown around the rooms and smashed without any plausible explanation. Kitchen glassware and crockery rolled off shelves and shattered on the floor.

The perplexed minister told his story this way:

"For two weeks and longer, the strangest things have been going on in the house. Miss O'Connell is my housekeeper, but she is in such a state that she cannot remain in the place.

"I realize how it sounds, but it is true nevertheless. I have seen pieces of furniture dashed to the floor and broken with no possible explanation at hand. It is all very mysterious.

"A few nights ago I was compelled to sleep on a cot just outside the room where Miss O'Connell and Mrs. Hoban and her daughter were sleeping, because they had been terrified by their furniture being dashed about the room in the dead of night.

"I had placed my alarm clock on a stand nearby and barely crept into bed when the clock was hurled down the stairs. I got the clock and again placed it on the table, for it was still going. Hardly had I gone to bed a second time before the clock was hurled across the room so violently it was broken. It stopped at five minutes past two o'clock."

Father Donoghue awoke the sleeping women and they all sat up the rest of the night in the downstairs parlor. In the morning, they found the women's beds upstairs ripped apart; sheets and blankets lay on the floor in torn disarray.

Historical records do not indicate whether there was a satisfactory explanation for the phenomena.

The Haunted Schooner

The old Iron Works Docks near Somerset, on Assonet Bay north of Fall River, was frequently thick with cargo vessels during the late nineteenth century. While steam was gradually augmenting—and eventually to displace—sail on the oceangoing vessels, grand sailing ships such as the *William H. Jordan* still called at ports up and down the Atlantic seaboard.

So it was that in mid-January 1886 the three-masted schooner *Jordan* was at the Somerset docks having off-loaded a cargo of coal. All went well with the unloading, but that was the last good thing recounted about the troubled ship.

It all began on a Saturday afternoon earlier that month when the ship's captain, Elias Theebar, was accidentally killed while overseeing the delivery of a new anchor at the railroad dock. A few hours later, the first mate and a cabin boy retired to their quarters at about nine o'clock.

The mate had just dozed off when he shot bolt upright at his late captain's voice, "Take hold of that anchor!"

"I thought it a dream," the mate said. He listened for several minutes, but all he heard was the gentle lapping of the water against the hull of the wooden vessel and the creaking of the aged timbers.

"At last I dozed but just then I heard something going on up forward on deck. I thought it might be the cook rolling barrels about and paid no attention to it until I heard a fearful thump on deck."

He rushed up top and looked around. No cook was about, indeed no other soul stirred. He waited awhile but then returned to his cabin. He lay awake until dawn.

"When I finally went back on deck," he recalled, "I found that the bower anchor had been dropped from the bows aft nearly to the waist, where the shore plank is. It takes a good many men to handle that piece of iron, and how it got there I don't know."

The mate didn't stick around to solve the mystery. He and the cabin boy quit the *Jordan* later that day, telling anyone within earshot that the captain's ghost had come back.

The mate's story spread so quickly that the owners were unable to employ a new crew and the *William H. Jordan* became one more cursed ship in the annals of maritime lore.

9

Better Left Unsaid

I fled, and cry'd out, *death*;
Hell trembled at the hideous name, and sigh'd
From all her caves, and back resounded, *death*.

—John Milton, *Paradise Lost*

WHO AMONG US has not spoken cruelly or in haste to someone we truly loved? Or cried out in frustration that the devil himself might be a welcome partner in overcoming some earthly complication?

Yet who among us has then faced our remaining days unable to recant those ill-conceived words when, perhaps, the person to whom they were spoken died a sudden and awful death?

Words spoken too quickly to take back are at the center of these Michigan stories of sentiments that ought to have been left unspoken.

The Spurned Suitor

Marie McIntosh was a Canadian girl whose unintentionally hurtful rejection of the love professed by a striking British Army officer could never be taken back. Her pitiable act so long ago condemned his ghost to forever wander the quiet woods of Detroit's Gross Isle, on the shore of Lake St. Clair.

THE STORY BEGINS in mid-1812. The month is August. The United States has been at war against Great Britain since June 12. Some historians identify the conflict as the second American revolution; today it is known better as the War of 1812.

The roots of the conflict are complicated. There were several long-term disputes between the two nations, including the stopping of American ships by His Majesty's Navy searching for deserters. The British were accused of then impressing into duty—kidnapping—anyone they found who was of English birth. An attack by the British on the *USS Chesapeake* two years earlier had nearly caused war at that time. Britain also imposed a blockade on France during the French Revolutionary and Napoleonic Wars, which had been a source of conflict with the Americans ever since.

The young United States government also disputed Britain's declaration of the border alignment with Canada and the Northwest Territories. Some belligerent members of Congress, primarily from the West and South, aspired to drive the British from Canada, and after that the Spanish—Great Britain's allies—from West Florida.

Within weeks of the declaration of war, however, it was clear that the American government was ill-prepared for such an undertaking: the treasury lacked the necessary funds, the regular army had fewer than 10,000 men, and the navy could muster only twenty seagoing vessels with which to confront the superior British naval forces.

The American military anticipated that a three-prong attack on Canada would overcome the evident weaknesses—from the bottom of Lake Champlain, from the Niagara River, and northward from Detroit.

All three campaigns failed.

An army marched north from Plattsburgh, New York, at Lake Champlain but then balked at crossing the border into Canada, and subsequently drew back to Plattsburgh.

Another American armed force briefly occupied Queenston Heights on the Canadian side of the Niagara River. The Yankee militia was overrun and captured by the British when New York soldiers refused to come to their aid.

But the third early battle and the most significant was the humiliating defeat of American forces at Detroit. General William Hull led 2,000 soldiers across the Detroit River into Canada, and directly into the waiting arms of troops commanded by British General Isaac Brock. His forces drove the Americans back across the river, capturing Hull's soldiers and Detroit in the process.

But what isn't so commonly known is that in the days before Hull's final surrender, a series of smaller clashes were taking their toll on both sides. In planning one of those skirmishes, General Brock made the decision that troops under the command of Lieutenant Anthony Muir would lead an assault on American soldiers at Mongaugon—now Gross Isle—on August 9, 1812. Even with their tough Wyandot Indian allies led by Chief Walk In The Water, the British knew it would be a dangerous mission from which the young lieutenant and a number of his men might not return.

MARIE MCINTOSH WAS the daughter of Angus McIntosh, a Scottish businessman living in British Ontario. She and her family lived in a grand home near present-day Windsor. Lieutenant Muir had been courting her for quite some time. But their courtship was rather chaste by today's standards, as was often the case in that proper era; their moments together typically came at formal gatherings or in the presence of their families. A young lady's reputation forbade any but the briefest of private exchanges with an eligible suitor, even one whose intentions were genuine and honorable. The lieutenant was an exceedingly shy man where women were concerned, despite his soldierly bearing; he did not speak often to anyone of his desire to marry young Marie.

Yet Marie knew in her heart that the handsome soldier was the man she wanted to marry, but she grew ever more restive at his bashfulness. In point of fact she found it quite annoying. She could not tell him of her abiding love, for that would have been quite unseemly without an engagement. Nevertheless it did not occur to Marie—not yet twenty years of age herself—that, despite words of marriage never having been exchanged, Lieutenant Muir would doubt her deep affection and devotion, nor that she would certainly agree to a marriage proposal.

Now, on the eve of the British raid on Mongaugon, Marie's shy beau faced a most harrowing assignment. He decided that he must tell Marie of his feelings and propose marriage. He imagined that the warmth with which she would greet his ardor might shield him from harm.

Thus on the night before battle, August 8, the lieutenant obtained a short leave from his company and stole away to the McIntoshes' home. Marie was alone save for her housemaid. He met Marie in the parlor and spoke forcefully of his love. Then dropping to bended knee he asked for her hand in marriage. He told her of the coming battle, that tomorrow he would face a perilous assault on the American forces, but that with her assent to an engagement he could face the enemy with confidence.

What then must have possessed Marie to do what she did? Was it coquetry? Was it her immaturity in dealing with matters of the heart? Or was she truly irritated at Lieutenant Muir's timidity in not making his intentions clearer before this night? We will never know.

Whatever her motivation, she turned away. She rejected his earnest proposal. The lieutenant was a serious young man entirely unprepared for such a stinging rebuke. He quickly rose to his feet and dashed from the room.

Now it was Marie's turn to be distressed. To her this was but a game in which she was softly scolding him for his timidity. She thought he would linger a few moments in the hallway before returning to press his claim for her hand in marriage. When he did not return, she hurried from the room and to the open front door. She saw that he was mounting his horse.

"Lieutenant! Anthony!" she cried, scrambling down the wide porch steps.

He did not look back as he spurred his horse away.

The commotion brought Marie's housemaid scurrying to her mistress's side.

"He must certainly know that I love him," Marie sobbed to the young servant. "Men are so stupid, so matter-of-fact. They take months to make up their minds to woo a girl, and if she does not immediately say 'yes' they feel themselves aggrieved and wounded."

The housemaid nodded sadly and held her mistress close.

MARIE AWAITED LIEUTENANT Muir's return. Nightfall came and still there was no sign of the young officer. At her maid's insistence, Marie at last went to bed. The maid drew tight the window shutters and pulled close the diaphanous curtains around the bedstead.

Sleep did not come. She went over and over the circumstances of that brief encounter with the one man with whom she wanted to spend the rest of her life but had rejected in a fit of pique. How could she have been so foolish! And now she was filled with so much regret at her thoughtless behavior.

As the morning sun began its ascent above the horizon, Marie fell into a disturbed slumber. Moments later she was wrenched awake as the door was thrown open. Rapid boot steps crossed the floor. Marie drew aside the bed curtain. Young Lieutenant Muir stood a few feet away, dressed as on the afternoon before. But that is not what caused her sharp intake of breath, nor why she shrank back against the pillow. His face was as white as death itself, a brutal gash angling across his forehead. Blood oozed down his pale cheeks, leaving long dark stains on his mud-spattered uniform.

"Fear not, my dearest Marie," came the lieutenant's distinctive voice. The hollow tone did not come from his mouth but rather seemed to envelop the entirety of his shattered body.

"Though the Americans were victorious, they will not long rejoice. England will soon triumph. I was shot through the head, yet I fell in honor. My body lies hidden in a dense thicket. I beg you for one final act of kindness. Rescue it from the wild beasts of the forest so that I may be remembered with an honorable burial. Farewell, my love."

With that he reached out and with a calm born of death he laid his fingers on her right hand. The coldness of that touch, the iciness of the grave itself, sliced through her skin. She fell insensible against the soft pillows.

THE SUN WAS high when Marie regained consciousness.

Her first thoughts were of that dream—for is that what it must have been? Yet it all seemed too real to ignore: of the lieutenant's frightful visit; of the touch that seemed more commanding than life itself. Reluctantly she glanced down. This had been no dream. Across the back of her hand were two deep, dark impressions. Marks from the fingers of a hand. The hand of Lieutenant Anthony Muir.

She leaped from bed. Calling to her maid, she hastily dressed and ordered that a horse be saddled. Her servants pleaded to let one of them accompany her. She ignored them and raced off to General Brock's encampment at Malden.

She knew Walk In The Water—the Wyandot Indian and British ally and an old friend of the McIntoshes—and haltingly told him of her dream. She pleaded with him to be taken to the battle site. He reluctantly agreed and together they went by canoe across the Detroit River. Once they reached shore, Marie moved as if in a trance toward a bramble thicket.

"This is where we shall find him," she whispered to her Indian guide.

It did not take long. The blood-spattered remains of Lieutenant Anthony Muir lay as he had fallen. In the cold light of a new dawn, the fatal bullet wound on his forehead was even more horrible than it had been during the fleeting glimpse she'd had of his ghost the night before. But she had found him. That now was all that mattered.

Walk In The Water and several of his men removed the soldier's body to Sandwich, Ontario, where he was buried with military honors.

At the funeral, Marie slipped a black glove onto her right hand. She never took it off.

MARIE MCINTOSH DID marry. A decent man who had heard the bittersweet story of Anthony and Marie courted her. They remained childless.

Lieutenant Muir's touch stayed with her for the rest of her life—a reminder that impetuous behavior and careless words can have consequences far greater than we might ever imagine.

On August 9, 1813, and for decades thereafter on that date, Marie slipped off her fine clothes, slipped on a pair of wood sandals and wrapped herself in plain black sackcloth. She went door to door from Windsor to old Sandwich as a mendicant pleading for money or goods for the poor. No church or churchman required such atonement for her transgression. She placed the burden of self-sacrifice upon herself.

Neither did the lieutenant slip away as an untidy footnote to a nearly forgotten war.

The shaded woods once plentiful in Grosse Isle—what was once Mongaugon—remained the soldier's ghostly home forever after, his bloodied form slipping quietly among the ancient oak trees toward the soothing river.

And the lieutenant's prediction came true. On August 16, 1812—just a week after Muir's awful death—the British forces of General Sir Isaac Brock marched triumphantly into the proud old French settlement that was Detroit.

Curse of the Pere Marquette

A Michigan trout fisherman named Herb might have avoided a most sorrowful chapter in his life had he been familiar with one Jabez Stone, the central character in Stephen Vincent Benét's classic story of a New Hampshire homesteader who proffers his soul to the devil in exchange for healthy crops and a happy family. What Herb desired most of all were not good crops, but rather a creel-full of fresh trout each time he waded into Michigan's famed Pere Marquette River. To achieve that end, Herb made a desperate pact with that region's version of the devil—a ghostly angler known to generations along the river as "The Man with the Catgut Beard."

Benét's story of "The Devil and Daniel Webster" details the unhappy fortunes of farmer Jabez Stone. His farm was a shambles: corn borers ruined his corn, blight covered the potatoes, and boulders the size of grown hogs seemed to pop up in his fields overnight making plowing all but impossible. Worst of all, his wife and children suffered the most from his failures. Finally, the day came when his problems became too much. On that morning, he'd broken a plow blade, Benét wrote, "on a rock that he could have sworn hadn't been there yesterday," his children had taken ill with the measles, his wife was sick, and Jabez had a mighty sore thumb.

That's when he cried out in frustration that the devil could have his soul if only some measure of success might finally come his way.

He got far more than he bargained for. That very evening, his capricious supplications brought a knock at his door. Standing at the threshold was one "Mr. Scratch"—a tall, dark stranger dressed in black who, when he smiled, presented sparkling white teeth, each one honed to a razor-sharp point. Jabez Stone kept his word and signed a blood oath with this devil in faint disguise.

Now, good fortune did indeed come to pass for the troubled farmer. His crops no longer failed, his children grew healthier and happier than he could have imagined, until at last Mr. Scratch came to take delivery of—his soul. He discovered—as others had before him and have since him—that if one wants out of such a bargain with the devil, he will have hell to pay. Stone demanded a trial at which he could argue out of his demonic agreement. It took Daniel Webster himself to extricate Jabez Stone from the contract during a frightening trial presided over by Mr. Scratch and twelve jurors plucked from hell itself.

NEAR AS ANYONE could tell, that fisherman named Herb wasn't a farmer like Jabez Stone, nor did he want for food or shelter. His passion was trout fishing, above all for rainbows and browns in central Michigan's Pere Marquette River, one of the finest recreational waterways and trout streams in all of the Middle West. Actually a large system of four distinct tributaries, the river includes some 380 lineal miles of river channel stretching across four counties.

The river formally begins at the juncture of the Middle and Little South branches, southwest of Baldwin, Michigan. The Baldwin River drains into this main stem a few miles downstream. Outside the village of Custer, the Big South Branch joins the Pere Marquette before it empties into Lake Michigan near Ludington. Sixty-six miles of the river are a federal National Scenic River and a Michigan Natural River.

Though trout anglers have been drawn to the river for decades, it is said that Herb's luck never held steady; he filled his old wicker creel mostly with fingerlings.

No one knows what Herb's last name might have been, but many of those who frequent the region of the Pere Marquette know his story. Herb's was an eventful encounter with the cursed, ghostly fisherman in the swallowtail coat, old cap, and catgut fishing leader growing out of his face, who himself had been condemned to wander the river in perpetuity by the ghost of Father Marquette after the nameless fisherman used a seine to haul in far more trout than was the legal limit.

Michigan poet, author, and historian Alfred Day Rathbone IV was among the first to describe the events of Herb's fateful encounter with the oddly bearded man. Rathbone self-published a small booklet with the poem, and it later appeared in a 1938 issue of *Country Life and the Sportsman* magazine. However, Michigan historian Bruce T. Micinski said the poem was actually composed at the Henry Rouse fishing camp near Baldwin sometime early in the twentieth century. Rouse was a famed river guide and angler.

What follows is Herb's story as it has been passed along for nearly a century.

> **Through** Michigan forests of spruce and pine,
> Away from the city's smoke and grime,
> There flows a stream of some renown
> That's filled with trout, both 'Bows and Brown.
> It's nearly always an even bet
> That you'll take fish from the Pere Marquette.
> The exception frequently proves the rule
> And this is the tale of a fishing fool
> Who whips that stream both night and day,—
> Yet never carries a trout away.

Herb is an awfully likeable chap
From his fishing boots to his fly-decked hat,
And his experience, both strange and weird,
Concerns the man with the catgut beard.
Herb used to fish the whole day through
And come back at night with just a few,
All smaller trout, say seven or eight;
You could spread them all on a dinner plate.
He never seemed to acquire the knack
Of hooking the big ones and bringing them back.
There was just one time that he filled his creel;
He got his limit—boy, they were real!
The finest catch that's ever been seen
From the rippling waters of that old stream,
But ever since then his luck's been down
And his largest trout is a six-inch Brown.

We used to stay in a fishing camp
With other chaps who loved to tramp
The rushing waters all day long,
Then liven up the night with song
And stories told with a poker face
As we'd gather 'round the fireplace.
One summer morn at break of day
Herb softly arose and stole away.
As he quietly waded into the stream
The mist was rising like clouds of steam;
'Twas like the grave, there wasn't a sound,
But a musty smell seemed to hover 'round.
Herb sniffed the air with a feeling queer,
He seemed to sense there was someone near,
So he glanced up-stream and all about,—
That something was there, he couldn't doubt.
Just then, down stream, at the next sharp bend
He beheld a sight that stood hair on end.
An apparition, amazing and weird—
It looked like a man with a long white beard.
But strangest of all were the clothes he wore;
An old plug hat from the Civil War,
A swallowtail coat that seemed too tight,

And a glimpse of a waistcoat, gleaming white.
He was wading the stream in those duds so odd,
And under his arm he carried a rod.
Then curtains of mist rolled swiftly in;
Herb chuckled aloud and thought with a grin,
"Some native trying to hook a trout,
I'll give him a hail," and he gave a shout.
The echoes answered with every wail;
No other replied to the cheery hail,
So Herb went splashing on down stream
To see who in the world it might have been
Out wading the river at break of dawn.
When he reached the bend,—the man was gone!
Herb stared around with a stupid grin,
Decided he'd better quit drinking gin,
Then he sniffed the air,—'twas that musty smell
That comes from old earth or an unused well.
Herb scratched his head and rubbed his ear
And declared the whole affair was queer,
But he tied a fly on his leader fine
And began to whip out a beautiful line.
As the day wore on and Herb wore out
In his strenuous efforts to hook a trout,
From his mind the incident slipped away,
Herb's catch was three little Browns that day!
Seated around the fire that night
With embers aglow and pipes alight,
Herb told the boys of his trip down stream
At the break of day and the man he'd seen.
Then spoke a fisherman old and gray
Who'd fished that stretch forty years to a day,
"Herb," said he, "that wasn't a ghost;
That man you saw was once my host
Who was cursed by the shades of Pere Marquette
For catching trout in a seining net."
From the bowl of his pipe he knocked the dottle,
And stretched out a shaking hand for the bottle.
He coughed a bit and heaved a sigh,
Then said, "There's no one knew of this but I.
This man, as I said, was once my guide

When my hand at fishing I first tried.
His name? No matter. Since he was queered,
He's known as The Man with the Catgut Beard.
He wears a waistcoat gleaming white,
A swallowtail coat that fits him tight,
And an old plug hat that's mossy green
And he's cursed to forever wade that stream.
He wasn't content to take his trout
On a hook and line,—no, that was out.
He wanted simply to rake them in
So he used a net,—'twas really a sin,
And I used to remonstrate with that guide,
But words were like water on his hide.

"You know, if you'd kindly pass that bottle
I could probably step on the verbal throttle."
The old man tipped the flask up high
And swallowed a drink with a choke and a sigh,
Then he lit his pipe and resumed his tale.
"Why, that fellow caught his fish by the bale;
What he didn't eat he fed to his hogs,
Which were fat as butter and heavy as logs.
Then one night while out on the stream
He slept on the bank and dreamed a dream
In which the ghost of Pere Marquette
Took him to task for his use of a net.
In stentorian voice the spectre said,
'Unless you cease, you'll wish you were dead!
If you should e'er make use of a seine
To take trout from my stream again,
On your old head I'll place a curse,
You'll catch no trout, and what is worse,
Your beard shall grow on lip and chin;
And from your neck and cheeks so thin
Instead of hair, I shall command
A growth of catgut, strand on strand;
Long and short with tapered end
Shall leaders from your face depend.
A finer gut you'll never see,
A walking leader box you'll be.

From your face you'll pluck a gut,
Tie it to your line,—and zhut!
The leader will have disappeared,
The trout will laugh; and from your beard
You'll choose another straight and strong,
And this you'll do your whole life long
And on into infinity—
'Tis my revenge, so you shall see.
I warn you man!' Then moaned the shade,
'Seine no more trout!—my curse is laid.' "

The old man paused and chuckled deep,
"That bottle, sir; and may I keep
It here to hand? There's little more
To this quaint tale of fishing lore."
The liquid down his gullet ran
And faintest flush spread o'er his tan.
He settled back within his chair;
Said he, "My guide swore then and there
That no more trout from Pere Marquette
Would find their way into his net.
But soon, as always, came a time
When trout would take no lure on line.
Like you these days, Herb, don't you see?
The guide went fishless, then to me
He said, 'Do you believe in dreams?
I know there's trout within these streams,
But I can't hook a single 'Bow,
And as for Browns, well, you must know
That I've returned with empty creel
So many times I think I'll steal
A final chance with my old net.
No ghost can scare me out—not yet!'
So, coming back from church that night
In swallowtail and waistcoat white,
And old plug hat so mossy green,
He slipped into the purling stream
And seined the creek from shore to shore,—
He caught a thousand trout or more,
Then started for his old log shack

A sack of trout upon his back.
That night I dozed beside the grate;
We'd fished that day until quite late.
The door burst open with a crash
I heard a shriek that seemed to smash
The echoes near and far,
And there, framed in the door ajar,
Stood the guide that I had known,
His face had changed,—'twas not his own.
A sort of mist enveloped him,
And from his lips and cheeks and chin
Long leaders draped themselves around
His legs and thighs in buckskin bound.
They spread out there upon the floor
And wafted in and out the door.
There seemed to be a musty smell
As though from some dark hole of hell,
And up I sprang in sudden fright
From gazing on that awful sight.
The figure groaned and shook his head,
And through the cloud of leaders said,
'Farewell, my friend, it is my fate
That I shall fish from dawn 'til late,
Day after day, year in, year out.
But I shall never more catch trout,
For leaders I must ever change
And new ones pluck in winds and rains.
This is the curse of Pere Marquette!'
And I can hear him moaning yet,—
Then, as the door swung gently to,
Deep in my heart I somehow knew
That I would never see again
My guide who took trout with a seine."

The embers in the fireplace
Threw shadowed glow upon the face
Of him who told the story weird
About The Man with the Catgut Beard.
Herb stirred himself, and with a smile
He rose to go. Then, "Wait a while,"

With flask in hand the old man said,
"Before you take yourself to bed
I wish to add this final line
To this old fishing tale of mine.
Many a fisherman now dead and gone
Has been in the stream at the crack of dawn
To see The Man with the Catgut Beard,
You're lucky, Herb, that he appeared.
On a muggy morning, all fog and mist,
When the Norway's top is being kissed
By the early rays of the golden sun
You'll see those coat tails on the run.
They're always just around the turn,
Billowing out like a flag astern.
Many who hear this tale have jeered,
But I *know* The Man with the Catgut Beard,
And I know if you catch him out some place—
Just borrow a leader plucked from his face.
Then tie it onto the end of your line
And the trout you'll catch will be a crime!
There won't be a one that's under a pound
And you'll have your limit, I'll be bound!
You see, it's all a part of the curse,
And makes his lot a great deal worse,
For leaders yanked from the end of his chin
Will work for *you* but not for him!"

Herb tossed in bed that starry night
And lay awake 'til dawn's faint light
Brought crimson hues through purple haze
Betokening one of June's best days.
Said he, "There couldn't be a bigger fool
Than I to let a silly legend rule
My normal, healthy human brain!
But I shall gamble just the same—
I'll find that Catgut Bearded Man
And beg a leader if I can!
I don't believe this yarn, and yet
Some fish I'll take from Pere Marquette
In spite of man, or beast, or shade—

My desperate resolution's made!"
Then, feeling like a simple fool
He visioned trout within a pool,
And stealing softly to the stream
He felt as though 'twas all a dream
No early beams of sun had kissed
Away the tears of morning mist,
As Herb stood doubtful on the shore
Where he had seen the ghost before
No sound disturbed the foggy air
While patiently he waited there,
'Til morning zephyrs, soft and chill,
Blew wispy mistrals o'er the hill,
And from Apollo's car of flame
Faint rays of early sunbeams came.
Disgusted, Herb had turned to go,
When from the river, soft and low,
He heard a piteous, tired cry,
And through the shifting mist his eye
Discerned a figure, quaint and weird,—
It was The Man with the Catgut Beard!
And as Herb watched him, from his chin
He yanked a leader, long and thin,
And tied it on his gleaming line
With feathered fly and hook quite fine.
In graceful curve the rod whipped back
The cast was perfect, but alack!
The leader simply disappeared,
And from beneath the catgut beard
A moaning cry of great distress
Betokened his unhappiness.
"Oh, Man with Catgut Beard!" cried Herb.
"With you I crave to have a word!
Once before at break of dawn
I was in the stream, but you had gone,
And all I saw in the morning wind
Were coat tails flying out behind."
The Man with the Catgut Beard then spoke,
And his voice was muffled behind the cloak
Of catgut whiskers adorning his face

And streaming down and all over the place.
"Young man," he said, in sepulchral tones,
"I don't know why I should trouble my bones
To help you out with your whimsical wish—
I know what it is; you want big fish,
And you'd pluck a leader from this beard
With which my bronzed old chin's veneered.
You'd tie it to your pliant line
And a catch you'd have in record time."
The shade then paused and in fiendish glee
His laugh rang out like a wild banshee.
His staring eyes glowed fiery red
And his whiskers whirled about his head,
And a horrible, musty, decaying smell
Surrounded this apparition of hell.
Herb shook in his boots and his face grew pale
And he gouged his palm with a fingernail,
But he stood his ground, although scared to death,—
While The Catgut Man regained his breath.
In a rasping voice that was hard as steel
The ghost outlined the terms of the deal.
"A leader from my face you'll take
But every trout you catch will break
An inch or two from tapered tip,
Until at length, just bit by bit
That ghostly gut will disappear,
And that will end your trout career.
From that time on you'll catch no fish
Save six-inch Browns,—and you will wish
With all your heart you'd never seen
The shade that haunts this grand old stream.
This is the price that you will pay
To catch big fish. What do you say?"
Herb shivered, much as with a chill;
His voice, he found, was small and still.
"I'll pay the price," he faintly said,
"I'll pluck this leader from your head
And trout I'll have for once, by gad,
To make the whole gang raving mad!
Although the future may be lost,

For that one catch I'll pay the cost."
"I've warned you, lad," the ghost replied,
"So choose a leader, true and tried;
Enjoy your fishing while you may
For you shall rue this deed today!"
Herb chose a gut, fine, thin, and long,
Well tapered, too, and extra strong.
With bated breath he gave a yank,
And as he did the figure shrank
Into the chilly mists of morn,
And with a quivering sigh forlorn
Completely disappeared from view,
While Herb stood wondering what to do.
"Well," said he, with knees still shaking,
"I'm shivering like an aspen quaking.
I'm not so sure I like that guy,
His fiery eyes or ghostly sigh.
But here's a leader from his face
And never was a better place
To try it out than in this pool,—
So, now we'll see if I'm a fool!"

There's very little more to tell—
Herb fished all day and did right well,
For fifteen trout, both 'Bows and Brown
Were in his creel about sundown.
The fish to Herb looked large as whales
And every one would tip the scales
Beyond the point that marks a pound,
But better still, he also found
His ghostly leader'd stood the strain;
He'd have enough to fish again.
And so it went for just a week;
Herb's trout career had reached its peak.
Of fishermen Herb was the champ,
And on his brow Fame placed her stamp
Of glory that can never fade—
His piscatorial name was made!
And then, with magic leader gone at last,
He faced the future scared, aghast.

The spectre's prophecy returned
And in his ears these phrases burned,
"From that time on you'll catch no fish
Save six-inch Browns,—and you will wish
With all your heart you'd never seen
The shade that haunts this grand old stream."

And so, alas, it proved too true,—
With all the fishing he can do
Herb fails to hook a single trout
That's big enough to talk about.
He whips that stream both night and day
Yet never carries a trout away.
His jaw is set, his face is grim,
He doesn't eat, he's getting thin,
And now and then he swears he hears
A spectral laugh and ghostly jeers.
Though others smile and turn away
And tap their heads as though to say,
"We think it's just a touch of sun,"
Herb lets them have their little fun.
He knows these mockings faint and weird
Are from The Man with the Catgut Beard.

Should you visit the Pere Marquette River region anytime soon, you will discover a beautiful sandy waterway drifting through overhanging bluffs, rolling hills, and the grassy floodplains of Central Michigan. Although German brown trout were introduced to the stream in 1884 and brook trout five years earlier, today it's the anadromous salmon and steelhead runs that draw thousands of anglers each year. Canoeists love this length of water because it is swift-flowing yet surprisingly free of dangerous rapids.

But will any among those thousands of anglers chance upon that vaporous fisherman with catgut beard, his coattails flying as he flees around a bend in the river? Or is the story a myth perpetuated by superstitious river folk?

You might be able to judge for yourself.

A few miles south of Baldwin on the banks of the Pere Marquette is the Shrine of the Pines, a unique public attraction featuring a northwoods lodge filled with several hundred pieces of pine furniture handcrafted from logs and stumps left over from the lumbering days of the early twentieth century. On a wall in that lodge hangs a drawing of the man with the catgut beard.

And if you're especially fortunate, someone in one of the many towns that dot the river might regale you with the ghost's most recent sighting. But beware. As writer Alfred Rathbone noted, "Like all unearthly creatures, his close acquaintance is a dangerous thing."

Entr'acte: Haunts of Ivy

Whom the gods love dies young.

—Menander, *Dis Exapaton*

A Soft Touch

WASHINGTON COLLEGE IS on Maryland's stunning Eastern Shore in the historic colonial city of Chestertown. The elite college has the exceptional distinction of being the oldest college in Maryland, having evolved from the Kent County School founded in the 1720s.

Yet, that is only one of its many unique qualities:

Its 1782 charter makes it the tenth-oldest liberal arts college in the nation and the only one named after George Washington while the first president was living (the fifty guineas he donated went for the purchase of scientific instruments; he served on the college's board until his election as president in 1789); the founding president, Reverend William Smith, later helped establish the University of Pennsylvania; the Sophie

Kerr undergraduate literary prize is the second largest such award in the nation—worth over $56,000 in 2006; less well known perhaps is that Washington College houses two of the more curious ghost legends on the Eastern Shore.

Few old college theaters exist which do not have their own ghostly inhabitants. Tawes Theater at Washington College is no exception, but unlike many other theaters, this old playhouse might contain as many as four ghosts, according to campus stories.

They include a custodian who might have hanged himself, a student alleged to have unexpectedly died in the theater, an odd little girl who skips up and down the theater's aisles, and the peculiarly named Tuxedo Man.

Tuxedo Man gets the blame for technical glitches during performances, especially of musicals, which he loathes. Could he have seen a production of *Carrie, The Musical?*

Although a former drama department head said he had never "heard, seen or had any experience" with ghosts in the theater, the same could not be said about the campus security office. According to published reports, several college cops sometimes avoided the theater on their nightly rounds. In one celebrated instance, the security office dispatcher got several phone calls originating from the office of a theater professor. A police officer checked the building, but he reported back that the theater was locked tight and the lights turned off everywhere he looked. The dispatcher got another call shortly after the cop relocked the office from which the calls had been coming. He went back. Again, he found nothing that would explain the calls. Finally, the investigating officer held the door open and waited. Sure enough, the dispatcher got a call while the cop held the door open. They apparently abandoned their efforts to come up with a plausible explanation.

Officers have also said some locations in the theater produce sudden icy cold drafts. Neither the building's cooling system, nor accidentally open windows, explain the sensation.

An incident also involving mysteriously-ringing telephones, as described in a story by one former theater student, might indicate that Tuxedo Man is an apt nickname for one of the Tawes ghosts. According to this account, students nicknamed the ghost "Noel," after noted British playwright and natty dresser Noel Coward, known for his fondness of formal wear.

In this episode, a technical crew of students had begun work to build a set for an upcoming production. They knocked off about noon to order pizza. After they placed their call from a theater professor's office, however, the phone rang several times. When they answered, no one was on the line. They took the phone off the hook. A phone in an adjacent office began ringing.

Two of the braver students went off to see if they could find some sort of technical malfunction. One of them later told the student newspaper about their adventures:

"Being theater techies, we knew the (building) inside and out, and we knew where the phone lines came into the building and where the main bus bar was. We headed upstairs to one of the lofts. The loft is nothing more than a hallway of sorts that runs the length of the theater from the stage to the lighting booth above and to the left of the audience seating. We use this area for storing props, and the dimmers used to be located there. We entered the dimmer room and looked down this hallway. Seeing nothing, we proceeded with flashlights in hand to the phones' main bus for the building. Everything looked to be in order. At the moment we decided everything was fine, the door to the dimmer room shut with a bang and three lights on the catwalk above us blew out in order. We almost killed each other getting out of there, down the stairs, and out of the building. The other three people in the office saw us run by and came to ask what was wrong. We sat outside and waited for the pizza guy, ate, and left, as none of us wanted to go back inside and work. . . ."

A DISTAFF WASHINGTON College ghost may occasionally show her face in the Hynson-Ringgold House, an eighteenth-century colonial masterpiece which serves as the home of Washington College's twenty-sixth president, Baird Tipson.

The house is one of the unique structures in a city of historic buildings. In 1767, Chestertown merchant Thomas Ringgold bought two houses quite near each other and connected them with a central wing. He later acquired enough land to extend his lot down to the Chester River and north to High Street. In the new, central addition, Ringgold built a distinctive antler, or double, staircase and installed paneling. During the Ringgold residency, the place acquired the nickname of The Abbey, apparently because one family member said it reminded him of an old abbey.

The Ringgold family owned the home until 1916 when it was sold to Henry and Ilma Pratt Catlin of New York. Washington College bought and renovated the house in 1946 and, since that date, every campus president has lived there.

While the Ringgold family still owned the house, according to one account, there were common "nursery tales of ghosts in the attic," but no verified sightings.

The Catlin family seems to have been the first to talk about a ghost in the house. According to a history of the college, their story was that a Jamaican maid fled back to her native country after complaining that a ghost would not let her get a good night's sleep in her room. The ghost—a woman, the maid insisted—brushed its fingers lightly across the frightened maid's cheeks. This particular ghost skulked about near the left side of the antler staircase, though its last sighting may have been by that maid.

Another legend, that the ghastly cries of slaves escaping via the Underground Railway are sometimes heard in the house, seems to be less well documented, and a product of yet a third legend of a secret tunnel extending from the old Customs House to the Hynson-Ringgold House and then on to the college itself. Long after the Civil War, black adults in Chestertown remembered that when they were children they were told by their teachers that runaway slave children were slipped into Chestertown via the tunnel and then taken by boat to freedom in free northern states or in Canada guided by no less a personage than famed abolitionist Harriet Tubman.

There seems to be scant evidence that such a tunnel existed. A deeply recessed alcove in the basement of the Hynson-Ringgold House seems to have given rise to at least part of the legend. Collapsed earth in the front yard of the Customs House suggested to some that there might have been a secret room. Records indicated that one or more underground storage rooms had been built under the front yard and adjacent to the

Customs House's basement, but nothing to show that a tunnel led onward from there. Further, an excavation for sewer and water lines in the area of the two houses found no confirmation of a tunnel between the president's house and the nearby Customs House.

Yet, as with many historic settings up and down the Eastern Shore, Washington College has had such a varied and colorful history that most anything seems possible, even traces of the once living that refuse to leave a most idyllic college setting.

The Glowing Specter

Coed dormitories with twenty-four-hour visitation policies were unknown on college campuses in the early twentieth century, and curfews were strictly enforced, especially on conservative Southern women's college campuses. So it was that on February 2, 1908, sweet Condie Cunningham and several of her girlfriends were up late at night cooking fudge on a stove in the kitchen of Main Hall, then as now a women's residence at the notable University of Montevallo, about thirty-five miles south of Birmingham, Alabama.

The girls weren't quite finished with their creation when the call came for lights out. Hurrying to clean up the kitchen because there were strict punishments for violating curfew, one of Condie's friends accidentally tipped over a bottle of cleaning alcohol, spilling it across the stove. The highly flammable liquid quickly burst into flame when it oozed onto an open burner.

The girls feverishly tried to smother the flames, but somehow Condie's housecoat caught on fire. She ran screaming from the room. Her friends managed to reach her in the hallway and smother her burning clothes, but not before Condie suffered fatal injuries. She died two days later in a local hospital.

And now for more than a century, the anguished ghost of Condie Cunningham has been heard crying for help in Montevallo's Old Main Hall. An unlucky few have even encountered her vaporous form running through the building, wrapped in a glow such as that cast from a fire.

At least that's the legend behind the most specific of at least six ghost stories passed down through the decades on this campus celebrated for its red-brick streets and paths, and for being one of the few colleges in the nation whose central grounds have been designated a National Historic District.

Founded as Alabama College, a state educational institution for women only, the school did not admit its first male students until 1956. Several years later, it was reorganized and renamed the University of Montevallo, after the small town of some 4,200 people that had offered its enthusiastic civic support when the campus was first established in 1896.

The 160-acre college grounds were designed by the Olmstead Brothers—brother Frederick planned New York City's Central Park—around several antebellum homes already in the area, including the 1823 Edmund King House, and Reynolds Hall, a Georgian brick house built in the 1850s and used as a Civil War hospital.

Both the King House and Reynolds Hall also harbor ghostly manifestations, but poor Miss Cunningham is Montevallo's saddest specter.

"When I was a student here, we thought it was just a made-up story," remembered Mary Frances Tipton, the retired head librarian, author of the school's centennial history, and a graduate herself of the university. "We loved to scare each other with it. We even reenacted it one time when I was an upperclassman for the incoming freshmen. All we knew is that the girl in the story had burned to death."

Although some of her classmates claimed to have seen the ghost in Main Hall, Tipton never met the elusive Condie. "What I would hear is that they saw something out of the corner of their eyes that looked like a flash of red, or of flames. But when they looked at it directly nothing was there."

But still Tipton thought the whole thing had been fashioned to thrill unsuspecting newcomers—ghost, horrific death, occasional appearances and all—until she returned to campus as an employee some years later.

"One of the professors did research for a history of the school. She hadn't been a student here and didn't know the ghost stories. Well, as soon as the book came out I started reading it. She had found in the board of trustees' minutes an account of a student being killed, even the girl's name, Condie Cunningham. Well, I nearly fell over," Tipton said. The trustees' record was similar to the campus legend of how the girl met her tragic death.

Tipton was amazed that the ghost story she first heard as an undergraduate was indeed based on fact and that it was still being handed down, generation to generation, after nearly a century.

The tragedy had an impact on school policies.

"I talked to elderly alumnae and they said they remembered how strict the school used to be about cooking in (dorm) rooms because of a fear that something like (Condie's death) might happen again," Tipton said.

But is there any real *truth* in this sad ghost tale of a young coed's continued presence at the scene of her dreadful fate?

Before its modernization some years ago, the four-story, colonnaded Main Hall had the atmosphere of many old brick college buildings thrown up in the late nineteenth century—high ceilings, tall windows, and heavy oak doors with transoms over the threshold.

"That dormitory was a spooky old building," Tipton recalled. "It's that fourth floor that seems to have the eeriest feeling about it. We don't know where Condie lived, but that's where the door was."

The door.

Condie's Door, some call it.

The door with the inlaid image of what some perceive to be a girl suspended upside down, her long, wavy hair cascading to the floor.

The door from a room on the fourth floor that the university finally removed from its hinges and put in a locked storage room because so many people were trooping through the hall to observe the odd likeness.

"I've seen it," Tipton said. "And it is strange looking."

But Tipton is quick to add that despite the campus legend, the door is most probably not original to the building and was not in place when Condie Cunningham lived there. There is no evidence to suggest that the room from which the door was taken might have belonged to her.

Not long ago, resident assistants guided several undergraduates to that storeroom where the peculiar door is kept, tilted against a wall in the small, dusty space. Some students claimed the door seemed warm to their touch. Still others reported a presence when they walked into the room. The image itself is indistinct, a matter of individual belief more than of photographic portraiture.

Yet students continue to be curious about Condie's story. One resident assistant said her charges insist they hear doors opening and closing late at night where no one should be. And sometimes in an otherwise silent and empty and darkened hallway there are those muted cries for help and quick footfalls as if from slippered, running feet.

IN REYNOLDS HALL, one coed says she was kicked. A young man claims that he feels the air currents change in the historic building. A spirit roams those hallways, he says.

Ghosts in college theaters are as plentiful as aspiring actors in Hollywood, and the University of Montevallo is no different—it has two of its own resident stage shades in two separate theaters.

The college's first president, Henry Clay Reynolds, might be the one who prowls the Studio Theater in his namesake, Reynolds Hall, the second-oldest building on campus, an exquisite example of 1850s southern antebellum Greek Revival architecture, now used for alumni and student organization offices, classrooms, and the small theater, a 175-seat performance space in use since 1923.

"I have had sensible faculty members tell me that strange things have happened in the building," said Mary Frances Tipton. "A good friend of mine was the chairman of the theater department. He is not an overly imaginative man, but he said that when he was there late at night, windows would slam up and down, doors swung open, and in the attic above the stage there are all sorts of noises. But I don't think he ever actually saw Captain Reynolds."

Captain Reynolds was a Confederate Civil War officer, a successful Montevallo businessman, and the person state officials turned to in 1896 as the school's president at the last minute when the original choice to head the school, noted Alabama educator Julia Tutwiler, who had the innovative idea to establish an Alabama college for women only, declined the position. She didn't think the state was committed to adequate funding on the new campus.

"Reynolds had a great deal to do with the success of the school," Tipton noted. "Although we're state-supported, the legislature had done very little to help us get started."

Reynolds used his business savvy and political connections in Alabama and Washington, D.C., to pin down funding for the school. It's generally believed that had Reynolds not been successful, Alabama College might have folded within a few years.

But the story of Henry Clay Reynolds does not end on a triumphant note. The college's board of trustees accused him of mishandling student funds and he resigned the presidency in 1899, just three years into his tenure.

It seems Reynolds owned a dry goods store in the city and officials said some of the school's money was being spent inappropriately at the store for school supplies. There were also accusations of improper bank loans and other charges that eventually resulted in several lawsuits and Reynolds's subsequent resignation.

"I don't know if there really was mismanagement or not," librarian Tipton conceded. "But it was a shame that he left such a bitter man. He really was responsible for the success in those early days."

According to most accounts, he moved to Florida and never returned to Montevallo.

Such an ignominious end to what had been a successful and celebrated career certainly might cause Reynolds to still wander the campus building that now bears his name.

Tipton thinks that if he does make an occasional appearance on campus, it's because he left as such an angry man. His presidential office had been located in the hall which, decades earlier during the Civil War, was an infirmary to treat wounded Southern soldiers. There is no truth to the campus legend that Reynolds was the officer in charge of its use as a hospital. Documents indicate he served as a lieutenant in Virginia campaigns.

The second theater ghost is more of what one might suspect—a former drama professor named Walter H. Trumbauer, who is said to inhabit Palmer Auditorium, an 1150-seat proscenium theater in Palmer Hall.

"I knew 'Trummy,'" Tipton remembered. "He was a darling little man; you just stood in awe of him."

Trumbauer was hard to please, but once students gained his approval they remembered it as a highlight of their college career, she said.

Professor Trumbauer was particularly noted for helping heighten the visibility of a traditional February program called College Night, an evening of competitive musical comedy programs entirely acted, written, directed, produced, and designed by students. There are even cheerleaders for each team, with outside professional theater professionals making the final decision on the winner.

"Trummy inspired the students to get more serious and professional about College Night," Tipton said. "He really did make it grow."

According to campus lore, the final night of College Night often marks an appearance by Trummy. As the concluding performances of each competitive group take place, a batten used to hold lights above the stage will begin to sway gently above the actors who will win. Is he accurate in his predictions? Alas, no one seems to have kept score.

Earlier in the College Night preparations, if Trummy really likes what he sees being rehearsed on stage, cast members will see a seat flop down somewhere in the house. That's the old professor come to watch.

As far as can be determined, no one has actually caught sight of the little man.

The same cannot be said for another of Montevallo's neighborhood phantoms.

If a visitor happens to stroll across the University of Montevallo's charming grounds late on a cool, misty night and chances upon an old man bent with age, carrying a lantern and a shovel, do not be alarmed. It's only the ghost of Edmund King, Jr., dead for nearly a century and a half.

King must have been a miserly sort. He didn't trust banks, and certainly didn't have faith that invading Union troops would not strip his property of all its wealth. That's why he is said to have buried a trove of gold coins in a peach orchard next to his residence, now King House, a centerpiece on the university's grounds. Though the orchard is long gone, speculation is that it probably stood where Harman Hall is now.

King was a wealthy Georgia planter who moved to Montevallo in about 1815 and later built a Georgian brick house with a wide center hallway and two spacious rooms up and two similar rooms down. The university uses King House to accommodate visiting professors and other distinguished guests.

But more than a few overnight lodgers there have asserted that Edmund King does not rest easily in the nearby cemetery, where he is buried along with other members of his family.

"We do know which room was Mr. King's bedroom upstairs," Mary Frances Tipton said. "And again I have had adults, and not just students, tell me they have heard these noises while they've been in the house. When the Yankees briefly used the house as their headquarters, King stayed there. He was old and sick and apparently couldn't sleep very well. Now you can hear him pacing back and forth not able to sleep. Sometimes you hear the clink of the coins he's counting at his desk."

The occasional student returning to Comer Hall from the library has also glimpsed a faint, moving light in an upper window of King House, as if from a lantern's glow. A curtain might be brushed aside and then quickly closed.

THE TWO OTHER prominent ghost tales on the Montevallo campus are a bit murkier, shall we say.

The figure of an older woman in a yellow dress is thought to show up on occasion sitting astride a rock in Main Quad.

"That might be Edmund King's first wife," Tipton said. "She apparently went through some hard times."

Another tale is rooted in a murder just off campus in the early 1970s. A young woman was choked to death by her boyfriend after she told him she wanted to break off their relationship. He was convicted and jailed. According to one account, the dead woman haunts a shack in the vicinity of where the murder took place, near the campus overflow parking lot.

Librarian Tipton attributes some of the stories to what she terms "the ripe imagination" of some students. But not all of them by any means. She is particularly intrigued with the story of Condie Cunningham because of its historical accuracy.

"When we found out what her name was, we were able to find a picture in an old annual of a group of girls that included her. She is one of them, but we just don't know which one" because names weren't attached to specific individuals in the picture, Tipton said.

Perhaps it would be sensible to make an enlargement of that photograph and post it in Main Hall—in that way one could say hello to her by name the next time she shows up.

Father Mueller

Spring Hill College in Mobile, Alabama, is one of the oldest of the twenty-eight Jesuit colleges in the nation and the first Alabama college to racially integrate, in 1955. Its programs in nursing and business are internationally recognized, while its 500-acre campus boasts not only beautiful live oaks and azalea-bordered walkways, but a lush eighteen-hole golf course. The college fields an intercollegiate golf team as well as men's and women's basketball, cross country, soccer, tennis, and men's baseball.

While the visible surroundings at Spring Hill College make it appealing to students, faculty, and visitors alike, an intriguing episode involving a legendary Jesuit priest who was also a professor of mathematics there gives it a ghostly history that may not be found in the college's official records.

The priest was Father Mueller, and although he died many years ago his presence was felt in more ways than one by a former student who eventually returned to Spring Hill College to also teach in the mathematics department. The student-turned-math-professor was Father Donovan. It was his story of a most unexpected encounter with Father Mueller's legacy that was related in a later report by Dr. Stuart Harris:

Father Mueller had inspired young priests, and so Donovan had studied and had graduated and had returned to teach math.

Unfortunately, Father Mueller had died. But shortly before his death, Father Mueller met the new professor and said, "You know, the reason the students always like me is I challenged them in the classroom."

If Father Mueller had a particularly bright class, he would give them several impossibly difficult problems to take home and try to solve. Rarely did they succeed.

So, Father Mueller gave Father Donovan copies of the problems. The problems had maybe fifteen steps that you had to follow in order to come up with the right answer. Perhaps it would take an hour, or two hours, to actually do your problem.

If you could complete it at all.

One day, in his best class of students, Father Donovan put the problem on the board. One student named George didn't like to be baffled.

Father Donovan wrote the problem. The students left class discussing how they were going to attack this thing.

The following morning, class started. The students filed in. Father Donovan stood up.

"All right, I'm going to write the answers on the board. Check your papers and see if you have this number."

He wrote the number on the blackboard, almost laughing, knowing that no one would have it.

He turned around, and George had his hand up.

"I have it, sir."

Father Donovan thought it must be a coincidence. George couldn't have the right answer.

"George, let's look at your paper," the priest said.

He checked out each step and the answer was right.

Father Donovan praised George to the class.

"This," Father said, "is the only time anyone has ever worked this for me."

When the class was over, George came up to Father Donovan.

"Father, I must make a confession," George said. "I had help on that problem."

Father Donovan didn't particularly care if several of the boys had gotten together to solve the challenge; it was still a great achievement.

"It wasn't a student who helped me," George said. "Last night, I worked on this problem for about four hours, sitting there at my desk in the dormitory. Finally, when I was about to give up in disgust, there was a knock at the door. I opened the door and there stood a priest. He had a long, white beard, a ruddy face, a very friendly look about him and he said, 'Hello. I have not met you, young man, and I like to welcome everyone to the campus.' "

George invited the elderly priest into his room.

After some small talk, the priest spoke: "Well, how is your homework coming along?"

"Father, I'm sorry," George replied. "I'm facing a problem tonight I can't work."

"Well, I have taught math before, so perhaps I can help. Let me look at your problem," the old priest said.

George showed him the problem.

"Oh, you've made a mistake here and a mistake there," he said.

The two worked together and solved the problem.

The next day George brought the solution to Father Donovan in math class.

However, Father Donovan didn't recognize George's description of the priest and wondered who he was. Certainly there was no one on campus any longer in traditional Jesuit robes and with a long white beard.

George went back to Father Donovan's office with him, where Father Donovan pulled out an old yearbook from his own undergraduate days on campus. He opened it to a class picture, showing a group of boys in the math club standing alongside the math faculty.

"Do you see the man who came to your room in this picture?" Father Donovan asked.

"Why, yes, it's quite obvious," George answered, pointing to one of the priests. "It's the man with the gray beard."

Father Mueller, late of Spring Hill College, was back to help the struggling math student.

Hanging Henry

His name was Henry L. Means. He was a medical student at the University of Vermont, Burlington, during the early 1920s. He must have been a perfectionist who suffered terrible bouts of depression because of what he considered his poor grades and his self-described ineptitude with women. It all got to be too much for the young man with such a bright future. On a day after final exams he climbed the stairs to the attic of Converse Hall and hanged himself.

The sad irony is that Henry Means would have finished that semester with straight As.

At least that's the story generations of University of Vermont undergraduates have come to appreciate, especially if they live in the castle-like Converse Hall, a brooding, 1895 stone pile with a spectacular view of Mount Mansfield from its upper floors. Originally built to house only male UVM students, it was designed by the architectural firm of the Wilson Brothers, Philadelphia.

The ghost of Henry Means—or just plain Henry, as most Converse Hall residents call their genial, if unseen, companion—is one of the most famous apparitions on any New England campus.

The five-story residence hall looks for all the world like a medieval English castle manor with its ivy-covered walls and U-shaped, Gothic design. A sharply sloping roof with church-like spires adds to its daunting façade. Air force and army recruits lived there during both world wars. Its mysterious and imposing appearance belies a most modern interior that today serves as a home for university undergraduates.

And Henry.

From most accounts, Henry is a gentle soul given to mischievous behavior. He'll hide the occasional prized possession, slam some doors, cause the lights to flicker, or announce his presence with quick-march footsteps.

He's particularly fond of proving his existence to those who may not believe in him, as this earlier written account by a university student might indicate:

"I and a few of my friends were in my room drinking a few drinks. We started having this conversation about Henry. One of my friends said, 'I don't believe in him. He's a fake.' So, he started to make fun of (Henry) and laugh. Just as he started, we heard these loud footsteps and the door slammed. Then, all of the empty (beverage) cans were thrown around the room. That night we were truly scared."

The convenience of having a ghost to blame for all manner of disturbances cannot be overstated, yet who is to say which problem is attributable to the natural aches and pains of a century-old fortress-like residence hall, and which might be truly the product of a ghost like Henry. In these incidents, collected by a former student at UVM, one is left to decide for oneself where the truth might lie.

At one time, Converse Hall housed married students, such as the couple who discovered that Henry might have been a devotee of candles. They wrote of what they learned:

"One of the strangest stories I know I heard from my sister. This happened to a friend of hers who also lived in Converse. She went to bed early one night with a candle lit on her bedside table. She really loved candles and had them all over her room. Her husband was working late that night and came home after she was asleep. She woke up frequently that night because she felt someone rubbing her nose. The feeling was really waxy. When she woke up no one was there. Her husband was asleep. Finally, she woke him up to tell him, but he thought it was just a bad dream. Later they both woke up when the mirror on the wall fell down. Now, in Converse back then the mirrors were bolted right into the wall, and when they checked it out the bolts were still in place. Her husband said he couldn't explain it but that they should just go back to bed. The next morning they found a trail of wax from her side of the bed to the door. Now, my sister isn't superstitious at all, but she saw the wax . . . and it convinced her."

There is a favorite saying in Converse—"Oh, well. It must be Henry." It might have originated with this story told a few days after the incident took place:

"Frankie, who lives just below me, has been complaining of noise from my room that wakes her up late at night. We tried to figure out what she hears, as I am a relatively quiet person. Two nights ago, I left my room at three in the afternoon and didn't return until the next morning. That night the noise was continuous, and sounded, according to Frankie, like all the furniture was being moved around and someone was pacing back and forth. I know no one was in my room. And so, what was the answer to the problem? The same explanation you often hear: 'Oh, well. It must be Henry!'"

Converse Hall had weekly parties in the attic that residents termed "Henry's Haunt," that sometimes included a dummy hanging from the rafters. But Halloween has often been

Henry's special time, as in this incident, written by one of the participants, when a couple of undergraduates decided to host a children's Halloween party in the hall.

"(We decided) it would be nice to have a party for kids in town, you know, turn out the lights and make it real spooky. We decided nothing fun ever happened in Converse. We were getting pretty silly and started yelling, 'Henry, will you join us?' As soon as we said that the lights started flickering on and off. At first we thought it was funny, but we went out in the hall and all the lights were doing it. Every time we said 'Henry,' it started up again. Then we saw that the door to the attic had popped open. It was always locked, you see. The door wasn't broken, it just came open. There was a really strong draft. We were scared, screaming and all."

Sometimes, it's been the smaller, quieter incidents that have led hall residents to think that Henry is out and about, as in this report by a student named Frank who was active in Converse activities:

"I was walking up toward Converse and saw the South door open really slowly, then close, just like someone went in, but no one was there. I'm sure it was Henry. Other people saw it, too.

"I was up here with my brother the summer they were renovating. We came in to see what it (Converse) looked like one Sunday afternoon when no one else was around. The whole time we were followed by noises like doors slamming and things being moved.

"Once Henry predicted a fire. . . . That Christmas vacation the entire basement was gutted. Henry predicted that no one would be hurt in the fire. The building was empty when it happened."

An undergraduate named Becky, described as being intelligent and sensible, took quite some time to be persuaded that Henry did indeed exist. An experience by a friend of hers convinced her otherwise:

"When (my friend) was a freshman she lived over in the East Wing in a triple (room). One of her roommates' mothers died but she didn't seem outwardly sad. (My friend) thought this was strange because she was close to her mother and should have been hurt. (After the funeral) a few days later they came back to the room and everything was soaking wet. All the walls were wet, like they were crying. They called the janitor but he couldn't find anything wrong. None of the other rooms were wet. It was like the room was crying."

Becky also sensed some strangeness in the room she'd been assigned in Converse:

"I used to get uncomfortable in my old room. I can't explain what it was, but I always felt like he was in there. That's when I started believing in Henry, living in (that room). He must like that room. . . . Maybe he lived there?"

As with many college campus ghosts, Henry adds a personal sense of warmth and belonging to the college scene that may be difficult for outsiders to understand. The college years can be a time of great stress for young people, a time of questioning one's own purpose in life, one's own beliefs, and one's ability to persevere in the face of academic and personal challenges. Perhaps the confidence that a student from the distant past loved campus so much that he simply cannot leave provides a kind of emotional safety net for contemporary students. At the University of Vermont, Henry might provide that connection, as spelled out by this former student:

"Of course I believe. I like Henry. He's pretty good to us, he never hurts us. He reminds me that school is not all academics and that you must give time to yourself and to your friends. That is why he killed himself, and that is why he is with us today. He plays with us when we are down, especially at finals time. Without Henry, Converse wouldn't be anything. Back in old Converse it was dirty and cold and spooky, and you could feel him better then. But the renovation didn't really change anything, because I still feel him here. All this luxury just hides him better. I'm glad he's here. I'm glad I believe in him. Maybe that's the only reason he's alive today, because we believe, or at least want to."

And for that, Henry is no doubt grateful.

Can a Ghost Pledge?

Most American college campuses feature Greek organizations for young men and women students. The off-campus houses for these fraternities and sororities are places where students can relax, study, and organize social functions like parties and dances. On at least a couple of campuses, an uninvited ghost or two may make their presences known.

At St. Lawrence University, Canton, New York, the ghost of the daughter of the first president of the university was thought to live in the Phi Kappa Sigma house. Her name was Florence Lee, whose father, John Stebbins Lee, helped get St. Lawrence off the ground in 1856. Little Florence lived in the house as a child until her premature death in 1860. She's been spotted wearing a long, flowing white gown, according to published reports. She'll also slam doors if she's upset with too much social activity, and turn off music systems that are playing loud music.

Meanwhile, halfway across the country at the University of Louisville, the sisters at the Chi Omega sorority house got along famously with a ghost named George. They knew it was a male because passersby looking through the large front window at night sometimes noticed a bulky figure wearing a suit and standing on the staircase. Just who it was no one seemed to know. In the absence of an identity back in 1984, someone took to simply calling him George.

The Chi Omega women didn't live in the house, so there weren't many instances of nighttime shenanigans by George. They did figure out that he seemed to live on a back staircase that connected with the kitchen because footfalls as if someone was trooping up those steps were heard during the daytime.

"We just use the house for meetings and stuff. It's a real old house, so no telling how long he's been here," one sorority member told a reporter. She added that she wasn't ever afraid of George, but his well-known presence made for some uncomfortable moments for her.

Once, when she was alone in the house, the lights started blinking on and off—his favorite activity—with no one near the wall switches. The *plink-a-plink* of single notes struck on the living room piano also alerted sorority members that George was about.

But, like Casper, George was a friendly being. "He's never hurt anybody," the sorority member reported. "I didn't believe all this when I came here three years ago. They just told me we had a ghost . . . but I didn't believe it."

George changed her mind.

The Colonel and the Cook

The young man, who once worked in Wiestling Hall, on the picturesque Penn State University–Mont Alto campus, made a compelling case for its supernatural attributes in an account he gave to a university publication:

"One day another student and I were cleaning up the now-recreation room, and there were two heavy wooden tables face down upon one another. I tried to move it but could not budge it, so I went and asked the other student to help me move it. When we returned, we found the top table perfectly balanced on the edge of the other table. We were the only students in the building that weekend because everyone else went home."

The same student said that one day, after turning off the three fans cooling the dining hall, he locked the doors to the building and left. He returned a short time later—unlocking the door to the building with the only key that was then accessible. Each of the fans was going full tilt. Absolutely no one else had been around.

Today, a visit to the modern cybercafé or well-equipped student center in Wiestling Hall on the rural Mont Alto campus might include more than an email chat with a former classmate or a homework question directed to a congenial professor passing by; a nighttime visit, in particular, may well mean encountering one of the two legendary ghosts inhabiting this circa 1803 building, the oldest structure in continuous use within the Penn State system.

You might have a sudden encounter with the building's namesake—Colonel George B. Wiestling—or it might be with one Mrs. Sarah Hurley Matheny, a onetime cook in the Wiestling Hall dining room who evidently liked to stir men's passions as well as potato soup. But there were those who didn't appreciate her bed-hopping. She came to a dreadful end when her life was cut short by discharges from a shotgun barrel wielded by one of her scorned lovers.

The bucolic campus and the surrounding woodlands certainly lend themselves to ghost stories, particularly during the fall of the year.

Nestled in the southern Pennsylvania forestlands between Gettysburg to the east and Chambersburg to the northwest,

Penn State–Mont Alto is the oldest campus within Pennsylvania's higher education system outside University Park. Dating back to its founding in 1903, PSU–MA began as the Pennsylvania State Forest Academy with a first year enrollment of precisely thirteen male students. It was the only state-sponsored forestry school in the country. Their classrooms extended to the nearby 18,000-acre Michaux Forest as a living, outdoor laboratory and, three years later, one of the first arboretums on a public university campus. The latter was opened as a means to propagate plant species using seeds from plants native to the United States and abroad.

The curriculum was unlike that found at most colleges. Fire-fighting was part of the students' course list, as was manual labor. Everyone wore military-style uniforms with Smokey-type wide-brim hats and tall boots both in the classroom and on what was termed forest patrol.

The school merged with Penn State in 1929—much to the chagrin of many Academy undergraduates, who prided themselves on what they considered their superior forestry major—and changed again in 1963 when modifications to the forestry program led to the campus becoming a comprehensive Commonwealth campus. That year also marked the entrance of the first females to the school's classrooms.

The 1100 undergraduates today either complete four-year degrees in several majors, pursue two-year associate of arts degrees—including forestry-related subjects—or take the first two years of college study before transferring to another Commonwealth campus.

While the Mont Alto campus is the second oldest in the system, the Franklin County village of Mont Alto and the property on which the campus now resides are even older. When the iron mining industry was established in the close-by hills, foundries to process the ore were built in Mont Alto in the first decade of the nineteenth century using East Antietam Creek for water power. Eventually two forges and a rolling mill were set up. Some 500 men were employed in their operations.

The village that eventually grew up around the iron foundries has many historic connections. The first Episcopal church in Pennsylvania west of the Blue Ridge Mountains,

Emmanuel Chapel or Mont Alto Chapel, was consecrated in 1854. It continues as an integral part of the Mont Alto campus.

Perhaps the most intriguing historical footnote in Mont Alto is the story of the burly, bearded man who arrived there in about 1859. He called himself Isaac Smith. But that was hardly his real name, as historian Reverend William Parker Neal explained in a previously published account:

"At first it was believed that he was a prospector getting ready to set up operations nearby. He took up residence in Chambersburg, but soon was operating a sawmill near Mont Alto. He explained to the people that the heavy boxes he was receiving were boxes of mining equipment. He was well-known throughout the area as he supplied charcoal to several furnaces. Though not an Episcopalian, he attended Episcopal services in Chambersburg and at the Chapel in Mont Alto. While leaving a prayer meeting at the Chapel on October 1, 1859, he was accused by a young girl of planning an insurrection. She predicted his death if he went into the South. 'Isaac Smith' ignored her warning, and fifteen days later with his 'army' of seventeen whites and five Negroes made his unsuccessful raid on Harpers Ferry, West Virginia. After his capture by troops under Colonel Robert E. Lee and J. E. B. Stuart, it was learned that 'Isaac Smith' was actually John Brown. He is reported to have received Holy Communion just before setting out on his unsuccessful raid on Harpers Ferry. The prieu dieu (kneeling bench or prayer desk) in the (Emmanuel) Chapel is supposed to have been used by John Brown while attending services in Trinity Church in Chambersburg. He was executed December 2, 1859."

Mont Alto tradition holds that John Brown taught Sunday school at Immanuel Chapel while he was preparing for his ill-fated raid on the U.S. Arsenal at Harpers Ferry. Not far away, the house he lived in at Chambersburg is open to the public. There is no record of where he might have lodged in Mont Alto.

The origins for a haunting at Penn State–Mont Alto rightfully begin in the waning months of the Civil War with the arrival of Colonel George B. Wiestling and two partners who bought the Mont Alto Iron Furnace. Wiestling had been a commander of the Twenty-third Pennsylvania Emergency

Regiment and, later, the One-Hundred-Seventy-Seventh Regiment, which had returned to civilian life shortly after the July 1863 Confederate defeat at Gettysburg and thus the beginning of the end of southern fortunes with northern incursions. Wiestling sustained wounds during his army service that left him partly disabled. Nevertheless, as the president and superintendent of the company, he enlarged the furnaces and quintupled their output to fifteen tons per day.

Wiestling was a devout man who insisted that the furnaces be closed from 10 P.M. Saturday to 10 P.M. Sunday in observance of the Sabbath. He began using the Immanuel Chapel for Sunday School shortly after he arrived in 1864, and served as its Superintendent until his death in 1891. Though some histories suggest that his passing was mysterious, there is nothing in the record to show that it was anything other than by natural causes.

Wiestling lived in the ironmaster's house for the thirty-seven years he spent in Mont Alto. That original 1807 log cabin, expanded and modernized many times over and covered with stone, is the core of today's Wiestling Hall. There is another legend that prior to the Civil War, the original ironmaster's cabin was a station on the Underground Railway, which spirited African-American slaves away from Southern indenture to freedom in the North and in Canada. Lying just twenty-five miles north of the Maryland state line, Mont Alto would have made a logical stopover on that famous route.

Another historical footnote adds that a force of some 25,000 Rebel soldiers under the command of Jubal Early passed through the village on their way to Gettysburg. They destroyed the iron furnaces on their way through town. Confederate troops also rode through town on their way to pillage and burn Chambersburg.

After Wiestling's death, the region's iron industry slowly declined and the ironworks closed. The state forestry commission bought the old works and 22,000 acres of woodland. The forestry school opened in 1903 and operated as an independent state school for twenty-six years before its union with the Pennsylvania State College system.

The ghost stories connected to Colonel Wiestling seem to have strengthened decades later, following the 1963 takeover of the forestry program by Penn State and the creation of Penn State University–Mont Alto as a comprehensive campus with full, four-year degree programs, although there is no clear connection between the two events. The ghost stories seem to have started on a lighthearted note. Students on this new campus decided to have some fun with a Halloween festival each year. It would include a male student dressed up as old Colonel Wiestling himself. The colonel galloped around campus astride a white horse, chasing after sophomore females. The festival didn't last long. It was canceled after a new residence hall staff member, who hadn't been told about the annual rite, called police when she grew alarmed when she spotted the ghost rider in hot pursuit of wildly screaming coeds.

Some believe that the ghosts of Mont Alto are benevolent beings whose singular purpose is to ensure the school's survival and success. But that's not to say there aren't episodes which have brought chills to witnesses, events which leave witnesses questioning their own judgment.

A former food service employee told a reporter in 1993 that he came to the campus "not believing in these things," but later changed his mind.

A day during Christmas vacation, for example, found him in Wiestling Hall. From a distance, a screen door slammed open, followed shortly by an inner door opening and closing, and then a back door doing the same. He checked the front door and found it locked with a security bar firmly in place. The employee was alone in the building.

Banging pots and pans often startle kitchen workers, such as the time before dusk on an early morning when the food service employee and a friend were startled by a sudden flash of light outside the windows. That was quickly followed by the plates, pans, and pots rattling in the kitchen cupboards.

Another time, the employee had a strange encounter with an automatic potato peeler that had a distinctive whirring sound:

"All of a sudden I heard it open up and the potatoes came out. There was nobody around. And that thing was closed tight. It couldn't have been an accident."

There is another candidate for the ghost of Wiestling Hall, a better one some say, since old Colonel Wiestling hasn't been heard from very much since a 1969 remodeling which moved the dining facilities to a new building and closed off the attic. It was in the attic that students used to sit and wait for the colonel, flickering flashlights gripped nervously in their hands. On more than one occasion, some reports indicate, batteries sometimes stopped working just at the point when things got interesting on that dark and musty top floor.

Mrs. Sarah Hurley Matheny was a real person about whom not a lot is known. Her blood-spattered ending came about because of her penchant for captivating multiple lovers, according to the stories about her. "It seems likely that she decided if one lover was delightful, two might prove doubly interesting," one account explains coyly. "A charming woman who loved not wisely, but too well."

She worked in the Wiestling Hall kitchen after the campus was taken over by the Commonwealth in 1903. Some years later, her boyfriend at the time apparently didn't like sharing her womanly attributes with others. He lured her to the back steps of Wiestling and let her have it at point-blank range with both barrels from a double-barreled shotgun. Her coworkers heard the blasts, and the head chef carried her lifeless body up a kitchen staircase to an upstairs room. Blood stains were said to appear regularly on the steps going up to the death room.

The Mont Alto campus band played outside the murderer's Chambersburg jail cell on the night before his hanging in April 1912. He was reputedly the last man hanged in that Franklin County seat.

Disturbances in the former kitchen area of Wiestling Hall are often attributed to Mrs. Matheny's restless spirit.

Visitors to Penn State University–Mont Alto have another opportunity to ponder this campus's mysteries. There is a 1907 photograph in the library that appears to show the hazy outline of a man some take to be Colonel Wiestling. He appears to be watching members of the 1908 class pose on horseback. The photograph has been around for some time, but it was not until the late 1980s that an undergraduate looking at it closely discovered the vaguely human form.

The college may be the only campus in the nation that capitalizes on a campus haunt in its promotional literature. A few years back, a brochure sent out to prospective students emblazoned the following on its cover:

PENN STATE MONT ALTO CAMPUS:
COMMUNITY, EDUCATION, TRADITION
AND AN OCCASIONAL GHOST!

Inside the front cover, a short paragraph encourages visitors to the library to take a look at the famous, century-old photograph and decide if the colonel himself is still hanging around, figuratively speaking, of course.

Seal Hall

Sometimes a person is especially *tuned in* to picking up the vibrations from a haunted place, or is particularly adept at identifying those locales with haunted histories. Such is the case with a woman we'll identify as Cathy, a former student at Western Illinois University in Macomb, who chanced upon a most peculiar situation some years ago at WIU's Seal Hall, a former residence hall but, at present, the quarters for various administrative and student affairs offices such as dining and housing services, the women's center, and student development and orientation. Her brief but persuasive account also illustrates the fact that bumping into an unknown entity for even a short period of time can be a truly alarming experience.

Western Illinois is a public university with some 13,000 students in fifty-three undergraduate and thirty-four graduate degree programs. Founded in 1899 as a teachers training college, WIU today has nearly sixty buildings on its 1,000-acre Macomb campus, about forty miles east of the Mississippi River in west-central Illinois.

Seal Hall doesn't seem to have a particularly remarkable history, other than for the tragic incident which Cathy relates

and which may have produced the residual haunting that Cathy
says she witnessed:

Manslaughter Charged in Shooting

"Clyde R. Johnson, a WIU freshman from St. Ann, Illinois,
has been charged with voluntary manslaughter in the aftermath
of the fatal shooting of Steven Hyde, a 19-year-old freshman, at
Seal Hall last Tuesday.

"Johnson, 24, will appear in court on March 15, for the setting of the date for his preliminary hearing. Two others . . . have
been charged with aggravated battery . . ."

—Western Courier, March 7, 1972

Cathy relates, "A friend of mine was involved with one of
the student organizations that had an office in Seal Hall. Since
there was rarely anyone there in the evenings, we often went
there to have a quiet place to study. The building always had
an eerie feeling, but we wrote it off as just our nervousness at
being in an old . . . building alone after dark."

"The apparent motive of the incident was a quarrel over the
payment of a debt, according to (McDonough County States Attorney H.D.) Sintzenich, who also added that a specific motive
for the incident would probably materialize in the trial. He
would not verify or deny any of the various rumors that are circulating on the causes of the incident, other than it was a private
quarrel and not a racial-oriented conflict.

"The altercation occurred shortly before 11 A.M. last Tuesday on the third floor of Seal Hall's east wing."

—Western Courier, March 7, 1972

"That changed one night. As we were leaving, we distinctly
heard footsteps—with no one there to account for them. At that
point we were more intrigued than scared. The next time we
went to Seal Hall, we took another friend, who also heard the
footsteps. (They) followed us down the stairs, but never up."

"The *Courier* verified the following sequence of events
through witnesses:

"Three men . . . entered room 314 shortly before 11 A.M. and began a conversation which evolved into an argument with Clyde Johnson, resident of the room.

"A fight ensued, in which Johnson received numerous lacerations of the head.

"In the course of the struggle, Johnson managed to take the gun that Hyde was allegedly carrying. (Ownership of the handgun has not been established officially, Sintzenich said.)

"The three men fled, running down the hall with Johnson in pursuit.

"On reaching the end of the hall, they ran into another third floor room, but were told to leave.

"Hyde (and the two other men) crossed the hall and started down the stairway."

—*Western Courier,* March 7, 1972

"Other things happened, like doors opening and closing. . . . The girl who was with us the second time we heard the footsteps is very down-to-earth and was sure she could find a 'logical' explanation. She decided the footsteps were caused by the way the staircase was built. I think she walked up and down every staircase on campus to test the theory."

"Hyde broke away and began descending the steps at which time Johnson fired two shots, hitting Hyde in the arm and in the back.

"Hyde continued to run, but collapsed in the stairway between the first floor and basement.

"Johnson turned and walked back down the hall where he laid down.

"When police arrived, Hyde was dead in the stairwell. Johnson was lying on his back in the third floor hall."

—*Western Courier,* March 7, 1972

"Several of the buildings were built around the same time (as Seal Hall), and in a similar architectural style. She thought those staircases would have similar sounds. None did, not even the other staircase in Seal Hall, or even higher or lower on the one staircase where we heard them. Just in the same spot."

With her friends, Cathy dug into the WIU library archives and found several articles related to the 1972 death by gunfire of Steve Hyde. She was not all that surprised about what she found.

"He died on the staircase after going down from the third floor—the same floor we studied on."

Seal Hall continued to house undergraduates for several more years until it was converted to administrative offices. Cathy thought there may have been other reasons than mundane ones for the conversion to an office building. ". . . No one wanted to live there because of the 'strange things' that went on," she said.

Postscript: The man accused in the shooting, Clyde Johnson, a decorated Vietnam War veteran, was acquitted in September 1972 on charges of voluntary manslaughter in connection with Steve Hyde's death. Johnson's attorney had argued that the WIU student was in fear for his life and shot Hyde in self defense. Johnson testified that his single thought was that he was going to be killed by the three men who assaulted him in his room.

Poor Mildred

The imposing old brick and stone centerpiece with its distinctive tower, on the picturesque Simpson College campus in Indianola, Iowa, a nineteenth-century masterpiece of campus architecture, is known today as College Hall. Planted squarely in the middle of the 1,400 student, seventy-five-acre campus, the hall was known until the early 1980s as Old Chapel, at this college founded in 1860 by members of the Iowa United Methodist Church. An extensive renovation led to its renaming and present use as the home of the Admissions Office and other departments.

But as with many other centers of learning all across North America, Simpson College can find its very own ghost story hiding inside a building used today for decidedly corporeal pursuits—in the case of this Iowa school, a story of a young woman who died too young in College Hall.

Her name was Mildred Hedges. A student at Simpson College in 1935, Mildred died in a fall off a third floor staircase in what was then Old Chapel. Was it an accident, as it was ruled those seventy years ago, or did she commit suicide?

The question still reverberates whenever a visitor to College Hall accidentally bumps into Mildred's . . . ghost.

The case for an accidental death is strong. A teacher at the time testified that the young girl was starting down the steep staircase with an armful of books when her shoe heel somehow got caught in the hem of her long dress. She lost her balance and pitched headfirst off the staircase. That heartbreaking event was confirmed some years ago by a Simpson undergraduate who discovered that the name of the dead girl was Mildred Hedges, and that she was killed in this awful manner. "She was wearing a skirt well below her knees," the student researcher said.

Though fact and fiction have tended to intermingle with the ghost of College Hall, there seems to be a rather strong case that something lurks in the old building. Many students over the years have spoken of meeting the apparition of a young woman on the staircase where Mildred fell. Some years ago, one student claimed the ghost had spoken to him. "She wants to be left alone," he said.

A security guard was badly frightened at meeting a translucent figure in an upper corridor. A cleaning lady told a news reporter that she knew mysterious things went on "all the time." She said that she and her coworkers consistently witnessed things they could not explain: basement lights turned on when no one was in the building, and third floor lights blinking on and off in an hypnotic rhythm, even when the electrical wiring is checked and rechecked by campus electricians.

Psychics held a séance in College Hall in late 1979, during which a student photographer may have captured the reflection of a female ghost sitting with the group there that night.

When the former Old Chapel was boarded up prior to remodeling, a number of witnesses claimed to have seen the face of a young woman peering from an upper window of the hall.

But the most telling evidence of all are the red discolorations that have been visible on the floor where Mildred Hedges landed after her fall. Some speculate that they are blood stains proven impossible to get rid of.

Music in the Night

The young professor was alone in his third floor music studio. It was late, perhaps one or two o'clock in the morning. He was a single, enthusiastic, first-year teacher on campus, so the long hours he had spent with his music on that day seemed to fly by. This night would be different. On this night the ghost came to visit.

"I heard a lady singing and there was no one in the building. It was real loud. It petrified me later when I thought about it. It was very real," he said later about the incident. When he told others about the experience, their reactions were mixed. Some people thought he was weird and crazy.

So genuine did the singing voice appear to be, so human in its origin, that he had a difficult time believing it could have been coming from a ghost. Yet he knew there was absolutely no one else in the building, nor were there any electronic devices about that might have accounted for a woman's voice suddenly bursting forth in song.

The professor should not have been surprised because the music building, Gates Hall, on the campus of Wayland Baptist University, in Plainview, Texas, the home of the music department until 1973, has one of the more well-known campus ghost legends in the American Southwest.

The young woman, in life a music major at the college, haunts the third floor of Gates Hall rehearsing over and over and over again a musical score that she did not perform correctly at her senior juries. Distraught at the thought of failure, she flung herself from a third floor balcony.

But then again she may have jumped from the roof.

The story is told both ways, according to a university historian.

And what was her instrument of choice? The piano. Or, maybe the flute. Then again she may have majored in vocal studies.

Again, one hears the story told in a number of ways.

While some details may be in dispute, what is certain is that the stories about the Ghost of Gates Hall go back at least sixty years, if not longer. At the fiftieth anniversary reunion of the class of 1941, for instance, class members remembered the time they put a live cow in the college president's office—located in Gates Hall—but were chased out of the building by the ghost.

Wayland has a long and distinguished history as the oldest university on the High Plains of West Texas. Founded in 1910 as the Wayland Literary and Technical Institute, today's Wayland Baptist University serves 1,100 students on its Plainview campus and over 5,000 on a second campus in Altus, Oklahoma. It is the third largest Baptist university in the United States.

Gates Hall is central to the life of Wayland. Named for the school's first president, the three-story brick-and-stone building is noted for its broad entryway with towering Doric columns spaced across the front. It was once the tallest building in Plainview. Administrative offices and classrooms occupy much of its space today. The third floor was once used as a men's dormitory—and later a women's dormitory—as well as the offices for the music department. The college president once lived in an apartment inside the hall.

The variety of uses to which Gates Hall has been put over the years makes it difficult to pinpoint the origins of the resident ghost—or *ghosts*, since two other candidates are sometimes mentioned.

The first president of Wayland—Dr. E.I. Gates himself—might return on occasion to check up on his old school, according to some. The days when the third floor housed male students gave rise to a story that a student was murdered up there and that it's his ghost that returns to haunt the place. But there is no evidence a homicide or a suicide ever took place in Gates Hall.

The atmosphere inside Gates is spooky, according to one former administrator, especially at night when one is alone. "You can hear doors slamming in the building and it creaks and groans."

But the normal creaks and groans in a century-old college building are quite different from a direct confrontation with some *thing* that is more authentic than one can imagine.

That is especially true with the music professor's experiences on the third floor, as he recounted to an Associated Press reporter:

"One time one of the security guys and I were out in the hall talking when something went by. It was like a cold breeze and it was a black thing. We ran out. There were many other noises in there. Many students talked about seeing something in the window long after I would be gone at night."

Yet, in the same interview, he stressed that he had an affection for the Hall which transcended its ghostly reputation.

"I used to go up there when I needed to think. That floor hadn't been remodeled. It still had fourteen-foot-high ceilings, and there seemed to be this spirit of Wayland there—people from its past."

The professor also offered an alternative explanation for the haunting of Gates Hall.

Before the music department moved to the third floor, an office was given over to psychologist Dr. North East West—his real name—a psychologist who also conducted experiments in parapsychology, at apparently the only other college campus at the time doing such work outside Duke University's famed parapsychology research lab.

The music professor's studio was once Dr. West's parapsychology lab. He thinks the stories of the third floor ghost might have originated—or at least grown in circulation—during the time of Dr. West's work.

And so, whether it might be old boilers and aging floors that cause the jitters in late night visitors in Gates Hall, or whether, as one university historian phrased it, "there are people who swear to you they've heard footsteps, stomping sounds, and doors slamming," the ghost of Wayland Baptist University's Gates Hall is not likely to disappear anytime soon from the retinue of stories passed on by undergraduates at this Texas campus.

C. Rafinesque

The midnight hour can, shall we say, be a bit disconcerting for the uninitiated who might find the occasion to wander the hallways of Old Morrison, the central administrative building at the singularly named Transylvania University in Lexington, Kentucky. A visitor to this circa 1834 Greek Revival historic landmark will find spacious hallways, modern computer facilities, a small chapel, offices for administrators . . . and the burial crypt for one of the school's early professors, one of the oddest characters in nineteenth-century American history.

Transylvania University—or "Transy" as it is affectionately known to students, faculty, and alumni—is an institution that has nothing to do with the Carpathian Mountains or blood-sucking vampires—the name is derived from the Latin for "across the woods." Nevertheless, it may be the only center of higher learning in the United States that incorporates a grave *inside* a campus building and at the same time struggles with an unsettling curse from the man entombed within.

The university itself is one of the oldest in the nation. Founded in 1783 as the sixteenth college in America and the first college west of the Allegheny Mountains, Transylvania has had a long and distinguished history. Its graduates include Stephen Austin, Jefferson Davis, John Hunt Morgan, Cassius Clay, and others. During the first half of the nineteenth century, the college rivaled Harvard and Yale for the quality of its faculty, students, and curriculum. The onset of the Civil War saw Transylvania close its doors, although Morrison Hall and other campus buildings were used as army hospitals by both sides. After the war and its reopening, Transylvania's curriculum included well-regarded schools of law and medicine, a seminary, and a liberal arts college. Since 1908, the school has been most noted for its liberal arts curriculum.

A National Historic Landmark because of its unique Greek Revival architecture, Old Morrison was designed by Gideon Shryock, who also oversaw its construction in 1833–34. It was built to replace an earlier administration building that burned in 1829. Colonel James Morrison had bequeathed $40,000–$50,000 to have it built. Henry Clay, then a law professor at Transylvania, was the executor of Morrison's will, and helped oversee the building project. The Revival style is exemplified at Morrison Hall by the six massive Doric columns stretching across its front exterior and large antepodia at the edges of the main entrance. It has held classrooms and churches, offices for the former law school, and the main library.

But Old Morrison Hall is unique in combining facilities for

the pursuit of higher education with the gloomy aspect of a cemetery crypt.

THE MAN WHOSE remains lie there is one Constantine Samuel Rafinesque, a pioneering yet exceedingly unconventional early American botanist and naturalist, who is revered even today as one of the most brilliant scientists in American history, a man of whom the *Smithsonian* magazine recently has written: "The intellectual breadth of the man was enormous."

During his life, Rafinesque collected, catalogued, and gave Latin names to thousands of plants and animals up and down the Eastern seaboard. In addition, while he taught in Kentucky, he located over a hundred prehistoric Indian sites in the state, published scores of scientific papers on nearly every subject imaginable, and taught courses in several disciplines. Amazingly enough, he was also a scholar in countless other intellectual pursuits, including geology, history, poetry, philosophy, economics, manufacturing, surveying, architecture, editing, and philology.

One nineteenth-century educator said of Rafinesque: "No more remarkable figure has ever appeared in the annals of science. But Rafinesque loved no man or woman."

It was that last idiosyncrasy that ultimately led to his inability to deal with the social, political, and behavioral requirements that his fame brought him. He died in 1840 at age fifty-seven, many years after he left Transylvania University, penniless and friendless in the cramped attic of a Philadelphia boarding house.

Constantine Samuel Rafinesque-Schmaltz was born in Galata, Turkey, near Constantinople, in 1783 to a merchant father from Marseilles and a German mother born in Greece. The Rafinesque-Schmaltz family first moved to France, and eventually to America during the Napoleonic Wars to escape European fighting. Earlier, however, Constantine had studied in America from 1802 to 1805. Later he spent about ten years in Italy studying botany with the notable British naturalist William Swainson.

Rafinesque dropped his mother's maiden name sometime around 1814 when he moved back to the United States with the rest of his family. A family friend in Lexington, Kentucky, one John D. Clifford, was instrumental in securing for him a teaching appointment at Transylvania University.

Rafinesque was considered one of the leading scientists of his day. He was acquainted with many of the other important early American scientists, including naturalist John J. Audubon, with whom he had a rather humorous first meeting, as recounted in an oft-repeated anecdote:

"A scientist friend of (Rafinesque) once sent him to John J. Audubon, who knew him by reputation but not by appearance, with a letter of introduction that read, 'I send you an odd fish . . .'

"Audubon took a glimpse around and asked for the fish. Rafinesque smiled, rubbed his hands together and said, 'I am that odd fish, I presume, Mr. Audubon.'"

Rafinesque taught botany, natural sciences, and languages at Transylvania from 1819 to 1825. His prickly personality—note his documented lack of affection for his fellow human beings—and, even worse in the reserved halls of academe, his penchant for self-aggrandizement and self-promotion, meant his relationship with fellow faculty, university administrators, and even his students was aloof at best and downright hostile on most occasions. He is said to have regularly canceled classes and gotten into habitual rows with most everyone with whom he came into contact.

His physical appearance was of no help with his social and professional lives—he was tall and thin with a rather hatchet-like face upon which was planted a long, aquiline nose under penetrating black eyes. He was given to wearing baggy black clothing and taking long walks in the woods, weighed down with a backpack within which he would deposit the plant and animal specimens he chanced upon.

His demise, however, came about when he irritated the university's president, one Horace Holley, once too often. Holley had grown tired of Rafinesque's unconventional behavior and casual attention to his classroom duties. But other versions of their dustup have Rafinesque insisting upon being granted a medical degree (Transylvania offered one at that time), or squabbling with Holley over the affections of a woman.

Whichever version, if any, might be correct, Holley ordered Rafinesque's belongings removed from his office while the young professor was on a field trip with his students. When he returned to find everything from his office piled in the hallway, he packed his bags and prepared to move back to Philadelphia, where he and his family had lived after fleeing Europe.

And that was when Professor Rafinesque placed a curse on Transylvania University that some say has come to pass—at least in part.

Precisely how he issued the curse is open to conjecture—whether he waggled his finger and shouted or screamed it over his shoulder as he scampered out of town are certainly two possibilities. Whatever the method, it seems to have worked. President Holley was forced to resign from the university within a short time after he argued with school trustees over a matter unrelated to Rafinesque. Holley died within the year. Later, the university's main administration building was badly damaged in a fire.

"Time renders justice to all," Rafinesque ominously noted upon hearing the bleak news from his former campus.

Transy experienced other problems, including a cholera outbreak on campus during a rebuilding project. Other difficulties and inexplicable problems showed up over the years as well. It was almost as if the old botany professor himself—shaking his finger and cackling in glee—might still have been hovering over the college grounds from which he was driven.

But that didn't stop Transy officials from making a kindly gesture that might have caused even sour, old Rafinesque a slight nod of thanks.

When Rafinesque died in squalor in that dingy, Philadelphia apartment in 1850, his body was carted off to a Philadelphia medical school for use by its students. A compassionate physician discovered what was going to happen to the famed scientist. He believed that a man celebrated for his many scientific accomplishments should not have such an ignominious conclusion and paid for Rafinesque's burial in a local cemetery.

There he lay moldering in the ground until 1919, when Rafinesque began his long journey back to Transylvania University. One Henry C. Mercer, an alumnus of the school, had heard stories about the early professor and decided to track down his humble grave. Mercer thought the university should at last honor him by reburying his bones on campus. Mercer eventually succeeded in persuading the university to go along with the idea and the remains of Constantine Rafinesque were secured in a heavy, lead-lined coffin in Old Morrison. Nearby is the epitaph: "Honor to Whom Honor is Overdue."

However, it didn't take long for mischievous Transy undergraduates to take advantage of the presence of a corpse in their midst. They created the Rafinesque Society, whose members, bedecked in black robes and black hoods decorated with a large *R*, held an annual torchlight parade. A ritualistic burning of a coffin followed each outdoor processional.

Another legend held that a light burning near his coffin must always stay lit or bad luck would befall the university. Rumor was that the light went out in 1969, just before Old Morrison was nearly destroyed in another fire.

In the mid-1960s, someone managed to haul the coffin to the Old Morrison chapel. It was recovered, put back in place and there it remains.

Rafinesque pervades campus in another manner. Most campuses have at least one restaurant where the campus community can enjoy a leisurely meal. Transylvania is no different. But theirs is called The Rafskeller, or The Raf for short, and it is indeed named after the legendary professor. Perhaps his frequent absence from classes had a particular resonance when the time came to name the place—after all, skipping classes to drink coffee and debate weighty matters is a grand tradition at any campus eatery.

If one believes in curses such as that thrown out by Rafinesque, then it is not too difficult to suppose that his has at last run out. The 1969 restoration of Old Morrison successfully expanded student and administrative facilities in the hall so that the building regained its status as the campus showpiece, and was nationally honored as one of the unique buildings in all of Kentucky through its designation on the National Park Service's National Register of Historic Places.

The Bearded Man

The chemistry professor never expected visitors in her third floor office at those late hours. It grew very quiet in the old brick hall, especially when the air conditioning had been turned off for the day. But then, on many nights, her quiet hours of grading student papers or preparing lectures would be interrupted by someone coming down the hallway toward her office.

The professor's curiosity and, truthfully, a bit of apprehension about being alone usually got the best of her and she'd poke her head out the door. No one was there. The footsteps proceeded right by her. She'd follow them down to the second floor . . . nothing. It happened time and again. Finally, she simply ignored it.

Which is what faculty, staff, and students at North Idaho College have done more often than not when the Union soldier of Seiter Hall is making his rounds.

NORTH IDAHO COLLEGE is situated on forty-five acres of beautiful landscape on the shores of Lake Coeur d'Alene, about fifteen miles east of Spokane, Washington. The 4,500 students on the two-year campus receive associate of arts degrees and other technical and academic certificates, or transfer to one of the four-year campuses in the state. Begun as a private school in 1933, North Idaho College is now a state college serving the Idaho Panhandle region squeezed between Montana on the east and Washington state to the west. British Columbia shares a forty-five mile border on the north.

The ghostly soldier in Seiter Hall might well have been stationed at the original Camp Coeur d'Alene. Founded in 1877 by General William Tecumseh Sherman, the fort stretched a half-mile along Lake Coeur d'Alene, on much of the same land now occupied by North Idaho College. Its original purpose was threefold: to watch the Canadian border, protect the northern Idaho frontier, and guard workmen putting in rail and telegraph lines in the region. A year later, in 1878, it became Fort Coeur d'Alene, and a decade later Fort Sherman.

The city of Coeur d'Alene grew up alongside Fort Sherman. An 1882 mining boom caused the city to rapidly expand, and the fort was finally abandoned in 1900. Most of the fort has been razed; however, the original chapel is a museum on the National Register of Historic Places. The former army officers' quarters are college faculty offices.

THE GHOST OF Seiter Hall is often depicted as a stranger in a dark blue peacoat similar to those worn by soldiers manning Fort Sherman a century ago. The hall is now home to science and mathematics classrooms and offices. One biology professor said sometimes the figure is glimpsed out of the corners of one's eyes, but never full on. He said that most often people hear footsteps, doors closing, and furniture being moved in unoccupied classrooms.

A common campus legend is that Seiter Hall was built over the Union soldier's grave, but there is no evidence to support that idea.

Several custodians who worked in Seiter Hall, and thus familiar with the ghost, told campus reporters about their experiences:

"Usually you hear things after 11:30 at night, after everyone has gone," said Dale Lemler, an NIC custodian. "You hear doors opening, people talking. But nobody's around."

Custodian Isabelle Marquez told another writer that she has heard noises and footsteps. "You just hear things and try not to pay attention, but sometimes I freak myself out. You hear everybody saying, 'Have you heard the ghost?' No, not yet. Hopefully if I do, I hope it's a nice one."

Lemler wasn't sure what kind of personality the ghost might have.

"A few years ago, when it happened the most, a set of keys was lost, and you'd have to check the sounds out. Nothing was ever there. A lot of people would think you're off your rocker, but other people have heard it. It never bothers anybody. After being in the same building for three years, you know something is there."

Former custodian Bob Trueblood seemed to be the one who identified it as a soldier.

A custodian who had seen it told Trueblood that it looked like an old man wearing a beard and was somewhat "translucent and fuzzy around the edges." He didn't approach that custodian, just stood back and watched him work. Finally, the custodian got frustrated and told the apparition to grab a mop and lend a hand. It didn't move.

Trueblood has his own tales.

"People tell you stories, and you find yourself listening. I've heard voices in a dark room. I don't open the doors and look in, but I make sure they're locked. One security guard won't go in that building late at night without his gun drawn."

Another custodian was skeptical that what caused the odd sounds originated with anything supernatural, although he had his own anomalous experience.

"I was cleaning a chalkboard on the first floor and I heard someone come down the stairs. As I snuck toward the hall, I heard the main door open. I ran and looked out, but no one was there. I've had similar things happen on the catwalk (which leads from the building's second floor to the library). I hear suspicious things—doors shutting, people talking—and I run out and check, and no one's around. I sneak up the back stairs . . . I never see anything. I can't speak for anyone else, but I'd say someone's there. He seems to be most active from eleven p.m. to one a.m."

Randy Brockhoff had worked for North Idaho College for ten years when he was interviewed. He, too, heard all sorts of strange sounds, especially after he'd walked out of the building for the night and started to walk away. "I know I just locked the building, but I'm hearing things."

Yet it was the chemistry professor who probably spent the most hours in Seiter Hall and who offered the most sanguine assessment of the Seiter Hall ghost.

"It's a completely benign presence, probably protective, someone affected in a positive way," she told a reporter. "Whoever it is has an intrinsic interest in the building, as if they are making rounds. I've never felt afraid, maybe a little spooked as anyone would be, but not with terror. When I'm in this building by myself, I don't like anyone else in here that I'm not aware of. I'm a skeptic, but let's put it this way: The ghost phenomenon is the best explanation possible."

It's an explanation that an old soldier on everlasting guard duty might appreciate.

Two Haunted Halls

Two of the most frequently cited centers of college ghostly activity seem to be in theaters and in dormitories. Perhaps it is because students in both locales seem to have plenty of time to pass along the customs and legends associated with both.

At Franklin College, about thirty miles south of Indianapolis, a modern, suite-style residence hall—Johnson-Dietz—is located where once stood Bryan Hall, a looming, stone edifice gutted by fire in 1985.

The new Johnson-Dietz complex is popular with students. The suites feature two bedrooms, a living room with bay windows, and separate bathrooms. A unique bubble room study lounge has glass walls.

But before Johnson-Dietz, there was Bryan Hall and the legend of a 1930s murder of a young coed. The details of the killing were murky, partially because of the claim that the death was hushed up so as to not offend the community. Her picture was alleged to have been deleted from the yearbook, and copies of the newspaper with references to the murder destroyed.

To add a ghastly note to all this, her body is said to have been stuffed inside a wall of the former women's dormitory, there to lie undisturbed for quite some time. When the bones were at last discovered, it was far too late to determine a cause of death. Or piece together any clues as to the identity of the killer.

For decades afterward, however, the residents of Bryan Hall heard the shuffling of slippered feet receding down the hallways, and faint moans late at night, seeming to come from nowhere and yet everywhere.

Precisely how a cover-up of such a horrific affair would have been possible on a college campus isn't clear from the skimpy details of the story. But since Bryan Hall is no longer, and the young men and women in Johnson-Dietz enjoy all the modern conveniences of college life, there is no longer reason to worry about a murdered girl's ghost returning to claim her old dormitory room.

Or is there?

Old Bones

Good friend for Jesus' sake forbear
To dig the dust enclosed here.
Blest be the man that spares these stones
And curst be he that moves my bones.

The verse written over William Shakespeare's grave at Holy Trinity Church, Stratford-upon-Avon, is arguably one of the most famous curses in history. The playwright's earthly remains are still there as far as anyone knows. But in certain other cases, the removal and reinterment of corpses has been connected to later assumed supernatural phenomena that can be, well, disturbing to the living.

The human remains workmen found in Albuquerque during the construction of Jeanette Stromberg Hall at the city's Technical Vocational Institute were moved to new gravesites, but if campus reports from 2002 are to be believed, some people think that fact could be linked to some strange goings-on people have claimed to have experienced in that building. Although a ghost as such has not been reported, there has been a considerable amount of what some consider poltergeist experience in the strikingly modern-looking building.

The main site of Albuquerque's TVI campus is near downtown, at Coal and University Southeast. The TVI's four campuses comprise the state's largest and most comprehensive community college. They offer certificates in health, business, trades, and technologies to thousands of students.

The planning for Stromberg Hall began in the early 1980s. Originally it was to be part of a larger complex that would have included facilities for the local public school system and a nursing school associated with Presbyterian Hospital. However, financial limitations caused the project to be scaled back. Ground was broken on the building in 1984 when construction crews tore into what had been a parking lot. But all that came to a halt when the remains were found of a small female child clad in a red velvet dress and encased in a glass coffin. One account claimed all of her hair was unscathed. Other pieces of scattered human bones were discovered. Authorities believed the site had been a pauper's cemetery. The girl's remains and the bones were reburied in a city cemetery.

Perhaps more attention should have been paid to that inci dent, for since Stromberg Hall was completed in 1985 have come unsettling stories from those who occupy offices there that make it seem that the building itself has, according to one report, an "almost sinister" theme connected with it. From sudden temperature fluctuations to water leakage to elevators that started and stopped on their own, some suggested the spir its of the angry dead were responsible. Others thought it sim ply construction problems. . . .

Whatever the cause, the troubles were cited by a number of building workers.

On the fourth floor, the clicking of a computer keyboard was detected in an unoccupied office. An instructor passing by the same empty room heard the shuffling of feet and paper being riffled.

Meanwhile, on the first floor, elevator doors sometimes open without anyone aboard and bathroom faucets will turn on for no reason. One report said, "The current residents of (Jeanette Stromberg) joke, with an uneasy undertone, about the toilets that flush and the doors that open, all on their own."

The "eerie feeling" even affected a security detail sent to the building after hours when something triggered an intrusion alarm. The officers scoured the building but found nothing amiss. However, when the investigators made ready to leave the building they heard a door slam from somewhere inside and then scampering footsteps.

"We rechecked the entire building, and still nothing," one of the officers told a reporter.

The TVI building seems to have been quiet for some time now. Other people who have taken classes there or work in one of its many offices dismiss the notion that the building is haunted in any way. Whatever the case, figuring out the truth of J. S. Hall adds a unique flavor to Albuquerque educational opportunities.

The Faceless Nun

At St. Mary-of-the-Woods College, five miles northwest of Terre Haute, Indiana, orientation programs include the usual information about classes, housing policies, cocurricular activities, and school history. But at this small women's Catholic college—the oldest such liberal arts institution in the country—there is another ritual that is passed along to incoming students . . . stories about one of the more famous ghosts on any Indiana college campus. Stories of her periodic visits to campus go back nearly a century.

She is the faceless nun. Those who insist they have encountered her describe a Catholic sister in a traditional habit but one whose face is without any recognizable features, a pale palette of blank flesh recessed deep within the veil which cloaks her head. Her origins are obscure, though most of those people familiar with the tale agree she was connected to the art department, as in this published account from a former student:

"There was a nun in the art department (who) liked to do portraits and she was doing a portrait of herself. It was very typical behavior for her, when she did portraits, she would paint the face in last. She was painting a self-portrait and before she finished she died so she didn't get it painted."

Was there ever such a portrait on campus? Probably not, although one was allegedly found in the attic of a campus building some years ago.

Another version of the nun's origin originates shortly after the campus's founding by Mother Theodore Guerin and five members of the Sisters of Providence. They left Ruille-sur-Loir, France, in 1840, to establish a church mission in Indiana. They settled in Thralls Station, near Terre Haute, and there founded a school for women, the first in Indiana. Thralls Station later changed its name to St. Mary-of-the-Woods. The heavily wooded campus is on a small plateau. The older buildings are of Gothic design. Its isolated location and sometimes fog-enshrouded grounds can be an ideal setting for ghost stories, both real and, perhaps, imagined.

The faceless nun might have been among the six founding sisters or another teaching nun in the years following the college's founding. According to this version, she was a fussy nun who couldn't bear to leave matters undone:

"(She) was called this because no one could remember who she was. She was a spirit who came back and could be seen occasionally in Foley (Hall), especially where the relics are of Mother Theodore. Supposedly she knew Mother Theodore before she died. All of this occurred in the late nineteenth century. She did no harm, and when asked why she was here . . . something had gotten fouled up about thirty masses said after her death so she had to get the matter straight."

The eminent campus keeper of the chronicles of the faceless nun was Sister Esther Newport, a member of the college's art department for thirty-three years until her retirement in 1964. After that, she lived in her order's mother house on campus. Though she never personally saw the faceless nun, she came very close on several occasions, as she later related in interviews with folklorist Michael Crawford:

"We had a couple of young women who were doing housework around the place. One morning, it was the middle of winter, around eleven o'clock . . . I came around to the art department. I came around to that big room with the big glass windows and I came in here and this little girl, we'll call her Catherine, was over dusting this table and Mary, the other girl, was over there and she had her back turned to us and was going about her business. When I came in, Catherine said, 'Sister, did you see that sister who was looking for you?' I said, 'No, who? Who was she?' She kind of fumbled around. I said, 'Was it Sister Celestine?' That was an old sister who used to come around and see me every once in awhile. And she said, 'No, no, I know Sister Celestine.' And she said, 'Sister, she kind of had like pleats down here, down the front.' And I said, 'Oh, maybe that was Sister Pauline.' She was a sister from Texas who was staying with us at the time and her habit had kind of a strange headdress with some pleats down there, in front. So I said, 'Oh, maybe it was Sister Pauline.' And she said, 'No, I know Sister Pauline.' And she got quite embarrassed. She said, 'Sister, Sister you'll think I'm crazy but she didn't have no face!' "

What makes Sister Esther's accounts so compelling is that she was specific and distinct in her accounts of these conversations with students and staff that saw the faceless nun. Sister had no reason to doubt the veracity of the teller, nor was her truthfulness ever questioned.

"In the same locality, another girl, a senior, she graduated that year, was in the art department. I came in one morning, about the same time of day, and she said,

" 'Sister, did you see that nun?'

"And I said, 'No, I didn't see her.'

"She said, 'Sister, you had to. I heard your beads.'

"We used to wear those beads, you know, that rattle.

"She said, 'I heard your beads. You were coming in the door and she was standing right here by me.'

"I said, 'Well, well, who is she? I didn't meet her. Maybe she went in this other door.'

" 'Sister, she couldn't. You were right there.'

"So I said to her, 'Well, who was she? What did she look like?'

" 'I don't know. She's the same one who is always coming here when I'm here. She always gets between me and the light; I never can see her face.' "

An art room once located in the former Foley Hall was the center of the ghostly nun's ramblings, as might be expected if she, indeed, was a former art professor. Earlier, it had been music rooms and even part of the lodging for grade-school children, who at one time boarded on campus.

Again it was Sister Esther Newport who had the closest of encounters, as in this incident during the time she was collaborating on a book with a Chicago author. Sister Esther was creating most of the illustrations, while her collaborator wrote the text:

"She came down to have a conference on the book, and we went around down to the big (art) room, the big studio, the one with the big windows. We sat down with our backs to the windows and facing the middle of the room where I had just finished a big picture, must have been about five feet long, and it was standing on the easel there right in the middle of the room right under a large light. The lights have been changed since then, but this was a big, 1,000 watt, just a bare electric light hanging down from the ceiling so that there was no possibility of any shadows or anything else around.

"I went to turn the picture, I was behind the picture. It was so large she couldn't see me behind the picture. She was standing over in another corner where the faceless nun comes around and she began to talk. I was over behind the picture but I answered her.

"She turned around and said, 'Where are you?'

"I said, 'Right here.'

"'Are you all over this place? You were right here a minute ago.'

"I said, 'I haven't been over there. I'm right here.'

"She was quite embarrassed. She's a professional woman and a writer and she wasn't accustomed to seeing ghosts, I guess. We came over and sat down in the middle of the room and began talking about the picture. We were facing the picture. Suddenly she grabbed me by the arm and said, 'My God, there she is again!' And she pointed right to the middle of the floor, right in front of this picture where there couldn't possibly be any shadows. She points a pathway of this thing she was seeing and it went over and went into a doorway and went downstairs. I didn't see a thing. I was looking hard, too. But she didn't say any more. We kind of laughed it off."

The oddity of the faceless nun appearing to only one individual in a room while other people were present was not confined to this one episode. It happened again right in the middle of one of Sister's art classes:

"We were having a . . . drawing class looking at the model up on the platform. There must have been ten, twelve, maybe more girls around sitting on the benches, you know the way they do in art classes. One girl way over in the middle of the room looked up and started talking. And I was way over there. Everybody in the room stopped. They looked at her, turned around, looked at me, the model pricked up his ears. Whatever it was she said I don't know, but I said, 'Saiver, were you talking to me?' And she said, 'But Sister, you were right here beside me!' And I wasn't. I was at least twenty feet away. She was embarrassed and everybody else seemed to think it was a little strange. . . ."

At some point in nearly every haunting there comes a time when those closest to the events say "Enough!" and explore ways in which the spirit can be laid to rest. In the case of the faceless nun, at least two methods were given a go, including simply telling the thing to be gone, as when Sister Esther recalled another nun getting plenty fed up with the spirit:

"She told me that she was sitting in this (art) room one time and footsteps came from this door, this place, and came over toward her and stood beside her. And she said, 'Go away.' She's a very stolid person; she wasn't having anything . . . so she just said that, not inquiring or anything. So the footsteps went away and then came back. And this time she said, 'Will you *please* go away and let me alone; I have work to do!' The footsteps went away and didn't come back."

DESPITE THE PHANTOM nun's obedience to such a stern directive, she continued to be such a persistent presence that Sister Esther finally talked to her order's Mother General. Sister Esther recounted the numerous episodes in which students or faculty would feel someone brush past them when they were speaking, although no one walked by, or the times in which a person would mistakenly begin a conversation with the ghost thinking it was one of the Sisters of Providence. The Mother General rejected the idea of an exorcism, but did approve of a special mass said for special intentions, in this case asking whatever it was that lived in Foley Hall to go away. "And so we did," Sister Esther said, "and I haven't heard of anything since. That was about thirty years ago."

Has the faceless nun finally vanished from St. Mary-of-the-Woods? Not quite, if current students are any indication.

A recent campus report describes the history of the faceless nun and says that "sightings have been reported time and again ever since her passing."

One student said she had seen the nun:

"I was walking down the hall one time and heard footsteps behind me. I stopped and looked behind me but no one was there, but I noticed a figure in the glass doors behind me. It looked as though a person was far away from the doors. I started walking again and heard the same noise; turning, I saw that person right by the doors. I booked it out of there!"

But another student was skeptical: "I think that they just

have her story because people think they see something and they relate it to the story. It is a scary story, because we make it that way."

Yet a freshman there seemed not to want to take chances: "I think that the story is true. I very much believe in ghost stories. I have not encountered the faceless nun, and I don't know if I want to, either!"

Even if the faceless nun has found peace, the young women at St. Mary-of-the-Woods can always turn to the legend of the poltergeist on "three back" at Guerin Hall, a circa 1913, four-story building which now houses administrative offices, classrooms, and student mothers with children. Formerly, it was a dormitory with both shared and private rooms.

The mystery of "three back" centered on room 334, a corner room, in which residents said they'd be startled by passing shadows, strange sounds, or moving objects—a wall-mounted crucifix is said to have once swung from side to side.

What was the origin of the poltergeist? A woman who attended the Woods in the 1930s told her daughter that a student had committed suicide by hanging in that room. But others dismiss that explanation.

Perhaps the prospect of both a faceless nun *and* a poltergeist might be more than any small college could handle.

No Exit

One of the universal traditions in legitimate theaters is that a floor lamp with a single, bright, bare bulb be kept lit on stage after-hours. The "ghost light," as it is termed, ostensibly prevents after-hours mishaps by actors or stagehands tripping over scenery, props, or electrical cords that might clutter the floor. Some believe, however, that its purpose is a bit harder to quantify—that it's there to illuminate the dark corners of dusty theaters where the shadowy residue of departed theater artists might hang about.

College theaters, like their professional counterparts, are often the site of interesting ghost stories. Just when the first appearance of a ghost as a *character* in a drama occurs is not recorded, but the appearances of ghosts who have become permanent residents of their favorite campus playhouses are not uncommon and often are quite remarkable, as the following stories illustrate.

THE THEATER DEPARTMENT secretary arrived at her university office early on that morning. The interior of the old building on the periphery of campus was gloomy under the best of circumstances, but that didn't impede her from being there in the early hours to finish some much needed filing before the daily onslaught of bustling professors and fretful students.

She got the folders she needed from a top drawer in her file cabinet, the type of unit in which the drawers slide back automatically once they're released. She turned back to her desk, but a slight noise from behind her made her quickly turn around. The drawer that she'd just used and had seen closing was now *moving outward on its tracks*. The drawer reached the end of the track and stopped. It stayed there until she reached out and pushed it shut again. This time it stayed closed. How could that be? It seemed impossible, and yet she had to believe what she'd just seen.

IN THAT OLD theater arts department office at Idaho's Boise State University, the secretary's experience was another in what by then was a growing inventory of encounters with their renowned, if reclusive, Dina, the ghost of Subal Theatre.

The Subal Theatre was located in the former Student Union Building, one of the three original buildings on the campus. Designed by Fritz Hommel in the 1940s for what was then Boise Junior College, the SUB was given over to the music and theater departments in 1967 when a new student union was built. A year later, a ballroom on a wing of the second floor was converted into a theater. It became known as the Subal, a blend of SUB and ballroom. The departments stayed in the building until the new Morrison Center for the Performing Arts opened in December 1983. The building is now the home of the communications department and campus broadcast facilities. The theater has been converted into classroom space.

Though Dina has been quiet for some time, her presence still dwells among those who've been long associated with the campus.

Dr. Charles Lauterbach is a retired professor and chairman of theater arts at Boise State and something of an authority on Dina. He is skeptical about the stories told of Dina, noting that there is hardly a theater in existence without some sort of ghost story connected to it. Ghosts in the green room—where actors apply makeup and relax before performances—are particularly common, he notes. Whenever theater folks gather, he adds, talk often turns inevitably to the ghosts that inhabit their specific theaters.

Lauterbach said Dina was a benign presence, if she does exist at all. Stories of her goings-on benefited greatly from the slightly gloomy atmosphere in the old Subal Theatre.

"The sunlight came in from the east through a small set of windows. The ballroom was a big room with Tudor arches that went up twenty or thirty feet into the air, so you had a kind of spaciousness to it. Now when the theater was built into it, the ballroom was cut off at the far end to form a small platform stage. They put in walls to form the theater. There were nooks and crannies all over the placé for storage, even under the eaves of the roof, and other 'found places' for storage of lights and costumes. They even built in a box office," Lauterbach says.

The story of Dina's origins began sometime after the ballroom was built into the former SUB in 1951.

"I came to Boise State in 1971, and there was already quite a bit of discussion about the theater ghost, and most of it centered on people who were in the theater arts department. Supposedly somewhere between 1951 and 1968, when the ballroom was converted into a theater, a young lady was jilted when the young man she'd invited to a school dance stood her up. She committed suicide in the women's restroom, which was just off the front entrance to the ballroom."

The problem with the story, Lauterbach notes, is that there is little factual evidence to back up the story. He's not heard of anyone who's been able to find any news accounts in the university archives to substantiate a suicide having taken place there in the 1950s or 1960s.

Another version of Dina's origins has the young woman killing herself in the 1940s, when the former theater building still housed the junior college's student union. The circumstances are similar, but this gathering was a Sadie Hawkins dance, where women ask men to a dance, but the man Dina had asked to attend decided he had better things to do and never arrived. However, a former president of Boise Junior College in the 1940s has said that he didn't recall any students taking their own lives during that time period.

None of the uncertainty of just *how* Dina came to be, however, can fully account for the numerous episodes of truly odd events reported in the former theater complex, including the secretary's experience with the animated file drawers and those which Prof. Lauterbach recalls.

Lauterbach said the incidents attributed to Dina often pointed to the work of a poltergeist, including one that involved the theater department chairman.

"He had an office right off the theater. One time someone tapped on his door. He went to the door and opened it. There was no one there. He thought maybe some students were playing games with him. He looked up and down the very short hallway and still found no one so he went back to his desk chair, which was right next to the door. There was another tap at the door. He reached up and opened it immediately. No one was out there. He said there was no way that anyone, even going lickety-split down the hallway, could have gotten out of there fast enough."

Lauterbach said the chairman could not find any obvious explanation for the knocking.

The same professor had another experience in the theater proper some years later. As he ended a rehearsal late one night, he waited for the student actors and crew to leave before he turned off the stage and houselights. As he walked toward the main light switch, the theater was suddenly cast into darkness. He called out to whoever had switched off the lights that he was still there, but he didn't get a response.

Again, he thought it might be a student prankster. Once he

got to the switch and flipped the lights back on he could see that no one was either near the switch or in the theater. And besides, he said later about the episode, he could easily have heard someone darting across the squeaky floors.

The professor said both of the incidents seemed typical of youthful student exuberance, but the failure to find any apparent culprit left him with what he called an eerie feeling.

Retired Professor Lauterbach thinks many of the incidents alleged to have been caused by Dina may have had simpler explanations, especially those related by imaginative theater students.

"A student in the building one night heard noises. He was working alone and called out, 'Who's there?' All he heard was a piano playing 'London Bridge is Falling Down, My Fair Lady.' The problem is that since the theater and music departments were housed in the building together immediately below the theater they had eight or ten music practice rooms with pianos and they weren't soundproof. They were open at all hours of the day and night for students, so it may have been someone who couldn't get in to play the piano until late at night. But still that was kind of an interesting occurrence."

And it was one that was passed along for years by students who claimed that Dina had a particular fondness for music.

Lauterbach said another oft-told incident involved the theater's technical director in the mid-1970s, Frank Heise.

Heise and a student technician were working late in the theater painting scenery panels for the upcoming musical production of *Stop the World, I Want to Get Off*. The horizontal panes were splayed out across the stage floor. Frank and his assistant put down their brushes and took a break. She left the theater while Heise sat in a house seat and made some mental notes of all that had to be finished for the production. When the student returned, she and Heise returned to the stage to see if the painted panels had dried. On several of the boards were the distinct tracks of a woman's shoes with pointed toes and small heels, as if someone had just walked through the wet paint. The student had not been near the panels. Further, the toes on her shoes were square-tipped and slightly larger.

Lauterbach has something of an explanation of how that

might have happened, but it is only conjecture and didn't satisfy those who sought a more ghostly explanation.

"Our storage in the building was such that instead of a place to store something like plywood, it got left out on the floor. It's possible that somebody, maybe one of the young ladies in our department, simply walked across the new wood and (her footsteps) would have left impressions in the wood. But it wouldn't show right away because of the more or less monochromatic appearance of the wood. But when you painted it and the paint dried then the footprints might have been seen because of the angle of the light. But that incident really did scare people."

Lauterbach told everyone that he was skeptical that there was a ghost in the theater, but that didn't prevent students from continuing their search for Dina.

"We used to have high school students who brought their sleeping bags and spent the night in the Subal looking for the ghost all night," he remembers.

Even he admitted that being alone in Subal did not top his agenda for late evening activities. "No one working lingered too late at night in that theater. (I was) scared to be the last in there."

But Lauterbach understands the power of suggestion. "I think we scare each other more just talking about it, but that's the nature of ghosts."

There were other, smaller episode of unpleasantness, which to some added up to a ghostly presence.

The ghost got the name she did because letters spelling out the name Dina once appeared mysteriously on a classroom chalkboard and were discovered on more than one occasion scrawled in lipstick on makeup mirrors.

The director of a play at Subal said he saw light coming from underneath the door of a vacant room, yet each time he opened the door the room would be dark.

In another production, a matchstick that failed time and again to light properly suddenly burst into flame and then soared across the stage. The actor handling the match was also to light a candle. Once he'd corralled the match and despite his best efforts, he could not keep the candle lighted.

Dina's final bow might well have been in the presence of another department secretary shortly after the theater's move into the Morrison Center. Not everything had been relocated to the department's new quarters, and she was chatting with a theater instructor inside an office near the old theater. The office door into the hallway was open. Suddenly a shadow fell across the threshold as if someone had stopped in the hallway just short of the doorway. Perhaps politely waiting for the conversation he—or she—overheard coming from the office to end. But when the secretary looked out the door, the hall was empty, not even the faintest of footsteps retreating.

HAS DINA MADE her final exit from the theater scene at Boise State?

The former SUB building and Subal Theatre itself were extensively remodeled into offices for the communication department and KBSU. The theater was subdivided into classroom space.

"Evidently Dina has never shown up for the communications people," Professor Lauterbach notes. He thinks that perhaps with the presence of so much electronic equipment, Dina might be reluctant to make an appearance. But in the stunning Morrison performance complex on the banks of the Boise River, Lauterbach notes, students and faculty tend to blame Dina whenever books are misplaced or somebody's costume ends up in the wrong place.

"They always say, 'See, Dina is at it again!'" Lauterbach laughs.

But whether it was the *reality* of a ghost or something far less substantial that caused her years of notoriety at Boise State, Dina's story may demonstrate a simple truth: ghosts in any theater have far more to do with memories than with disembodied, disappointed coeds who might once have been stood up on a date.

"We've got nice offices and we've got a nice theater," Lauterbach says of the Morrison Center. "The facilities have great equipment and all that sort of thing, but we don't have any ghosts."

Not yet, anyway.

TWO-HUNDRED AND FIFTY miles across the state from Boise, the Pocatello campus of Idaho State University is not to be outdone by their neighbor to the west when it comes to the supernatural on stage.

Not only does Idaho State have a luminous modern performing arts center that was built to replace an antiquated theater complex, as does Boise State, but it boasts its own theater ghost who may—or may not—have decided to take up residence in the new theater. He is a gentleman nicknamed Alex, and so prominent is this ghost of Frazier Hall he's featured in university publications.

Although the ISU L. E. and Thelma E. Stephens Performing Arts Center will be the center of theater performances for decades to come, the circa 1924 Frazier Hall with its spacious, 800-seat auditorium and intimate Powell Little Theater is scheduled to retain at least some theater performances into the near future.

That's good news for Alex, who seems to have made several appearances over the years. A young woman theater graduate from the 1980s told a reporter that she was responsible for naming the ghost. Her first acquaintance with him occurred during a theatrical performance one winter's night. As she sat on the steps backstage waiting to go on, an outside window above her head that was supposed to be sealed shut against the cold kept opening. She would get up to close it each time. Finally, in exasperation she called out to Alex that she was cold and didn't appreciate the constant draft and would he please shut the window! The window quietly slid shut and stayed that way.

The Alex stories are legion. An ISU newspaper chronicled his time in Frazier Hall, with perhaps more than a slight acknowledgement to the date on which it was published . . . Halloween:

Former drama professor Reed Turner was hanging lights on the main stage at Frazier Hall in the wee hours of the morning. He and a student were the only ones in the building. As they prepared to leave, they noticed the side stage door open slowly, and then swing slowly shut again. Moments later they "perceived something" said Turner. "There was someone on stage." But it was more of a sense of a presence rather than a specific being.

Again, late on another night, a drama student sat in the darkened dressing room beneath the stage, trying on makeup. She had lit a candle for effect, since the makeup was for Halloween. Without warning, the candle flickered and went out. Annoyed, she went upstairs to get a match, only to find upon returning that the candle had been relit.

Kevin Korn, a student scenery technician who was building sets for a production, slept all one night on the main stage. He reported hearing noises, and described a "screech—like something (that) was being dragged" across the stage floor.

"More than one person at different times has seen it," said the former professor, Reed Turner. He found "it" hard to describe and could not attribute clothing or facial features. He termed it a form, like a "blue-gray glow . . . I sensed he was older."

All those who have described the ghost said it was an elderly male. Some have felt him as simply a strong presence. Others have heard a piano playing, to find no one there only seconds after the music stopped. Unlike at Boise State, there are no music practice rooms near the theater.

Though firm evidence eludes them, many people share Turner's conviction when he said, "I think there is something here . . . paranormal."

To the teachers, students, workers, and performers at Frazier Hall, the ghost is simply known affectionately as Alex. Turner did not know who the ghost might have been in its earlier life on earth. For years students have speculated, however, that Alex was a teacher who spent much of his time at the old theater and still keeps watch over it.

Alex has been sensed, seen, and heard all over Frazier Hall, but he seems to frequent the main stage and various creaky walkways, according to Turner. "Things just move a little bit, doors close and open." That's how Alex announced himself.

"He's been here and he's done nothing vicious," Turner said. "More than spooky, our ghost is friendly—it does pranks." That does seem to be the case with most theater ghosts, perhaps continuing with the sense of exuberance often associated with youthful actors in college plays.

Dr. Donald Asboe was a speech and drama instructor for

over forty years at Frazier Hall. He told a campus reporter that he would probably have said they are not ghostly pranks, but "structural" pranks.

"This old building can scare the hell out of you," Asboe said. He demonstrated how drafts, squeaky doors, and fluttering curtains create illusions in people's minds.

He attributes the screams, wails, and deep moans he's heard to the steam heating system in the building. He has never seen the ghost.

But he also admitted to something else about the Frazier Hall haunting: "It's scared me out of my wits."

By their very nature, according to Asboe, theaters arouse the imagination and intensify perceptions—"and there are your phantoms." He acknowledged, however, that some events, such as the candle that relit mysteriously, are hard to explain.

Whether the ghost actually exists or is a product of lively imaginations may never be resolved. Everyone seemed to have their own answers—skeptical, rational, or gullible—when faced with the stories about Alex.

NAMED FOR CHARLES R. FRAZIER, an early president of Idaho Technical Institute, Frazier Hall is over eighty years old, and for all that time it has been the home of the theater and communications department at Idaho State. Through the doors of its classrooms, costume shops, theaters, rehearsal rooms, and design studios have passed students who have gone on to great success on stage and screen: people such as television star William Peterson; film and stage actress Sue Ann Langdon; movie producer John Foreman; and pianist Roger Williams. Theatrical performances at Frazier Hall are scheduled to be phased out over the coming years. And who knows but that the new theaters at the Stephens Performing Arts Complex may engender their own unique ghost lore?

As for old Alex's future, a campus publication may have put it best recently, when an anonymous correspondent wrote: "The truth could be that the ghost of Frazier Hall is the collective spirit left behind by the throngs who have passed through Frazier since 1924. The spirit lives on between the building's halls and beyond its walls in the lives and memories of thousands of students who entered the doors of Frazier with hesitation and vague aspirations, and left with the self-confidence and knowledge to pursue and fulfill their dreams."

THE EVENING PLAY rehearsal had ended a short time earlier. Director Jim Zimmerman sat poring over his notes spread out on a table propped over the backs of several seats about midway back in the theater. The last actor had bid goodnight and slipped out the stage door. It was late, about ten o'clock, and Zimmerman had had a long day working as managing director of the summer theater and then guiding this run-through of summer stock perennial *The Music Man* as it made its way to opening night a week or so away.

Zimmerman scrawled a few notes to pass along to his cast the next day. He was about ready to wrap up, turn off the lights, and lock up for the night when he became aware that someone was on stage.

"I didn't notice him until I felt somebody walking on stage. I looked up and there he was. I don't know where he came from," Zimmerman remembered, "other than from stage right. He walked over to center stage, somewhat downstage. He stood looking at me."

He was a slightly built man of medium height who appeared to be somewhere in his thirties. He had longish hair and was clad in a red, short-sleeve shirt and blue jeans. His face was partially cast in the shadows from the stage work lights overhead. In any case, Zimmerman didn't recognize him.

"Do you want something?" Zimmerman called out.

The stranger didn't answer. Not even a reaction that he had heard the question or wished to acknowledge the man asking it.

It was the beginning of a brief, albeit significant encounter that leaves the theater veteran puzzled to this day.

JIM ZIMMERMAN WAS the managing director at the St. Croix Valley Summer Theater for over fifteen years, beginning in the late 1980s. He also directed at least one of the three or four shows staged each summer. The stock company still performs each summer in Davis Theatre on the campus of the University of Wisconsin–River Falls, in far western Wisconsin, about thirty miles east of the Twin Cities of Minneapolis and St. Paul, Minnesota. Zimmerman is a professor of theater at the university.

As a theater veteran, the normally unruffled Zimmerman is not unaccustomed to vivid stories breathlessly recounted by actors and theater technicians about everything from bizarre auditions to haunted theaters. But little did he realize that on this one particular summer evening in Davis Theatre, Zimmerman would come upon a situation that would result in his own intriguing addition to theater lore.

Although the outsider standing on stage maintained a stony silence while he looked out into the theater house, as the auditorium seating area is termed, Zimmerman figured it was not a problem, that it was perhaps a campus visitor who had wandered in by mistake. It happened once in awhile. The main doors to the fine arts building in which the theater is housed are often kept open past midnight, as is the case on many college campuses.

"I wrote a few more notes," Zimmerman said. "Then this man crossed from a little bit stage left of center over to the stage left side. He stood there for awhile, and then he crossed back behind the backstage draping. That's when I lost sight of him."

Altogether, Zimmerman estimates the man spent about a minute on stage.

The middle of the stage was bare, although both wings (the sides of the stage) had partial sets under construction for the upcoming Meredith Willson musical. The reason Zimmerman hadn't seen the stranger before he appeared on the stage itself is because the partial set on stage right could easily have blocked his view of anyone coming from backstage until they were well on the main stage itself.

Whether it was his preoccupation with finishing the rehearsal notes or the lateness of the hour combined with his fatigue from having already put in a sixteen-hour day, Zimmerman didn't immediately register too much apprehension about the unexpected visitor. But the manner in which the incident occurred was unexpected and strange, he agreed.

However, when the man didn't come back into sight, Zimmerman put down his pencil and considered the situation a little more carefully.

"The only people in that theater in the summer were company members or folks I knew. I'd hired them all, I knew them all, and I didn't know this guy. Here he is at ten o'clock at night, walking around, not answering my question," he said.

Zimmerman decided at that point to "find out what's going on." If it was someone who'd wandered into the theater by mistake, he could direct the person to where he needed to be. But Zimmerman knew he also had a responsibility to take action should the person be an intruder bent on mischief.

As he climbed onstage, Zimmerman considered the options. The only way the man could have left the stage from where he'd lost sight of him was through a door in the back stage wall leading to a hallway. Beyond that door and to the left a few feet was the locked door into the theater shop. The scene shop does have a set of wide doors leading to an outside loading dock, but they were locked that night because the shop crew had gone home.

Through the stage door and to the right, about eight feet away, was a long hallway that runs alongside the theater.

"He had to have gone out that (stage) back door after I'd lost sight of him. So I got up and looked. He was gone. He'd left. He couldn't have gone down the spiral staircase," Zimmerman said, referring to a narrow, twisting set of metal steps that lead downward from one corner of the backstage to storage rooms for props and stage furniture. "I would have heard the 'clunk-clunk-clunk' of his footfalls."

Therefore, Zimmerman reasoned, he must have gone out the back door.

"There's a very limited traffic pattern outside that door. Someone has to go in one specific direction (to leave the building). So I went out the door and right where the two hallways meet, at that 'T' intersection, were a couple of the actors. I asked them if they'd seen this guy in a red shirt and blue jeans come out the door. They both said no, that no one had come out. I asked them how long they'd been standing there and they said they'd been chatting since rehearsal ended. He had to have gone someplace. I knew he hadn't gone down the spiral staircase. He just had to have gone out that door. But he didn't. So I didn't know where he went. It's that simple."

Zimmerman knew of no reason why the two actors would obfuscate the truth on the question of whether a stranger had come out the stage door or would want to mislead him in any way. Everyone associated with the theater company paid particular attention to building security issues because of the valuable props, costumes, and shop equipment that could be damaged or stolen.

The fact that Zimmerman didn't recognize the man, even though the theater house lights and the stage's work lights were still on, raised his concerns as well about his intentions. Yet, the man's apparent nonchalance at being seen hardly seemed to be the tactics of a would-be thief.

"So I don't know where he came from—backstage, from the shop or . . . He could have come in from (the shop), been strolling around for a time, and then come out onto the stage. When I first (glanced up) I thought it was an actor who'd stuck around after rehearsal and maybe wanted to talk to me. But then I didn't recognize him and I didn't recognize that he was any part of the university," Zimmerman said.

Even if the man had come in from the shop area, Zimmerman couldn't figure out how he would have gotten in there in the first place. All the shop doors were locked. The actors he talked to in the hallway seemingly would have noticed a stranger about.

The other oddity is that Zimmerman didn't hear any footsteps.

"That made me wonder, too. That was weird," he said. The wood stage floor is located above the theater's props and scenery storage rooms. It does creak a bit under a person's weight, Zimmerman added.

ZIMMERMAN SPENT A few more fruitless minutes looking for the intruder before locking up and heading home. He was still without any sort of explanation about the man's identity, where he'd come from, or, more importantly, where he'd gone to.

"At the time, I didn't think much about it except for wondering where the guy went," Zimmerman said. "It went to the back of my mind. But then I shared it with someone a few days later and that person said I saw Sanford Syse. The shape of his body, his relatively slight build, seemed to match (Syse's) description. The red shirt and the blue jeans were often what he was wearing. I'd never met him; I'd never seen his picture at that time."

This explanation seems straightforward enough. Sanford Syse designed the theater complex, helped found the summer theater with which Zimmerman was associated, and taught at the university for many years.

The problem?

Sanford Syse died in 1973.

The possibility that Zimmerman had seen the ghost of the theater's founder stunned him. He hadn't thought of a supernatural explanation for the stranger's appearance.

"He was as real as you or me," Zimmerman emphasized.

Even during his later conversation with another staff member, Zimmerman didn't present the problem in any context other than it being an issue of a stranger prowling around the theater.

"I was talking about it in reference to keeping the theater doors locked after hours. Here was a stranger walking around on stage and he could get hurt, or rip us off or something. I was talking from a security standpoint. I said I didn't know where he'd gone or how he got away or who he was. The person I was talking to made the connection to Sanford Syse."

Syse was an assistant professor of speech and theater at the university. He died of cancer at the age of forty on November 28, 1973, at a Madison, Wisconsin, hospital. His funeral in Blanchardville, Wisconsin, was notable because Syse had planned the entire service, down to who the eulogists would be and the hymns that would be sung. He received undergraduate and graduate degrees from the University of Wisconsin–Madison. Before joining the River Falls faculty in 1963, he was an assistant technical director for theater at the University of Illinois at Urbana. Before his death, Syse established a theater scholarship at River Falls and, more recently, the university's "black box" theater was renamed in his honor.

But on this night, Zimmerman knew little about Syse.

"I DIDN'T KNOW much of the history of Sanford Syse except for his name," Zimmerman recalled. "Now, subsequent to that night, I've learned a lot more. But right at the time I didn't think much about it except for wondering where the guy went. I'd never met (Syse); I'd never seen his picture. I saw it later at the dedication of the black box (theater) and I wish I would have known then what he looked like because I might have recognized him. I could see (the stranger's) face, but I just don't remember it."

The renaming of the black box after Syse did not take place until several years after Zimmerman's nighttime summer theater encounter.

Zimmerman found that there seemed to be some history among students and, perhaps, others with the ghost of Sanford Syse. He said that when he later described the incident to people, several noted that the attire of a red shirt and blue jeans is the way they see him. Zimmerman seemed somewhat surprised at the equanimity with which his encounter was treated by people who seemed unruffled at the prospect of discovering the theater might be haunted.

"I never thought it was a ghost at the time," Zimmerman said. Since the person he saw appeared for the entire world to be a fully three-dimensional human being, he had little reason to believe it was an apparition. "He looked absolutely real. It was only after I'd mentioned it to somebody that this guy was wandering around on stage during the season that they said it was probably the ghost of Sanford. I did not tell them the story to get a qualification on what it might have been or who it was."

While Zimmerman said it is still possible that the person he saw was simply a late night campus visitor who somehow ended up on stage, he doesn't think it likely.

"It could have been somebody from outside. Somebody who might have come in from the shop area. There are those big doors that connect the shop to the theater on the right side. He might have come through there and then onstage."

But he doesn't think that's the case. The man's rapid disappearance and odd behavior make him skeptical about that explanation. "He had to have been on the center of the main stage a good twenty or thirty seconds. He just looked around. People just don't do that (late at night). And he didn't say anything."

Zimmerman never saw the man again, nor was he ever able to pin an identity on him other than that offered by the people to whom he told the story—Sanford Syse.

"I wasn't looking for a theater ghost," Zimmerman laughed. "Believe me, I was just trying to get my job done that night. Somebody else brought up the idea of a ghost. To this day I don't know if it was a ghost. I do know it was a bunch of anomalies that I can't answer in terms of why he wouldn't answer me, why he just stood there looking around, why he physically disappeared out of a door that nobody saw him leave through."

Zimmerman is a professor on the university faculty. In all the years since that one summer night, he has never seen anything the slight bit anomalous—supernaturally speaking—in the university theater. He seems comfortable in talking about this single visit by what he has come to believe was the ghost of Sanford Syse. And he thinks he knows why he came back.

"I think he did a good job of designing the theater. For a space that was built in the 1970s, it's still functioning pretty well today. That might have been his motivation (in coming back). It certainly would have accounted for the body language I saw when he seemed to be looking around the space, looking around the theater. Studying what was there."

Zimmerman believed Sanford Syse—if that's indeed who he saw—had a mission in being in Davis Theater. He was there for a reason. But he wasn't going to discuss it with the new professor.

NORTH CENTRAL COLLEGE is situated on fifty-six beautiful acres in the heart of one of northern Illinois's most picturesque small towns, Naperville. The college's nearly 2,000 students come from twenty-five states and dozens of foreign countries to pursue studies in over fifty undergraduate majors and graduate programs.

But outside the theater department, few of those students may know that the college's main auditorium—Barbara Pfeiffer Theater—has something of a legacy of ghostly goings-on.

Pfeiffer Hall itself is named after the mother of a major college benefactor. The large theater accommodates over 1,000 audience members on the main floor and in the balcony.

Some audience members are permanent residents.

According to a former theater student, in the late 1980s, late night flash photographs taken in the theater seemed to reveal some interesting subjects, especially at the top of the balcony around the light booth. It's some sixty feet long and eight feet wide. The booth had three exits, one on each end and one closer to the middle. One photograph taken inside the booth facing the west side apparently revealed a face in the door window. No outside lights were on, nor was anyone standing outside the door.

The former student said an enlargement of the photo revealed what looked to be the fully three-dimensional head and shoulders of an older man.

That could also explain the curious sensations visitors sometimes sense in the light booth.

"The usual feeling in the booth is one of being watched," the former student said.

It might be that the watching is carried out by one of the three ghosts said to reside in Pfeiffer Theater:

The first is an unnamed drama teacher who, according to the legend, shot himself in the head after suffering a bout of depression. His office is near Pfeiffer Theater. The office door has slammed open and shut without anyone nearby and, in the old office itself, a jar of pencils once had the tendency to slide from one side of a desk to another.

A second ghost is reputedly Barbara Pfeiffer herself. She is known as the woman in the second seat of the second row. According to one story, she died while watching a play in the early part of the twentieth century. Her body was taken to the cloakroom before being removed from the building. The old cloakroom is one massive cold spot, the former student said.

Finally, there is Charlie, the theater janitor, who died unexpectedly at home. His main haunt is on the west stairwell and in the balcony. His face is that of the man who mysteriously appeared in the photo taken inside the light booth.

FREDRICA "FREDDY" SHATTUCK was a celebrated drama professor at Iowa State University. The university's old Shattuck Theater was named in her honor, and though that playhouse was torn down nearly a quarter century ago, Freddy's lingering presence, according to some, is still felt in the modern Fisher Theater, which sits atop a beautiful grassy knoll on the southeastern edge of campus.

Freddy's presence may be in more than just the memories of old-timers.

A former professor of theater told a newspaper reporter that "some weird things have happened in (Fisher Theater). Actors have heard voices; technicians have heard people call out to them. Sometimes, when I've been in there alone or with just a few other people, I could swear I've heard the chairs move as if there are people sitting in them."

The professor said whoever haunted the theater was the benevolent spirit of someone who was happy simply to remain involved with the ISU theater. That's why he thought it was probably the ghost of Freddy Shattuck. For instance, Miss Shattuck's old wheelchair was still in the prop room. Whenever it was used in a play, students claimed it would roll across the stage under its own power, stop, and then swing around toward the audience.

He also cited a story about a theater student working in the shop area who received a telephone call that an aunt was critically ill with cancer. Upon hearing the news, she ran to the restroom for a good cry. When she got back, a box of tissues had suddenly appeared in her workspace.

"Miss Shattuck is taking care of us," the professor observed.

"Good evening, Vincent."

An ordinary enough greeting one might say . . . unless it's being used to bid hello to a theater ghost.

That's what happens on occasion at the university theater in the eleven-story Price Doyle Fine Arts Building on the campus of Murray State University in Kentucky.

- During one particular performance, student technicians communicating with one another via headsets and microphones couldn't identify what caused a "lub-dub, lub-dub" echo in the headsets. It sounded just like a heartbeat.
- A student whose hands were full of soft drinks was startled when a stage door opened for him to pass through, and then closed after him.

- A couple of students misplaced a wrench they were working with and immediately blamed the ghost. "Vincent! Bring it back!" they shouted. The wrench suddenly reappeared with a decided *clunk*.

Most of the time, students and some staff said it was just a general feeling of being watched. But that isn't unusual in a facility where *watching* is a fact of life. The former tech director noted that theaters are places where fantasies are lived out by imaginative people. So he's not sure if Vincent really exists or not.

But whenever he arrived at the theater, he was always careful to greet Vincent by name. He didn't think it could hurt.

10

A Stately Presence

The ghost . . . reminds us that death is the one thing certain and the thing most uncertain; the bourn from which no traveler returns, except this one.

—Robert Aickman, *The Fontana Book of Great Ghost Stories*

CHRIS COWMAN HAS seen lots of strange things during his career in government and in the media, but little prepared him for that encounter in the Minnesota State Capitol building.

"It was something I'd never felt before," Cowman remembers of the evening in 1998 when he saw what he believes to have been a ghostly presence.

Cowman had an office on the second floor of the majestic 1905 Italian Renaissance-style building overlooking downtown St. Paul. At the time he was working in the legislature's internal communications department. During the capitol's early years, his workspace had been part of the original state

Supreme Court chambers complex, a large and airy room with high ceilings, but had since been divided into many smaller office cubicles. Cowman's small office had two doors, one leading out of the office and into a long, interior hallway; the other led into a larger room which also held a few small desks, office supplies, and a shared coffeepot.

"It was during a late night legislative session, probably ten or eleven o'clock," Cowman recalls. "I was in the office all by myself. I thought I heard something in that other office."

He got up from his desk and walked over to the door leading to the adjacent room, which was closed at the time. He peered through the door's glass panel into the other room.

He couldn't believe his eyes.

"What I saw was a white 'thing' behind the door."

The "thing" was in motion, moving as he watched it.

Cowman pushed the door open and went in. The object—whatever it was—had departed. He quickly recognized, however, that all was not quite correct.

"I felt something like a cold breeze. It just hit me. I can't even describe it. I felt something that scared the shit out of me. I looked around a little bit and wondered what it had been; then I thought, I'm getting the hell out of here."

He walked out without looking back.

In the days and months that followed, he never *saw* anything like that again.

Yet all through his time at the capitol he had what he termed "feelings" that would make him leery about staying in his office, especially after dark.

"I'd be in the office . . . and just get chills. Who knows what it was. But it was definitely something. When I talk about it, like even now, it still gives me a chill. It was something I've never felt before. Or since."

Chris Cowman now lives in Washington, D.C. and works in television news production. He is not alone with his suspicions that something more than memories of legislative boondoggles or eccentric politicians remains behind in the dim, nighttime hallways of the century-old Minnesota Capitol.

Over the years, different employees say they've seen ghostly figures or have had strong suspicions that the capitol is haunted.

A former Supreme Court marshal reported seeing the

murky form of a tall man in a dark suit lingering near a staircase; a cleaning woman was visibly distressed when something comparable to white smoke came rumbling through a
doorway, turned around, and then went back through, slam-
ning the door on its way out; a legislative aide says he always
had the sense he was being watched; and the retired director of
the house of representatives public information office had his
own encounters with the supernatural.

So routine did the sightings become and so common were
the discussions about the eerie experiences, that likely candidates for the spirits themselves were identified—the first, a
long-since-departed Minnesota Supreme Court justice, and the
other, one of the building's original workmen who, according
to legend, died in a fall from the capitol's unique suspended
cantilevered stairwell.

But after extensive interior remodeling to the building over
the past decades and more multi-million-dollar restorations
in the planning stages, the ghosts may at last be fading away.
Yet, the stories told by people like Chris Cowman of strange
shapes and odd noises, of fleeting glimpses of long dead public servants and sudden unnerving cold breezes, will probably
never completely vanish.

THE YEAR 2005 marked the centennial of the Minnesota State
Capitol building, a palatial, stone edifice perched on a high hill
overlooking downtown St. Paul.

The designer was St. Paul architect Cass Gilbert, a Zanesville,
Ohio, native who was virtually unknown at the time the Minnesota legislature awarded him the capitol commission in
1895. Formally opened nine years later, on January 2, 1905,
the state's foremost public building cost a then-considerable
$4.5 million to build. Gilbert's Minnesota successes catapulted
him to national prominence—he went on to become president
of the American Institute of Architects. Among his other note-
worthy architectural achievements were the Arkansas and
West Virginia state capitols, the United States Supreme Court
building in Washington, D.C., and one of the world's first sky-
scrapers, the Woolworth Building, in New York City. Gilbert
died in 1934.

Gilbert also decorated the building's interior and supervise its physical construction.

"In the old days, the architect, the painter, and the sculpt were frequently one and the same man. There is no reaso why they should not be so now," Gilbert wrote of his amazin abilities.

The Minnesota Capitol design and construction won acc lades from architects and designers from around the worl Many of Gilbert's design achievements were distinctive for th era: the lofty marble dome; the uses of multiple types of stor and marble in its construction; a magnificent and airy interi highlighted by historical murals; and a distinctive, fre standing staircase rising four stories, from the lower groun level to the third floor legislative galleries.

The exterior view of the capitol—built of white marbl and granite in the style of a Renaissance palace—is dom nated by a soaring dome over the central, three story rotund A brass ball covered in gold filigree sits atop the dome. Th Georgia marble and St. Cloud granite on the exterior are b two of the twenty different types of stone used throughout th building.

At the base of the rotunda is a sculptural grouping of fou golden horses pulling a chariot, called the *Quadriga*, or *Th Progress of the State*. It, too, is covered with gold leaf. Aroun the interior of the dome, regional and national artists create murals depicting the history of Minnesota and the Northwes Also along the rotunda walls are glass cases holding flags ca ried by Minnesota regiments in the Spanish American an Civil Wars.

Architecture critic Larry Millett wrote of the building more intriguing furnishings:

"Like other major public buildings of its time, the capito also is a gigantic repository of art in the form of painting sculpture, and various hortatory inscriptions designed to en courage pure and noble thinking. Much of this zealous, hig minded art seems merely quaint to modern eyes, yet there also something deeply touching about it."

Each floor has its own unique function. The main visitor en trance is on the first level, which also houses the Governor Reception Room. A Cass Gilbert-designed mahogany table i the centerpiece. Press conferences and various public events are held in the room.

The second floor holds chambers and offices for both the State Senate and the State House of Representatives and legislative staff members. Until they moved to a new building, the state Supreme Court offices, in the area where Chris Cowman worked, were also on this floor. The court continues to hear oral arguments in its second floor judicial chambers, which have been partially restored to their early twentieth-century appearance.

The house and senate public galleries rim the third floor.

A cafeteria is located on the ground floor, which is actually one level below the first floor. Cass Gilbert and assistant E. E. Garnsey laid out the restaurant to look like a turn-of-the-century German dining hall. It, too, has been restored to its original 1905 motif. The restaurant is open to the public when the legislature is in session.

But what of the less obvious capitol characteristic—the persistent perception that it also harbors a ghost or two?

To hear the stories is to think it unlikely that all of the witnesses have simply been putting in too many long hours poring over legislative minutiae.

The young Supreme Court marshal noted earlier happened also to be the daughter of a retired Chief Justice of that court. She told a reporter that she saw a "presence" near an elevator in the East Wing of the building. The "tall man in an old, dark suit" seemed to be beckoning to her.

Appropriately enough, one of the building's cleaning women saw a strange white, misty substance on a Friday the thirteenth, as she later explained to a reporter:

"I was reaching down for an extension cord while vacuuming and something white came out of this door, like smoke, and then it went back in and slammed the door. There are probably lots of (ghosts) in this building. I've heard doors rattling before at night."

A legislative aide came away from his capitol spirit encounter with feelings similar to others who think the place is haunted—that the entity is not at all frightening. The aide worked in the East Wing and often had the impression that he was being "watched."

"(The ghost) is pretty mild mannered; it seems to be there

just out of curiosity. Actually, I think it adds a little character to the capitol," he said at the time, adding that he believed it might have been the ghost of a Supreme Court justice. "It seems there is an aura of authority, like that of a justice."

ONE OF THE witnesses who talks most eloquently about the ethereal incidents at the State Capitol is LeClair "Lee" Lambert, the retired director of the house of representatives public information office.

Lambert spent nearly seventeen years working there and doesn't shy away from a discussion of the haunted side of the capitol, nor about his belief that history is about people and their relationship to a specific *place* and *time*, a far more personal connection than what may be found in books and mortar alone.

Further, Lambert's own, earlier, experiences in New York City with what he took to be the supernatural perhaps make him more attuned to the State Capitol's otherworldly denizens of the dark. Not only did he have some personal encounters with the capitol's supernatural side, he has developed something of a philosophy about whom and what these things might be.

"I would think that one reason ghosts appear is that (the capitol) is a place they loved and that was theirs in a way. They didn't want to move on or go anywhere else. Or maybe they couldn't find their way out. But I do think it all connects to the past, to some kind of history in a structure," Lambert says.

He notes that while ghosts sometimes prowl outside—in the open air as it were—it seems to be more common that they are usually inside enclosed spaces.

Lambert grew up in Amityville, N.Y., a town with its own association to supposed supernatural events. He studied at Hampton College in Virginia, Harvard University, and the University of Munich.

Lambert did not come lately to the world of ghosts and haunted places. It was during his time at Time-Life Books, where he was a researcher and writer, that Lambert had his first encounter with a ghost. He lived in an apartment in the West Village area of New York City, on the second floor of an old but nicely remodeled brick fire station on Twenty-First

Street, around the corner from the Chelsea Hotel between Eighth and Ninth Avenues. The time was the late 1960s.

The apartment on the first floor was vacant. Another apartment above him was rented by a different tenant. Lambert didn't know anything about the history of the building.

Of his suspicions that the apartment was haunted, Lambert says he didn't realize at first what had happened.

"A friend of mine was going to stop by and visit after I got home from work," he remembers. "But I got home early and decided to take a nap. It was an old fire station, so once you left the street level there was a staircase directly up to the second floor."

Each floor featured a separate landing for each apartment. Once visitors got to Lambert's second floor apartment, they had to follow a long railing around the stairwell to his main apartment door.

"I had left the door open downstairs on the street and also the door to my apartment. If you walked directly into my apartment there was a very small bedroom. If you turned right there was a bathroom and you could go through that and end up in the kitchen. A big bedroom was behind the kitchen. Well, I decided to take a nap in the small bedroom so at least he would know I was already home from work."

But Lambert's friend had a most unsettling experience.

"Later he told me that when he came up the stairs to my landing and made a turn around the railing he saw me standing in the doorway to my apartment. That would have been about twenty feet away from my front door. But when he got down to the doorway I wasn't there. He thought I'd gone through the bathroom and into the kitchen."

It wasn't Lambert standing in the doorway. He was sound asleep in the small bedroom.

"When he told me the story he asked if I'd been playing tricks on him. I said I'd been napping, that he'd seen me sleeping. I couldn't have come back through the living room, the kitchen, and the bathroom, and into that small bedroom without him seeing all that. He asked if I had a ghost or something. That was the first time I knew."

It was an experience that would change his perspective of what is real and what is not real.

"The next time *I* actually saw something," Lambert says. It was under equally perplexing circumstances. He's still not certain of just exactly *what* or *whom* he saw.

"I was having a dinner party with ten people, total. I had a large table around which we could sit on the floor, sort of a 1960s table with candles. It was a large, oriental table that everyone could easily sit around. Dinner was ready and I counted ten people, but I hadn't included myself. I did it again, and again there were ten people around the table waiting to eat. There should have only been nine people at the table because I was the tenth person. And I knew I hadn't invited an extra person, which was why I counted twice."

Lambert knew all the people relatively well. As he counted, though, he took note only of the "figures" he saw and didn't look carefully at their faces.

"I brought an extra plate out," he adds. "That's why I knew for sure I'd counted twice. I thought, well, okay, I guess I'd invited one more person and forgotten about it. But when I sat down there was an extra plate. I would have recognized a stranger. I thought I'd miscounted, that's all. But then I connected it to the time my friend came over and saw someone he thought was me standing in the door."

Lambert lived in the converted firehouse for about two years before leaving to study art history at the University of Munich. He sublet his apartment while he was out of the country. All of the odd incidents occurred before he left for Europe.

A third incident took place on a night when Lambert threw a party and had an apartment full of guests.

"I had the lights down low, a typical sixties evening with candles all over. One of my friends came over to me and asked who the person was sitting on my stereo console. I looked over. It was a man and he was dressed similarly to everyone else. He looked like he belonged. I said I wasn't sure who it was since the room was kind of dark. I thought it was rude to sit on someone's stereo. I walked over but by the time I got across the room he wasn't there. It was crowded, so by the time I'd made my way through the crowd he'd disappeared. I looked around the apartment but couldn't find him. I thought it was very odd."

Lambert moved to Minnesota in 1974 and took a job with the Urban League. He remained there for six years before joining the African-American Cultural Center where he helped draw up plans for a museum dedicated to African-American cultural and historical contributions to Minnesota and to the United States. Fund-raising efforts fell short of their goals and the museum was never built. In 1986 he accepted a job as assistant deputy sergeant-at-arms and coordinator of educational programs. He remained at the legislature until 2003, eventually rising to become a director of public information, supervising all the written and electronic communications disseminated by the State House of Representatives.

Along the way he also became something of the resident expert on the capitol ghosts.

"I'd heard that there was a ghost on the stairwell that goes from the ground level all the way up to the top," he says. "It's a floating, cantilevered staircase. If you look over the balcony it seems like you'd go straight down. I understand that one of the workers in the building died when he fell off the staircase. His ghost had been seen there."

Lambert also knew about the elderly gentleman ghost the young court assistant had seen near the former second floor Supreme Court chambers.

"I'd heard all those stories, but I hadn't heard about the one I saw," he offers. The one Lambert caught sight of was in the same second floor vicinity as the mysterious encounter Chris Cowman had with the formless white mass.

Lambert's office was in a former Supreme Court justice's office. It connected to a second, larger office that was also used as a storeroom. A water cooler, a small snack bar, and the office coffeepot were in there as well.

"I had gone into the connecting office to get water or coffee, I don't remember which specifically. So I was facing east with my back to the door that I had just come through, the one that connected to my office. And in the corner of that room I noticed a movement. When I turned to face it there was a hazy form, kind of wispy, that went across the room and out the main door into the hallway. It wasn't really a human shape as such, but a wispy, smoky kind of thing, like a plume. Grayish, not white. Very thin and almost as high as the room itself."

Lambert said the form floated slowly across the room in a "curvy" sort of movement.

"It wasn't moving very fast because I certainly had enough

time to see it. It just went out the door and into the inner hall-way. I thought, well, that's different. We must have another ghost or something," he recalls with a laugh. "I didn't think it was natural because it happened so fast, for one thing."

Lambert mentioned the incident to his assistant at the time.

"He told me that he'd never said anything but that he'd felt (a presence) in the office. That 'something' was there."

Lambert never had the sense that whatever was lingering in the capitol was an evil being or an angry presence. Quite to the contrary, he found that any time he had the sensation of someone watching him, or some invisible presence standing about in the same room, it was reassuring, almost comforting somehow, to know that a few of those thousands whose careers had been spent in the capitol loved the place so much they refused to move on.

Even when Lambert thought his eyes were deceiving him he didn't flinch or draw back. Such was the case when the offices were being renovated and Lambert, with his assistant, decided to check on the progress of the reconstruction.

"We decided to go up about five o'clock. The door was open to 216D, which were our offices. There was lots of plaster dust and so forth. We walked down the hall and into the conference room. There's a door back into our office from the conference room. The door was open when we went past it. We went on down and into the conference room. Nobody was around. Just bare walls. We came back through the conference room and the door that had been open was closed. Now, these are old, heavy oak doors that do not close by themselves."

Workers had gone home for the day. No one was about, Lambert said.

"The temperature had also changed," he adds. "There was definitely something different when we came back through there with the door closed. It was like someone was in there, a presence. We felt something. And not just the temperature change. It was also the feeling, like someone was watching us in there."

Lambert calls the sensation a sort of "aura."

"You know how if a group of people have been together and they've been arguing or debating and angry and you feel the tension? That's what I mean by aura. There was something intense in the air."

Lambert doesn't think the presence in that office was the same one seen by the young Supreme Court marshal sometime before. The marshal was the daughter of a former Supreme Court justice. She had spent a lot of time visiting her father's office over the years and had several encounters with the very distinct ghost of a tall man wearing a dark brown suit. She saw him near the second floor elevator. That ghost, some believe, is reputedly Justice Brown, a member of the Court from 1909 until 1913, when he died.

"If I remember correctly," Lambert says of the courtly ghost, "she had also seen it standing in its long black robes near the old Supreme Court chambers."

Lambert also cites the case of a senate staff member.

"It was about six o'clock at night. People had gone home. It was a day on which there was no senate session. He was in his office on the senate side of the building when he looked up to see someone standing in the doorway."

The senate staffer asked if the person needed some assistance. The person in the doorway turned on his heels and walked away. The staff member got up and walked after him. The hallway was dark and empty.

"He hadn't heard any of the ghost stories," Lambert says. "He told someone what happened. The other person said it was just the ghost of the capitol."

Lee Lambert grew used to the doubt with which he was greeted by others when he described the experiences he'd had.

"Some people believed it, but others were skeptical. I think after the renovation (of the capitol) there wasn't much left of a presence. Maybe Justice Brown couldn't find his way around any more."

He thinks the most important element in his encounters with the capitol spirits is that he's had an open mind, a willingness to suspect that some things exist beyond the here and now.

"You have to see (a ghost) objectively, and not be afraid, especially when you see it for the first time. Being cognizant of the fact that (the supernatural) does exist has a lot to do with it, or at least believing that it does exist."

Lambert did not leave the ghosts behind when he departed from the capitol. A longtime friend named David died suddenly shortly after Lambert retired. Yet his friend remains a central part of Lambert's life.

"David exists, I know that for a fact, because he comes and goes all the time. People look at me strangely when I say that, but those who knew David believe that."

Lambert says that in the past he saw David's spirit, but those occasions are becoming less frequent.

"I don't see him anymore, but I feel his presence. I consider him my guardian angel. He protects me."

Free guided tours of the Minnesota State Capitol are offered each day year-round on the hour by members of the Minnesota Historical Society. Sightings of long-departed Supreme Court justices are not guaranteed.

11

Find My Bones

He lives, he wakes,—'tis Death is dead, not he.

—Percy Bysshe Shelley, *Adonais*

ANN BELL ADAM politely excused herself when her close friend Virginia Gregory answered the ringing telephone. The call was from Virginia's doctor-husband who was out of town on business. Mrs. Adam, who had dropped in for a chat on that warm October afternoon, didn't want to intrude on the intimacies of the couple's conversation. She headed toward the kitchen in the Gregorys' rambling, ramshackle mansion on the outskirts of Gulfport, Mississippi.

As she pushed through the kitchen door, however, she was startled to see a boy in his early teens with the extension telephone pressed to his ear. He was obviously listening intently to the Gregorys' exchange. Odd, too, because Mrs. Adam thought she and Virginia were alone in the house.

"Son, Mrs. Gregory is talking to her husband on the telephone. You shouldn't be listening in. Put down that phone," Mrs. Adam admonished.

He looked over at her, his face expressionless. He meekly obeyed her orders, replaced the phone in its cradle, turned on his heel, and walked out the back door.

Within a few seconds, however, Mrs. Adam realized something was very wrong. The Gregorys had seven children in their blended family and this boy *was definitely not* one of them. Nor had she ever recalled being introduced to him as a family friend during one of her numerous previous visits.

Clearly he was a stranger who had no business sneaking about the house.

She quickly followed him out the door, yet he seemed to have vanished into thin air. Within the brief few moments he had been out of her sight, she doubted he could have found a hiding place so quickly in the wide open yard outside the kitchen door.

Just at that moment, Virginia came out the back door searching for her friend, who turned to her and said:

"Virginia, I do believe I've just seen your ghost!"

Perhaps most startling of all, however, is that Virginia Gregory wasn't all that surprised. That ghostly young man was but one of the several ghosts with which she and her family had become intimately acquainted over the preceding six years and which they would see again in the future—including this poignant revenant of a teenage boy, the fourteen-year-old son of former owners, who was killed decades before when the tractor he was driving overturned on the property, crushing him underneath.

Mrs. Adam's accidental encounter also reinforced for Virginia and her family the accurate, albeit notorious, reputation of being in one of the most haunted houses in the United States, so named by noted parapsychologist Dr. J. B. Rhine, who interviewed the family and visited the home. He told them that he'd never come across such a "variety of manifestations" in any house he'd heard of in the United States. They included at least two other ghosts, adult males; poltergeist-type activity, such as knockings and raps; disembodied voices and unsettling moans; and cold spots that sometimes followed family members about.

Interestingly, Ann Bell Adam—who has since passed away—had a family connection to another infamous American haunting. She was a direct descendant of a family that had their own run-ins with the supernatural, in the form of the so-called Bell Witch of Tennessee, Kate Batts.

While the casual observer might dismiss Mrs. Adam's claims, and wonder why Virginia did not do the same, she described her friend as someone she "knew well, she was my best friend," and certainly not the sort of person to create teenage eavesdroppers out of whole cloth.

There is another mystifying angle to that particular afternoon's adventure, Virginia said: "I didn't hear any of that (exchange) and I was on the extension sitting in the living room. I didn't hear him hang up, I didn't hear their conversation. You always can hear that on an extension, but I didn't."

THE GREGORYS' HOME was not an archaic antebellum pile of timber and brick tucked away at the end of a long drive under sheltering white oaks, as might be expected, but rather an "enormous, unattractive frame house," in Virginia's words, that had been built in 1915 by one of Gulfport's founding families, including the daughter of one of the city's founders, Captain Joseph Thomas Jones.

Jones and Gulfport's other founding father, William Harris Hardy, were businessmen associated with the Gulf and Ship Island Railroad Company in the late nineteenth century.

Hardy was a lawyer who suggested that a railroad line be built from the Gulf of Mexico to Jackson, Tennessee, while he was surveying the right-of-way for another rail line, the New Orleans & Northeastern Railroad. Where the two roads would intersect, the city of Hattiesburg was founded. It was named for Hardy's wife. The north-south railroad he proposed became the G&SI. The site on the gulf that became the terminus for the road became the struggling city of Gulfport. Hardy hoped that his new city would one day rival New Orleans and Mobile for industrial commerce. He died in 1917.

Jones, on the other hand, was a Pennsylvanian who attained

riches from oil wells in his home state. Captain Jones—he was wounded in the Civil War as a nineteen-year-old conscript—spent a large portion of his oil fortune pursuing his childhood fascination with railroads. He took over the G&SI when it went bankrupt in 1895 without completing its leg to Jackson, Tennessee. He finished the job. When the government turned down his request to dredge a channel between Ship Island and the railroad terminus at Gulfport, he invested millions of his own dollars dredging the channel, building Gulfport Harbor and investing in city construction. In his later years—he died in 1916—Jones became known as the "Grand Old Man of Gulfport."

ALTHOUGH THE HOUSE was built by members of Captain Jones's family, there is no evidence he lived in it since he died less than a year after it was built.

Several families moved in and out of the house over the next forty years until Dr. Kendall Gregory and his wife, Virginia, bought it in 1957 from Virginia's ex-husband, who had acquired it as an investment property. By the time the Gregorys moved in, the house had a reputation for being haunted, although little verifiable information had been available to them about the circumstances surrounding the rumors.

"It was a little subdivision," Virginia said of the area of Gulfport in which they lived. "There were some medium-price houses a block before you got to our house, then some very nice houses that went up the street past our house toward Bayou Bernard and our harbor. They were perfectly beautiful places, so they were all very nice. Ours was by far the most bedraggled. Just a towering, awful-looking thing. . . . It didn't have any saving virtues except that it was big enough for us and our children." She and her husband bought it for what she termed a "reasonable" price.

Despite the dilapidated condition of the old house, its beautiful location near a bayou on the outskirts of the city nearly made up for its appalling defects. The house's physical setting was a delight, Virginia said, especially the graceful oak trees that dotted the lawn, which itself swept down to their own private small harbor on the bayou. Wisteria and azaleas grew in abundance along a lengthy trellis leading down to the shoreline.

"But old houses decay as the years pass by. By the time we got out of there I can't tell you how happy I was," Virginia conceded.

The family didn't put many resources into remodeling because its general deterioration, even before their arrival, made it virtually beyond repair. By 1969, twelve years after setting up housekeeping there, the Gregorys moved out and rented a house elsewhere. They had plans for subdividing the five acres of property on which the house sat and perhaps rebuilding, but that didn't pan out.

A few months later, an arsonist torched the mansion.

"The house was notorious anyway," Virginia said. "Everybody knew it was haunted, and so teenagers were in there all the time. We couldn't keep them out."

Although the Gregorys identified a suspect for police, Virginia said, no one was ever arrested or prosecuted for burning down the house.

THE GREGORYS WERE a blended family—Virginia and Kendall, whom she called Greg, had children from previous marriages, and three of their own. She had two boys, Parham and Ricky; his children included Grier, later an attorney; and Tucker. Together the Gregorys had Kendall, Jr.; a girl, Virginia, called "Sister" by her family; and John, the baby of the family.

Skepticism was the order of the day from the beginning that all the unusual, albeit intermittent, incidents for which they kept records didn't add up to anything more than coincidence or the natural rasps and groans of an old wood frame home plagued by the intense moisture that comes from living in the Deep South, and in desperate need of repair.

They certainly didn't want to characterize the place as haunted, Virginia Gregory emphasized.

"We didn't believe in (the supernatural), nobody did. We thought 'how ridiculous.' We just had to be absolutely certain" of everything.

Even when visitors and family members first started talking

about particularly odd occurrences, the idea that they were supernatural in origin didn't immediately occur to them. Nonetheless, Virginia started paying more attention to the stories she was hearing from her family and from visitors. "People did have very peculiar things happen to them," she said.

For example, one woman friend staying overnight talked to Virginia about waking up in her bedroom to find a man standing beside her bed. She didn't have the reaction one might imagine . . . she could see the opposite wall through his body.

"But, you know, you can't believe 90 percent of what people tell you. So I looked upon all that with a jaundiced air, to tell you the truth," the mother and stepmother of seven children said.

However, when Virginia enumerates those small "things," their sheer peculiarity makes one wonder that any family wouldn't think some unseen forces might have been at work. She itemizes them with astonishing clarity.

"A rock came through the window one night into the children's room," Virginia said matter-of-factly. "On another night, I heard something banging on the window when everyone was gone. I called a neighbor and she sent her husband over with a gun to walk the grounds with me because I was so scared. We couldn't find anything. The ground was soft, so he said look (tomorrow) to see if there are any footprints in the soil. I did and of course there were no footprints."

She never did figure out who or what was causing that. It happened two or three times at the window on the long porch just off the Gregorys' bedroom on the second floor. This porch, termed a sleeping porch in the old days, was a screened-in room on which family members would sleep at night during humid summers before air conditioning eliminated their usefulness. It ran the length of the three bedrooms. There were no tree branches nearby, nor any loose siding or wobbly windowsills, according to Virginia.

"It was as if someone was throwing dirt clods against the window screens," she added, noting that it was highly unlikely anyone would have been doing that in the middle of the night.

Virginia had been tossing and turning on a different night, unable to sleep. A sudden clicking, as of long fingernails against the couple's headboard, nearly sent her shooting straight up into the air. It also awoke her husband who threw on the lights and looked all around the bed. Nothing was to be found. They turned the lights back off and tried to settle down.

That wasn't the end of it, she told writer and paranormal expert Susy Smith: "I lay there and thought 'What am I going to do if this thing starts banging on the headboard of the bed?' About thirty or forty-five minutes later I found out. There was this resounding crash, as if somebody had taken the flat of his hand and slapped the headboard. It was the loudest thing I ever heard. I screamed!"

Again, Kendall got out of bed to check out the room. The couple tried to duplicate the loud slap but could not produce anything that came even remotely close to it. Kendall even went downstairs to the den—directly underneath their bedroom—and jabbed a pool cue against the ceiling to see if that approached what Virginia had heard. It did not.

On another day, a metronome began to tick away on its own, almost as if somebody was frustrated that it wasn't keeping a proper beat.

But what finally convinced Virginia that the house might well indeed be haunted by an entity trying to *communicate with them* were the series of "candle incidents" in the summer and fall of 1963, at about the same time that Ann Bell Adam came upon the boy in the kitchen.

Virginia explained: "Grier and I had taken a kitten to the veterinarian and came home with it at about ten o'clock in the morning. We walked into the kitchen so I could warm some milk for it, and I reached under the sink to get something. And there was a little, red candle burning down there. I thought my maid had put it there for some reason. I went upstairs and asked her why she was burning a candle under the kitchen sink. She said that she hadn't put it there. It was the second one she'd found. The other one had been in the glasses cabinet. She'd decided not to mention it to me" because she thought it might have been someone out to frighten her.

Virginia called her husband, who was at work. The children were at school. At Dr. Gregory's suggestion, she notified the sheriff because she thought someone might have gotten in the house while she'd been gone and was trying to harm the family or perform some sort of mystic ritual because the house was "haunted."

"It hadn't been burning long enough to leave any of the soft wax on the wood that it was standing on. They weren't even our candles; it was a little red candle like on a birthday cake. It just didn't make any sense at all, but you don't think that way. You think somebody is trying to burn your house down."

The maid had been working for many years for the Gregorys and wasn't a suspect in the mischief. "She was incapable of doing anything like that," Virginia said.

A few months later in 1963, a frightening episode involving young Parham's jacket persuaded Virginia that perhaps they were dealing with something not readily explainable.

Parham had come home from school, greeted his mother, and gone up to his room. He came rushing back downstairs with his blue school jacket in hand. Across the back of it were several burned holes, several still smoldering. He told his mother that the jacket had burst into flames when he entered the room. He'd put out the fire and took it to show Virginia.

Parham denied any culpability, and his mother believed him. There didn't seem to be any reason for him to ruin the jacket.

"I was meant to find those burning candles and that smoldering jacket," Virginia believed. Any of those incidents, if left undiscovered, would have burned the house to the ground. She further believed that the small fires were a way in which "someone" was trying to contact the family, trying to call attention to himself.

It was at that point that Virginia felt compelled to contact the family of the young boy who had been killed there. She first got in touch with the child's aunt. Oddly enough, Virginia discovered that the aunt and her family were in the fire protection business.

"She came over and talked about how haunted the house was," Virginia recalled. It turns out that nearly everyone who lived there before the Gregorys had had peculiar experiences, she said.

Eventually the dead boy's mother came for a visit as well. She indicated which room had been her son's as they walked through the house.

"I told them the boy had been seen around the house. (The

mother) wanted to see him as well," Virginia said. However, that did not happen.

Meanwhile, the ghost boy made several more appearances.

A woman who worked for the Gregorys drove up early one winter morning to see a youth of about fourteen in the yard looking up into the trees. She parked, got out, and went over to ask him what he wanted. He vanished.

Once he came walking down the driveway, Virginia said. A man working for the family doing some cleaning saw him through the living room windows and went to the front door to let him in. The boy walked on by and headed toward the back kitchen door. Curious, the man who'd been cleaning went back to the kitchen, opened the door, and went out. The boy never showed up.

Oddly, the young boy was never seen in the same place twice.

It was not long after the boy's mother and aunt visited that Ann Bell Adam had her run-in with the kitchen boy. Thinking there might be a connection between the dead child and Mrs. Adam's experience, Virginia got hold of a school picture of the boy taken around the time of his unintentional death. She showed it to Mrs. Adam, who was reluctant at first to identify the picture as the boy. She didn't want to upset Virginia, nor did she want word to get back to the boy's mother that her son was "earthbound."

Later, she admitted to Virginia Gregory that the boy in the picture was the same person she'd seen in the kitchen, and signed an affidavit to that effect, which she provided to writer Smith:

"When I arrived at Mrs. Gregory's house a little later she showed me a small, clear picture, of the type taken at schools for the children's class pictures, depicting the head and shoulders of a young boy. I was very certain and I am still convinced that it was the same boy I had seen that afternoon; however, I told Mrs. Gregory that I couldn't be sure one way or the other. Mrs. Gregory then told me that the picture was of the boy who had formerly lived in that house and had been killed there. On my arrival home I told my husband what had happened and that I identified it as the same boy."

Later that same fall, in November 1963, there was a bizarre

incident in one of the upstairs bedrooms. Two of the Gregory boys told their mother they'd found blood on a windowsill. When Virginia looked, she found two blood smears. Her husband took it to a hospital lab where it was determined to be of human origin. None of the children had cut themselves but the littlest boy, Kendall, did have a nosebleed, his mother said. However, she thought it unlikely he would have smeared blood from his nose in a bedroom in which his brothers were sleeping. She didn't think the blood smears had "happened normally."

"THAT SORT OF thing went on" all the time, Virginia said. For those first six years between 1957 and 1963, the Gregorys continued to be cautious in assessing the origins of the cockeyed events at their mansion. They especially doubted some of the complaints raised by their children.

"There was this racket on the third floor, but it was empty," she noted. "We had a pool table up there, but we didn't use it. When we first moved in the children talked about sounds from that third floor like somebody was rolling a hoop, and going up and down the stairs. This happened before we accepted the fact that the house was haunted."

THEN NINETEEN-YEAR-OLD GRIER saw "the ghost in the study."

At least as it concerned Virginia, that event moved her from mere suspicion that her house was haunted to an absolute certainty that several different entities were likely at play in her sprawling home on the bayou.

She talked about that night and what her son told her about the event: "The air conditioner had gone out in his bedroom so he went downstairs to spend the night sleeping in the den. Nobody knew he'd gone down there. I came downstairs for breakfast about the time he came out of the study. He said 'I hate to tell you this, but this house is haunted.' We'd already suspected that something slightly awry was going on."

Grier told his stepmother that he had been sleeping on the couch when he was awakened well before sunrise by the den door slowly opening and then closing shut. He looked over in that direction. A young boy about the age of his stepbrother was standing in the doorway. At first that's who Grier thought it was, his stepbrother.

But it wasn't Kendall, Jr., at all.

This youngster in the den was translucent. Grier saw the wall paneling through his body.

He watched the unnaturally bright, slightly smoky figure walk slowly across the room with the sort of motion one associates with a low-grade video surveillance camera, a jerky kind of movement in which the subject appears to move only every few seconds. Further, the den seemed to be aglow from a soft light radiating from the boy. He appeared to grow in height until he reached a corner bookshelf and then disappeared. The room darkened upon his leaving. Grier turned on two lamps so that he could look more closely at the area where the figure vanished. He didn't find anything amiss, turned off the light closest to the couch, where he laid back down. He eventually fell back asleep.

His first inclination when he awoke a few hours later was to think the earlier episode had been but a dream. However, he saw one of the lights he'd turned on still burning—the one next to the bookcase—and that there were signs of rain outside the windows. He'd remembered hearing the rain during the boy's sudden vanishing act.

THE CONTINUING SKEPTIC in the family was Dr. Kendall "Greg" Gregory, a faithful man of medical science who didn't believe—or would not admit to believing, Virginia said—that other than purely explainable phenomena occur in the world of the living. She remembered amiably that researcher J. B. Rhine called him "the good doctor mundane" for his careful manner. Dr. Gregory died in 1974.

"He didn't even believe it when Grier saw the ghost. He didn't believe anything," Virginia said.

Disbelief was more difficult to maintain for the good doctor after a particular November night . . . when he himself was awakened by horrifying moaning in the couple's bedroom that seemed to come from absolute nothingness. The spacious bedroom with its own built-in fireplace was situated directly above the den.

The doctor described the experience in an affidavit for writer Susy Smith:

"I listened to (the moaning) for perhaps a minute. It seemed to be right in my bedroom, so I got up as quietly as I possibly could and moved toward the window away from the side of the bed to see if I could pinpoint the location of the sound. I finally walked toward the dresser so that the moaning was between me and the bed. This was approximately the last time I heard it because I then advanced very quickly to the spot where it came from and it stopped. When I turned on the light there was not a thing of any unusual nature to be seen in the room."

Virginia Gregory did not hear the moaning because she had the habit of wearing wax earplugs to bed. Later, her husband told her what had happened. She was a bit more colorful on what he said his actions were at the time, as he related them.

"He got up out of the bed and 'surrounded' it," she said. "He walked around the room to be sure it wasn't coming from outside (the house). He got in between the sound and the fireplace to be sure it wasn't coming *out* of the fireplace. It was in the center of our room. I slept (through it) because I had those earplugs."

Once the moaning stopped, there was little else he could do and he went back to bed. He didn't tell his wife about it until later and even then in a general sort of way. Virginia said her husband didn't discuss the incident in great detail. "He was a great believer in not upsetting things any more than they were already upset. I guess he figured that if he admitted it, we'd all go berserk."

Others in the house also heard the moaning on that night, according to Virginia. The doctor's own younger son, Tucker, heard it from a bedroom down the hall from his father's and stepmother's. Virginia Gregory's older son, Parham, heard the moaning from his room at the other end of the hallway. She said neither boy could pinpoint its source.

Virginia, however, didn't have long to wait for her own introduction to the foul racket that had so disagreeably disrupted her husband's sleep.

"I was writing in my report to Dr. Rhine. I had kept a journal and I was trying to think about how to describe the moaning sound," she said of that day soon after her husband told her about the nighttime commotion. She kept the journal, at Dr. Rhine's request, to write up the various phenomena as they occurred. Usually her entries were made at the writing desk in the master bedroom. She was having some difficulty putting into words her husband's experience as he had related it, since she had not personally heard it.

At that moment, a cry such as she had never encountered burst from the center of the bedroom.

"It was horrendous. I can't compare it to anything . . . an indescribable, bubbling moan, a horrible, hideous sound as if someone was in unbearable agony. It lasted about fifteen seconds," she said.

The thought that her children might be playing a nasty trick on her crossed her mind. They were such over-the-top groans that it seemed to be something straight out of a Hollywood horror movie. She checked around the house to see where the children were and what they might be up to; her husband was away. One older boy was studying in his room. The smaller children were taking their baths. A quick check to see if a dog outside might be the culprit was equally unproductive.

"Then I went into the kitchen and drank a glass of milk to try to calm my nerves," she told writer Smith. Heading back for her bedroom, she got her second surprise of the evening.

"As I returned across the living room, in the far end toward the den I saw a very round, white, clear flash of light. The lamps were on in the other end of the long room, but the place where I saw the light was rather dimly illuminated. The flash was like the light that would come from a camera flash bulb, but small, round, and bright. It was followed by a 'flick' sound like the one that occurs when lightning strikes close to your house. The weather was quite calm, however."

The weather may have been calm but Virginia was not. She was terribly frightened by the harrowing noises and now the equally strange flash of light. As the night wore on she found it difficult to get to sleep. She got up and telephoned a friend from the bedroom extension, hoping that the sound of another adult voice would calm her tattered nerves. The voice did, but not a man's heavy tread she now heard coming her way from the sleeping porch. She put the telephone down and cautiously peered through the porch door. No one was about, as she had somehow expected. It wasn't the first time there had been distinct footsteps coming from out there.

"THE QUESTION WE had the whole time we lived there was: *Why* is this particular house haunted?" she noted. "When Dr. Rhine said it was the most haunted house he'd ever heard of . . . that became the question. Why? You could understand if the same (activity) went on over and over and over again, but all this was an entirely different kind of thing. They'd play odd little tricks. Like the time the man came to tune the piano in the study. He had an electric work light that he put down inside the piano. When he got into the study, the light wouldn't work. He went out to the living room, plugged it in, and it worked just fine. Then he tried all the (electrical) plugs in the study. The light worked in all of them except the one by the piano." Virginia believed it was another "joke" being played by one of the resident ghosts.

NEARLY EVERYONE IN the household was affected during the twelve years the family spent there, including the youngest of the children.

"Kendall, who was about four or five years old at the time, said he didn't want to sleep in his room any more because there was a 'bogeyman' in there," Virginia remembered.

Now, a sentiment such as this is hardly the exception for small children squeamish about creatures skulking about in the nighttime. Bogeymen in bedroom closets may be as old as time.

But what if the bogeyman itself could very well *be real* because, of course, the house itself is *haunted*?

"I woke up one night when I was about five and the closet door of my room was moving back and forth," Kendall, Jr., said later in an interview. "I didn't think much about it and went back to sleep. Later I woke up again and there was something staring at me in the face. It was leaning over with its face close to mine. It looked like a boy, but I couldn't see it clearly."

Kendall leapt out of bed and turned on the light, but the thing had disappeared. Another late night visit a few days afterward was of a different sort, as his mother remembered:

"He saw the closet door open and a type of light come out," his mother said he told her. "It passed across the room, opened the other door, and went out. Now, why it opened the door, I don't know. I said, 'Honey, you just had a bad dream.' Finally we had to move him out of the room. I couldn't leave him in there any longer because he was just too terrified."

Virginia said they never discussed ghosts in front of their small children for fear that it might upset them.

There were four bedrooms on the second floor. Kendall and Virginia used the largest of them as the master bedroom, the boys still living at home shared two others, and little Virginia, or "Sister," had the middle bedroom.

Sometimes when visitors stayed overnight, Sister had to sleep in a spare bunk in little Kendall's room. That's where her first encounter with the family's haunted side of life took place, when she was about six, according to Virginia Gregory, though no one had mentioned anything to her about the house being haunted, and it came well before Kendall's own experience with the resident bedroom "bogeymen."

On one of those nights when she was sharing Kendall's room, something awoke her. She looked over toward the closet and saw the door slowly open, a light emerge, float toward the hall door, which itself then opened. The light went through the door, which closed behind it.

Though Sister told both Kendall and her mother what happened, neither one was inclined to believe her.

Then the light came again. It was sometime later, and again Sister was staying in one of the bunk beds in Kendall's room.

"I woke up about two in the morning and the closet door opened and it came out," the girl told writer Susy Smith. "It wasn't like fire, but looked like the heat waves over a fire . . . but glowing. It was exactly like that. I couldn't get the covers over my head like I usually do at night when I'm scared. I was struggling and trying to get under the covers but I couldn't and finally it went through my feet and I could feel this cold chill coming up my legs. It came around, like through me. I had my eyes shut. All of a sudden it got real dark, and then it got light again."

In September 1967, Virginia said her stepson, Grier, and two fellow law students—both young women—decided to test the family's theory that the den seemed to be the center of supernatural activity. They organized an informal séance that commenced shortly before midnight and stretched on into the early morning hours.

"We'd been through all kinds of hell," Virginia said, "but (Grier) wanted to see it, he wanted to see what would happen. And he wasn't afraid; I don't know why . . . I was terrified."

According to a later interview with writer Smith, Grier said he and the girls sat up all night, usually with the lights turned low or off. Only a bit of light from some outdoor lighting came in through the curtained windows. Within the first few hours, they heard sounds like that of soft music, talking, and laughter. It was usually muffled, but clear enough that they thought it came from one specific corner of the room. A "tinny" recording of an old vocal jazz record was equally discernible.

A light on an electric coffeepot they'd had in the den seemed to bounce around, even following their verbal directions when they told it which way to move.

At various times during the night, the trio claimed to have been able to see indistinct figures moving about the room—a man in a striped shirt, another wearing a sort of white robe. Another appeared to be staring at them as he leaned against a card table.

Among the furniture in the den was a square coffee table situated in front of a circular sofa in the same corner Grier had seen the ghostly figure on the night his bedroom's air conditioner broke down.

On this night one of the dim figures they'd seen swirling about the room made an unusual personal approach. "Grier said this figure came and sat down on the edge of the cocktail table," Virginia said. "Grier reached out his hand, the figure reached out its hand, and they passed through one another."

One of the women excused herself to get a drink of water in the kitchen. As she returned the other two noticed that a tall man in formal wear followed her back in. He leaned up against the door frame and stared at them.

The final specter was that of a little girl with Shirley

Temple-like blond curls. She wore a sweet, ruffled party dress. On her tiny feet were dainty ballet slippers. Her arms extended out to Grier and the young women as if in supplication, or perhaps appealing for assistance of some sort.

The three young people could not identify any of the figures as individuals with whom they were familiar or had ever seen before, alive *or dead*.

What Grier's experience did do, according to Virginia, was solidify a belief that at least a few of the explanations for the supernatural events in the mansion extended back to a raucous era during the Second World War when the place had been used as a non-commissioned officers (NCO) club for armed forces personnel stationed in and around Gulfport.

Later events would buttress that conclusion.

But on this night of the young trio's strange encounters, at least some of what they experienced might have been caused by sitting for too long in dim light or darkness, Virginia believed. It's possible some of it came from imagining things, she said. But she insisted that the clearly defined figures—especially that of the child and the male figures—were the product of genuine late night phantasms.

Another complication stemmed from one of the young women, however, who later declined to verify the account of the other two. She thought some of the music and singing they heard might have been caused by the whine of the air conditioner; however, the unit was not on that night, according to Grier and the other woman. It was late September and the heat was tolerable.

The reluctant witness did assert that what most impressed her that night were the swirling pinpoints of light that she thought could have been stirred up by air movement, with reflections caused by the faint light in the room. She did not want to verify the other appearances that night. Her friends think she may have rationalized away her own experiences. Virginia suggested that "maybe she didn't want the notoriety. . . ." But she said all three agreed in the beginning on the events of that night.

Some validation of that night's weird reports may have occurred two years later—in the summer of 1969—when two couples, also close friends of the Gregorys, asked to spend the night in the den. They were mature, sensible people who knew little about the specifics of what had occurred in that room. They were stunned by what took place overnight, according to Virginia.

"They heard what seemed like a cocktail party going on outside the room, upstairs or perhaps next door. A piano, ice clinking, a woman singing," she said. Of course, there was nothing of the sort happening anywhere in the house.

SWIRLING FIGURES WERE not just confined to the den.

Another of the couple's sons watched in fascination as a shape floated through the bedroom in which he was sleeping. There were two beds in the room. The Gregory boy was in the smaller of the two, while a buddy staying the night was in the larger one. He woke up and saw the dark form of what he thought at the time looked like a woman in a long gown floating above him and quite near to the ceiling. There was some light in the room coming through the windows from the upstairs porch light. The figure lacked details, but it was darker than the surroundings. He said it had the appearance of gas fumes or heat waves coming off an asphalt highway on a summer's day, a description similar to what Virginia saw on one occasion.

The same teenager spent many nights listening to the old floorboards creak in his room the minute he turned off the lights, Virginia said. He said it sounded like a man's footsteps. They would stop the moment he turned on the lights.

Was it the natural process of an old house settling or groaning in the wind as during a storm? A person's senses may be more acute at night, as well.

The boy didn't think that was the case. He said during a storm the house's walls rumbled a bit in the wind, but never the floorboards. He also pointed out that the only time the floorboards made that distinctive sound was when an actual *someone* walked across them.

Family members also noted that running footsteps up and down the staircase abruptly stopped when someone approached the steps, but would resume when the observer returned to another nearby room.

VIRGINIA AWAKENED ONE night in 1969 to see a man standing at the foot of her massive canopy bed.

"I couldn't see his face, but I knew who it was. It was Greg, my husband."

At the same moment she saw him standing looking down at her from several feet away . . . he was sleeping soundly beside her. To say that she was astounded is to greatly underestimate her shock.

"That's who it was, though, that I saw at the foot of the bed. It took me awhile to figure that out (because) I couldn't see his face. He was raised off the floor, standing so I could see everything but his shoes. Remember how Jack Benny used to stand with his elbow in one hand and his chin in the other? That's how he was looking at me. Kind of like saying, here I am. He looked as if he were amused by the whole thing. I was appalled."

Virginia was able to identify the filmy figure as her husband because he was wearing a brown plaid sports coat she had given him. But it took her some time to come to the conclusion that it was indeed her husband.

"I didn't know anything about out-of-body experiences at the time. The whole time I lived there I wondered what I'd do if I woke up one night and (a ghost) is standing at the foot of my bed. That's exactly what happened. Of course you don't believe it at first because your mind rationalizes what it doesn't understand. I couldn't understand what in the name of God was going on."

When she saw Kendall at the foot of the bed, Virginia closed her eyes and turned away. She opened them and looked back. He was still standing there, intently staring down at her. She briefly closed her eyes again. When she dared to look again, the figure had become a faint silhouette; and then it was gone. She still had not been able to see his facial features.

"Why he was there, I have no idea," she said of what she now concludes to be an authentic out-of-body experience. Her husband never awoke during the entire experience.

Dr. Gregory died five years later, in 1974. She did not believe it was a precursor to his death, nor a harbinger of any other future family events.

"THAT WAS FASCINATING," she says succinctly about the memory of one particular episode and certainly one of her husband's more bewildering incidents.

This particular day had begun when her husband brought home a medical article about a rare affliction one of his patients was facing.

"It was a condition in which your heart 'shoots out' blood clots all over your body. He had a patient in the hospital with it," she remembered.

Her husband wanted to study the article in preparation for treating the man. He brought it up to the bedroom and read it before he went to sleep that night. He put the pages on the nightstand and turned off his light.

As she, too, drifted off to sleep that night, Virginia was thinking about another piece of writing, though a much different one. It was a recipe for a particularly delicious casserole she had made in her previous home whenever they entertained larger gatherings. She was thinking of it now because she and her husband had made the decision to move.

"I was so ashamed of the condition of the house and thinking, thank God because (if we move) I can have people over for dinner again. That's when I thought about the old recipe. But I hadn't seen it since we moved into the house. It would feed a lot of people . . . twenty-two or so I think."

The next morning the couple got up, dressed, and ate breakfast. Dr. Gregory returned to the bedroom to retrieve the article. It wasn't on the nightstand. He scoured the room for the pages, which were wrapped in a bright, orange cover. He called down to his wife, who came up to help him search. Still nothing. By now, he had to leave for the hospital, and he asked his wife to continue looking. It simply could not have walked off of its own accord.

Or could it?

Virginia talked about what happened next in an interview with writer Smith:

"Greg left for the office, and soon I went to the grocery store. When I returned I sat down and started thinking about the pamphlet. I got some kind of impression about it—I guess you could call it 'psychic,' wouldn't you? I thought, 'If the spook has taken Greg's pamphlet, he has carried it to the third floor, and if I go up there I'll find it.'

"I went upstairs and entered the big room over our bedroom. Then I walked on through it and into the little storeroom back of it. The first thing I saw on the floor was my lost recipe! It is in a little booklet that was lying in the center of the floor. No, indeed, it had not been there the last time I was in that little room and it couldn't have fallen off something and landed where it was. It was right out in the center of the bare floor. I picked it up and took it downstairs.

"Greg came home for lunch and looked all over the bedroom again for his pamphlet. He still could not find it. Shortly after he returned to the office, I was watching one of the television soap operas I am hooked on, and right in the middle of it, it suddenly occurred to me, 'If the purpose of all this was for me to find the recipe, I have found it. So the pamphlet should be back where it was.' I walked over to the bedside table and it was there! We could never have missed that brilliant orange cover when we looked so carefully before, if it had been there then."

Today, Virginia Gregory is absolutely certain there was a purpose behind the case of the missing medical pamphlet:

"I was supposed to find this recipe. When I called him up and told him I'd found his pamphlet, he asked where. I told him on the bedside table, but he said that was impossible, it hadn't been there. Of course it wasn't there: 'they' were playing little games."

BOTH VIRGINIA AND her husband had some early thoughts that their children could have been playing games, could have been responsible for many of the "hauntings" by inventing stories or carrying out pranks. They questioned the children and were quite frank in telling them they thought some of the ghost sounds might be of the children's making. But neither parent thought them capable of that behavior, especially with this sort of activity.

"We never elicited anything from any of them that was in the least suspicious," Dr. Gregory later wrote.

Casting additional doubt on such a theory is that Mrs. Gregory, her husband, and family visitors and friends had various encounters when none of the children were home, or they were occupied in ways that would have precluded them from playing childish pranks or creating creepy effects.

THE VISITORS WHO heard odd sounds, or saw mysterious images, were often so perplexed that they didn't know what to say or how to react.

Sometimes a visitor might hear the tinkling of glass from an elaborate candelabrum that stood on the fireplace mantelpiece in the den—even though such an item hadn't been in the house since the time of the original owners. Virginia likened it to the ticking of a clock on the mantelpiece, again long after it had been removed from the house.

On a summer's evening, about a year before the Gregorys moved out in 1969, a young lawyer friend and his wife came for dinner. The Gregorys and their visitors all adjourned afterward to the family's long living room. The comfortable room was filled with chairs and sofas and had matching fireplaces at either end. The couple sat on a sofa in front of the fireplace closest to the dining room. At the far end of the room, a matching fireplace was in the wall, on the other side of which was the den.

All evening long, the attorney complained of a chill, even though it was quite a humid evening. He also said that he kept hearing a low growl coming from the other end of the room, from the floor in front of the far fireplace. He was stumped because the three others—his wife, Virginia, and Kendall—heard nothing. He said it sounded like a dog's low snarl.

The Gregorys were stunned.

Their dog, Thor, was curled up at their feet.

He was inside because of what had happened earlier that day to the family's other dog, Chester. He had been struck and killed by an automobile.

Normally both animals were kept outdoors, but Thor had been whining so much that Virginia had let him inside to sleep for the night. He didn't show any signs of hearing the growl—perhaps Chester's?—about which the visitor remarked.

DURING THE TWELVE years the Gregorys lived in the house, they employed a number of individuals to work as cooks or housekeepers. Several of them were as befuddled as the family members by the bizarre sights and sounds.

Myrtle was the family cook and housekeeper for many years. She said that one day when the Gregorys were gone, and she was alone in the house, she saw a man she did not recognize go into the den. He was attired in a gray sweater and pressed trousers.

The cook told writer Susy Smith: "I did not know it was a ghost then. I just thought it was one of the boys who come in here sometimes, but I didn't recognize him. When he didn't come out . . . I got my sister-in-law . . . who was also working here then, and we went in and looked for him. There was no one there."

She once mistook a household ghost for the head of the household. It happened as she prepared the morning's breakfast. As she busied herself at the stove, she saw out of the corner of her eye a man come in and stand at the far end of the kitchen table reading the newspaper. He wore a suit, as Dr. Gregory normally did, so she didn't think much about it and continued her work. A few minutes later, Virginia Gregory came in asking for the morning paper. Myrtle said Dr. Gregory already had come in to pick it up because she'd seen him reading it. Virginia said her husband was still upstairs, as it was Thursday, his normal day off. The children were still sleeping. The newspaper was still rolled up on the table where the housekeeper had placed it earlier that morning.

On another occasion, Myrtle and her sister-in-law were cleaning the upstairs when they heard an enormous crash from downstairs. The family had several cats at that time, and the two women feared that one of them had knocked over a lamp, or perhaps a picture had fallen off a wall. They scurried downstairs, but nothing was out of place or broken. Later, they discovered the cats had been sleeping upstairs anyway.

A chance encounter by another household worker helped the family identify who one of the ghosts might have been in life. And it was another thread in the cord that linked the Gregory house with the infamous era during which it had been an armed forces NCO club.

Susan was the employee's name. As she stood folding laundry at the kitchen table one afternoon, she was startled by a man walking out of the bathroom that opened off the butler's pantry next to the kitchen. He stopped and stared at her for a long minute. She noticed that he wore black trousers and a crisp, white shirt. On his head was a white cap, such as that sported by 1930s English drivers who favored sporty convertibles. He was an obviously solid figure, who for all intents and purposes looked like he absolutely belonged in the house.

Perhaps he did.

After lingering a moment, as if to wonder who this strange woman might be, he stepped out of the kitchen, across the living room, and up the staircase toward the second floor.

Although not a little frightened—her hair was "drawing up," she told an interviewer—Susan followed the man at a short distance. She heard him ascend the staircase but didn't actually see him on the stairs. A few moments later, she followed up after him. Susan found Virginia Gregory in her bedroom, who told her that she hadn't heard or seen anyone else. Together the women hunted through the house for the intruder—or more likely a ghost, they now concluded—but went away empty-handed.

Virginia said the staff also told her that on numerous occasions when they heard something upstairs, they'd take Bibles in hand if they mounted a search for what it was they heard. "They saw many things," Virginia concluded.

VIRGINIA GREGORY BELIEVES that an explanation for the haunting came in the form of several historical events either in or near her former home.

The first was that heartbreaking death of the fourteen-year-old son of former owners. The several times the spectral teen boy was sighted—inside and outside the house—he seemed to want to communicate with the family, Virginia said. Further, she believed she was meant to find the burned candles and her son's smoldering clothing. The teen had no intention of injuring anyone. "(He) never did us any harm, besides scaring us. But I don't think he scared us on purpose. I think whatever was there wanted one of us to know (he was) there and wanted some kind of communication because (he) called out to my children."

She cited, as an example, the night Parham heard someone call out his name. He told his mother it sounded like a child's voice calling through a length of pipe. The incident happened late of an evening when Parham had been helping out at a bridge tournament at which his mother was one of the contestants. He had stayed to tidy up after the event and got home after everyone else had gone to bed. Just after he got to sleep, he awoke with a start at a sharp smack on the floor. A book had fallen off his desk. A moment later, he heard someone calling his name from out of the darkness. A shadow moved slowly across the swath of light coming in through the window from an outdoor lamp. He carefully got up to look around. Near the mantelpiece came a sudden rush of cold air. It followed him back to bed, where he spent a restless night. He told his mother the next morning that it was one of the most unsettling nights he had ever spent there.

A SECOND EPISODE tying the Gregory home to a period of history that might have resulted in a handful of lingering specters deals with the city of Gulfport's historic connections to its waterfront and its strategic importance during both world wars.

Within four years of the community's founding in 1898, the first harbor was completed and the young community became the Port of Gulfport. During the ensuing century and more, the city has been inextricably connected to its harbor facilities, and no time was more important than during World War II. In 1942, the U.S. Navy chose Gulfport to host one of its Construction Battalion sites.

Meanwhile, the house into which the Gregorys would one day move played an important, albeit quite *different* role for the armed forces. It was leased by the U.S. Government to operate as a non-commissioned officers' club.

What went on in her former home during that era, Virginia Gregory believes, has accounted for several of the adult male ghosts her family encountered.

"The NCO era was ghastly, it was a really bad place," she said, adding that she spoke with numerous individuals who had been involved with the club, including the man who owned it at the time.

The enlisted man chosen by the armed forces to operate the club was a sergeant nicknamed Frenchy. According to reports at the time, and in subsequent research by Virginia Gregory and others, Frenchy was not averse to hosting illegal activities of most any sort. He lived in one of the bedrooms and filled the others with gambling equipment and prostitutes. The club's reputation for all manner of unspeakable enterprises grew to be such a blight that the government eventually closed it down.

Frenchy himself might have been the man that Susan, the household worker, saw come out of the bathroom. Her description of him as short and swarthy seemed to fit. His clothing matched the sergeant's favorite working attire—black pants, white shirt, and a sporty cap.

Virginia also set out to verify Susan's account of the story.

"After she told me about him, and she described him so perfectly, I went to (the previous owner) when it was an NCO club. I asked him if he knew who it might be. He said, yes, that's Frenchy all right. I had described him according to (Susan's) description of him. He had on that white cap with a snap bill, black pants, and white shirt. He had acne scars on the bottom of his face."

Frenchy had died a few years before in New York City. Not much is known about the man, although he did reportedly return to the house after the war to retrieve savings bonds hidden in a window seat on the third floor.

VIRGINIA BELIEVED THAT something terrible took place at the house during Frenchy's reign. The moaning and screaming, she said, and what sounds like a heavy body being dragged across the floor might be lingering vestiges of that era.

Paranormal expert Susy Smith thought it might be something more. "Perhaps some of the grotesque things that happened then still remain captured in the atmosphere of the house. They may be memory images of some kind."

Parham Gregory may have encountered one of those images on another occasion. He had gone downstairs early one morning searching for a bite to eat. A soft moaning seemed to be coming from the den. He paused to listen, though he could not pinpoint the location from which the sound came. A woman's faint voice cried, "Get out! Get out!" An intense but not especially shrill scream rose and fell, before all was quiet once again. He went on to the kitchen, found his midnight snack, and made his way back toward the stairs. Lights were now on in the den, though he knew no one else in the house was up. He debated whether to check out what was going on, but decided against it.

BEFORE THE HOUSE succumbed to arson, shortly after the Gregorys moved out, writer on the supernatural Susy Smith visited Virginia Gregory and her family in an effort to discover the identities of the ghosts and, if possible, to put them to rest by holding a séance . . . on April Fool's Day, no less. Smith had earlier discovered that she might have possessed some abilities as a medium.

The results were mixed.

"I kept hoping, in a halfhearted sort of way, that one of those famous cold-blooded moans would come just back of my right ear in an area of the room where no human could have produced it," Smith wrote of her experience. While she wanted some indication of the ghosts' presence, Smith "had no desire to be taken over or influenced in any way by the Gregory ghosts."

Though no ghosts materialized during the evening, Smith did have several distinct impressions and reactions: "Once, briefly, I thought that a man dimly observable across the circle from me took on the appearance of a woman sitting there cuddling a boy in her lap. Then, right at the end of the evening, I had a feeling of incredible yearning, a real sadness, and I knew it was for that child, invisibly in our presence. . . . Why did he remain in the house? Was he clinging after death to his earthly surroundings because he enjoyed the pleasure of trying to attract the attention of the young people in the family? Or did he feel left out of things? Might he somehow be lost and in need of enlightenment and liberation?"

Smith and Virginia Gregory thought that their reaching out to the young boy brought some positive results, "that he does not have to remain there as an unseen presence, that he can move on to a fuller and more rewarding existence with enlightened spirits who are just waiting for his acquiescence to help him."

OVER THE ENSUING three decades, Virginia Gregory has revisited the memories of her twelve years in a haunted house on numerous occasions. The memories and the fallout have been mixed blessings.

"When we first discovered the house was haunted, I was absolutely enthralled with the idea, fascinated by it," she says. "But I made the mistake of telling people about it. I should never have done that. They thought I was a nut."

Which Virginia clearly is not.

She was called a "pioneer" by J. B. Rhine, who told her that nobody understands the kinds of psychic disturbances she and her family experienced. "You just have to live it day by day," Virginia says he told her, adding that "you have to understand that whatever these are cannot hurt you."

At one time, Virginia thought that perhaps a member of her family was an unwitting medium, outing the ghosts whenever he or she was there. She's discarded that notion, as no single family member was present for everything that happened over those years.

"No single child was ever there when all the things happened," she adds, noting, too, that sometimes she and her husband were both or individually absent when an entity suddenly materialized, or something else took place.

After Dr. Kendall Gregory's death in 1974, Virginia decided to learn all she could about psychic phenomena and moved to Charlottesville, Virginia, with her family, to study with a professor at the University of Virginia who was researching the paranormal.

"I wanted to know what he had found," she says, "so I offered my services as a research assistant. I worked for him for about seven months, looking at all fifteen hundred case histories in his files. Some of them are irrefutable. A lot of them are full of holes."

She attended the University of Virginia and later got her master's degree and doctorate at the University of Southern Mississippi. She teaches poetry and fiction writing.

"IT'S TOO BAD that we live in such an age where nothing is allowed that isn't scientifically demonstrated," she says. "You can't believe in anything or people will think you're (crazy)."

But those years remain a central element in her life.

"I've never heard of a house like it, never lived in another house like it, and I hope I never live in another one like it. It completely changed our philosophies, one hundred and eighty degrees. We didn't go to church, we never did, but it changed all of (our beliefs). Greg, too, before he died. Somebody once asked him if he believed all of this and he said, every word of it. That was after twelve long, miserable years. . . . His colleagues asked me all kinds of questions. Once, when I was visiting my cousin, he had a professor over for cocktails to give me the third degree. He was a great skeptic. He said there are no such things as ghosts, that he knew it and was positive of it. I started telling him some of the stories, but he said there was a logical explanation for everything. I told him the stories that seemed to show there was some kind of deliberate reason, or method, that there was some kind of intelligence behind the activity."

By the time Virginia finished recounting the episodes, her skeptical professor appeared to be something at a loss for an explanation.

She has continued her interest in psychic phenomena, including a visit to an English clairvoyant in London.

"He told me stuff that absolutely no one in the world could have known. He said there was a woman (present) who had crossed over a long time ago and she wanted to talk with me. Her name was Jean Anna. I said I didn't know any Jean Anna; I'd never heard of Jean Anna. Three days later I realized that was my paternal grandmother's name. Now what are the odds of me walking as a stranger into a place far from the United States and then having that man pick up on that name?"

In the end, however, the Gulfport haunting may not even have been about the *house* proper but rather what went on at the site years before. But it's a history nearly impossible to verify one way or the other.

Virginia Gregory suspects that perhaps events which unfolded decades or centuries before there was a Gulfport or even a United States may have played a crucial role in the haunting. Native American settlements were not uncommon all along the coastal region. Battles among the various tribes and later clashes between white settlers and the native peoples may have taken place near the old Gregory home, considering its proximity to the bayou.

"My take is that something happened there a long time ago. I think there was a thinning of the wall between the living and the dead" that caused the haunting, she said. "It's possible I was hearing the moans of the dead. That possibility just dawned on me about a year ago because I wondered why in the world that place was so haunted, and with such a variety of events. It wasn't the same old thing over and over again, like you might find (elsewhere) with vibrations or whatever you might call it; some woman just going up the stairs. The same thing never happened twice."

She believes there may have been an Indian village or settlement where the house was located. Her children regularly found arrowheads on their property. Archeological sites were routinely demolished in those years Gulfport was founded, so if there were any traces of an ancient community it might very well have been destroyed.

"The house wasn't that old," she adds, noting that it was the first house on the site. Neither was she able to find any unsolved or suspicious death there, "no tragedy other than (the boy being killed). It just didn't make any sense."

Virginia's research into the burial customs of Gulf Coast natives indicated that many of their practices were rather cruel according to modern sensibilities. "They did the most brutal, terrible things you ever heard of in your life. They strangled slaves to accompany a dead chief, put rawhide around their throats . . . or choked them to death. Mothers threw babies into funeral pyres."

To explore the possibility that the haunting stemmed from what went before, Virginia and a friend convened of an evening to consult a Ouija board. She said it seemed to provide them with an intriguing clue. Though it didn't give her any substantial information about the house, the board did seem to communicate something about a man who had been killed by Indians not far from the house.

Several times, the Ouija board's planchette glided across the smooth surface, forming a single phrase:

Find my bones. .

But even with that disturbing command, Virginia Gregory had no interest in doing any more digging into the long-ago.

12

The Weeping Woman

Oh, howe sadde it is to see
A piouse woman lose her minde
All through a seeing such as sight
Which neither was so good nor kinde.
Take heed ye maydens in thy youthe
To persevere in prayer and truth,
Lest ere it be too late to finde
The devil he hath turned thy minde.

—*Epistolas Ecclesiasticum et Apostolicum*,
March A.D. 1501

THE YOUNG WOMAN tearfully told police that someone had kidnapped her two young boys, Alex and Michael. She didn't know who had taken them or why. Her pleas for their safe return were carried by world media in that fall of 1994. Her name was Susan Smith. Soon her story unraveled and she confessed that she had drowned her children after her boyfriend said their presence was a reason he could not go on seeing her. Police found the boys' bodies in eighteen feet of water in South Carolina's John D. Long Lake.

Smith was convicted of murder and sentenced to life in prison.

Some headlines about the case used a term unfamiliar to most readers. *TIME* magazine, for instance, said Susan Smith was a "modern day" *La Llorona*.

That is her Spanish name: *La Llorona*. The Anglos know her as *The Weeping One* or *The Weeping Woman*. Sometimes it is *The Wandering One*.

But by whatever name she is known, this character was unknown to most of those readers who followed the tragic story of Susan Smith and her murdered children. What kind of mother would so cold-bloodedly take the lives of her own offspring?

To millions of Spanish-speaking peoples, there was no mystery. La Llorona is a bansheelike character who has figured prominently as the most significant ghost of the Southwestern United States.

For over five hundred years she has drifted through South and Central America, Mexico, the American Southwest, and then to Spanish-speaking communities throughout the United States. She wears a white, frayed, blood-soaked gown. At one time a beautiful woman with jet-black hair and a flawless complexion, she is now to be feared and to be avoided. Her cries are enough to send shudders through even the strongest hombres. *"Ay, mis hijos, mis hijos"*—My children, my children. She is looking, frantically looking, along the rivers and dry streambeds for her small murdered children—dead by her own hand, the innocent victims of infanticide.

Despite obvious similarities to the tragic Greek character of Medea, La Llorona seems to be based to some measure on actual historical personages, according to historians and anthropologists. She is a synthesis of fact and of Indian and Spanish culture and traditions.

One of the earliest references to a similar story comes from Tenochtitlan, an Aztec city, where the goddess Chihuacoatl appears as a striking dark-haired woman attired in a white dress. She wanders the night crying, *"Ay, hijos mios . . . ya ha llegado vuestra destruccion. Donde os llevare?"*—Oh, my children . . . your destruction has arrived. Where can I take you?

To the Aztec, her cries are now thought to have been meant as a forewarning against the coming destruction of their civilization.

Another of the early New World traditions to have some of La Llorona's characteristics was the legendary ravishing Aztec girl *La Malinche,* the mistress of the Spanish conquistador Hernando Cortés. She was his translator and is said to have borne him at least one child before he left her to marry a prosperous Spanish woman. La Malinche's pride thus insulted, she set out to avenge Cortés's betrayal of her love. She killed her offspring, the children of Cortés, and helped plot retribution against the Spanish subjugators.

By a different account, La Llorona might have originated with Doña Luisa de Olveros, a beautiful Indian princess who fell in love with a Mexican nobleman, Don Nuño de Montesclaros. The year was 1550. So deep was Doña Luisa's love for Montesclaros that she gave birth to his two children, some accounts say twins. Although he didn't promise marriage, Luisa prayed for the day when they would be wed.

While Luisa waited and prayed, Montesclaros lost his passion for her. At length, she decided to confront him over his desertion. Late one evening, she ventured to his family's lavish home. To her surprise, Montesclaros seemed to be the center of a gala party in his honor.

It was his wedding day.

He laughed when Doña Luisa fell to her knees to ask why he had forsaken her. Marriage had always been out of the question, he sneered. She was an Indian and thus beneath his station in life. She was thrown out of the house.

Doña Luisa ran through the muddy streets, choking back sobs and crazed with anger at her humiliation. When she reached her home, Luisa exacted her retribution. She found the dagger Montesclaros had given her as a present and with it she slit the throats of her children and threw their bodies in a river.

For days she wandered the countryside, babbling incoherently, her clothes ripped and smeared with the blood of her children, until authorities found her and discovered the crime.

The courts found her guilty of infanticide and "sorcery." She was publicly hanged, her body left to dangle for hours from the gallows as a warning to any other woman who might entertain the same homicidal ideas as Doña Luisa.

The ghost of Doña Luisa de Olveros is La Llorona, the weeping one, her bloodied hands reaching out to passersby as she searches for the children she so wickedly slaughtered.

To folklorists today, a purpose in the La Llorona story is to warn children of what might happen to them if they stray too far, or venture alone into the night. Impoverished but pretty teenage girls might also read it as a cautionary tale about not falling in love with higher-born boys who wear fancy clothes and drive flashy cars. The boys will use their status to pursue the girl for their own greedy sexual pleasure, but will never consider marrying her.

There are many accounts of La Llorona's appearances and behaviors, including these:

In the environs near Las Cruces, New Mexico, La Llorona has sometimes been called "Monica." She is known through several variations, according to an account by historian Mrs. J. Paul Taylor, of La Mesilla:

La Llorona was an independently-minded young woman with several children to whom she paid little attention. One night she left her children alone to be with her lover at his home, only a few houses away. Somehow her house caught fire. She rushed home to rescue them, but both she and her children were burned to death.

Ever since that time, this thoughtless mother has become the ghost of La Llorona. She is known for showing up wherever there is a fire, including at cookouts along New Mexico's Rio Grande River. She screams and beats her hands against her face, crying out for the children dead through her own selfish and pitiless behavior.

LA LLORONA WAS making love with a handsome young man when a flash flood swept through the Mesilla Valley, according to another Las Cruces-area story. The woman's children were swept away by the rapidly rising water. Her sorrowful cries echo across the water whenever flash floods occur in south-central New Mexico.

THE FACT OF La Llorona being a single woman is nearly universal. In yet an additional version from Las Cruces, she had a child born out of wedlock. To bring the child home would have led to her being banished from the community and disgraced. Instead, she threw the child into the Rio Grande River. Suddenly overcome with grief and remorse at what she had done, she threw herself into the roiling river waters. She is seen along the river's banks weeping for her children.

SOMETIMES THE WEEPING one becomes something of a "child thief" as well.

If a woman has a child near the Rio Grande when La Llorona is happening by, the ghost will try to snatch the child to replace her own.

A PARTICULARLY GRISLY version of the La Llorona story states that the woman is a lazy, unfit mother of two small children. When she discovers that she is pregnant with a third child, the thought of taking care of three children is more than she can bear. She kills the two children she had—both daughters—before the new baby arrives. She takes them to the banks of the Rio Grande ostensibly for a picnic. But in reality she plans to drown them. At the riverbank, though, she finds a herd of wild pigs rooting in the mud. Instead of drowning the children, she throws the girls into the midst of the pigs, which promptly eat them. So great is the physical exertion in this despicable act that she gives birth prematurely on the banks of the river. In pain, she rolls into the river and drowns.

Now those who drive along the river looking for La Llorona now and again discover her presence in the bloody scratch marks in the car's wax finish.

Another version of the legendary story was written by author Joe Hayes. A girl called Maria lives in a poor village, yet no one who had seen her imagined that there was a more beautiful girl in the world. And she was very conceited; she bragged that she would marry the most handsome man in the world, Hayes wrote:

One day into Maria's village rode a man who seemed to be just the one she had been talking about. He was a dashing young ranchero, the son of a wealthy rancher from the southern plains.

She knew just the tricks to win his attention. If the ranchero spoke when they met on the pathway, she would turn her head away. When he came to her house in the evening to play his guitar and serenade her, she wouldn't even come to the window. She refused all his costly gifts. The young man fell for her tricks.

In time, everything turned out as Maria planned. Soon they were married. They had two children and they seemed to be a happy family together. But after a few years, the ranchero went back to the wild life of the prairies. He would leave town and be gone for months at a time. And when he returned home, it was only to visit his children. He seemed to care nothing for the beautiful Maria. He even talked of setting Maria aside and marrying a woman of his own wealthy class.

Maria was angry with the handsome ranchero and began to feel anger toward her children, because he paid attention to them, but ignored her.

One evening, as Maria was strolling with her two children near the river, the ranchero came by in a carriage. An elegant lady sat on the seat beside him. He stopped and spoke to his children, but he didn't even look at Maria. He whipped the horses on up the street. A terrible rage filled Maria, and it all turned against her children. And although it is sad to tell, Maria seized her two children and threw them into the river. But as they disappeared down the stream, she realized what she had done. She ran down the bank of the river, reaching out her arms to them.

But they were gone.

Villagers found Maria's body the next day on the riverbank. She was buried there. But she did not rest.

On the night of her burial, villagers heard strange sounds coming from along the river. They thought it might only be animal sounds or perhaps the wind. But in time they knew the eerie sound was that of a woman's wail. The dead woman was walking and crying for her dead babies.

The villagers saw a woman staggering up and down the bank of the river, dressed in a long, white robe, the way they had dressed Maria for burial. On night after night they saw her walk the river bank and cry for her children.

Thus Maria became La Llorona, the weeping woman. And by that name she is known to this day.

The moral is clear: children must never, ever venture alone to the riverbank. La Llorona may be there to snatch them and take them away. Forever.

IT IS CURIOUS that La Llorona has merged with another traditional ghost, the hitchhiking woman in white, in some American locales. For instance, in Gary, Indiana, in the now-vanished community of Cudahey, now an industrial neighborhood of the city, La Llorona and the woman in white were both said to have visited the old streets of that locale, as this author noted in an earlier book.

The hauntings were centered on Cline Avenue, near its intersection with Fifth. The dank Calumet River and a railroad track cross Cline just north of there. It is grim area, even in the full light of a sunny, summer afternoon.

Little is left of Cudahey. It was once a thriving neighborhood of Mexican-Americans who worked in Gary's legendary steel mills. Most of the old homes have long since been torn down, their owners moving to more desirable communities as they settled into their adopted homeland and advanced in their places of work.

But on occasion, one can still hear whispered stories of the mysterious, weeping woman who begs unsuspecting drivers for a ride in their car. She is dressed in white, her black scraggly hair hanging in dirty strands about her face. This "ghost woman of Cline Avenue," this woman in white, could very well be a Midwestern adaptation of La Llorona.

Historian Philip B. George wrote: "It is possible that the Mexicans, settling in the Indiana harbor area and in Cudahey, heard the tale of the woman in white from the Anglos. . . . Within the Mexican community the ghost became identified as La Llorona. As the economic situation of many of the Mexicans improved, they moved to newer communities where day-to-day contact with Anglos was more common. The Anglos could then have picked up the tale from the Chicanos in its new form as the White Lady."

There are differences in the habits of La Llorona and the woman in white, however.

The woman in white is known for hitchhiking. She stands near the Cline Avenue overpass, under which flows the muddy Calumet River. She hails a taxi from there and requests a ride to nearby Calumet Harbor. But less than a half-mile later, the driver suddenly discovers that the woman has vanished from the backseat.

Sometimes the ghost doesn't even bother to hail a cab. She just appears mysteriously in a car as it speeds along the boulevard, only to depart without having said a word a few minutes later. At other odd moments, she will be glimpsed gliding across Cline Avenue in the direction of old Cudahey.

But unlike other women in white in American ghost lore, the Gary ghost did not die on her way to or from a dance. Rather, she is said to have killed her illegitimate children by drowning them in the Calumet River.

Once, some years ago, area media decided to investigate Gary's mysterious ghost and converged on the area with camera and microphones. Several hundred spectators joined in, all of them scouring any wooded area near Cline and Fifth for a glimpse of the ghost. The press and the spectators hoped to capture the elusive spirit—at least on videotape if not in the "flesh." On that night, however, it seemed that no self-respecting specter showed its transparent face.

WHETHER IT IS the traditional La Llorona in the Southwest, or its Anglo Indiana version, there are thousands of people who believe this ghost will never know peace. Not until, that is, she reclaims the souls of her slaughtered children.

13

Disturbing Deeds

All houses in which men have lived and suffered and died are haunted houses . . . Death is but a veil and through that veil we may now and then, as through a glass, see darkly.

—Mary Roberts Rinehart, *The Red Lamp*

GHOSTS PAY LITTLE heed to the fame or fortune of those they haunt. That might be the lesson one derives about these properties that came furnished . . . in more ways than one.

The Mystery Writer's Mystery

"THERE'S SOMEBODY IN the garden!"

With those disquieting words, young Alan Rinehart pointed out the window so that his mother might also see the glowing white orb drifting above the formal flower garden some forty yards away.

"As we looked it left the garden and started down the lawn away from the house," said Alan's mother, famed mystery author Mary Roberts Rinehart. "It looked like the round light of a pocket flash, turned consistently in our direction, a thing unlikely if it were being used to guide the footsteps of whoever carried it."

Whoever carried it? Or *whatever* carried it. The latter may be more accurate because the single, intense white light was not just turned toward the house, it did not illuminate any surrounding space as would have been the case with a flashlight.

Mother and son stared transfixed as the light rolled on until vanishing into a marsh at the foot of the Rineharts' expansive lawn.

"That disappearance was as puzzling as anything else," Mrs. Rinehart said. The only path through the marsh was over two hundred feet from where the light faded away.

A mysterious light was not the only anomalous incident during Mary Roberts Rinehart's summer-long residence at the rambling oceanfront mansion she had rented on Long Island. Mrs. Rinehart, two of her three sons, and some household staff put up with nearly a dozen inexplicable, and in the minds of at least some of them, possibly paranormal events that neighbors eventually confessed to her did not surprise them at all—the place had been haunted for years!

THE TIME WAS June 1918. The nation was riveted on the war news flowing out of Europe. Mrs. Rinehart's husband, Dr. Stanley M. Rinehart, remained in Washington, D.C., hoping to be sent overseas as part of the war effort. Her oldest son, Stanley, was already in Europe serving in the armed forces.

Mrs. Rinehart decided to rent the rambling and remote Long Island mansion to finish work on her next novel, *Dangerous Days*, a psychological thriller of unhappy married life. It was published a year later and eventually adapted into a silent film starring Lawson Butt and Clarissa Selwynne. In many ways, the novel would mirror Mrs. Rinehart's own dismal marriage. Dr. Rinehart was entirely dismissive of his wife's literary efforts, especially of what he termed the "trashy" popular fiction she wrote. He resented her growing celebrity status. The fact that he chose to stay in Washington while his wife and the rest of the family were on Long Island could fairly be seen as adding to their marital strain.

Mrs. Rinehart, at age forty-two, was already an accomplished author of magazine articles, novels and, most popularly, mystery and detective fiction. Her first two mystery novels—*The Man in Lower Ten* and *The Circular Staircase*—had been bestsellers shortly after the turn of the century. The latter was adapted by Mrs. Rinehart and Avery Hopwood into a popular stage play, *The Bat*. It is still performed by amateur and professional theater companies.

Mrs. Rinehart wrote scores of other works of fiction and nonfiction, including a series of popular novels featuring the globe-trotting female character Tish, and the Miss Pinkerton series with nurse/detective Hilda Adams. Mrs. Rinehart herself had been educated as a nurse in her hometown of Pittsburgh.

Her literary output was not limited to the printed page. She landed on Broadway as one of the earliest American female playwrights of note with the 1907 comedy *Seven Days*. The achievement is even more amazing when one considers that she was just thirty-one years old, and at a time when women could not even vote!

In many of her novels, Mrs. Rinehart extols the pleasures of having children, but makes it clear she resents brutish husbands who disparage any independent successes their wives might enjoy. She did try to please her own husband by writing so-called "serious" literary fare, including *Dangerous Days*. It wasn't until 1929 that she returned to the genre of her earlier successes, mystery and detective fiction.

For nearly half a century, and despite her husband's withering sarcasm, she remained one of the world's most popular novelists. Several of her titles remain in print a century later.

HER SUCCESS MEANT that she could afford the summer rental of the fully furnished mansion. The very large and extremely comfortable home was situated at the end of a long driveway off the main highway. A gardener's cottage was at the entrance to the drive. The expansive grounds were filled with a formal garden, a small pond, and thick groves of trees. "It was isolated, of course, but bright and sunny," Mrs. Rinehart said. The ideal retreat for a mystery writer. She settled in with the other two of the couple's three sons, Ted and Alan; her aged mother (who usually lived with her daughter and son-in-law), a personal secretary, an aunt visiting for part of the summer, and several maids to run the household and cook the meals.

The couple's son Stanley would go on to help found the prominent publishing house of Farrar and Rinehart.

Now with most of her family happily situated at the gracious residence, Mrs. Rinehart thought she'd be able to finish her novel undisturbed by nothing more than the occasional minor domestic dilemma.

"But that summer contained much more than the usual routine," Mrs. Rinehart recalled in her autobiography, *My Story*. After a time, she and most of the rest of her family and her staff came to believe the house was plagued with ghostly disturbances, despite her determined reluctance to arrive at such a conclusion.

"I am not a . . . spiritualist," she wrote, "although to say that nothing exists which we cannot see has always seemed to me to be nonsense." She said she had a firm belief in conscious survival after death, which she laid to her Christian faith, and even thought that an invisible world might exist all around us even though we may not understand the laws which govern it.

The mysterious lighted orb Mrs. Rinehart and her son witnessed rambling across the garden late that night was but a near finale to earlier events involving her and most of the members of the household—and which would test her skepticism that "so-called physical manifestations prove nothing" about the existence of the supernatural.

And it took some time for Mrs. Rinehart to even pay attention to the complaints by those around her.

The family cook was subjected to the first of many anxious moments within days after the family moved in. One morning she protested to Mrs. Rinehart that not only did she hear constant footsteps in an unused storeroom above her own bedroom, but that a rocking chair next to her bed rocked back and forth during the night. She could take the footsteps, but the animated rocker was just too much!

Another of the family's staff soon joined the fray.

"One night I heard a scream," Mrs. Rinehart remembered in her memoir. "The laundress rushed in to say that she had been starting up to bed, and she had seen a man on the staircase, also going up."

Mrs. Rinehart, her two sons—with Alan toting a lethal shotgun—and her secretary scoured the house looking for an intruder but found no one.

They marked up the incident to the vivid imagination of the women involved. But that dismissive attitude would soon change.

It came about because an earlier Rinehart novel, *The Amazing Interlude*, was being considered as a stage play. Silent film star Marie Doro was up for the lead role of Sara Lee, a young woman who joins the European Red Cross in 1914 and is thereby changed forever. At Mrs. Rinehart's invitation, the actress came to spend the weekend at the Long Island estate to discuss the play and her character. Although she had some stage credits, Doro was best known for a series of popular silent films, including the title role in the earliest known film version of *Oliver Twist*.

The visiting actress got caught up in the remarkable goings-on during her first night with the Rineharts, as Mrs. Rinehart recalled:

"To my astonishment, (Marie) carried her breakfast tray into my room the next morning, while I was still in bed, and said that she had not slept at all, that someone had walked up and down the hall outside her door all night."

Mrs. Rinehart added that, as in the instance with the laundress, a careful search of the house failed to turn up any plausible source for the annoyance.

By now, nearly everyone in the household, with the exception of Mrs. Rinehart herself, had taken notice of some sort of odd, perplexing clattering in the night—usually in the distinct form of a heavy-footed man climbing the old main staircase and then shambling down the upstairs hallway only to linger outside one of the bedroom doors. Mrs. Rinehart tried to eliminate all the usual suspects—creaking timbers of old homes, wind soughing through the trees, or maybe an errant mammal. Setting traps didn't turn up any signs of rats, squirrels, possums, or other critters.

Then the mystery writer herself became involved in the mystery. It began innocently enough with a series of what she called "little occurrences" which, when taken with the man on the staircase and inexplicable footsteps, led her to believe that despite her better judgment, perhaps something otherworldly was at play in the old mansion.

The first incident involved a small brass reading lamp the writer kept on a table in the dressing room next to her bedroom. She had turned the dressing room into her small office—during the day she wrote at the table, a plain old kitchen type outfitted with paper, pencils, typewriter, and chair.

"At night the connecting door stood open, and after I had put out my reading lamp it seemed to me that night after night I could hear this lamp moving. I would get up, turn on the ceiling light, and look about, to find that the lamp was just as I had left it," Mrs. Rinehart wrote. She was never quite certain if it wasn't nerves wreaking havoc with her consciousness.

Nevertheless, Mrs. Rinehart always doubted that the supernatural was at work in the house. Son Alan apparently agreed. He bought his mother a revolver to protect herself from someone breaking into the house at night. But even he couldn't set aside every episode. One night he threw open his own bedroom door, gun in hand, to confront whoever it was he had heard heavily climbing the staircase, only to then stop outside his bedroom door. When he peeked out the hallway was quite empty.

Mrs. Rinehart's secretary—whom she described as a no-nonsense young woman with long red hair who stayed in a room in a wing at the opposite side of the house—disparaged talk of ghosts and the uncanny. That attitude didn't last long, Mrs. Rinehart wrote:

"She burst into my room, hair flying and brush in hand, to gasp that someone was hiding in the enormous hamper for soiled clothing which stood outside her door. She had been brushing her hair and twice the lid, which squeaked, had raised and lowered. I caught up my revolver and ran back, entirely prepared to riddle the family wash with bullets if necessary, and loudly addressed the hamper: Come out of there! Nothing happened. Come out, or I'll shoot! But the washing remained silent and at last, revolver poised, I raised the lid. Of course it contained nothing but what had a legitimate right to be there."

LITTLE BY LITTLE, the woman who had dealt only with fictional mysteries learned that the puzzling events in the house didn't surprise the estate's full-time gardener. She spoke carefully to him one morning after a particularly uneasy night when she was kept awake by the steady thumping coming from an old warming pan near the bedroom fireplace.

"Hearing noises all night? Well, I wouldn't wonder," the gardener allowed.

"What do you mean?" Mrs. Rinehart shot back.

"Oh, I don't mean anything," he replied. "But my wife, she wouldn't stay in that house at night for a million dollars. She tried it once, and about one a.m. I heard her ringing the bell like mad for me."

The bell on the porch outside the kitchen had been used to summon workers at mealtime. The gardener's wife claimed that something had taken hold of the blankets on her bed and dragged them to the floor.

While he wouldn't go so far as to claim the house was haunted—perhaps wanting to protect his steady employment—he encouraged Mrs. Rinehart to carry out an experiment that sounded like one he had tried.

"You move one of those pictures in the living room and the next day you'll find it back where you took it from."

For whatever reason Mrs. Rinehart didn't take him up on the challenge.

DURING ALL THAT summer nothing as straightforward as a wailing specter manifested itself in a way to provide unequivocal evidence of a haunting. Mrs. Rinehart brushed aside the one time she *might* have seen a ghostly figure. It was at dinner one night. The room was dark save for lighted candles on the table. She saw someone standing in the pantry doorway. She took the person to be the cook trying to get the attention of the maid serving the meal. However, Mrs. Rinehart was told the cook was at that moment cooling herself on the porch steps outside the kitchen door. Mrs. Rinehart thought that the gloomy semidarkness in the room might have caused her to imagine the figure.

Nevertheless, the inability to discover a cause for the various incidents that could not be brushed aside led Mrs. Rinehart to become progressively more uneasy. Were some of the peculiar noises or events simply the results of that apprehension? Which of them could be put down to objective truth? Was there indeed an occasional prowler determined to bring harm to the family, as her sons seemed to think? Try as they might, no one in the household could think of anyone who wanted to do them harm.

Yet that latter possibility—that someone unknown was lurking about the estate—seemed to the family more probable after a dog they were taking care of was shot to death. The dog belonged to the house's permanent owners and had the run of the place.

"None of us had ever heard of a ghost who carried a revolver, and I began to wonder if, after all, the house was being entered at night by some intruder," Mrs. Rinehart wrote about the shooting.

And so, at an hour before midnight on a night soon thereafter, Mrs. Rinehart, her sons, her secretary, and the gardener stationed themselves in various rooms around the house. Ted and Alan were positioned in the living room and sun parlor respectively. Each was armed with a shotgun. The gardener was in the gunroom in a wing on the opposite side of the first floor; Mrs. Rinehart, with a revolver in hand, and her secretary situated themselves in the dining room. From there she could see the hallway and staircase; the large bay windows provided a clear view of the back lawn.

Mrs. Rinehart described the episode:

"It was a nervous time. The furniture creaked, we spoke in whispers, and the hall candle I had placed in the hall, was burning low. At one o'clock I glanced toward the hall and saw a strange and shapeless figure crawling toward us through the doorway. In that semidarkness it looked like some hideous animal, and I opened my mouth to shriek. Then I summoned all my courage, raised the revolver and said loudly if shakily, Speak, or I'll shoot!"

"For heaven's sake, mother! You've scared him off!" cried Alan Rinehart as he got up off the floor.

"Who?" demanded his mother.

Alan ran to the bay window and pointed toward the lawn. Both of them watched in awe as a solid white light appeared to float over the flower beds some distance from the house. As mother and son gaped in astonishment, the mysterious object turned away from the garden and floated down the lawn and on toward the marsh. Oddly, the light seemed to Mrs. Rinehart to be directed toward the house the entire time. Yet both wondered how that could be if it was being used by some unknown person to guide his—or her?—path away from the house. And the lack of any radiance made it doubtful that someone was holding a lantern. The glow finally disappeared into the marsh. From her account, that was the first and last appearance of this mystery light. No one in the household investigated any further.

"I have no explanation for that light," Mrs. Rinehart wrote of that late night mystery, "as I have no explanation for the other things which occurred. I went on working. I was working rather better than I was sleeping, and the brass lamp was quiet enough when I was there."

But that doesn't mean all *else* was quiet. Alan Rinehart came galloping up the stairs to his mother's bedroom some days later claiming that as he got some crackers from the kitchen cupboard for a midnight snack, a teakettle slid across the stove top.

A BIT OF the mystery may have been solved once Mrs. Rinehart finished work on *Dangerous Days*, and could visit more with her friends and neighbors in the area. At one dinner party she passed along to the other guests some of the strange incidents that had befallen her over the summer. The next day the party's hostess stopped by the house. What she said seemed to settle the matter: The house had been known for years as being haunted, she told Mrs. Rinehart. Several years before, it had been the subject of a feature story about its mysteries in a New York newspaper. A photograph of the house had even been included.

MARY ROBERTS RINEHART would go on to have one other mystifying experience with ghostly phenomena—this one complete with what seemed to be a resident poltergeist—in the Washington, D.C. apartment once owned by the late Pennsylvania senator Boies Penrose.

But these two amazing episodes were not enough to persuade the famous mystery writer that she had stumbled upon phenomena from another sphere.

"I have lived in several houses, without imagining that they had other tenants than those who were paying the rent! I still have my fixed belief that if there is an invisible world about us, it does not and cannot manifest itself physically," Mrs. Rinehart wrote in her autobiography.

However, like all good authors, she took from that summer vivid memories she later distilled for *The Red Lamp,* a suspense novel published six years later, in 1924. In that book, middle-aged William Porter inherits an isolated and possibly haunted lakeside estate Mrs. Rinehart named Twin Hollows. Porter and his wife are not dissuaded from moving in even when they hear rumors of the place's ghostly reputation. That all changes when they see a dim apparition beckoning to them from the glow of a single red lamp. They don't know if it's a dangerous stranger trying to frighten them away, or a visit from the dark recesses of the hereafter.

That of course was the unanswered riddle of Mary Roberts Rinehart's own very strange summer on Long Island.

And what she later wrote in *The Red Lamp* could well have mirrored that experience:

"This is Twin Hollows. A place restful and beautiful to the eye; a gentleman's home, with its larkspurs and zinnias, its roses and its sun-dial, its broad terrace, its great sheltered porch and its old paneling. Some lovely woman should sweep down its wide polished staircase, or armed with basket and shears, should cut roses in the garden with its sun-dial—that sun-dial where I stood the night the bell clanged. But it stands idle. It will, so long as I live, always stand idle."

The Ghost and Mr. Loewe

The famous Broadway composer didn't mind the isolation that came from staying in rural New York State while he and his partner finished work on their next show. Nor was Loewe necessarily caught up in the superstitious belief that bad things are said to happen in threes.

No, what Frederick "Fritz" Loewe most definitely didn't want to encounter again at the rural New York farm owned by his collaborator, Alan Jay Lerner, was a third visit from what he took to be the ghost of Revolutionary War hero General Mad Anthony Wayne.

Especially since that last time—when the long-dead general flushed the toilet!

AS THE GENIUSES behind such musicals as *My Fair Lady*, *Brigadoon*, and *Gigi*, composer Frederick Loewe and writer/lyricist Alan Jay Lerner formed one of the great Broadway partnerships of the twentieth century. The men had met in the late 1930s at the Lambs Club, a famous New York nightclub. Lerner was a radio writer with theatrical aspirations. Loewe, a child musical prodigy in his native Germany, had immigrated to the United States at the age of twenty in 1924. He had met with only marginal musical and personal success. But with Lerner as the wordsmith and Loewe creating the music, the pair would find universal acclaim in their Broadway musicals filled with such well-known standards as "Almost like Being in Love," "I've Grown Accustomed to Her Face," "Gigi," and "If Ever I Would Leave You."

IT WAS THE habit of the two men to isolate themselves while writing their shows so they could avoid unwanted distractions and interruptions. One of those places was at Lerner's Rockland County, New York, farm in the Dutch country of the Hudson River Valley. Lerner claimed the farmhouse had been built in 1732 by General Wayne's father.

But from what Fritz Loewe experienced, he thought some of the Wayne family may still have been there.

"When I purchased it I was forewarned that the ghost of Mad Anthony patrolled the premises," Lerner wrote in his autobiography, *The Street Where I Live*, although he disavowed ever having personally seen the ghost.

His musical partner may have wished he could have said the same thing.

BORN IN PENNSYLVANIA in 1745, Anthony Wayne earned the nickname "Mad Anthony" for his rash and impulsive behavior during his decades of political and military leadership. An early agitator against British colonial policies, Wayne organized and commanded a Chester County, Pennsylvania, regiment at the outbreak of the American Revolution in 1776 and later was put in charge of a Pennsylvania battalion. Soon promoted to the rank of general, his most famous accomplishment was the daringly successful nighttime assault on the British fort at Stony Point, in present-day Rockland County and not far from Lerner's farm home.

After the war, Wayne served in Congress, in the Pennsylvania legislature, and as the commissioner of the Northwest Territories. He died in 1796 at the age of fifty-one.

The fact that the general passed away in the next state over—Pennsylvania—did not dissuade Messrs. Loewe and Lerner. Something had so jarringly disturbed Fritz Loewe in two earlier working trips to Lerner's spacious farmstead that in 1955, during the team's final long haul to complete the book, score, and lyrics for *My Fair Lady*, the composer refused to stay with Lerner even though it would have been more convenient. Instead Loewe rented a home from his close friend, the actor Burgess Meredith, a short distance away.

So what really *did* happen on those earlier occasions?

In his autobiography, Alan Lerner provided the only known written account of Loewe's encounters with the ghost who might have been General Wayne:

"The first . . . had occurred the previous October. In the guest room there were two double beds. One night Fritz was asleep in one bed and Virginia, the woman with whom he was living, was in the other. He was awakened suddenly by the sound of heavy footsteps coming up the hall that seemed to pass right through the locked door and into the room. The room turned ice cold. He thought for a moment he was dreaming, until he heard Virginia cry out from under the covers of the next bed: 'Go away! Leave us alone! What did we ever do to you?' The footsteps and cold air then seemed to pass through the wall and out into the night. Fritz turned on the light. The door was still locked, but there was no question they had both heard and felt the same presence.

"On the New Year's Eve before we left for England, they were again fast asleep and again heard the footsteps coming up the hall and walk through the door. But this time the footsteps continued on into the bathroom where, a few seconds later, they both heard the lavatory flush. Then the steps continued through the wall and disappeared into the forest. When I awoke the next morning and went to their room, Fritz and Virginia had gone. They had gotten up immediately, dressed, and driven back to New York."

Loewe left a short note addressed to Lerner:

Dear boy, a ghost who wakes me up in the night is one thing, but a ghost who goes to the bathroom and takes a crap is more than I can stand. I will call you tomorrow. Fritz.

Fritz Loewe's assumption that it was the ghost of Anthony Wayne is apparently based on Lerner's assertion that he'd been told the house was haunted. The episodes did indeed occur as Lerner described them, according to Francine Greshler Feldmann, Fritz Loewe's companion for the last thirteen years of his life. But from her perspective, Loewe and Virginia may have done more than *heard* strange noises. She thinks they may have *seen* something as well.

"That's all absolutely true. He told me the same story. He and his girlfriend at the time both saw the ghost and rapidly split and went to stay with his very good friend, Burgess Meredith," Feldmann said. She adds that Meredith told her the same story.

"STORIES FROM THE lips of Lerner and Loewe must be watched with great care," cautioned Larry Hartzell, a music professor and a Frederick Loewe biographer.

"While Fritz never really lied—his stories always had a true fact behind them—like Lerner he would definitely expand the story to fit a particular emphasis. The best way to approach both men was given by the conductor Andre Previn. Although Previn was talking about Lerner, his comments apply just as well to Loewe. (Previn said) if Alan had to decide between telling the story or the 'myth,' he always told the myth."

Hartzell said it's important to keep in mind that Lerner had not seen or heard anything unusual in the more than seven years he'd owned the house.

"Also, there was a second person in the room with Fritz who agreed with him as to the particulars," Hartzell added. "(Loewe) was, among other things, a superstitious person. If he believed he saw a ghost, he saw a ghost."

Could it have been a ghost, but not necessarily that of General Wayne?

"I have not heard about any local legends of Anthony Wayne's ghost in this area," said Linda S. Zimmerman, a Rockland County and Hudson River Valley historian. "There are many stories about Revolutionary War soldier sightings in the county, and as often happens in such cases, people are not content to believe they have seen an ordinary soldier. Everyone wants to see the ghost of a general, or some other famous person. I think Aaron Burr's alleged ghost holds the record for appearing in the most locations."

Zimmerman maintains that since Anthony Wayne died in Pennsylvania, "it's unlikely his ghost would be wandering around over here."

Professor Hartzell said the setting of Lerner's farm in the Hudson River Valley, a district that's rife with ghost stories, may have had something to do with Loewe's experience.

"The Old Dutch settlers were very good at developing and expanding upon such things. Washington Irving's 'Headless Horseman' did not just accidentally come from that region. It is possible that Fritz heard one or two stories about Mad Anthony when he conversed with local townspeople and with his imagination did the rest."

Aside from the few paragraphs Lerner included in his own autobiography, Fritz and Virginia seem to have told only a few close friends of their ghostly encounter. Perhaps the famed composer didn't think these two singular nights worthy enough to stand alongside his other achievements.

Professor Hartzell found no mention of the story in Loewe's own personal writings, nor any indication that Loewe had further supernatural experiences.

Yet, to him, that gives the episodes a ring of authenticity.

"To me this makes it extremely probable that 'something' happened on those two nights. I am not willing to say it was the ghost of Anthony Wayne, but I have no trouble believing

Fritz and Virginia saw, heard, or experienced something very unusual."

Shadows on Wilmarth Place

It was dark and cold outside. Inside the imposing stone and brick Georgian Colonial home in the small city of Wantagh, on the southwest shore of Long Island, the two women and the little girl were not expecting anyone home for another few hours. Gail Fitzpatrick was the older of the women. Her husband, Jim Fitzpatrick, was an airline pilot not scheduled to return from one of his trips until later that night. With her in the house was her daughter Gillian, nicknamed Gill by her family, and her daughter-in-law Lisa Fitzpatrick, still in her late teens but married to Gail and Jim's son, Larry, who was away at work.

Gail had earlier fixed dinner for herself, her teenage son, Samuel, and little Gill. Lisa had dinner in the basement apartment she shared with her husband. Once the table was cleared and the dishes put away, Samuel followed his nightly routine and retreated to his second-floor bedroom, where he closed the door and turned up his stereo.

The time was not yet eight o'clock in the evening. Gail and Gill were downstairs for a visit with Lisa in the apartment in which the couple was living. Money was tight for the newlyweds—Larry worked two jobs to help make ends meet—so the couple stayed for a time in the spacious but simply decorated quarters.

The two women and Gill sat and chatted in the apartment's main room about all manner of household subjects and concerns. The house above was quiet. They'd all wait up for Jim Fitzpatrick when he got home a few hours from then.

That's why they were startled when they heard the kitchen door that led outside bang open upstairs.

"We heard the back door open and close, and then a man's heavy footsteps above our heads," Gill remembers of that night. (She is now Gillian McNamara, married and living elsewhere.)

Whoever it was seemed to be going toward the doorway that led out of the kitchen and to the main hallway.

The footsteps suddenly stopped.

"We expected to hear Jim's voice calling for Gail, since (it) sounded just like him." Jim often used the back door later at night in order not to awake anyone who might have been sleeping.

Gill says that she detected somebody murmuring from above.

"You know how you can sometimes hear low voices, so low you can't make out what they're saying? We heard that but nobody 'freaked out,'" she says. "We all just assumed my father was home." Perhaps he had brought a friend or colleague over for a visit.

Gail Fitzpatrick ran upstairs to let her husband know that she had been visiting with Lisa in her apartment.

"She said she would see me (the next day)," Lisa says. Her mother-in-law went up the stairs. Gill stayed downstairs with Lisa.

Gail Fitzpatrick didn't stay upstairs.

"Perhaps ten minutes later she came back down. No one was up there, she said. The back door was locked. She had looked all over the house, even out toward the garage to see if he was out there," Lisa says.

Gill recalls her mother calling out at one point, "Lisa," from upstairs in a voice that sounded tense. All three of them ended up in the kitchen. The only living creature in the kitchen was Poopie, the family's miniature schnauzer. Now he was cowering in the corner of the kitchen whimpering.

"It was so bizarre," Gill says. "We talked about that for the longest time. There was high drama in the house. We all ran around asking what the hell that was. Do you believe that? What was it? Those sorts of things."

Lisa said she and her mother-in-law had an idea and it had nothing to do with group psychosis or mass hysteria. The kitchen walker added another layer to other strange experiences they'd had in that house.

"We guessed it was a ghost, but we had no idea why one would be walking across the kitchen," Lisa Fitzpatrick says. Over the course of the seven-plus years the extended Fitzpatrick family lived in their Wantagh home, the family came to the disquieting conclusion that their home was haunted.

THE FITZPATRICKS' IMPRESSIVE home on Wilmarth Place was built in the late 1920s by the same man responsible for the famed Lido Beach Hotel in Long Beach, according to Gill Mc-Namara. William Reynolds built the Lido Beach Hotel after he was defeated for re-election as Long Beach mayor. The dredging of a harbor that bears his name opened Long Beach as a resort community.

"He built several other homes on the same street . . . for his children as they married and needed their own places," she says. "But they were English Tudor style. Ours was the only Georgian Colonial."

The two-story residence with a red tile roof, magnificent stone and brick façade, included intricate stonework set in graceful arches around the front doorway and the downstairs windows. Attached to the side of the house was a separate entryway that also served as a summer porch.

The main entrance foyer was constructed with matching black marble floors and walls. A glowing crystal chandelier hung from the ceiling just inside the doorway to greet family and guests. Twin leaded glass doors with crystal doorknobs opened onto a hallway, off which doors led into the main rooms. Most of the ceilings were at least ten feet in height. A graceful hallway staircase with an imported Italian brass banister led to the second story. A coach light set into the banister was kept lit in the evening, providing a warm welcoming glow in the hallway. The home's hardwood floors were of herringbone pattern mahogany; plaster crown ceiling moldings were incorporated into most of the rooms.

The home's main floor design was straightforward. On the front, right-hand side of the hallway a formal dining room behind a set of leaded double doors, and a roomy kitchen behind it in the back. On the opposite side of the hallway, a spacious living room toward the front, and at the rear and through a set of Italian leaded glass doors, another, smaller room that Jim Fitzpatrick used as his home office.

One ascended the hallway's long flight of stairs to a landing from which a sizeable window looked out over the backyard.

The upstairs hallway was another three steps up and around the corner. On one side of that hall were Gail and Jim Fitzpatrick's master bedroom suite and master bath. Bedrooms for Samuel and Gill were on the opposite side with separate bathrooms.

"When we first moved there, it was a beautiful residential, suburban area," Gill remembers. "But by the time we left seven years later, they'd torn down an old house behind ours that was on a large piece of property and built a new telephone company building. That really changed everything. Suddenly there was a ten-story building behind us."

But that house served as more than just a lovely architectural jewel for the family—it also served as a frequent reminder that there are ordinary places where revenants of lives long past might linger into the present.

THE FITZPATRICKS MIGHT have guessed much earlier that their lives on Wilmarth Place would be anything but ordinary.

After all, it's not every family that finds bullet holes in their kitchen wall.

Not long after the family moved into the house in the mid-1960s, they found what Gillian and Lisa say were bullet holes in the wall directly opposite the kitchen door.

"My mom wanted to take down some hideous wallpaper," Gill says. "(My parents) ended up putting up paneling. But when they peeled the wallpaper off, I remember (them) saying, 'holy shit, look at this.' There were bullet holes all over the walls."

The family had been given to understand that the builder, or an early owner, had ties to the mob and that the bullet holes might have had something to do with that era in the home's history.

"I think what my family surmised is that (someone) might have been killed in the house, in the kitchen. I don't think they knew for sure (but) the kitchen was where we kept hearing all the footsteps and the voices," Gill says. There were even rumors that it was the builder who'd been killed there, though they had no solid evidence of that. The Fitzpatricks did not buy the house from the original owners.

LISA FITZPATRICK REMEMBERS the disturbing frequency with which unmistakable voices and memorable sounds would result in fruitless searches for their sources.

"Gail was in the hospital with pneumonia . . . ," Lisa recalls of one particular episode. "It was evening and Gill and I were downstairs in the apartment gabbing when we both heard the back door opening and Gail calling out as if she had just come back from a trip and was looking forward to seeing her daughter. Gillian and I looked at each other; she said 'mom's home!' and I said, 'your mom's home!' at the same time. She wasn't expected for several days at least. We went running up the stairs."

There was no one in the kitchen, or anywhere else on the first floor. The back door was still closed and locked as were the other doors and windows. The only other person they found was Samuel, who was in his room upstairs with his door closed and the music blaring.

"I was thinking Gail had taken a turn for the worse, had died, and was saying good-bye," Lisa remembers. "So I called the hospital room. Gail answered and told Gill that she'd just been thinking of her. But she said she was fine and would be home in a day or two."

Gillian McNamara says the idea of her mother being able to "throw" her thoughts from a distance so that her voice seemed to float through the house did not necessarily surprise her.

"My mom was a little bit psychic. Before we had Caller ID, I remember seeing her walk over to the telephone and put her hand on it. It would ring. She'd pick it up and say (the woman's name telephoning) and it would be her friend."

WHILE MOST OF the incidents in that house on Wilmarth Place could be categorized as merely puzzlements or nuisances, others caused alarm and sometimes fright in the recipients who were beset with the unwanted and unpleasant skirmishes.

Lisa Fitzpatrick remembers one episode in particular that frightened her the most. It was especially memorable and upsetting because she was pregnant with her first child, and home alone with only the two small dogs for protection.

"Initially, it was because I thought some (person)—not a

ghost—was in the house and had to be up to no good and would probably murder me if they realized I was there. I had a door from the basement to the outside and could have grabbed my dog and ran for it, but I couldn't leave my mother-in-law's dog upstairs to be hurt or possibly killed while I ran like a big coward."

PERHAPS WHAT MADE her think less of a supernatural explanation and of something far more human in origin is that all this happened in the bright sunlight of an early afternoon.

"I heard the back door opening, but not closing, and then someone walking across the kitchen floor in what seemed to me to be a somewhat stealthy manner, as if someone was stopping to listen, and then moved on a few steps. I thought maybe someone was checking out things on the countertops. It was not the tread of someone light in weight. At first I thought the next-door neighbor might have come in the house, as he was wont to do, without knocking. I wondered what he was up to being so sneaky, but the tread sounded too heavy even for him. I was also upset to think that my mother-in-law had left the house with the door unlocked." Lisa couldn't barricade herself downstairs as there was no lock on the basement door.

Her dog ran over to the steps going upstairs, looked up, and whined. He then scrambled back across the room and hid under a desk. Lisa tiptoed over to the bottom of the steps and listened in a cold sweat, unable to move any farther as the footsteps proceeded across the kitchen floor. She heard her mother-in-law's schnauzer, Poopie, growling from somewhere overhead.

"I'd never heard him growl like that before or since; the growls almost sounded like screams and it went on and on. I knew for sure that the person wasn't the neighbor because the dog knew him, liked him, and vice versa."

Lisa thought then that someone "really bad" was in the house. She was petrified. Any thought of "ghosts" was far from her mind as she wondered what weapons might be on hand with which to protect herself. Strangely, the footsteps seemed to fade away as they neared the doorway leading out of the kitchen. But she heard the schnauzer standing in the hallway at the top of the basement stairs, still growling. She grabbed a hammer off a nearby table and tiptoed up the stairs.

"Several steps from the top I could look under the door and see the dog's feet. I strained to listen over the growling to see if I could hear anyone moving about and where they were. From the way the dog was acting I thought whoever it was had to be standing in the kitchen doorway. I was wondering what the heck (the intruder) was doing; it seemed like someone was just standing there watching the dog going berserk. I was prepared to leap out if I saw feet moving toward where the dog was standing."

After a few minutes of listening and looking under the door, Lisa says she got "really annoyed" with herself for cringing in fear and not taking some sort of decisive action. She noticed, though, that Poopie had abruptly stopped growling. He didn't seem to have left the basement door.

"I thought whoever was there must have moved away from the kitchen doorway, so I finally screwed up my courage, raised my hammer . . . opened the door quickly, and leaped out into the hallway."

She prepared to "whack" anyone who might be there.

The house was silent. No one lurked in the kitchen doorway. No one was quickly exiting through the back door. Little Poopie the schnauzer was wagging his tail.

"I stood still for a few minutes listening. Then I started checking the doors and the windows. The back door was closed and locked. I had to unlock the foyer door to go check the front door. It was closed and locked. All the windows were intact, closed, and locked."

She went through the second floor as well, but found nothing amiss. There didn't seem to be any *worldly* explanation for the terrifying ten or fifteen minutes she'd just gone through, but Lisa had one straightforward proposal: "I hoped whoever that was wouldn't visit anymore."

AS ANYONE WHO has lived in a large old house is well aware, noises emanating from furnaces, heating ducts, and through drafty windows can startle the unsuspecting. But on Wilmarth Place, the cold drafts and furnace room *clanks* came accompanied by something more visible.

The basement apartment was not heated so the furnace room door was left open to heat their living quarters, Lisa Fitzpatrick says.

"At this time my 'living room' area was set up directly across the stairs and my 'bedroom' was directly opposite the door leading into the furnace room. Against the wall next to the furnace room—perhaps six feet from the furnace room door—I had a coffee table with a large old-fashioned mirror sitting on top of it which, from the floor to the top of the mirror, would have been a little over five feet tall. My puppy, Cinnamon, was under the bed. I was sitting in bed reading and it seemed to me to be getting colder. I never thought much about that because it was always chilly in the basement." Her husband was in bed reading next to her.

Lisa looked up from her book when she thought she heard a noise in the furnace room. For some reason, that dark room always gave her an "uncomfortable" feeling, even during the daylight hours. She would have closed the lockless door but that would have shut off the only source of heat the young couple had.

"I sat there looking toward the open door into the darkness of the furnace room waiting to see if the sound would be repeated. I can no longer remember what it sounded like . . . but I remember it got my attention. My dog started growling, even though he was the sweetest, most even tempered dog I've ever owned. I got down on the floor to look under the bed to see what he was growling about."

She saw little Cinnamon staring out from under the bed and into the furnace room, and though she called his name and tried talking to him, he would not shift his eyes away. He continued growling but didn't move to confront anything.

"I started to look up again and a movement caught my eye from the direction of the mirror. Something had moved from left to right in front of it and was gone in a few moments. It was as if I was looking at a reflection of clear, bunched-up cellophane, except there was nothing in front of the mirror to reflect anything. I tried to see what it might be as it was moving but could not make out any details. However, it covered the entire height of the mirror as it moved, as if someone had just walked slowly in front of it.

"As the whatever-it-was was almost all the way across the mirror, I turned my head and asked my husband 'are you seeing this,' and though he had heard the noise, thought it was colder, heard the dog growling—he remained blissfully unconcerned, with his nose buried in his reading material. When he glanced up he saw nothing."

The couple's dog then crawled out from under the bed wagging his tail. The room got warmer. Lisa shut the furnace room door for the rest of the night, though she had to reopen it in the morning to heat the apartment. She also left a few lights on and made sure her flashlight was working.

"I was probably nervous for several nights thereafter but I figured that my dog could see and hear things I couldn't, so as long as he wasn't acting differently I quit worrying about it."

And, she adds, the couple wasn't harmed in any way.

THERE WERE TO be more incidents involving odd, floating masses that didn't seem to Lisa Fitzpatrick to have been caused by anything *natural*.

"One evening at about nine or ten, shortly after my husband and I were married and living in the basement apartment, he had gone upstairs to use the bathroom. We were already in bed with the lights off and he didn't bother turning one on. At that time, our 'bedroom' was directly across from the long, steep flight of stairs and the only nightstand and light were on his side of the bed. One would have to walk in front of the open furnace room door to get up the stairs, and also to reach the overhead light switches. After he got upstairs I heard voices. His parents were in the family room watching television and they wanted to chat for a few minutes. Being nosy, I turned over to see if I could better hear what was being said. I couldn't hear the exact words and lost interest. As I started to turn back over, a whitish mass floated out of the furnace room above the floor, and then very, very slowly across the room. It paused a couple of times. When it was about halfway across the room I dove for the table lamp, switched it on, but my 'guest' had disappeared."

Lisa described it as a kind of a cloud, about three feet in

height, and stretched out in a vertical direction. It wasn't particularly luminous, and though she could see nothing else in the darkness of the apartment, she clearly detected it. The next day she bought another flashlight to keep under her pillow.

THE BASEMENT APARTMENT was not the only location in which Lisa discovered anomalous activities.

"One afternoon, perhaps about five p.m., I was helping my mother-in-law fold towels. I had carried an armload (to the second floor) to the linen closet while she started dinner. My husband and I were invited to dinner that night, and (Gail) was a terrific cook, so I'm sure my mind was focused on that as I climbed the staircase. As I got to the small landing, I glanced out the window, and as I turned to climb the last couple of stairs a shadow passed right in front of Gill's room, moved across the hall, and turned left into the master bathroom, disappearing as soon as it passed through the doorway. The shadow looked exactly as it would against the wall with the light source from the window behind me, and then having a person walk across the hall."

Only it was a shadow sans person.

Lisa says it took on the appearance of a light, gray overlayment when it reached the doorway to the bathroom.

"I was surprised and interested, but not really frightened. Perhaps because it happened so quickly. I told Gail about it. She asked me not to mention it to Gill so as not to frighten her."

ANOTHER INCIDENT LISA attributes to, perhaps, a type of poltergeist activity:

"Gill and I were alone in the house, down in the apartment, shortly before Gail got home from grocery shopping, so it was probably around four p.m. We heard a loud crash that sounded to me like the crystal chandelier in the dining room had crashed onto the table. The noise was very loud. I went tearing up the stairs thinking that Gail was going to be upset at the damage. She kept her house just so. I expected (to see) the remains of the chandelier on the table and a big hole in the ceiling, with plaster all over."

But what she found was a perfectly clean and orderly dining room, obviously without a smashed ceiling fixture.

"Samuel and one of his friends came home shortly after this happened, while I was in the process of checking the rest of the house. At that time, Jim had a large fish aquarium that he kept in his office off the living room. Either Samuel or his friend mentioned that and I thought, oh, no, maybe the noise was the tank breaking. Nope. Absolutely nothing was out of place, no windows were broken, nothing had fallen anywhere in the house. And nothing outside the house appeared to be out of order."

No one was ever able to figure out what the source of the crash might have been. The house was too well insulated for it to have occurred too far distant. Both Lisa and Gill were convinced something had produced it from inside.

THROUGH THE DECADES, Lisa Fitzpatrick still can't explain much of what she heard and witnessed in that house in Wantagh.

"I really have no idea as to the identity or identities of the unusual 'guests' in the house. The footsteps and the dog growling incidents where I really had a sense of evil—probably compounded by the dog's reaction—were the only times I was truly terrified. I think I had a vague fear that if these ghosts had not passed on to where they were supposed to go, then they might possibly 'get' me with some psychic attack and possibly hurt me physically if they were 'bad' and noticed me. In the back of my mind was the feeling that if I was experiencing this stuff I might be enough a part of their world to be affected by it."

But Lisa had no desire on her part to be anything "other than an observer."

It seems that the incidents were more or less occasions on which whatever entity the family thought lived there got out once in awhile just to make its presence known.

Samuel Fitzpatrick had a fright shortly after midnight one evening after he'd returned home from work. He'd parked his car in the driveway. A long pathway led from the driveway, around the back of the house, and in through the kitchen. As Samuel passed by a window to a utility room in the back, he saw what he described as a "face" pressed against the glass looking out at him. He ran into the house but found no one awake. He managed to look around the house for a few minutes but found nothing amiss. "It just scared him to death," Gillian remembers.

As a little girl, at times, it was almost too much for her to take, Gillian says.

"I remember coming in the house from playing and hearing my mother's dresser drawers opening and closing, over and over. It sounded strange because they weren't being opened as you would if you were looking for something. They just opened and closed, quickly and repetitively."

Gillian had been at the bottom of the stairs when she heard it. She listened for a few seconds before going up.

"I assumed it was my mother because they were definitely her drawers that I heard. You can identify certain sounds because you hear them so much. As I reached the top of the steps, I called out her name."

The sound from her mother's bedroom stopped. Gill crept inside but didn't find anyone.

"I had been alone so I got very scared I ran outside where the sun was shining and that always somehow made things seem less scary."

Gillian searches her memory of those years for hints as to what might have brought out the home's psychic energy.

One explanation might be the bizarre occasions on nights of the full moon when Gail Fitzpatrick would hold what she termed Dummy Suppers.

"I remember being very scared as a little girl," Gill McNamara recalls. "She'd wait and look at the calendar until the full moon. We all dreaded it. It had to be the full moon, and right on that day. That night. She'd make all of us sit in the dining room."

She set the table backward, Gill says, putting out enough place settings for the children and her, but set an additional one for a "guest." Once the children were seated around the table, Mrs. Fitzpatrick snapped off the lights and placed a record on the turntable. She always played a creepy composition called "Fear" from an album of music from the science fiction television series *One Step Beyond* recorded by the Harry Lubin Orchestra. Other tracks on the album included such titles as "Bullfight" and "Weird."

"She'd walk backward setting the table; she'd put the plates on the table from behind her back. And she'd go all the way around the table before leaving an extra plate, usually at the head of the table," Gill remembers. Jim Fitzpatrick did not approve of his wife's actions and never attended one of the Suppers.

"Then we'd all sit there in the dark and wait. I don't ever remember anything happening, but just being scared out of my mind and hating it," Gill says.

Her mother hoped that a spirit or ghost would materialize at the Dummy Supper, but Gillian never saw one. But that may not mean something was not *watching them* in this peculiar ritual.

Once, however, Gill says, Larry and Lisa, her brother and sister-in-law, tried their own version of a Dummy Supper.

"They were still dating then, and sitting in the dinette just off the kitchen. So what they did was to sit in the kitchen without the lights on to see if anything would happen. There was a bell ringing far away, but it got louder and louder and louder and they panicked. He ended up taking her home."

ALTHOUGH GILLIAN MCNAMARA was in grade school during her family's life on Wilmarth Place, the mystery of what caused the puzzling noises and the origins of those fleeting shapes has stayed with her all her life.

Whatever it was, was definitely "related to that house," Gill says today. And she believes it was linked to the original owner.

"After living in that house, I believe there are ghosts. But they weren't the kinds of ghosts that go shooting across the room. It's nothing like that. It's much more subtle. This house had a lot of eerie things happen in it while we lived there, but never once did we feel threatened or as though someone was trying to drive us out."

GAIL FITZPATRICK HAS passed away, and the three children live in different parts of the country.

For her part, Lisa Fitzpatrick says her strange experiences on Wilmarth Place haven't adversely affected her.

"It's something interesting and scary . . . and a great story to tell when I'm around people who are interested in those things. Odd things have happened (to me) in other houses, so this wasn't terribly unusual, even though there was quite a lot of activity for the year and a half I lived there.

"Most houses I've lived in feel okay; very few have made me feel 'creeped out.' I only felt scared or uneasy in that house (on Wilmarth Place) while the incidents were taking place or for a short period of time afterward. Except for that furnace room, I really liked the house. I do tend to pay attention to how a house 'feels' to me."

And, imagination or not, if the atmosphere in a house doesn't feel right to Lisa Fitzpatrick, she does not want to be there.

14

The House on Hanging Hill

"Poor, poor Ghost," she murmured; "have you no place where you can sleep?"

—Oscar Wilde, *The Canterville Ghost*

I had barely closed my eyes when I heard the sound of a key turning a door lock, followed by the slow rhythmic tread of footsteps echoing through my apartment. I jumped from my bed, put on my robe, and walked quickly to the living room. The front door was just as I had left it, securely locked, and no one was walking about. Once again, I decided I was merely overwrought. I returned to the bedroom, but my ghostly visitor accompanied me. His footsteps, very audible, followed me. . . .

THE WORDS ARE those of Lynne Gause in an unpublished personal remembrance of the intersection between her life and the haunted history of Wilmington, North Carolina's, celebrated antebellum Price-Jones-Gause House. With her husband, Tom, Ms. Gause lived in the house for many years and grew to appreciate the legends associated with its nearly two centuries of recorded history. But what separates her story of the resident ghost apart from most others is that her first encounter with it didn't take place at that house on Market Street, but rather in her apartment in the time before her marriage to Tom Gause. She might have been followed back to her apartment by the spectre, and, based on her description, her future husband identified it as looking much like his great-grandfather, Richard J. Jones, a prominent Wilmingtonian. Most other accounts of the ghost considered it more likely to be a revenant left over from before the days when the house was built in 1843 and the site was atop a mound of earth grimly known as Hanging Hill. Convicted thieves and murderers were hanged from gallows on that very ground during the late 1700s and early 1800s. If no one claimed their bodies, they were buried on that very knoll.

On the night of those phantom steps, Lynne Gause had been on a date with her future husband. They'd gone to the beach, but Lynne developed a severe headache. She asked Tom to take her back to her apartment. He readily obliged before returning to the Price-Jones-Gause House where he lived.

While Lynne relaxed on the sofa in her apartment, the headache disappeared, but then she had an entirely new problem, according to her written account:

"While lying there, I felt what seemed to be a strange cold hand on my shoulder. Startled, I glanced up, and on the darkened TV screen, an image appeared. It was the face of a distinguished, elderly gentleman with white hair, a goatee, and piercing blue eyes. The hint of a smile played on his lips and he held a pipe in his teeth. I searched the corners of my mind for a clue as to his identity, but my search proved futile and as I watched, the face slowly faded away.

"Being an unemotional person, I tried to rationalize about

this phenomenon. I glanced at the lamp close by to see how colors had reflected in the black and white TV set, but, just as I thought, the set was unplugged. Finding nothing awry, I decided that I must have dozed off and dreamed the entire episode.

"After reaching this decision, I told myself, 'enough of this foolishness' and immediately began preparation for bed. But . . . I was to get little or no sleep that night!"

The key in the lock and following footsteps beleaguered her until, finally, she fell asleep.

Lynne and her future husband had scheduled a lunch together for the next day. When they met, she described what she had seen.

He said the description fit photographs he'd seen of his great-grandfather, Richard Jones.

"I wonder if our well-known family ghost could have visited you last night," Tom Gause wondered.

Jones had been secretary-treasurer of the Tidewater Power Company, and active in several local charities. At age ninety-seven, and upon his doctor's orders, he stopped walking to work. He died three weeks later.

"I think he approves of you and we should get married right away," Tom said. Within days the couple was engaged, and several months later they married and moved into the historic family home.

THE BEAUTIFUL BRICK home, known over the decades as the Price-Jones House before the newer owners' name was added, was designed and constructed by a family that spared little expense with its exquisite furnishings and unique architectural flourishes. Originally twelve large rooms and a wide hallway graced the house, with a spiral staircase leading to the vast second floor. Imported wood was turned into banisters, floors, and moldings; the material used to make the fourteen-inch-thick brick walls had originally been used as ballast in sailing ships; and the wide hardwood floors were held together with pegs and not nails.

The Wilmington Chamber of Commerce used it as their headquarters for many years, before it was converted for other business uses.

During those Chamber years, countless individuals reported strange and unexplained incidents there. But recent years provide merely the dark frosting on this eerie devil's cake of a story.

Not long after the Price family moved into their new house in 1843, stories circulated about unseen presences there—of chains rattling in the early morning hours, of shuffling feet and of muffled voices. Those who heard the disconcerting disturbances thought it likely they were consequences of those condemned men whose last breaths were taken on that very site.

It is extremely difficult, of course, for historians to identify the anonymous dead from centuries before, but writer J. Fred Newber offered one possible candidate for the ghost of Market Street:

"James Peckham (was) a man accused of stealing a jeweled purse from a distinguished Wilmington lady in the late 1700s. Throughout his trial, Peckham maintained his innocence, but the accused was found guilty and sentenced to be hanged at Gallows Hill. As the noose was being slipped around his neck, Peckham saw the jeweled purse in the hands of a seedy character who had come to watch the execution.

" 'That man has the purse!' Peckham screamed desperately.

"The shifty-eyed individual was immediately seized, but a search of his possessions failed to produce the piece of evidence which would have exonerated Peckham.

"The doomed man insisted that the purse must be nearby . . . that the onlooker had somehow managed to dispose of it. Despite his pleas, the hanging went on as scheduled, with Peckham declaring his innocence to the end."

There is no reported evidence that Peckham was buried on the hill, though his last earthly struggle for breath might be enough to suggest that he hasn't given up his hope for vindication.

BURIED HUMAN REMAINS were found several years ago when workmen disturbed a very old unmarked grave. Bits of cloth and metal were found with the bones; however, no records existed of any family members being buried there. Speculation extended to one of the hanged criminals, or perhaps a slave or Native American from the Colonial or early-Republic eras.

One version of the final disposition of the bones indicates they were decently reburied underneath the basement's brick floor with the intention that the departed soul would rest in peace.

The virtuous gesture did not work for either the departed or many of the mansion's residents over the years.

From the first days the Price family moved into their new home in 1843, the mysterious presence made itself known. The first evidence is said to have occurred after a leisurely dinner in their spacious dining room. Family members clearly heard the heavy tread of a man climbing the long staircase and then plodding along the upstairs hallway. The men in the family rushed to confront the trespasser but the footsteps fell silent and they found no one. When they returned downstairs, however, the measured tread resumed. Once again they searched; careful to post one of their number at the head of the staircase should the intruder try to make his escape. They need not have worried. An investigation inside closets, beneath beds, and even on the roof outside the open windows produced nothing of consequence.

So it continued over the ensuing years and decades. The family grew accustomed to its unseen tenant, mindful that it had never caused harm to anyone, nor did it seem to grow in intensity. Visiting friends or relatives might become upset at the sudden steps tramping along beside them down the hallway, or the rocker that might suddenly start swaying, but once they were assured of the ghost's genial nature, they usually calmed down.

The single propensity of the ghost that *did* upset family and visitors was its proclivity to move objects about or even at times hide them all together. Thus we have the makings of a house inhabited by a ghost with distinct poltergeist tendencies.

A most common occurrence was the taking of bedspreads off unsuspecting sleepers. They'd feel the blanket slowly being pulled toward the end of the bed until a final, definite yank sent it tumbling to the floor.

On another occasion, a woman visitor gazing in her bedroom mirror and adjusting her hair noted a smoky substance float across the room toward her and cloud the mirror. She wiped the vapor away, but it reappeared on the mirror seconds later. Taking up a cloth, she wiped more vigorously than before, and at the same time heard an older man's low hum and caught the strong scent of a man's acrid pipe smoke. At that moment the temperature dropped precipitously—it had been a typically humid summer's night—before edging back up. She moved out of the room shortly thereafter.

Rhythmic, sequential tappings on the walls distressed the family. The peculiar noise would start at the top of the house and work its way downward, almost as if someone were searching for a soft spot in the walls. Once it reached the basement, the noise ceased.

Clock hands have been found turned to different hours on each of the house's clocks, but never to the same hour.

This ghost displayed an appetite as well, but a teenager's habit of leaving soiled kitchenware about. A cook around the turn of the twentieth century complained to the family that dirty napkins and grimy dishware were being left in the kitchen, apparently from a midnight snacker whose presence surprised each and every family member. Among themselves they denied being the culprit, but wisely chose not to inform the cook that it was the resident ghost munching its way through the night.

The respected Gause family inherited the house in 1934 and with it the legendary spirit. It was during that family's tenancy that their daughter-in-law and noted poet Lynne Gause wrote her short memoir:

"I was unprepared for the role that ensued as mistress of the Price-Jones-Gause House. My first night in the beautiful old home is one I shall long remember. A chill enveloped the house, although it was late summer. I thought I had solved this problem when I found several patchwork quilts on the shelves of the linen closet and tucked them tightly across the bed before I drifted off to sleep.

"My slumber was rudely interrupted when I felt a strong ethereal force pulling the covering from the bed. I awakened Tom and he told me quietly that this had happened before. I began to believe the tales of the ghost that haunts the old dwelling.

"The next morning, to add to my convictions, my bedroom mirror suddenly clouded over as if covered with steam. However, when I ran my hand across the surface, the glass was not even damp.

"Later that day, I noticed an antique rocker gently moving back and forth. This (was followed by) footsteps climbing the spiral stairway in the hall. To add to the mystery, the following night the lights in the heavy, overhead chandelier dimmed and slowly went out. These scenes were repeated many times during my stay in the haunted mansion.

"Intrigued, more than frightened by these ghostly manifestations, I questioned my husband about the history of the house. I learned that several years before a grave containing fragments of human bones had been located in the side yard by workmen erecting a fence. The remains were never identified. However, if the ghost was Richard J. Jones (Tom Gause's great-grandfather), the bones were probably not him. His resting place is known to be in a local cemetery.

"Although I no longer live in the Price-Jones-Gause House, I have often wondered if a restless soul could move his earthly remains closer to the spot where he spent the most active years of his life."

SOMETIME AFTER THE Wilmington Chamber of Commerce bought the house in the early 1970s, the ghost came to be known casually as George, perhaps because it was better to stick a name on the thing than to merely refer to it as A. Ghost.

A chamber official told a Raleigh newspaper that he'd cleaned up innumerable messes he thought George had caused.

"I can't tell you how many nights I've been called back to the office to fix something George did, or undid," he said. "Most times it's to reset the burglar alarm (or to) turn off water spigots, lights, and electric typewriters he left running. The thing is, we know, we *know* we turned them all off when we left. And we've checked with the janitorial service, and they swear they didn't turn them on. The police are constantly calling me to come let them in because the burglar alarm went off. And it's triggered only by sound."

Another alarm is activated by movement only. It reportedly went off in the middle of the night with no one—alive— present. The aroma of baking sweet potatoes and pipe tobacco, similar to that smelled decades before by the house guest, has been detected.

Another former chamber official told the same newspaper that although he wasn't a believer in things supernatural, ". . . a lot of things that happen here can't be explained. I've heard creaking stairs and running water and whistling sounds when there's nobody else in the building."

While some of those events might be attributable to the ancient structure itself, other mischief pinned on George is not so easy to dismiss.

That same official expanded on his comments to columnist Dennis Rogers, and added an unsettling footnote . . . George occasionally manifests himself:

"One time I was here alone and had to go downstairs to put water in the boiler. After I got back upstairs, I heard water running. It sounded like it was coming from the bathroom, and I knew I had turned the water off downstairs. I went into the bathroom and both faucets were running full blast. Those are screw-type faucets. Something had to turn those faucets on."

The visible George was spotted by the executive secretary of the chamber, but when she turned to look full at the ghost it wasn't there any longer.

That last chamber official had a much more direct encounter.

"I was in here using the copying machine," he told the newspaper. "I thought I heard something in the hallway, so I looked up at a security mirror that shows down the hall. There was no light on in the hall, just the light from the front porch. I saw a figure in silhouette standing there. It raised the hair on the back of my neck, and I left as fast as I could."

However, the incident that is still one of the most plausible encounters with the ghost of the Price-Jones-Gause House came in 1967 when the Wilmington newspaper sent a team there to write a Sunday feature. The newsman, Jerry Tillotson, and the photographer, Andy Howell, roamed through the house on a couple of occasions, noting its unique antebellum architectural features, spacious rooms, and graceful atmosphere, according to reports of their activities.

Toward evening, the two men were quietly chatting in the drawing room when they heard a door close from somewhere in the house. The creak of footsteps on the staircase sent the men charging out the door. Though they saw nothing, both men said they continued to hear the steps groaning under the weight of someone going up to the second floor. The photographer snapped a picture of the empty staircase.

When he got back to the newspaper office and processed the film, the photographer was flummoxed. In the photograph he'd taken of the staircase, a filmy figure was clearly discernible, though it lacked a distinct profile. It was solid because none of the details of the staircase or wallpaper could be seen through it. What seemed to be shoulders, a neck, and two arms—but no head or legs—stood out in relief and was captured on film.

Is it the ghost's shadowy portrait, or a trick of light and film and imagination? It's safe to say that believers and disbelievers have had their say over the ensuring years, but both groups might acknowledge that in the end only George himself knows for sure.

PERHAPS THE MOST celebrated ghost in the Wilmington region was not a human revenant at all but a mysterious light that scores of witnesses reported seeing in the Brunswick County countryside not far from the juncture of North Carolina Highway 87 and U.S. Routes 74 and 76. It's a speck on the map called Maco. The Maco Light, or Joe Baldwin's Light, as it has been known for nearly a century and a half, has been seen by everyone from a former president to high school boys angling to thrill their girlfriends. *LIFE* magazine ranked it as one of the great "true" American ghost stories.

But if research within the last few years is correct, the suggestion that a man named Joe Baldwin had anything to do with its origin is erroneous. A North Carolina geographer has found that old Joe might never have existed, and that the railroad man whose death precipitated one version of the legend may have been *Charles* Baldwin, and that he may have been killed years before the accident to which the legend alludes, according to Wilmington newspaper reporter Ben Steelman.

Legend and history have always entwined in the telling of the light's origin, as in the account from one of this author's earlier books:

It had rained hard all day and now, in the late night hours, a fine drizzle fell, like a beaded curtain. The freight train rattled along between scrub pines and deep underbrush, headed for the village of Wilmington, on the southeast coast of North Carolina. The year was 1867.

To conductor Joe Baldwin the chugging of the old stream engine made a comforting sound, especially as the train neared the end of its long day's journey. Joe liked his job on the Wilmington-Florence-Augusta line and felt fortunate to have secured such a fine position. Some of his friends who had returned with him following the Civil War had not been so fortunate.

Although tonight there were no scheduled freight pickups or drop-offs before Wilmington, Joe called out each station in turn. That was his job. Now as the train neared Maco Station, he slid open the rear door of the next-to-last car and expertly leaped across the network of pins and couplers. But as soon as he landed on the last car he knew something was wrong. It had lost momentum. Beads of sweat stood out on his forehead. With sickening dread, he realized what had happened. The last car had become uncoupled and was rolling to a stop. He also knew a passenger express train was only minutes behind.

Joe seized his lantern firmly in one hand and jerked open the rear door of the car. Then, stepping out onto the platform, he peered down the tracks. The engine headlamp from the distant passenger train was growing fast. He frantically swung his light in great arcs to signal the oncoming engineer. His screams were cut off as the screech of metal striking metal punctured the night air; soot and sparks showered the brush on either side of the glistening rails as the locomotive slammed into the stalled car.

Joe Baldwin's mangled torso was discovered sprawled across the tracks. He had been decapitated, but his head was nowhere to be found. He was the only fatality.

Not long after that tragic accident, local residents said a mysterious light appeared by the tracks outside Maco Station, a scattered handful of farmhouses and a general store a dozen miles outside Wilmington. It was unlike anything that had ever been seen before. After newspapers picked up the story, mobs of people converged each evening upon the tiny hamlet to watch for the eerie glow. Many hundreds claimed to have seen it during its earliest years. Within a few decades it was being talked about far beyond the North Carolina borders. A company that operated a caustic soda terminal not far away incorporated the story as a booklet into their promotional materials. Later, two newspaper photographers on separate assignments to "capture" the light came back with pictures showing some sort of whitish, though indistinct masses.

Some witnesses believed the light to be Joe Baldwin's lantern still swinging its futile warning to the approaching train. Others thought the light was the glowing spectre of the conductor himself—searching for his bloody head. One man claimed to have seen the light in a swamp near the place where his lantern landed on that fateful night.

John Harden was a newsman and a collector of Carolina legends. He wrote that, "the Maco light is first seen at some distance down the track, maybe a mile away. It starts with a flicker over the left rail, very much as if someone had struck a match. Then it glows a little brighter, and begins creeping up the track toward you. As it becomes brighter, it increases in momentum. Then it dashes forward with a rather incredible velocity, at the same time swinging faster from side to side. Finally, it comes to a sudden halt some seventy-five yards away, glows there like a fiery eye, and then speeds backward down the track, as if retreating from some unseen danger. It stops where it made its first appearance, hangs there ominously for a moment, like a moon in miniature, and then vanishes into nothingness."

The light's appearance was unpredictable at best. It might show itself night after night, especially if a fine mist was falling, or, again, it would disappear for weeks at a time.

A second light began appearing in 1873. This one traveled west rather than east along the rail line, and the two sometimes met. More than one frightened engineer, believing another train was coming toward him on the track, yelled at his brakeman, squeezed his eyes tightly shut, and prayed. At the dreaded moment of impact, the light vanished. Finally, signalmen began carrying both red and green lanterns. Given a green light, an engineer could push fearlessly down the tracks past Maco.

The light disappeared following an 1886 earthquake. Three years later it reappeared, same as before. President Grover Cleveland reportedly was riding a train toward Wilmington when it stopped at Maco Station to take on coal and water. While he was waiting, the president decided to take a stroll down the tracks. Seeing a signalman swinging a green lantern in one hand and a red one in the other, he asked about the curious signal. He was then told the story of Joe Baldwin. Some believe Cleveland actually saw the famed light itself.

Countless attempts were made to explain the phenomenon. Reflections from automobile headlights coming from nearby roads have always been a popular explanation for anomalous lights. On one midnight, all roads near Maco were supposedly cordoned off for an hour with guards posted to turn back motorists. The light still appeared, hovering about three feet above the tracks and traveling, as per usual, in an easterly direction.

Others believed it might be swamp gas. At least one attempt was made to destroy it with gunfire. A machine gun detachment from Fort Bragg was sent out to investigate. The men fired repeatedly at the light, but it merely hopscotched ahead of them on down the track.

EVEN THOUGH THE old Atlantic Coast Line railroad tracks were torn up nearly forty years ago and even though there have been no recent confirmed sightings of the mystery light, interest remains high in the true nature of the gleaming orb. And now with new historical research by geographer James C. Burke, as reported in the *Wilmington Star*, at least part of the mystery may be solved, at least that which deals with the identity of the beheaded trainman.

Burke was completing his doctorate in geography at the University of North Carolina, Greensboro, researching antebellum railroads in the region. He discovered the Maco legend almost by mistake. Intrigued, he began looking into the origins of the so-called Joe Baldwin. What he found is that *Joe Baldwin* may have actually been one *Charles Baldwin*. The problem is that Charles Baldwin's death came in 1856, and not a decade later as the Maco legend holds, and it occurred due to his own negligence.

Burke found the following in the January 5, 1856, edition of the *Wilmington Daily Star*:

> Just as we were going to press, we learn that an accident occurred upon the Wilmington and Manchester Road last

night, at Rattlesnake Grade, by which several persons were more or less injured, among them Messrs. Charles Baldwin and E. L. Sherwood, of this town. Mr. Baldwin's injuries, it is feared, may result fatally.

What happened is that the "working of the pumps" on the night train malfunctioned, according to a later newspaper account. The engineer uncoupled the rail cars and drove the locomotive the eight miles or so into Wilmington for repairs. Once they were completed, he sped back. He was going too fast, however, and plowed into the idled rail cars. The engine was damaged, as were the rail cars. The mail car was crushed.

E. L. Sherwood was the mail agent and not seriously injured. The conductor was Charles Baldwin. He, on the other hand, suffered severe head injuries and died a few days later, on January 7, 1856. He was buried at Oakdale Cemetery.

Although it was the engineer at the locomotive controls, a coroner's inquest found that Charles Baldwin was at fault in the collision. According to a newspaper account of the proceedings, the inquest found that the conductor (Baldwin) had not placed a lantern on the abandoned cars so that the engineer—Nicholas Walker—knew when to slow down. That was his job; he failed and it cost him his life.

Burke's research established that Rattlesnake Grade and Maco Station were one and the same. It was originally called Maraco before residents shortened it to Maco and dropped the "station" designation. Before that, the small settlement was known as Farmers Turnout and before that, at the time Charles Baldwin was killed, it was called Rattlesnake Grade after a high trestle over Rattlesnake Creek.

Writer Steelman found the only *Joe Baldwin* from North Carolina around the time of the Civil War had no apparent connection to Wilmington. Steelman speculates that perhaps the Charles Baldwin whose death can be documented might have become the *Joe Baldwin* of legend. And instead of a negligent conductor responsible for his own death, Charles was transformed into a genuine railroad hero trying to save innocent passengers from certain death.

But still unexplained is the ten year gap between the actual accident and the date of *Joe* Baldwin's celebrated death.

How is that possible?

As Burke told reporter Ben Steelman, there might be a simple answer:

"History becomes legend."

SHOULD THE NORTH Carolina ghost light hunter want a more contemporary location in which to search his prey, he will have to decamp for a location about two hundred and fifty miles to the west of Wilmington—at the prosaically christened Brown Mountain, hardly a mountain at all but a sort of geological tabletop spread across the Blue Ridge foothills at an elevation of a mere 2,600 feet, straddling Burke and Caldwell counties about fourteen miles northwest of Morganton.

Brown Mountain lacks any monumental distinguishing geographical characteristic—except at night. Then mysterious multihued lights rise above the treetops, shimmering and dancing, disappearing, then reappearing.

Even more astounding is that variations of them have been reported for nearly two centuries.

It is the rare intimation of the supernatural that's been acknowledged by the federal government. The United States Forest Service has erected an official government wayside on North Carolina Route 181 near Morganton detailing the history of the Brown Mountain Lights.

No one knows when the puzzling lights first appeared, but legend has it that they were visible well before the Civil War, possibly as early as 1850. In that year a woman of the region allegedly disappeared. Neighbors suspected that her abusive husband murdered her. Shortly afterward, while search parties scouted Brown Mountain in search of her body, strange lights bobbed above them in the night sky. Some of the more superstitious among the searchers suspected the victim's spirit had returned to haunt her murderer; others thought the lights had been sent as a warning to end the search, while some believed they would be led to the woman's corpse if they could just determine where precisely the lights had originated. Her remains were eventually found below a steep cliff. Her manner of death was never determined.

Ever since that time, the lights have appeared with some

regularity. They are well-known to North Carolinians and to thousands of out-of-state visitors.

Descriptions of the lights vary among observers. One person reported seeing a bright red light that vanished in less than a minute. Another said he observed a pale white light whirl inside a halo, disappear for twenty minutes, and then reappear. A minister described the light as cone-shaped and "larger than a star;" presumably he was referring to its brightness and not its actual planetary size. When two more of these "star lights" arose, he and his sons watched through field glasses. The lights rose high in the sky and faded out.

Other persons said they saw yellow lights that moved upward, downward, *and* sometimes horizontally. Sometimes clusters of lights appear and rise so fast that it's impossible to count them. When viewed through a telescope, the lights resemble balls of fire.

Many theories abound as to this weird visual anomaly. At first the lights were thought to be a will-o'-the-wisp, a phosphorescent light hovering or flitting over swampy ground at night, possibly caused by the combustion of gas emitted by rotting organic matter. However, there is no marshy ground in that section of the two counties.

Could it be foxfire, a luminosity produced by certain fungi found on rotting wood? Probably not. That's usually a weak, pale light that does not appear as colored globes, floating in the sky, as has been reported at Brown Mountain.

An amateur explorer once claimed that he'd found a piece of pitchblende, a radium ore, at one end of the mountain. But the rays from the radium *are*, of course, invisible. Geologists have since confirmed that Brown Mountain is composed of ordinary cranberry granite.

Then there's the moonshiner theory. These scofflaws once operated a plethora of stills near Brown Mountain. To prevent detection by federal agents, they sometimes screened their stills to conceal the fires, but when the covers were at last removed and the fires raked out, clouds of rising steam reflected the firelight from below. But the era of moonshining has—*most* folks say—long since passed into mountain lore. The lights still appear.

The possible presence of St. Elmo's fire was explored for a

time. St. Elmo's fire is an electrical discharge from sharp objects during a thunderstorm. Ocean-borne sailors heading through lightning are well acquainted with it because it often appears as electricity crackling around a mast top. But the phenomenon requires a solid conductor and never occurs in midair. More problematic is that the lights have appeared on clear nights with no storms brewing anywhere in the region. Interestingly the lights are not reported after a long drought.

For a time, an observation made in the Andes Mountains of South America was offered as an explanation for these North Carolina lights. The so-called Andes Lights incidents were observed in these high Chilean mountains when silent discharges of electricity passed through clouds and onto the mountain peaks. These discharges often produced round, shimmering lights that could be seen sometimes for more than three hundred miles. However, that idea was eventually dismissed when it was determined that the Andes events occurred only at elevations over fifteen thousand feet, not at the much lower altitude of the Blue Ridge foothills.

The United States Geological Survey has made at least two formal studies of Brown Mountain.

The first geologist determined that the lights were caused by headlights of locomotives and automobiles in the Catawba Valley, south of Brown Mountain. But three years after his report, a massive flood washed out railroad tracks and bridges and turned the primitive roads into quagmires. No traffic of any kind moved. The lights appeared as usual.

Later, a second geologist came to Burke County to survey the lights. He carried with him an impressive array of scientific equipment. Each time the lights were sighted, their appearance was checked with train schedules. After two weeks of diligence, the investigator announced his findings. He said 47 percent of the lights originated from automobile headlights; 33 percent from locomotive headlamps; 10 percent from fixed lights; and 10 percent from brushfires. He believed that the lights radiated from a deep valley several miles away and that atmospheric conditions caused the lights to appear to rise over Brown Mountain. Mist and dust particles rendered the lights colorful.

Despite these prosaic scientific explanations, at least some of the mountain folk and the many visitors each year continue to believe the lights are of supernatural origin.

John Harden, in his book *The Devil's Tramping Ground*, quotes a former state fire warden, J. L. Harley: "If God could make Brown Mountain, could he not also make the lights? . . . I have fought forest fires on every mountain from Linville Falls to Blowing Rock at all times of the night and have seen these lights a great many times from Grandfather Mountain above any human habitation. It is true there were hunters with lanterns, but please tell me whoever saw a lantern ascend up into the elements where no game exists? . . ."

A summer night after eight o'clock is often the best time to look for the Brown Mountain mystery lights. There are several popular vantage points: Beacon Heights, just off the Blue Ridge Parkway near Grandfather Mountain; Wiseman's View, on North Carolina Route 105 near Morganton; and, of course, the federal government's designated wayside on North Carolina Route 181.

15

Grave Secrets

Disguised as man; filled with alarm.
An enemy's bullet could yet slay
This woman's life—or cause me harm.
Who would remember me today?

—Anonymous, *The Woman Soldier*

Vivia Thomas

JAMES BARRY RECEIVED a medical degree in 1814 from Edinburgh University and then served in the British military for over four decades. Dr. Barry later became the chief inspector of British army hospitals in Canada. Not until his death was it discovered that James Barry was in truth Miranda Barry, a woman who had successfully passed as a male since her teenage years.

Frank Mayne achieved the rank of sergeant in the Union Army during the Civil War but was killed in battle. That's when his fellow soldiers discovered that he was a she: Frances, not Frank.

On the Vicksburg Battlefield's Illinois monument is the name of Albert Cashier. He survived the war and filed for a pension in 1899. Albert's actual name was Irene Hodgers. She was from Ireland. Her proper sex was not discovered until 1911 when she was involved in a car accident. The surviving members of her regiment were stunned. One said of her: "Cashier was very quiet in her manner and she was not easy to get acquainted with."

All told, over five hundred women dressed as men and, passing as such, fought for both the Union and the Confederacy. Many died, but many more survived to continue their charade, or decided to return to civilian life and resume their feminine identity. Some of the women were discovered, as described in this excerpt from an 1863 letter from a soldier to his wife: "We discovered last week a soldier who turned out to be a girl. She had already been in service for twenty-one months and was twice wounded. Maybe she would have remained undiscovered for a long time if she hadn't fainted. She was given a warm bath which gave the secret away."

The ruse of a woman dressing in men's clothing to pass as male is not such an uncommon theme in history and in popular entertainment. From Joan of Arc's manly haircut and asexual battle attire to Hilary Swank's Oscar-winning performance in *Boys Don't Cry*, women have often chosen to pass as the opposite sex in order to achieve their objectives.

During the Civil War, some of the women masqueraded as men to be closer to other soldiers and better ply their trade as prostitutes; however, most of the women joined up and went in disguise to be with husbands, brothers, or fiancés.

At the U. S. National Cemetery in Fort Gibson, Oklahoma, is the Circle of Honor grave of the only woman to ever serve in the United States Cavalry dressed as—and assumed to be—a man. Therein lies not only a tale of a woman who succeeded in passing for a male for over twenty years, but also one of Oklahoma's enduring ghost stories, though one in which fact and fiction have melded into one.

Her name was Vivia Thomas, born to prominent Boston parents in the early nineteenth century. Though she grew to womanhood dissatisfied with life in the staid East of the era, she nevertheless acquiesced to the tacit understanding that a woman's role was seldom anywhere but in the home. There simply weren't many opportunities for women other than marriage, thus Vivia was paraded through the various cotillions and dinner parties in the years before and during the Civil War.

Shortly after the war, Vivia attended one particular ball at which she met a most handsome and dashing cavalry officer. He wooed her and won her hand. He asked her to marry him. She accepted.

But there was one problem. He had been assigned to Fort Gibson, Oklahoma, in Indian Territory. He asked Vivia to wait awhile. He would send for her and then they would be wed.

But there was something in his offhand manner that caused her to have misgivings about his proffered devotion and pledges of fidelity. Once he'd left for Fort Gibson, she devised a plan, one which would certainly allow her to escape the stifling life of a society matron. Vivia shaved her hair down to her scalp, bought a range of roughhewn men's clothing, and, dressed as a fair-haired man, joined the army.

To twenty-first-century eyes, a woman successfully passing as a man and then enduring the rigors of military training seems almost impossible to believe, yet it was not so difficult a century and a half ago. Physical exams were usually perfunctory and quite modest by today's standards—rarely was the patient touched, for instance. The physicians often looked only at hands and feet— and if the woman had tightly bound her breasts and wore baggy clothing typical of the period there was in all probability little chance of discovery. The pants worn by Civil War soldiers were generously cut in the front and back. Little bathing occurred, and if it did it was conducted with the person wearing long johns, considered to be the same as nudity in prim Victorian times.

Thus Vivia Thomas became a soldier. Fortunately, she was able to follow her fiancé into the cavalry and wangle an assignment to Fort Gibson. Her femininity was not difficult to mask. She was slight of build, with small hands and feet, but her comrades thought little of it as long as she could do the work. She kept to herself and didn't talk much.

All the while she was able to keep an eye on her lieutenant. He didn't have the slightest notion that the slender fellow in the baggy uniform who always seemed to be close by was in fact the woman to whom he'd earlier pledged his love.

As Vivia had feared, his fidelity presently waned. A Cherokee Indian girl who frequented the fort caught his eye. He was soon spending evenings at her home. Vivia was incensed. Night upon night she would cautiously follow them on their assignations. It all became too much and on a frightfully cold December night in 1869, she lay in ambush near the girl's house. As he left, Vivia shot him dead, and then stealthily made her way back to Fort Gibson.

Vivia of course was never suspected. The military concluded that someone in the girl's family shot the lieutenant because they did not want her falling in love with a white soldier. But no witnesses were ever found, nor could they place any of the girl's family at the scene of the killing. The case remained unsolved.

But it was not so simple for Vivia Thomas.

She did not understand the depth of her love, nor how her heart would be broken by her one imprudent act. She began to visit the lieutenant's grave, but always late at night. Her grief was overwhelming. Night after night, she threw herself on the grave, crying out through her sobs the sorrow she felt for what she had done and the remorse that she was suffering.

There it all might have ended. Her heart would have healed and maybe she would have stolen away from her army life to once again become Vivia. But then a most unexpected thing happened.

The lieutenant's ghost came calling.

Vivia ran away on that first night, but so deep was her grief that she could not stay away. And each night his ghost arrived to keep her company.

Holding out a bony figure in an accusatory manner, but never uttering a single word, he hovered above his own grave so that she was overwhelmed with even more anguish and regret. On a particularly bitterly cold night early in January

1870, she contracted pneumonia and collapsed at the cemetery. She was found and taken to the infirmary.

With an understanding that her time was short, she confessed her guilt to the Fort Gibson chaplain. Vivia Thomas died on January 7, 1870. Only upon her death was her true identity discovered.

Vivia had used deception and trickery to become a soldier, but her cavalry mates were nevertheless impressed with her bravery in enduring the harsh and dangerous life of a frontier soldier. She was buried beneath a plain marker in a place of honor at the federal cemetery.

The Number Six Mine

The ghosts of dead miners killed in underground disasters seem to inhabit hundreds of deep shafts all across the nation. Quite often the unexpected visits by these shades affect the ability of the mine to reopen. A 1904 explosion that killed one hundred and seventy-nine men nearly caused the mine to go out of business because, once it reopened, workers claimed the ghosts of the dead were keeping them from doing their work. Most of them quit and left for other mines. The owners brought in Montenegrin immigrants to replace them, but they, too, saw the ghosts of all the dead miners. They quit as a group five years later.

A ghost "ran wild" in another mine, as recounted in this published report from 1904:

"Two miners who never have been known to prevaricate are our authority. They state that they have frequently seen a white apparition loitering around the room in which they are employed, but of late it has become bolder, and frequently stands upright with fingers pointed toward them as they enter the room, but always vanishes when they approach it with their lighted lamps.

"The story has it that the ghost is the spirit of a young man of foreign birth who was instantly crushed to death in the room where the spectre is seen, shortly after coming to this country and procuring employment. The skeptical claim that the young fellow had a secret which he longed to divulge to someone, or a message which he desired to send home, but his tragic death prevented him from making known his wishes.

"The circumstances of his death are well-known among the miners, and they frequently narrate the story of his sudden death, which occurred only a few hours after he began work, and probably before he had formed the acquaintance of a single person in the mine where he was working. He met death in a most violent form.

"A party, it is claimed, of persons picked for their courageousness will visit this underground place of the spook at a dead hour of the night and endeavor to hold a conversation with the apparition.

"A man who claims to have held frequent communications with spirits will accompany the party, and will broach the ghost with interrogations which, he contends, will induce it to relate the secret it desires to unfold. Then, according to his theory, it will return to the rendezvous for spirits and will never again be seen on earth.

"Should the spirit relate a story worth printing, we are assured by the spiritualist that we will be given it for publication."

There is no record of another story "worth printing." Apparently the problem the ghost was having was easily solved.

The ghost of a woman in white led to problems at the Number Six Mine near Buck, Oklahoma.

Miners once believed it to be bad luck if a woman went anywhere near a mine, thus the ghostly woman was taken to be a sign that disaster was imminent. Young Charley Withers was an exception. He was a shot-firer who lived with his mother. What happened next was explained in a written account by mining historian George Korson:

"His mother shared the fear of the other miners and begged him to quit his job, but Charley only laughed at her. Each evening she met him halfway down the hill as he came out of the mine and walked home with him. Finally he yielded to her pleas and promised to quit his job. They were to meet halfway down the hill from the mine for the last time. This, however, happened to be the day when the maiden wraith, her face more troubled than ever, reappeared before the miners working on an early shift. They dropped their tools and hurried out of the mine. Charley Withers met them as he was going to work and they warned him not to enter. Charley, however, laughed at their fears and continued walking. Twenty minutes after he had started working an explosion tore up the mine, hurling tons of debris high up in the air and completely destroying the super-structure. Charley and another shot-firer named Sam McKinney were killed instantly—on the very spot where the vision of the maiden in white had appeared. It took a long time to re-cover Charley Withers's body from the debris, but his mother, ever faithful, waited as usual halfway down the hill from the mine."

What were the origins of the superstitions about women in mines?

One version claims it came from Russian miners who them-selves believed the superstition may have originated with peas-ants who claimed to see the "vampire souls of women leaving their river caves for their flight through the night air in search of prey."

16

Terrible Tilly

When the merry wag doth hush his voice
And cower . . . then shall ye know
That ghosts do walk within this ancient Tower
Fact or fantasy, truth or tale,
As shadows shorten and the skies grow pale,
Can ye with certainty stand and claim
That voices called—but no man came?

—Shelagh Abbott

SEAFARERS LIKE NOTHING better than a good ghost story. Their favorite, of course, is the legendary Flying Dutchman, a phan-tom vessel under the watchful command of Captain Van-derdecken and his crew of ambulatory, albeit drowned seamen.

To see it is a fate to be scrupulously avoided for to do so is to be given fair warning of impending disaster.

The Dutchman story was often told at dramatically situated and historic Tillamook Lighthouse, located on a tiny rocky outcropping about a mile off Tillamook Head on the Oregon coast near Ecola Bay State Park. The lightkeepers nicknamed the rugged outpost Terrible Tilly for what has come to be seen as obvious reasons. It is perhaps the most physically isolated lighthouse on the entire Pacific coast, nearly unreachable even under the most favorable seas. So difficult were the circumstances that lightkeepers' families had to remain behind on the mainland. The men themselves remained at the light for all but ninety-six days per year. The only human contact came via the supply vessel every three weeks that brought mail, provisions, and reading material.

Therefore, storytelling came naturally to the daring men who operated the station.

One misty afternoon, the keepers were talking about their various experiences sighting ghost ships at Tillamook and elsewhere when a ship broke the northeast horizon.

The men on duty jumped up and pressed against the glass trying to see through the gloom.

"Ah, looks like the Flying Dutchman," one keeper cried.

"Damn ship looks like it's heading right toward the rock," the head keeper replied.

But another light man and one with keener eyesight set his companions straight.

"Say, that's no *ghost* ship, that's the Manzanita."

The Manzanita was the coal tender, carrying fuel and supplies to the lighthouse. It arrived about every three weeks. All supplies and personnel were off-loaded using a derrick boom with a cargo net or a breeches buoy.

The youngest man on the crew, having not heard about Captain Vanderdecken's ship, later asked the veteran head keeper how the Flying Dutchman came to be. And so the stories always began.

THE LIGHTKEEPER COULD just as well have started with the stories at Tillamook Lighthouse itself and its gripping history.

Originally planned as a warning to ships turning into the Columbia River, and built at a then-substantial sum of $50,000 in 1879–1881, Tillamook Light was one of the most difficult to construct in the history of Pacific Northwest navigational aids. Part of it was due to its location on a slippery slab of basalt rock poking out of the Pacific Ocean. Even before that, however, the Native American communities along the Oregon coast whispered that Tillamook was a cursed place. No tribe ever attempted to land there.

An 1894 report describing the lighthouse graphically summarized its location: "Rising from the ever-restless bosom of the Pacific Ocean and towering aloft to the height of about one hundred feet stands Tillamook Rock on the summit of which are located a light station and a fog signal. Rugged, broken, and of irregular form, it constitutes a prominent and notable sea mark to all who pass up and down the coast, or enter or depart from the mouth of the Columbia River."

The first attempt to survey the rock for a lighthouse was in June 1879. That ended in near disaster. The construction engineer charged with surveying the site barely managed to land on the rock himself, but failed in every attempt to unload his surveying instruments. He resorted to a tape measure and estimates for his figures.

With the engineer's rough figures transferred to construction plans, John R. Trewavas was hired to head up the work crew that would build the light. It was September 1879. He decided to go out before the main crew to more thoroughly inspect the place. But when he tried to climb aboard the rock from his swaying boat, waves caught him and sucked him under. His body was never recovered. Amazingly enough, considering the inhospitable location of the site, he was the only man killed in the construction.

Eight workers managed to land on the rock in October 1879 and began drilling out a level plain for the lighthouse foundation. The men stayed through the winter of 1879–1880, with only a six-by-sixteen-foot tent for shelter against gale force winds and pelting rain. The cornerstone was not laid until June 22, 1880; the lighthouse became operational on January 21, 1881. The seventy-five-thousand-candlepower light shone across the water from a position some one hundred and thirty-four feet above the rock. Navigational charts warned ships not to come within fifty feet of the light or risk being smashed against the rocks.

Tillamook Lighthouse served the Pacific Northwest shipping lanes for seventy-six years before its powerful beacon was taken out of commission in 1957. Yet on some midsummer evenings when the sun slides beyond the western horizon, some mainland residents swear the old beacon flashes once again. Nonsense, say others, it's only the sun's reflection on the polished glass. Whatever one believes, there is little doubt that Tillamook Lighthouse is a place of misfortune . . . and mystery.

The most enduring tale associated with the lighthouse, and a favorite among lightkeepers for decades, is the tragic fate that befell the thirteen-hundred-ton British bark *The Lupatia* just a few weeks before the light became operational. Her entire sixteen-man crew was lost when the ship ran aground there on January 2, 1881.

According to the lighthouse's superintendent of construction, Captain H. S. Wheeler, and *The Oregon Journal*, here is what happened:

The weather was misty with a strong southeast wind blowing. At 8 P.M. the lighthouse workers heard loud voices penetrating the ghostly gloom.

"Ahoy! . . ." came the cry above the pounding surf.

The superintendent realized a ship must be in trouble. He ordered lanterns to be lit and a fire started atop the rock. Soon his men could see the running lights of a great sailing ship bearing down on the rocky outpost.

Though the lighthouse's lamp was not yet lit, Captain Wheeler assumed the ship saw the lanterns and bonfire as it disappeared into the foggy night.

Sadly, that was not to be the case.

The Lupatia, inbound from Japan and heading for the Columbia River, had run aground on the rocky shoals. With the morning's first light, Wheeler and his men could see the topmost section of the mizzenmast rising several feet above the ocean's now calm surface. Debris floated on the water. There were no signs of survivors. Search crews later found the bodies of nine men along Tillamook Head, all dressed in light clothing unsuitable for survival at sea. Four other crewmen were presumed dead though their remains were never recovered. Incredibly, the ship's dog was found alive. An Astoria family nursed it back to health.

WITH THESE EARLY deaths at Tillamook Lighthouse, and the reluctance of Native Americans to venture there, it is little wonder that it soon gained the reputation for being haunted. Strange groans were heard on the stairway leading to the light. Yet with the habitually strong winds and rough seas, it is easy to find all sorts of natural explanations for the odd sounds lightkeepers encountered.

Coast Guardsman James A. Gibbs served part of his tour of duty at Tillamook Light. In one section of his autobiography of his career at sea, Gibbs wrote about Tillamook and what can happen to even the most sober-minded individuals given just the right isolated surroundings. Especially if he stumbles upon another chilling tale of another haunted lighthouse in the Caribbean. This is Gibbs's account of his first midnight-to-dawn watch at Tillamook Light, according to his published memoir, in which he encounters ghosts real and, perhaps, imagined:

"I suddenly found myself alone in the kitchen (of Tillamook Lighthouse) with four walls staring at me. I looked up at the old Regulator clock on the wall, which slowly ticked away the minutes. When the time came for my first rounds, I went outside into the cold, windy night to check the visibility. The atmosphere had cleared somewhat and a slight drizzle pricked my face. The roar of the sea was intense and all around was a black abyss, except when the probing beams of light from the beacon cut the darkness like a knife. For obvious reasons it was scary outside and I was glad to re-enter the fog signal house.

"Continuing my rounds, I headed for the tower and began climbing the spiral staircase to check the light. As I ascended, my shoes clattered against the iron grates. The sounds called back at me, echoing off the tower walls. Just before I reached the watch room, I detected another unrelated noise, strange, haunting. Stopping in my tracks, I stood motionless. There it was again, a whispering moan, like one in pain.

" 'Oh, not again,' I thought to myself. But this was different, and the utterance smacked of something human. Could one of the (other) keepers be trying to frighten me? 'Oh, you foolish soul,' I thought. These old duffers had better things to do than go around playing ghost. Then I got to thinking of the conversation at the dinner table. Were there really such wraiths, I wondered, or were they only a figment of the imagination. I looked all around trying to figure out the source of those strange sounds but could draw no logical conclusion. Thus I hastily parted company with the unseen apparition, scurried into the watch room, and then climbed the ladder to the lamp room.

"I started back down the ladder, satisfied that all was well in the lamp room. Suddenly my thoughts were diverted back to the ghost in the tower. Sure enough, those same sounds were again audible in the same area. I was certain the three keepers were fast asleep at that hour, so it was just the spook and me. Then my eyes fell on a small door near the landing which I had evidently overlooked in surveying the lighthouse. Going back to the kitchen to get a flashlight, I returned to investigate. Could it be that the strange noises were coming from behind that door?

"As if playing a role in a mystery movie, I automatically tiptoed toward the entrance. My hand reached for the handle. Timorous, I stepped back as it creaked open. Gathering my self-composure, I bolted inside. The air was dank and there was barely enough headroom to stand erect. As I flashed the light around, shadows played on the wall like hobgoblins around a witch's brew.

"Finally I found a light bulb on the ceiling and pulled a protruding chain. At first it didn't respond, but finally a dim glow flooded the room which, as I was later to learn, had been created after the original metal lighthouse roof had been holed repeatedly by sea-thrown boulders. It was a storage area of sorts and a place to keep books sent from mainlanders who related to the lonely role of the lighthouse keepers. From the looks of the place nobody ever used it; cobwebs were everywhere. It was like the attic of an early American residence, with a littering of castoffs. What a perfect home for the lighthouse ghost— and certainly a shadowy hideaway that needed future scrutiny. The floor creaked but the moaning sounds I heard in the tower were not in that room.

"As the flashlight fell across the sagging bookshelves, I removed two volumes and returned to the more pleasant surroundings of the kitchen.

"Making my entry in the log, I sat down to study the literary gems I had taken from the upper room. Blowing a collection of dust from the first, I discovered the auspicious title *Tom Swift and His Motor Cycle*. Casting it aside, I picked up the other, which told about the old U. S. Lighthouse Service and some of its problems. I thumbed through to an article on the Navassa Lighthouse on a rock pile in the Caribbean and—wouldn't you know—on this night of all nights, there was an account of the supernatural. Inasmuch as it was an isolated seagirt lighthouse like Tillamook, my curiosity was naturally aroused and I read on. It went something like this:

The head keeper (in the Caribbean lighthouse) was an individual of twenty years' experience in lighthouses, quiet, practical, and certainly not a believer in supernatural things. He was chosen to handle the station after oppressive heat and miserable privation had delayed its completion until 1917. There was an indescribable something about that small island on the sea road to Panama (near Haiti and Cuba), rumor persisting that it was cursed, a holdover from the days when black laborers with white overlords off-loaded its guano resources. A mutiny among the workers had created a blood bath in which several were killed.

That first evening, the keeper-in-charge ascended the tower staircase (just as I had done that very night) and became conscious of the reverberating sound of his feet on the grates. After tending the light and while returning to the dwelling for coffee, he was aware of the damp, humid night, despite a clear, star-laden sky. Then he heard it—a loud, rhythmic wailing sound coming from outside, a sound resembling a man with a high-pitched voice accompanied by a shallow drum. Not believing in spooks and such trivia, despite having served in several lighthouses all claiming ghosts, he believed in a logical explanation for everything. Still, curiosity prompted the keeper to open the door and listen until the whistling wind finally drowned out the sound.

Nevertheless he took his lantern and inspected the area. Satisfied that no intruders were about, he started back. When he reached the dwelling, a loud cackling laugh from the sea pierced his ears. Believing it a strange combination of shrieking sea birds, he dismissed it from his mind, not sharing the experience with his assistant.

Two nights passed without consequence. On the third, it happened again. The keeper distinctly heard the same dull throbbing of the drum. While his assistant was winding the weights that turned the lens, he stole silently out into the night. Scurrying toward a clump of wild growth a short distance from the lighthouse, he hid himself from sight. Again the drums began beating, slowly and quietly at first, then gaining momentum and volume. The pulsating beat was mingled with the cry of birds and the incessant wind. Then came the same haunting voice that had startled him the first night, this time in a chant. The words sounded like, "Go 'way, white man, go 'way before it's too late!"

It was the call of one troubled, seemingly warning of impending doom. But how could this be? There was nobody else on the rock but the two attendants of the lighthouse. He wondered if the oppressive island possessed some strange mysticism. The tempo grew into a wild chant, the apparent warning continuing with greater rapidity, as the drums grew ever louder.

While the listener crouched in the thick growth, the chanter's message, in broken English, seemed to be telling of the brutality heaped upon the blacks before the awful Navassa riot of yesteryear. Numbed by it all, the keeper made no attempt to capture his taunter nor was he able to see any clear image. Instead, each night when not on duty he returned to his secluded listening post to hear the chant. The entire episode smacked of voodoo, and this the keeper knew, but try as he would he could not resist the strange magnetic pull. The keeper became progressively morose and nervous. Alarmed by such behavior, the assistant watched his superior stare for hours on end at the vast sea, tapping his fingers on the table in the same tempo as the voodoo drums. Sometimes he was incoherent, neglecting his duties.

One day, as if in a trance, the troubled man came back to the lighthouse pale as a ghost, chanting a strange jargon and beating his chest in drum-like rhythm. He was stark mad. By running up distress flags, his frantic associate was able to attract a passing ship, but after signals were exchanged the vessel sailed away and it was two harrowing weeks before a lighthouse tender arrived off the island to remove the demented keeper.

The drums were then suddenly silenced and the voodoo chant was heard no more, nor was its originator, if any, ever found.

For a decade after the incident, the lighthouse service maintained personnel at the service, but few could stand the awful privation, the bloodsucking insects and fever. Voodoo rumors persisted all the while.

Finally, in 1929, the Lighthouse Service authorities threw in the sponge, admitting that Navassa was not fit for human habitation. The lighthouse was in turn automated at considerable expense and is still operated with occasional servicing from a buoy tender out of Miami.

"It was almost ironic that I should come across such an article on my first night as lighthouse keeper. I was careful, thereafter, not to take the ghost of Tillamook lightly.

"It was one of the longest nights of my life, but finally out of the east a pale glow appeared over towering Tillamook Head, a giant monolith rising from the mainland beach a mile or so east of the rock. A sea mist hung low and the ocean had calmed somewhat. Through the night I had imagined all kinds of things in the shadows and none of them seemed pleasant—clammy, wet, miserable things—the kind that make one wish for desert sunshine. In the days that followed, strange and ghostly visitations were seriously discussed and often considered as omens to be heeded. For some reason, lighthouses seem to spawn more than their share of ghostly tales and supernatural happenings.

"My entry in the lighthouse log that morning was routine, for who would have believed my experiences of that night?"

FOLLOWING ITS DECOMMISSIONING in 1957, Tillamook Light-house fell into gradual decline as it passed through the hands of several private owners. Eternity at Sea bought the property in 1980 and renovated the building and grounds. It's now a National Historic Monument and a federal wildlife preserve. Eternity at Sea offers mortuary space in the lighthouse as a columbarium for people wishing to have their ashes interred in one of the most un-usual final resting places in the world. Over forty thousand niches were made available for prospective clients, from the lantern room at the top to far beneath in the lighthouse basement. Income from the mausoleum-above-the-sea provides for the on-going maintenance of the private property.

If there were indeed ghosts when Tillamook Light was oper-ational, they are surely pleased to have been joined by newer arrivals to spend time without end at one of the most remark-able lighthouses in the world.

17

Ghosts Along the Pecos

> ... generally our modern ghosts seem to do and say as
> little as their nineteenth-century counterparts. As in the
> 1880s, the banality of 'real' specters stands in sharp
> contrast to the horrendous and frightening powers they
> wield in literature or in television and the cinema.
>
> —R. C. Finnucane, *Ghosts: Appearances of the
> Dead and Cultural Transformation*

THE PECOS RIVER rises in Mora County, in southeastern New Mexico, before snaking its way through Southwest Texas—Big Bend Country—from Red Bluff Lake to its confluence with the Rio Grande River southeast of Langtry, Texas, the ghost town site of the Judge Roy Bean Saloon and Museum. Judge Bean, the "law west of the Pecos," is said to have named the settlement after the celebrated English actress Lillie Langtry. Bean fell so in love with her photograph that he re-named the town in her honor. Ironically, the two never actually met. The only time she ever visited "her" town was shortly after Bean died in 1904. He had bequeathed her his pistol, which she gladly accepted. It's now on display at an English museum featuring her memorabilia. Langtry and its museum are but two reminders that the Wild West is not that far distant. All along its nine-hundred-and-twenty-six-mile waterway, the Pecos River flows through some of the wildest and most storied landscapes in all of North America.

Through this country known as the Trans–Pecos is the most spectacular scenery in all of Texas. In the northeast, the Pecos Basin sweeps into the Great Plains, while in the soaring Guadalupe Mountains along the New Mexican border in the northwest is the state's highest peak. Indeed, all Texas mountain peaks over five thousand feet are in this part of the state. On the vast western ranges west of the Pecos, land is abundant but people are scarce—ranches average twenty-thousand acres, while the population averages less than one person per square mile, and that proportion is declining.

Despite the dwindling populace and virtually trackless expanses, Texas from the Pecos River on the east to the Mexican and New Mexican borders on the south and northwest has produced some remarkable ghost stories. Here the visitor might find haunted lakes and spectral baby snatchers; buried bullion in Socorro or the black-masked *El Tejano*, The Texan, who guarded his gold even after death; or the odd events at Devil's River. Cowboys have doubtlessly spent many a night around lonely Texas campfires telling these stories.

The Ghost Steer

The lone rider came hard through the windy winter dusk. Reaching the ranch corral he slid from his winded mount.

"You musta' seen a ghost," another cowboy said wither-ingly, and then he laughed.

"Well, I seen a steer," the first cowboy insisted, his face pale, his eyes wide. "But then I didn't see him. He was there and then he wasn't there. Jus' like that."

THE COWBOY WASN'T joking . . . he'd seen the storied brindle bull calf branded MURDER, a young steer that had been dead for decades.

The story of that strange branding begins in 1890 in rugged Brewster County, Texas, hard by the Rio Grande River. A one-armed cowboy and Confederate Army veteran, Henry Harrison Powe, was shot to death in a dispute over a yearling calf.

Powe had migrated to Texas in the hardscrabble years after the war. Bullets that shattered his left arm in a skirmish at war's end forced his buddies on the battlefield to cut away his jacket sleeve and amputate the useless limb.

Once in Texas, Powe settled near Crystal City to run cattle, and then moved farther west near Fort Davis in the Davis Mountains as the Southern Pacific Railroad extended its track westward.

Powe's killer—the oddly named Fine Gilliland—was tracked down by Texas Rangers and killed when he tried to flee.

Cowboy friends of Powe found the calf that had been at the center of the argument and branded the word MURDER on its hide. For decades to come and for far longer than it should have been alive, the steer roamed the rangeland, cast out from every herd it tried to join. That's what cowboys argued when they returned to their bunkhouses bug-eyed after encountering the mysterious animal.

As a teenager, R. M. Powe, Henry Harrison's son, was riding roundup with his father when he witnessed the cold-blooded murder. In 1935, he provided a graphic written account for his younger sister that seems to contradict the oft-told legend:

"DEAR SISTER"—HE WROTE—"YOU wanted me to write the story of the killing of Father. It is just as plain to me now as if it happened only yesterday, so I'll tell the whole episode as I saw it.

"First, I want to dispute a (newspaper story) I saw in which it seemed to pin the blame on Father. One mistake was, the roundup wasn't given by this large cattle company that they referred to, though the man that killed Father was working for this large cattle company they speak of. The company was Dubois and Wentworth. Fine Gilliland wasn't working with the roundup—just came there about twenty minutes before the killing. To thoroughly understand this, one will have to be familiar with cowboy phrases.

"On January 28, 1890, there was a roundup operating at Leoncita [note: perhaps today's Leoncita Ranch between Fort Stockton and Alpine] given by the small cattle owners in that country for the purpose of branding calves that had been missed in the fall roundup. Eugene Kelly was in charge of the work. There were two or three thousand cattle in the herd and among them was a brindle bull yearling, unbranded, but wasn't with its mother. Gene Kelley and Frank Rooney came to Father and told him that the brindle bull belonged to an HHP cow, which was Father's brand. Father asked them if they were positive that this calf, the brindle bull, belonged to his cow; Kelley said he was positive and could swear to it.

"Separating cows with unbranded calves began and Kelley told me to hold the cut. There had been only a few head cut out when the brindle bull came near the edge of the herd and Father cut it out and then rode back to the herd. Then Gilliland came to where I was and asked me if that calf had a mother in the cut. I told him it didn't but that Kelley had told Father that it belonged to an HHP cow.

"Gilliland said Father would play hell getting it unless he produced the cow, and rode in and cut it back to the roundup. It passed near Father as it went into the roundup and he looked back and saw Gilliland was driving it, so he rode out and met him, but I wasn't close enough to hear what was said.

"Father then rode to where Kelley was and apparently talked to him a few seconds. I suppose in regard to his certainty that the calf belonged to Father's cow. Then Father rode in the roundup and started to drive the bull out. Gilliland went to where father was in the middle of the roundup. They stopped there together a few seconds and father then rode to the far side of the roundup and stopped there with Manning Clements. I saw father reach into the saddle pocket and knew what it meant for I knew Manning always carried his pistol in his saddle pocket.

"Father went back into the roundup and drove the bull out toward the cut. Gilliland came in a run and tried to drive the bull back to the roundup while father was trying to put it in the cut. Gilliland stopped and unbuckled his saddle pocket where he, too, carried a pistol. He took his rope down and overtook the bull and tried to rope it but missed. Father then shot at the bull.

"By this time, Gilliland had dropped in behind father, had gotten off his horse, and was squatted down on one knee with his pistol in both hands aiming at father's back. I yelled to father to look out, that Gilliland was going to shoot; by that time he had fired directly at father's back. Father started to get off his horse and Gilliland shot again. By this time father was off his horse, and, being a one-armed man, had to wrap the bridle reins around his arm. The horse, being afraid of the shooting, was trying to get away, and came near jerking father down.

"In the meantime, Gilliland ran up to within five or six feet of father, and by that time father had got straightened up, facing Gilliland, and they both shot at almost the same time, then both shot again.

"Father's gun was empty then, for there were only three cartridges in it. Gilliland grabbed father's pistol and shot him again. Father staggered a few steps and fell on his face dead.

"I was so excited I hardly knew what was going on, but I heard someone say, 'For God's sake, don't kill that boy!' and on looking up I saw it was Manning Clements. Gilliland had two pistols in his hands. He told Manning to give him his horse, which Manning did, and Gilliland got on the horse and left in a run. I then started to Alpine to notify the (Texas) Rangers.

"In about five days from then Gilliland was overtaken and when resisting arrest was killed by two Rangers, Thalis Cook and Jim Putnam. However, he was killed after shooting Cook in the knee and killing two of the Rangers' horses and a dog. I was told that some of the cowboys had branded the brindle bull as follows: MURDER on one side and JAN 28 90 on the other side. Later this was found to be true.

"I suppose I am the only person living that knows what became of the noted bull. There was a man by the name of Bill Allen driving a trail herd to Montana. I asked him if he would take the animal out of the country. He said he would and I got the animal and put him in the herd and went with it to the Pecos River, at Horse Head Crossing—that is where they crossed the river and that is the last I ever saw of the brindle bull."

THE RUTHLESS MURDER of Henry Harrison Powe and the Rangers' killing of Fine Gilliland excited much public fascination, even in those days of well-oiled trigger fingers and swift, often lethal justice. As author Barry Scobee said in his account of how the legend of the brindle bull came about "fatal fights over calf-brandings were not uncommon." Powe and Gilliland both no doubt believed they were the aggrieved party and fully justified in defending their respective points of view that the brindle bull belonged to their particular outfits.

"The original affair was one that could scarcely arise today . . ." Scobee noted. "Powe was an honest and reputable citizen, but he was of the War Between the States. He had seen killing, had himself been wounded and lost an arm. He was of the Western frontier. Law by the gun was a common rather than a rare thing. It was the habit of men to so settle their hot disputes" in deadly encounters over calf brandings. Gilliland was said to have been a good cowboy and a basically decent man. He probably thought, too, he was defending the financial interests of the cattle company that employed him.

However, the story of the bizarrely branded bull seems to have taken on a life of its own. Gunfights were nothing out of the ordinary, even if it was a merciless slaying over a seemingly minor dispute such as that which erupted between Gilliland and Powe. But to undeservedly brand this young calf MURDER seemed especially pitiful. Author Barry Scobee says one story is that the calf wandered across the rangeland alone all its life. Its rusty red coat eventually turned gray.

"Cowboys drove it from their herds and ranges," Scobee wrote, perhaps out of fear for what its presence might inflict among the drovers.

ALTHOUGH POWE'S SON claimed the brindle bull was taken across the Pecos River in a herd heading north, stories of the mysterious ghost steer were told and retold for generations: that it would quietly appear on a distant hillock before vanishing in the night; that a cowboy would have an additional steer in the herd and realize it was the brindle bull huddled by itself away from all the others; that there'd be a sudden stampede set off by a quick, dark shadow passing through.

BARRY SCOBEE WAS familiar with that cowboy who insisted he'd seen the mysterious steer take part in a vanishing act.

But anyone who encountered the steer had a tough time convincing his skeptical bunkmates.

After that ranch hand briefly described his encounter, he found other ranch hands had come over from the barn and saddle-shed.

"You saw the ghost steer, that's what you saw!" one of them called out.

"He's a liar by the clock, that's what he is," jeered a third man. "He went to sleep in the saddle and saw a boulder or a bush."

"I saw a yearling," the troubled cowboy persisted. "And when I rode over toward him he jus' wasn't there."

In time his companions agreed it had been no mistake, no delusion. The cowboy had seen the steer branded MURDER.

The Restless Spirit of El Tejano

He rode a coal black stallion with a saddle made of the finest Spanish leather and inlaid with silver buckles. To confuse his trackers, he nailed on his horse's shoes backward so it always looked like he had moved out in the opposite direction.

His face was hidden behind a mask made of black silk.

He robbed the banks, the rich, the occasional lone stagecoach . . . but *only* if it carried bullion being shipped East by wealthy mine owners. He never, ever took money from the poor traveler or newly arrived settler.

He was the enigmatic desperado known as *El Tejano*. The Texan. The Robin Hood of Texas.

Though El Tejano is thought to have roamed the American Southwest far and wide—from Arizona's Santa Cruz River north and east into New Mexico and Texas, to Piacho Peak to Cerro del Gato and far beyond—this nameless bandit took much of his ill-gotten gain to Texas where he doled it out to the poor and to the desperate.

The posses that chased him were countless. So many in fact that rather than be slowed down by so much booty as he escaped another lawman, El Tejano secreted a great deal of his stolen wealth in countless mountain caves.

People who heard of his actions searched for the treasure as soon as they knew El Tejano had left the territory, for they didn't want to cross him.

El Tejano trusted only one person—a young Mexican boy who would run errands for him. If El Tejano needed supplies, he would approach the boy's house and whistle. If the boy whistled back, El Tejano rode in—no one was about. In time, though, the large reward must have become too tempting for El Tejano's youthful amigo. One day El Tejano appeared and whistled. The boy whistled back. The bandit rode directly into the blazing guns of one of the biggest posses ever to have been organized to bring him to justice. His body was riddled with scores of bullet holes. At his funeral, those who at last saw his bare face were shocked to realize he'd been an ordinary citizen whom they all knew. He had worked as a blacksmith and was known for his kindnesses in running errands for the elderly in town.

BUT THE FUNERAL did not end El Tejano's legend. His spirit will not rest until all of his hidden riches have been found.

That is what a teenage boy and his father discovered as they were hiking one day.

"I KNOW WHERE there is a cave in these mountains, and I am sure there is treasure hidden inside," the boy told his father. El Tejano's treasure, he said. He pleaded to go in and get it.

The older man knew that it would not be so easy.

"You had better not go unless you have the nerve and the courage to face up to the Tejano," the father warned, afraid to tell his son that he himself would never set foot in such a perilous place. "Be sure you can answer his spirit when he talks to you."

As with most boys, the young one bragged that he was very brave and set off for the cave with two gunnysacks into which he would stuff enough treasure to last his family many lifetimes. Indeed, he did find money and silver and gold that he crammed into the first bag. Some of the smaller trinkets he thought worthless and tossed aside. At the moment he started to fill the second bag, a voice distant and hollow roared toward him:

"All or nothing! You take it all or you take nothing!"

The boy looked around, frightened and starting to shiver. He could not see anything, but he knew it was the ghost of El Tejano somewhere close by. Then he fainted.

Far down the hillside, the teenager's father waited and waited. When his son did not return, he carefully climbed through the rocks and found the cave entrance. He peered into the gloomy interior. The boy was inside just regaining consciousness. He sat up and dazedly looked around. The bags were empty. Nothing remained of the riches.

"Where is the treasure?" his son cried out. "When I came in, I already had one sack filled and had started to fill the other one when I heard a voice say, 'All or nothing, you take it all or you take nothing.' Then I passed out."

"There is not a sign of anything here, son. What did you find?"

The boy quickly explained the piles of cash and mounds of silver that he had shoveled into the gunnysack. He said some things appeared worthless so he tossed them aside.

His father nodded.

"That is why El Tejano came," the old man explained. "For his spirit to rest, *all* of his treasure must be found . . . everything must be used. Nothing can be left behind. All is to be taken. Or nothing."

Too Close for Comfort

At one time the residents around Socorro had plenty of ghost stories circulating in their community. Pancho Villa's storied treasure—guarded by an hombre of indistinct lineage—is thought to have been buried under a cross of white stones somewhere in the vicinity.

East of Socorro at a place called Hill of the Virgin passersby sometimes noticed firelight that is said to betray the location of ancient Indian silver mines. At this hill, old-timers have told of the instances when the translucent forms of an emaciated warrior wearing only a breechcloth, and a rangy, slavering dog once leaped in front of a young man and his girlfriend. "To him who does no harm, no harm will come," the Native man intoned. The astonished couple fled in the opposite direction.

The old witch of Mount Franklin places a curse on anyone who dares search for buried gold on "her" mountain.

For sheer bravado, however, it is difficult to improve upon the antics of a ghost named Don Mauro, in the house he once called home near San Elizario, according to Texas writer and historian Charles Sonnichsen.

The sprawling adobe home had been the scene of many intrigues in the middle of the nineteenth century, but when Don Mauro passed away it fell into some disrepair and an endless turnover of tenants.

Perhaps it was because Don Mauro kept putting in appearances.

One couple had been shown the location of buried gold by Mauro's ghost, but only after they promised to use it for Catholic masses so that his soul might be redeemed. They reneged on their promise and fled to Mexico. They started a business with their ill-gotten gains, but it failed, and the wife died unexpectedly.

But that was not to be the end of Don Mauro.

Antonio and Bonifacia Maciel lived in the house for a while. Antonio worked late hours so Bonifacia went to bed well before her husband got home. It seems that the ghost of Don Mauro decided that she needed some company on those nights when her bed was half empty.

"Every night I go to bed by myself, because my husband is

working and comes home late," Bonifacia eventually confided to a friend. "And every night the ghost of an old man with a long, white beard comes and gets in bed with me. When my husband comes home and wishes to go to sleep, he has to say, 'with your permission,' before the old man will let him get in bed."

But that wasn't the half of it. Not only did the befuddled husband *see* old Don Mauro, but he had to crowd in because the ghost refused to get out.

"It sounds like Don Mauro," nodded her friend, who had lived in the neighborhood for a long time. "He used to be fond of the ladies."

And then she whispered, "Quite a lover he was, too!"

"He still is," said Bonifacia slyly. "Oh, yes he still is."

ELSEWHERE IN SOCORRO there were many stories of old men and old women who secreted their money and their valuables in all manner of odd places rather than trust any local bank. It seems that most of these hiding places were eventually looked after by the ghosts of their owners just as scores of other buried treasures in the Southwest are protected, it is thought, by mysterious, supernatural forces.

Manuel and his wife Concha discovered just how disruptive such a situation could prove to be after they moved into an old adobe house. Their landlord was a nasty old woman who insisted on keeping a personal eye on the place. Nearly every day she walked into the house uninvited to peer into every room and nose through the couple's few personal possessions. When she wasn't doing that, she made certain that no strangers ventured into the yard. It was her house, so Manuel and Concha did nothing to stop her. What could they do? They were simply grateful to have a roof over their heads.

One night they discovered more was at play in their simple home than a nosy old crone.

"Jesus! Mary! Joseph!" Manuel cried, nudging his wife as he cowered under the thin blanket that covered them. "Concha, do you see that, too?"

"Yes," Concha stammered.

A bony woman in white was bending over in the doorway of their bedroom, her thin hand scooping at the floor. Manuel could see something gleaming in her hands. Gold coins. She rose up and dropped the coins behind a mirror. They trickled down along the wall until they vanished into the flooring. All the while she stared at the frightened couple, a tight smile on her face. Finally, she backed through the doorway, raised her hand toward Manuel and Concha, and beckoned them to follow.

They went after her and watched as she backed toward the aqueduct behind the house, walked along the bank and then into the water. Her hand was still raised in a kind of plea. At last she disappeared under the water.

Who was she?

Did her odd behavior mean a treasure was buried under the flooring of the house?

Manuel and Concha didn't wait to find out. They left within days. No riches on earth outweighed their fear of seeing again such a horrible image.

Time passed. Manuel and Concha were blessed with three children—David, Eduardo, and Carmelita. Several years later, they found themselves living just down the street from their old house. They'd not forgotten what had happened there, but their memories had been softened. It was a good street with many children with whom their three little ones could play.

One afternoon the neighborhood children were busy in some typically noisy games. A bit of a squabble broke out about something or other. Little David wandered away from his playmates, found a nice bit of earth, and started digging at it with a stick. Suddenly, the door of the house into whose yard he had wandered flew open. It was the house his parents had first lived in, but of course there was no way he could have known that. The same spiteful old woman lurched out onto the steps and screamed at the boy to get away from her house and yard. He ran crying all the way home to his mother. When he blurted out the tale, Concha and Manuel nodded. They patted their little boy on the head, hugged him tightly, and said everything would be all right but he mustn't ever again go into the old woman's yard. He said he wouldn't and skipped back outside.

The couple whispered to each that this was certainly a sign that treasure was indeed buried somewhere under the old woman's house or in the yard. That was surely why she objected so stubbornly to a little boy's innocent fun.

Coastal Warnings

Hundreds of miles to the east of the Pecos River is the semitropical, Gulf Coast city of Corpus Christi, a rapidly growing metropolis of nearly three hundred thousand people at the northern tip of the Padre Island National Seashore, the longest barrier island in North America. Discovered in 1519 by the Spanish explorer Alonzo Pineda, Corpus Christi wasn't permanently settled until 1838 when Colonel Henry Lawrence Kinney established a frontier trading post on the site. It was Kinney's Trading Post, or Kinney's Ranch, until the U.S. Army arrived in the mid-1840s under the command of General Zachary Taylor. Taylor set up camp in preparation for a war with Mexico. The Army remained as it established a permanent southern U. S. border.

The settlement took the name Corpus Christi—Pineda had landed on the Roman Catholic feast day of Corpus Christi, literally the body of Christ, always the eighth day after Easter—following the post office's request for a more permanent postmark for letters and documents being mailed from the region. The city was incorporated in 1852 and a mayor and city council elected. However, another quarter century would elapse before a city charter was written, and it was not until 1879 that the first ordinance passed—one that banned hogs and goats from running loose in the streets.

The city has thriving arts centers, public museums, the first birding trail in the nation, a thriving ship harbor, and enough other activities to keep visitors busy for many weeks in a climate that averages seventy degrees year round.

Less well-known perhaps are some of Corpus Christi's ghost tales.

THE PRIEST FROM Laredo was sleeping in a guest room of the Diocese of Corpus Christi's chancery building. It was long after midnight when he suddenly awoke. Standing next to his bed were the iridescent presences of two priests and a nun. All three stared intently down at him.

"I wasn't dreaming," he told a diocesan newspaper. "They

weren't hazy, but were as clear as day. I wasn't frightened at all, because I think they were just very friendly spirits who were there to tell us they were okay, or to ask me to pray for them."

The priest and others thought one of the priests might have been the second appointed bishop of the Corpus Christi diocese, Emmanuel Ledvina, and for good reason. During his tenure in office, from 1921 to 1949, the present Corpus Christi Cathedral was erected, as was the chancery office, in which several eerie encounters have been described. The building served as Ledvina's residence, as well as that of diocesan priests.

The nun may have been the long-deceased and somewhat irascible former diocese archivist, Sister Mary Xavier Holworthy. Secretaries at the time reported that on quiet nights they heard her trademark door-slamming followed by some rapid footsteps in the unoccupied quarters of the chancery.

A former assistant chancellor of the diocese said the incidents didn't appear to be "malicious," but, he added, were certainly "strange things . . . that are hard to explain."

That same assistant chancellor, and the diocese chancellor himself, told a reporter that once they'd separately heard footsteps in the hallway outside their bedrooms and then watched in fascination as their rooms' doorknobs turned. But neither door opened.

The incidents didn't stop with nighttime visitations or wandering nuns.

Two priests saying their evening prayers on the third floor were startled when the elevator suddenly started up from the first floor and then stopped down the dark hallway near them. The doors opened. No one came out.

Oddest of all, however, were the instances in which priests living in the chancery said they'd awake in the night but were prevented from sitting up because a weight seemed to be pressed against their chests. A seminarian, it is said, was sleeping next to a crypt in the basement of the cathedral when he had that sensation . . . the same night that the assistant chancellor said it happened to him.

EARLY IN WORLD WAR II, a busload of sailors traveling from Houston to Corpus Christi paid little attention as a nun dressed in traditional habit climbed aboard a bus at one of its stops along the route and started chatting amiably with the young men. She said she was returning to her Corpus Christi convent from a recent trip on church business. What startled the sailors, however, was her prediction that 1942 would see the war's end.

Minutes later, they noticed that her seat was vacant. She'd somehow disappeared off the bus even though it had made no other stops along the way.

Several of the men decided to check out the convent the nun mentioned. They told their strange story to the convent's Mother Superior, who stared at them. No sister had been visiting in that area, nor had she expected any member of their religious order to arrive back from any travels in the region. At their request, she showed them a scrapbook of convent history and photographs of present and past nuns. They all took note of one nun in particular and said that was the person they'd spoken with on the bus.

The Mother Superior looked at them with suspicion. The nun they identified had been dead for years.

IT SEEMS THAT this part of Texas is favored more often than not by visits from distaff spirits who haven't found eternal peace.

The sixty miles of highway that separates the cities of Alice and Encino, southwest of Corpus Christi near the fabled King Ranch, is the terrain favored by a Texas version of the world's fabled ladies in black.

This Texas beauty was in life one Leonara Ramos, wife of wealthy rancher Don Raul Ramos. The story goes that the couple had been married but a short while when Don Raul sailed for Spain on business. He returned months later to discover his wife was pregnant. A meddlesome acquaintance told him the child was not his. Despite his wife's protests that the child was indeed her husband's, Don Raul dragged her into her bedroom and ordered her to change into her black mourning clothes. He then dragged her from the room. He rounded up several of his ranch hands, ordered them to tie her up and take her in a buckboard a day's ride away. They were to find a solid tree from which to hang her and leave her there.

The vaqueros were upset at having to carry out their gruesome task but dared not cross Don Raul. Several hours away, the men found a towering pecan tree with a thick horizontal branch some ways up and threw the stout hanging rope over it. They stood her up in the buggy, put the noose around poor Leonara's neck, pulled it tight, and whipped the horses forward. She was left hanging from the tree.

Perhaps Don Raul realized too late his awful mistake, for his men found him sprawled on the floor, blood congealing on the floor from a gunshot to his head. His fingers still grasped the pistol.

Now those venturing along Highway 281 between Encino and Alice, or on the lonely ranch roads outside Concepcion or Ben Bolt or Falfurrias, might see this woman in black, her head flopping gruesomely from her swollen, broken neck.

THE LADY IN the silky green dress who visited her dying fiancé at the James McGloin home in San Patricio County has the distinction of being the out-of-body extension of her *actual self* . . . very much alive at the time in Mexico City.

Her name has been lost to history, but her betrothed was Mexican Army Lieutenant Marcelino Garcia, commandant of Fort Lipantitlan. He was critically wounded in the early 1830s in one of the first battles between Mexico and the United States. He was taken in by his friend James McGloin, who did his best to tend to the deep wounds. A note was sent to Garcia's fiancée in Mexico City about his grim prognosis. A few nights later, the McGloins found the dim form of a woman standing next to Garcia's bed. They watched as Garcia tried to touch her arm. Night after night she came back, always silent, always attentive to the lieutenant. The lieutenant died of his wounds, but the lady in green returned to the bedside for nearly a quarter of a century.

In time, the family realized she was no longer a part of the household routine. A message arrived telling them that the woman Lieutenant Garcia had been engaged to had died an old woman in Mexico City . . . at nearly the same time her ghost had stopped visiting the house in San Patricio. She had never married.

That old McGloin house on Round Lake is within a pioneer settlement of Irish immigrants. In the same neighborhood is the

1875 Dougherty House, a rambling frame house formerly used as a schoolhouse, but now within a privately held bird and nature sanctuary. The Dougherty House has been visited by paranormal investigators looking into several ghostly occurrences.

There might be a good reason that particular area is haunted. It lies directly off Farm Road 666.

WHEREVER SPANISH-HERITAGE PEOPLE have settled in North America, stories of the ubiquitous La Llorona, the Weeping Woman, have followed. Corpus Christi and southeast Texas are no different. Here her name was said to have been Luisa and she wanders the riverbanks looking for her children, whose lives she ended in the dark waters.

She was a stunningly beautiful peasant woman with whom rich and aristocratic Don Muno Montes Claro fell in love. He wanted to marry her, but his family forbade it. He did not entirely obey his family's wishes. He did not marry Luisa, but instead built her a small house. Don Muno spent his nights with her and eventually fathered several children. In time, he stopped attending to Luisa. She panicked and rode to his ranch. The servants would not let her enter—Don Muno was being married the next morning. In a rage at this betrayal, she rode back to her home, took her children to the river, and drowned them. She was captured and imprisoned where she died a mad woman, calling over and over again for her dead children and for her lover, Don Muno.

SHOULD YOU SEE a wandering slip of a lady wearing an organdy dress, pause and say a brief prayer for the repose of the soul of one Chepita Rodriguez, for that is whom you have seen. And it means that a Texas woman has been unjustly accused of a crime.

Chepita went to her death on October 13, 1863 for a crime she likely did not commit. Though she pleaded innocent, she refused to say any more. It might have been because she wanted to protect the actual killer—her no-account son.

Chepita's life began well enough. Her father had been a well-regarded soldier in the battle for Texas sovereignty. Unfortunately, he had been too busy fighting to provide for his family, and so when he was killed, they were left destitute. Young

Chepita left home while still a teen and took up with an outlaw. She had a baby son, but the child grew to follow his father's path and not his grandfather's more honorable traditions. Father and son abandoned poor Chepita, who turned to managing a rather disreputable public house. One John Savage checked into the hotel of an evening. It's thought he was traveling with saddlebags filled with gold. Mr. Savage permanently checked out soon thereafter. A flour sack was discovered floating in the Neuces River. Inside was the unfortunate gentleman, his body cut into many, many pieces. There was no sign of his gold.

Chepita was arrested and charged with his murder. Despite her protestations to the contrary, a jury found her guilty of murder and sentenced her to death. Her supporters claimed she'd recognized her long-vanished son racing from the hotel with Savage's saddlebags, and rather than turn him in refused to speculate about another suspect.

She died at the end of a rope suspended from a mesquite tree along the Neuces River.

THE NEUCES—WHICH flows from northwest of San Antonio through Southeast Texas, Lake Corpus Christi, and then into the Gulf of Mexico at Corpus Christi—is a waterway known for abundant wildlife and ecotourism.

It's also known in some circles for the two headless horsemen said to prowl its banks near Corpus Christi.

The first is a rustler tracked down and decapitated by lawmen "Bigfoot" Wallace and Creed Taylor. They tied his headless corpse to his horse and let it go. It was a warning to other would-be scalawags that their crimes would not be tolerated. The horse was eventually stopped, the rustler's body buried. Yet some claim that the rider still roams the countryside astride his stallion looking for his lost skull.

One Muerto del Rodeo might have been a Kentucky native who settled in the area to search for gold. Someone crushed his skull in the belief he had struck it rich. He'd found a small vein of gold, but not nearly enough to please the unknown killers. Now del Rodeo wanders the riverbank trying to piece together his compacted cranium.

Two other spectres are said to occasionally make appearances along the Nueces. Oddly, they are always engaged in a brawl with one another. Reports are that these Spanish gentlemen might be two pay wagon guards whose sizable treasure was stolen in an ambush. They're still looking for the spoils in the thick mesquite along the river's embankment.

18

The Uninvited

How common these dead, nameless, unreckt things grow.

—Anonymous

THE REFRAIN MIGHT read like a twisted nursery rhyme: *Old Mac-Dougall was a ghost, eeii, eeii, ooohhh; with a cackle, cackle here, and a cackle, cackle there, here a cackle, there a cackle* . . .

But this flippant ditty surely would not have been welcomed by the South Kings County, Washington, family that suffered the predations of the late John Francis MacDougall, Ghost. In their cozy, older brick and cedar home, the former owners said that was not the half of it, because along with Mr. MacDougall came white and green mist floating in the hallways, bathroom mirrors that moved of their own accord, the sweet smell of roses in the house—*during the winter*—and, in the nighttime, voices and noises, always the voices and noises.

The deceased John MacDougall is buried alongside his wife, Sarah, in a graveyard not far from the family's home. The family was given the pseudonymous name of "Williams" in published reports at the time of the haunting.

"Even now when I think about what happened when Mr. MacDougall was here, I can't sleep at night," the family's daughter, Becky, with a curious degree of respect for the unbidden visitor, told a reporter. "It's best not to think about it. Every time I hear the wind blow a tree limb against a window or some other little noise in the house, I think, 'Oh, no, could it be happening again?' "

The circumstances of John Francis MacDougall's arrival are obscure. Suffice to say that his *stay* is not so ambiguous— it lasted a frightfully long four years. His disappearance on an October day in 1979 was equally unexpected but nevertheless welcomed by the beleaguered family. As with his unexplained appearance, MacDougall didn't offer any readily apparent rationale for the termination of his visits.

The MacDougall ghost normally signaled his presence in the form of a white or green mist in the hallway. The mist's sudden departure was as upsetting as its arrival. Sometimes the mist would be accompanied by a man's voice seeming to come from the house walls and its attic. Once young Becky Williams heard the voice in the corner of her bedroom mumbling over and over the words "murder, murder, murder!"

The most difficult part of those long months and years is that few believed Becky Williams and her family. But so traumatic was the experience for the young woman that she moved out of the house when she turned eighteen. The strange voice in the corner was one factor in her leaving, but not nearly so disturbing as those times in the middle of the night when she awoke because her bed was shaking so violently that it threatened to toss her onto the floor.

Once the ghost left under his own power, Becky came back to live again with her brothers and father.

"We don't see things floating through the air now," Becky said at the time. "We don't see people walking down the hallway who are not members of the family. But I still prefer not to be here alone at night."

The sometimes green, sometimes white mist that the family believed was actually MacDougall's airy form nearly became a constant in the haunting.

"I saw the mists, sure . . . but they never really had any real shape. I mean they weren't square or rectangular. You couldn't measure the depth of them."

The mist also formed outside the house.

"Have you ever seen leaves floating down from a tree? Once I saw a mist floating upward in the same kind of motion. My dog was barking at it. I could see the mist as long as it was in the tree. After it got past the tree, I lost it. It was too light, I guess," Becky Williams remembered.

The overpowering aroma of roses got so bad that family members sometimes had to step outside to recover. In the winter, they'd return home, open the front door, and nearly be overcome. It was as if each room was scattered with rose bouquets, even though no flowers were kept in the house, nor did anyone use a rose-scented spray.

Old John Francis MacDougall might have left because the family members—minus Becky, who had moved out—stopped being afraid of him. They'd been told that ghosts make more mischief if people fear them.

Becky Williams, for one, said that though MacDougall was gone, she'd always remember the mists, the moving furniture, and the voices. Because of that, she had developed some specific qualifications should she ever be in the market for a home.

"I like old houses but I don't think I could ever own one now," she told a reporter. "Those are the kinds of places where you imagine ghosts might be. You never know what might be in them."

And you may not want to find out.

"Come Out and Help Me!"

Rachel, a young widow, sat quietly in the kitchen of her pleasant house on Tacoma's South Eighth Street. It was late in the evening; her mother, also a widow, had gone out and Rachel was waiting up for her.

From the front of the house, she heard her mother call to her: "Come out and help me!"

Rachel got up and walked through the dining room and into the living room where her mother seemed to be calling from. Both rooms were empty. She knew the only other people in the house, her younger sister Brenda and her own eighteen-month-old son Benjamin, were fast asleep.

A few minutes later, Rachel heard the same voice and the same words, but again found nothing to account for it. Her mother didn't in fact return home until sometime later that evening.

A SERIES OF quite extraordinary and quite unexplained incidents in that Tacoma home led the family to believe it was haunted. Located only a few blocks from Jefferson Park, southwest of the University of Puget Sound, the house held four members of the same family: Lucille, a forty-one-year-old widow; her daughter, Rachel, also a widow; Rachel's year-and-a-half-old son, Benjamin; and Lucille's fourteen-year-old daughter, Brenda. Their real names were not used in news reports.

When the story of the Eighth Street haunting broke in the local newspapers, Lucille's extended family had lived there for about nine months. Within two weeks of the time they moved in, they recorded the first episode, but didn't immediately connect it with what they came to believe was supernatural activity.

They thought mice or other small animals had burrowed into the walls and into the attic because one of the first noises they heard was simply a scurrying noise in the bedroom Lucille shared with her daughter, Brenda.

"(Brenda) called me and I came in and we both listened for three or four minutes," Lucille told a reporter. "I remember saying, 'That can't be mice because workmen had just finished blowing insulation into the attic.' Then the noise stopped and we just sort of shrugged it off."

Not for long.

Tiny mice feet morphed into noises that were distinctly identifiable. Like a door slamming in Lucille's bedroom one night when guests were present.

"It was as though someone were angrily opening and then slamming the door shut. It happened three or four times before I could get over the shock and run down the hall to find out what it was," she said. She came back to her guests as shaken and as perplexed as she had been a few minutes earlier.

The episodes grew in number. The family got more anxious:

• On a late night, strange moans came from the dining room and dishes began rattling in the kitchen cupboards.

- A chandelier that started to swing on its own volition was halted in mid-swing by Lucille herself. When she let go, it once again began arcing.
- Running feet raced through the house on another night. Lucille and Rachel listened for minutes on end to this footrace by undetectable marathoners.
- As Lucille and her small family pulled up outside the house one other night at about 11 P.M., Lucille pointed out to Rachel that a light was on in her older daughter's bedroom. The light was off by the time they got inside.

Just as oddly as the unsettling events began, they ended in May, about eight months after they'd begun.

"We thought it was over," Lucille told a reporter.

It wasn't that easy.

A few weeks later, on a Wednesday night, the family was gathered in the living room when they all heard from the kitchen what sounded like a doorknob being violently twisted by a very strong individual. Jumping up nearly simultaneously, all four rushed into the kitchen, but it had stopped by then.

Lucille said she couldn't afford to leave the house. "Every penny of our savings was in it," she told the local newspaper. That's when she began her search for a haunt buster, one sure technique in achieving parity with a ghost.

Uncle Chad

The two women who lived in another Tacoma house had oddly similar experiences to Lucille's family on South Eighth Street, except that in this case the haunting continued for thirteen years.

The initial news reports claimed a ghost seemed to have encamped shortly after Mrs. Usher and her middle-aged daughter, Mrs. Price—not their real names—moved in. The women were never harmed because they thought the ghost was probably their late Uncle Chad, gone at that time for a quarter of a century.

But that's not to say the ghost—even if it was good old Uncle Chad—didn't frighten them on occasion.

A scratching noise *inside* the back door sent a chill through Mrs. Usher late one evening because it sounded like something was trying to get out. She couldn't find evidence of scratch marks in the light of the next day.

The local police even became involved when Mrs. Usher opened the basement door and saw what she took to be the shadow of a man on the wall at the bottom of the steps. She called the police but, search as they did, they couldn't find anyone.

It had all started years before and appropriately enough in the dark early morning hours.

"The doorbell rang at four in the morning," Mrs. Usher told a reporter. "It frightened me because there was no doorbell, only wires hanging out. Nothing was connected." She wasn't able to replicate the sound, even when she spliced the old doorbell wires together.

From then on something new happened on an almost daily basis. Some of it was clearly poltergeist-type activity: cups and saucers launching themselves across the kitchen, bathroom towels going missing and then turning up in odd places, door raps, faint voices calling the names of the house's occupants, and the clank of metal coming from beneath the living room floor. While some of the creaking and clanking might be attributed to the natural proclivity for houses to settle on their foundations as they age, the other reported events were puzzling. Even the lights had minds of their own, which isn't unusual if the family is dealing with an alleged poltergeist.

"I wouldn't sleep in my bedroom for quite a few years because the light in the walk-in closet would switch on and off by itself in the middle of the night," Mrs. Usher told a reporter.

Sometimes the entity got assertive. Mrs. Usher said that someone once pushed her across the bed though she was alone. She said it felt like the hand of a small person, perhaps a woman, against her back.

Sometimes the entity got helpful. As when Mrs. Price, Mrs. Usher's middle-aged daughter, remembered the night when her son George came home to find both doors locked. He knocked. The door opened. The problem was that his mother and grandmother were both fast asleep.

And sometimes the entity got confused. She recounted the

time when Mrs. Price's daughter had a friend stay the night at a slumber party:

"I had tucked them in and they were in their nightclothes. But when they got up in the morning they were fully clothed. They didn't know how that happened."

In some desperation, Mrs. Usher said they hired a fortune-teller to read tarot cards in an attempt to figure out what inhabited the house, other than the corporeal residents. She said that a man murdered his wife there many years before. The crime had taken place in the basement—thus the shadow on the wall.

"But I'm not convinced," Mrs. Usher said to a reporter. "I've talked to my neighbors, who have been here many years, and they don't remember anything like that."

The hauntings began to diminish after Mrs. Price talked about them under hypnosis. She was a bit sad to see the ghost leave. She missed the kind of spiritual sentinel Uncle Chad had apparently become.

For her part, Mrs. Usher was glad to see the ghost, even if it was Uncle Chad, vacate the house. "I'm fearful of them," she said.

A Pack of Poltergeists

The late *Tacoma News Tribune* columnist Bob Lane suggested in one of his newspaper essays what is often the case in cities and towns across the nation—that no matter how large or how small they may be, every community has its collection of haunted places and more than a few people willing to share their perplexing adventures in them.

Tacoma's Old City Hall, for example, had a spate of odd incidents during the winter of 1978–1979, when the tower bells chimed—despite the fact that the ringing mechanism was disconnected. Room lights were mysteriously flickering on and off. Searches by police and other personnel could find no one hiding inside, nor any logical explanation for the incidents.

In February 1979, the burglar and fire alarms were repeatedly set off and vacant rooms would suddenly glow with electric light.

Guards complained that they were ending up chasing shadows, Lane wrote.

Back in 1904, former Ambassador and Mrs. Hugh C. Wallace donated the four large bells to the city in memory of their late daughter. They were installed in the City Hall tower. Long rods connected the sixty-pound clappers to the clock mechanism, but had been disengaged, according to a building manager.

Nevertheless they rang at least once during many nights, city maintenance workers claimed.

The building manager took the highly unusual step of spending the night in the tower. He came away a believer that something out-of-the-ordinary was afoot up there.

"I can tell you . . . there is a spirit up here. Have you ever been alone somewhere and you knew somebody was standing near you?" the man told columnist Lane. Just *who* that somebody might be was never divulged.

Guards said that chasing shadows through the building was not part of their job description. One night watchman lasted only a week before he called it quits. Too many unexplained incidents for his taste.

Meanwhile, Tacoma's Historical Society Museum had a problem of a different sort—the ghostly figure of Mary Todd Lincoln materializing near a display of the President's memorabilia, according to one guard. He had worked at the museum for two decades and was said to be a "sober and sincere" man, Lane wrote. What would Mrs. Lincoln's ghost be doing in Tacoma? It's hard to figure out, although there have been reports of spirits materializing near their worldly possessions, even if those objects are many miles distant from the ghosts' last known earthly address.

The same guard claimed to have witnessed a chair slide across the marble floors without human assistance. Mrs. Lincoln was not in it.

The museum's elevator had a mind of its own as well, another guard told Lane.

As he was making his rounds one night, the guard got off the elevator on the first floor, left the building, and locked the door behind him. He went around the outside to the third floor where he found the elevator waiting for him.

Did he unconsciously press the third floor button as he got off inside? He didn't think so.

"It makes you think twice," the guard told Lane.

Columnist Lane found a haunted house on the city's North Sixth Street. A woman who may or may not have died in one of the bedrooms might have been the cause of some seriously strange behaviors.

Like those old joke plastic teeth that clatter away when they are wound up, a family there had a problem with a noise in the dark that sounded just like that. The clicking of a set of false teeth. It would come from midair. In the middle of the living room. At night.

A cold spot in the doorway to the dead woman's bedroom never seemed to go away. It wasn't a draft, just a single icy swirl of air at that one place, the residents told Lane.

A direct approach to the problem seemed to work. A young man in the house got so fed up with the disturbances that he sat down in the bedroom one night and declared that he was staying put in the house. No ghost was going to chase him away!

The teeth clattering stopped, the cold sweep of air went away. All was well. At least for the time being.

The Phantom Engineer of Eagle Gorge

The railroad tracks through the Cascade Mountains' Eagle Gorge on the Northern Pacific's Tacoma–Washington line were a grueling stretch of steel under the best of conditions. Some said it was the most dangerous section of track in all the company's twenty-five-hundred-mile line. In the early days of steam locomotives, train engineers fortified themselves as best they could before taking the run through the gorge. They knew that a single miscalculation could send them, their passengers, or freight and hundreds of tons of iron and steel plummeting into oblivion.

And if that happened they'd join Tom Cypher, the most famous phantom engineer in all the Pacific Northwest.

Despite the thousands of miles of rail line that have been torn up and reseeded for bike trails and walking paths, phantom trains and their unearthly engineers are as ubiquitous in American ghostlore as the congregation of specters lurking alongside American highways. From states as diverse as West Virginia, Michigan, and Tennessee, the mysterious moving lights along old rail beds aren't thought of as swamp gas or the reflections of passing automobiles, but as the penetrating high beams from an ancient steam locomotive bound for nowhere.

What makes the Tom Cypher story unique is an account by a former Northern Pacific engineer, J. M. Pinckney, of what happened to him on the night he hopped aboard an NP locomotive to see for himself if the legends of the phantom train were true or not.

Pinckney knew all about Cypher's death, as did nearly every trainman in the West:

Tom was at the control of Engine Number Thirty-three on that winter's night when his immaculate safety record came to a deadly end. He was said to be an expert trainman with years of experience among the mountainous peaks and valleys of Washington and Oregon. But none of that was of any use when his engine hurtled off the tracks at Eagle Gorge, carrying freight and passengers and himself to oblivion. Tom was a well-known figure along the route. Not many of the residents familiar with his presence could imagine that his life had been taken in a train wreck.

For months afterward, however, reports circulated that Tom Cypher's engine never did leave the tracks—enough people saw it steaming full-bent for glory that word about that phantom train became the talk of the entire line. It'd pull into a station with its coal hopper empty and no one in the engine cab. Within seconds it was gone.

Or at least that's how the stories went until J. M. Pinckney decided to ferret out the truth. He had a hard time believing that Tom Cypher still rode his Number Thirty-three. There was only one way to find out and since his work was on a different part of the route, he would have to hitch a ride on a locomotive going through Eagle Gorge.

Thus it was that on Sunday night, January 3, 1892, Pinckney sat crunched in the cab of a passenger train's locomotive heading for Eagle Gorge, courtesy of another member of the Brotherhood of Locomotive Engineers. Pinckney was quizzing the engineer and the young fireman about the Cypher sightings and regaling the untested coal firer in particular with stories of near misses and runaway locomotives. The fireman wasn't amused by Pinckney's casual attitude toward what he took to be horrific events.

The trip began uneventfully enough, but just before the train entered the gorge, they encountered something that Pinckney said, according to his later account, "made his hair stand on end."

In a news account of that night, published the following Sunday, January 10, in the *Seattle Press Times* newspaper, Pinckney said this is what happened:

It was clear late on the night of January third. The sharp rays from the locomotive headlamp flashed along the track. Straining to be heard above the pounding steam engine, the men were spinning yarns while keeping a sharp look as they neared Eagle Gorge, the scene of many disasters as well as the reputed section of track haunted by Tom Cypher's steam engine.

The engineer was nearing the conclusion of a particularly grisly story when he suddenly grasped the throttle, and in a moment "threw her over," that is, reversed the engine. The air brakes slammed on and the train came to a sliding standstill. The train was within just a few feet of where Cypher met his death two years earlier.

The passengers were thrown about and confused about what circumstances had led the train to stop in the middle of the mountains. The conductor rushed forward to ask about the sudden stop, but the engineer was unusually calm as he fiddled with some of the apparatus in front of him. He mumbled something about a piece of the machinery being "loose" and that he needed to tend to it.

He peered back out the side window and then got underway. Pinckney turned toward him, and asked:

"What made you stop back there? I heard your excuse, but I've run too long on the road not to know that your excuse is not the truth."

The engineer glared back and then pointed through the open window.

"There! Look there! Don't you see it?" he barked.

Pinckney edged toward the window and looked out. Some three hundred yards down the track he saw the distant glow from a headlight of a locomotive running ahead of Pinckney's train. The rays of red, green, and white light pierced the dark forest alongside the tracks and splayed sharp streaks of silver as it bounced along the rails.

Pinckney jumped away from the window.

"Stop the train, man!" he cried out, trying to wrest control of the gear lever from the engineer.

But the engineer blocked Pinckney's way and said in an eerily calm voice, a tiny smile playing across his lips:

"Oh, it's nothing. It's what I saw back at the gorge. Tom Cypher's Engine Number Thirty-three. There's no danger of a collision. I know the man running it ahead of us can run it faster backward than I can this one forward. I have seen it before. Yes, twenty times or more. Every engineer on the road knows that engine, and he's always watching for it when he gets to Eagle Gorge."

Pinckney picked up the story.

"The engine in front of us was running silently, but smoke was puffing from the stack . . ." he recalled. "It kept a short distance ahead for several miles, and for a moment we saw a figure on the pilot. Then the engine rounded a curve and we did not see it again."

A small station whizzed by in the gloom, but no one was about. At the next station, the telegraph operator warned Pinckney's train to stay well back from a runaway locomotive that had just gone by. Pinckney and the engineer did not make a reply. Neither man was afraid of a collision with *that* engine.

Pinckney, however, could not avoid checking on down the line.

"Just to satisfy my own mind on the matter I sent a telegram to the engine wiper at Sprague, asking him if Number Thirty-three was in," he said. "I received a reply stating that Number Thirty-three had just come in and that her coal was exhausted and boxes burned out."

J.M. Pinckney didn't expect the reporter or the newspaper readers to believe his tale, knowing full well that it strained credulity. Laugh if you will, he seemed to be saying, but also know that you weren't aboard that train a week earlier as he had been.

It was a difficult story to verify, he noted. "Just ask any of the boys," he suggested, "although many of them won't talk about it. I would not myself if I were running on the road. It's unlucky to do so."

19

The Wild Rose of Greenbrier

My life closed twice before its close;
It yet remains to see
If immortality unveil
A third event to me . . .

—Emily Dickinson, *My life closed twice
before its close*

I have so much trouble sleeping on these nights. Thoughts of you will not go away. Thoughts of your lush and long curly ebony black hair framing the porcelain complexion you were so proud of. Of your giggles turning to wild laughter at the silly shenanigans one of your seven brothers pulled on some unsuspecting visitor. Of how this child of mine had become so very pretty that all the young men in the neighborhood were suddenly smitten with this astonishing Circe in their midst. Then of your hasty marriage, a union that I had opposed with all of my being. You just smiled and said that it was for the best. But he was such a frightful man. An evil man who had already thrown away two wives and one cold in the grave, but then had taken you as his third bride, and he claiming to be twenty-nine, and that not bloody likely I whisper to no one but myself.

And finally, long after midnight, come the darkest

thoughts of all, the ones that I cannot even wish away, the ones of my little Zonie hardly into her twenties all twisted and pitiful at the bottom of the staircase like some raggedy doll and of what your last thoughts must have been before death closed in forever. Were they of me and of your father? Were they of your brothers, my strong sons, that you will never see again? Were they of the winding roads among the scattered cedar and scrub pines on our Little Swell mountain that you raced up and down on so many summer afternoons? Or, God help me, were they of that face, his dreadful face, looming before you, and then of his strong hands clamping down on your long, slim neck. He who promised to love and cherish you with all his being but became the instrument of your destruction? I want so much that you, my only girl child, that you my Zonie might come back to me one more time, so that I might know that it was him that did this to you, and in that way to give me the evidence, the instrument of his ruination. Only then may I go to my own eternal reward and be with you always.

I doze. But I am pulled back from the half-sleep that is all for which I can hope in the cursed dark. I hear something. A shadow moves across the floor. Is it you? Oh, yes, it is, thank God, my child. My Zonie. What is it? Tell me. Tell me how he squeezed the life from my precious flower. Tell me so that I might exact revenge on his worthless soul. Please child tell me!

But the child does not speak to the mother. The ghostly mouth moves, yet there are no words issuing from this shade. She turns her back to walk away. She stops. Her head twists round on her shoulders . . . my God . . . and she is looking back at the woman who gave her life.

Please child, please, I want to know.

But it's not to be this time. Zonie does not say that . . . but I understand what it is she is not saying. That tonight is not the right time for her to reveal the truth. That I must wait. And that is so very, very hard to do.

Zona Heaster Shue's body was discovered on Saturday, January 23, 1897, at the foot of the stairs in her simple, two-story log home at the settlement called Livesay's Mill, near Lewisburg, West Virginia, in the Richlands section of Greenbrier County. Eleven-year-old Andy Jones found the body. He did chores in the neighborhood, and often helped out Mrs. Shue and her husband Erasmus Stribbling (Trout) Shue.

Trout Shue had been working in his blacksmith shop when he asked Andy to go to his home to find fresh eggs, and then to ask his wife if she needed Andy to go to the store for anything.

Zona, or Zonie as she was nicknamed, was twenty-four. Her husband stated on his marriage license three months earlier that he was twenty-nine, but that was a lie. He was thirty-five.

There was much about Trout Shue that was not truthful.

When Andy finished hunting for the eggs, he knocked on the door to the house but got no answer. He went inside. That's when he found the body. He later said that Zonie looked for the entire world like she was merely resting. Her dark brown eyes were open, her lips slightly parted as if she were about to speak. Her curly black hair spread out on the floor, a limp yellow ribbon was pinned above her ear. She lay on her back, legs straight and her dress neatly smoothed. An arm lay draped across her midsection, the other at her side, palm slightly curled. The boy looked closely and did not need anyone to tell him that his mistress was dead. She did not move, there was no hint of shallow breathing; he found her skin hard and cold when he dared touch her arm.

Within minutes he had raced home to tell his mother—"Aunt" Martha Jones—and together they hurried to the blacksmith's shop where Trout, clad in bibbed overalls and a sweat-stained hickory shirt, was bending over an anvil. Despite the cold January day, the forge was so hot that sweat dripped from his long, black moustache. They told him what the boy discovered. All three hurried to the house. He ordered them to fetch the coroner, Dr. George W. Knapp. Mother and son did as they were directed.

By the time the doctor got there, nearly an hour later by most accounts, he saw that Trout had taken his wife's body upstairs to their bedroom and dressed her in her best Sunday-go-to-meeting clothes. He had tied a bright scarf around her neck.

He was holding her in his arms and crying in what to the doctor appeared to be understandable anguish at his wife's tragic death.

Dr. Knapp didn't take long in his examination. He noted some discoloration on the front of Zonie's throat, but backed off taking a look at the back of her neck when Trout objected that it was a profane abuse of his wife's remains.

The doctor was surprised at her death. He'd been treating her for a few weeks for some "trouble," but there was nothing that he'd found to indicate an imminent death. A newspaper story later stated that she'd died of the "everlasting faint."

Another account more sadly said Zonie died of "childbirth."

Neither would prove to be correct.

The unraveling of the circumstances surrounding Zona Shue's inexplicable death and the role she herself might have played in solving the crime have provided the grist for one of the most enduring ghost tales in West Virginia history. A roadside marker tells the story of "The Greenbrier Ghost." It is a story still known and retold in that section of West Virginia, even though there is strong reason to doubt its authenticity. But that's never gotten in the way of a good ghost yarn.

WHEN DR. KNAPP finished with his cursory examination, he found two young men to ride the fifteen grueling miles over to Little Sewell Mountain to give Zonie's parents the terrible news. Her father, Jacob Hedges Heaster, scraped together a living from hiring out as a general laborer and from what animals and crops he could raise on his small farm. Together he and his wife Mary Jane Robinson Heaster had eight children. Seven boys. And Zona.

Zonie's body evidently remained in her bedroom until the next morning, a Sunday, when it was taken in a plain pine coffin to her parents' home at Little Sewell. Trout did not stray from his wife's side during the arduous journey to her parents nor during the wake and Monday burial.

Those who attended the wake and burial do not agree on their recollections of Trout's behavior. Some said they were truly moved by his tears and attentive ministrations to his wife's remains. Most accounts say he often wrapped his arm around her head when friends and relatives approached the coffin and talked about how "pretty" she was. He put additional pillows in the coffin to help her "rest." He pointed out that the scarf was one of her favorites and thus the reason he chose it for her to wear. It did strike some as odd that her head was swaddled by heavy wadding material.

But most people in the neighborhood remained suspicious that Shue had somehow gotten away with murder, or at the very least knew much more about his wife's death than he was letting on. They questioned how a young woman in seemingly good health would suddenly die and why it was that Trout didn't let anyone get too close to the body. A few thought her head had seemed "floppy" when she was laid out at her parents' home and perhaps that was why her husband had insisted upon the additional support.

Nothing came of the doubters' gossip . . . then.

Zona Heaster Shue was laid to rest in Soul Chapel Church Cemetery on Monday, January 25, 1897.

TROUT SHUE WAS the perfect subject for small town rumors. He was a brawny, dark-haired, blue-eyed, boastful newcomer to the isolated mountain settlement, who made his living in the searing heat of a blacksmith's shop. He was a prevaricator who lied about his age—most accounts have him at least five to ten years older than he stated on his marriage license to Zona Heaster—and had been sent to prison in 1889 for horse thievery.

He had two marriages before the one to Zona. His first wife was Allie Estelline Cutlip, whom he married in 1885, and by whom he had a child, Girta. Trout told folks that Allie had "abandoned" her husband and child and that Girta was being raised by her grandparents. However, there is a strong indication that his version of that first marriage is not entirely accurate, though there is little to show that the first Mrs. Shue ever spoke extensively about her marriage to Trout. The couple was divorced. It may have been an abusive relationship and Trout might have resented the presence of a child in the marriage. It does appear that the divorce occurred during the time he was serving his prison sentence.

His second marriage engendered the most discussion subsequent to Zona's death.

In 1894, Trout married Lucy Ann Tritt, and together they lived between the villages of Rupert and Alderson. She died less than eight months later, also under puzzling circumstances. The story is that Trout was building or repairing the cabin chimney. He asked Lucy for a glass of water. She brought it out to him and was killed when falling bricks from the repair job fell and hit her in the head. Several of her family members thought he'd intentionally thrown the bricks at her, though it doesn't seem that he was formally accused of any crime, or that anyone ever proved that Lucy's death was anything but a horrific accident.

The circumstances under which Trout Shue and Zona Heaster met and later married are also something of a mystery. He apparently showed up in Greenbrier County in the early fall of 1896 and married Zona Heaster soon thereafter, perhaps within weeks of their meeting. The Greenbrier newspaper reported a marriage between "Mr. E.S. Shue and Miss E.Z. Heaster" on what would have been October 20, 1896. Trout, of course, had attracted immediate attention when he moved to rural Greenbrier County and opened the blacksmith shop. He was handsome, newly single, and so he might have been considered a "good catch" in the parlance of the times.

There is an alternative theory, one proposed by historian Katie Letcher Lyle, the most knowledgeable authority on the death of Zona Shue and from whom we've learned most of what we know of this case.

Zona and Trout were married soon after they met, this supposition goes, because she told him that she was pregnant; since Trout assumed he was the father he did the "right thing" by marrying her. Perhaps she did die of "childbirth," as the coroner originally wrote, and which could have been code for a miscarriage or even a self-induced abortion. Young Andy Jones said in later years that he recalled seeing a trail of blood on the floor beside the body. Or, perhaps Trout somehow discovered that he was *not* the father and killed his wife in anger. Jones later said Trout struck and killed his wife and had dragged her body to the staircase to make it look like she'd fallen.

The difficulty with this premise may be that the couple seems to have married within just a few weeks of having first met, hardly enough time for even a barely-literate mountain woman to comprehend that she was pregnant. However, according to Lyle's research, one woman who had been a child at the time and remembered seeing Zona said she was "fat," at Christmastime, about two months after the marriage ceremony, which contradicts other descriptions of Zona at the time as being slim and rather pretty.

In truth, no one today will ever really know how or why Zona Shue died.

But a week or two after Zona's burial, Mary Jane Robinson Heaster thought she knew *exactly* how her child died.

She said her daughter's ghost pointed its cold, dead finger right at Trout Shue. And that is where begins this famous tale of a dead woman returning from her grave to ensure her killer's punishment. The story continues to be told over and over again, even if there is room to doubt its accuracy. Then again, verifiable truth has never gotten in the way of a good ghost story.

BY MOST ACCOUNTS, Mrs. Heaster was inconsolable in the days after Zona's death, could not sleep more than a few hours at a time, and spent nearly every waking hour longing for her child and praying that somehow the truth would come out. She is said to have told anyone who would listen that Trout Shue had gotten away with murder.

According to her later statements, however, Mrs. Heaster was able to go even further in her attempts to bring Trout to justice. The ghost of Zona Heaster Shue paid a visit to her mother and spelled out precisely how and why she had been murdered.

"She came back and told me that he was mad that she didn't have no meat cooked for supper," Mrs. Heaster said, according to newspaper accounts. "She came four times and four nights; but the second night she told me that her neck was squeezed off at the first joint, and it was just as she told me."

For well over a century now, the same story has been told:

Trout Shue was convicted of murder based on the testimony of the ghost of his dead wife who appeared to her mother to give the evidence necessary to imprison her cunning husband.

Despite this oft-told version of the events, and even Mrs. Heaster's later claims, the first indication that suspicions surrounding Zonie's death were moving beyond mere speculation had nothing to do with midnight visits by reanimated daughters. On February 25, 1897—about a month after she was buried—a Greenbrier newspaper ran the headline "Foul Play Suspected," over a story that revealed there had been an exhumation and autopsy of Zona Shue's remains. No mention was made of a ghost playing any role in that decision.

The reasons for the autopsy were quite clearly spelled out in the story, even though by today's newspaper standards they would be considered reckless—the anonymous reporter noted that "rumors" of Zona Shue's murder had led law officials to suspect "foul play" and that Trout Shue was suspected of having a hand in her death.

A published account of the proceeding states that three doctors, including Dr. Knapp, performed the autopsy in a makeshift morgue at a local school building. Five laymen attended as witnesses. Incredibly, Trout Shue was also in attendance, although by some accounts he sat in the corner "whittling."

The doctors carried out a fairly standard autopsy for the times by first slitting open the corpse's front body cavity and examining the stomach contents—which they found to consist of bread, butter, and some fruit preserves. Since it appears that the month-long illness for which Zona had been seeing Dr. Knapp did not improve, perhaps the doctors were looking for signs of poison. Having found nothing suspicious, and with only primitive instruments and under flickering kerosene lamps, they continued their inspection of the other vital organs. Again, there was nothing to raise an alarm. Most significantly, they apparently found no signs of a miscarriage or an attempt by Zona to induce an abortion.

At that point, the doctors turned their attention to the external body. There were apparently no signs of cuts or bruises, no fractures or broken bones to indicate she had fallen down the stairs, or even to the floor. Eventually the trio of doctors looked closely at Zonie's neck, which to some observers at the funeral was unusually "floppy" and around which Trout Shue had conveniently wrapped a scarf. Further, it was recalled that as he sat next to his wife's body through the wake and funeral, Trout often had his arm around her head, ostensibly cradling her in grief. He would not let anyone, even her parents, get too close.

It was in the neck area that the doctors found what many had suspected would be found, an indication that Zona had met with foul play.

A record of the formal autopsy has never been located. It is doubtful that one was kept, thus the only extant accounts of the proceeding are from newspaper writers who may have been present or interviewed the doctors and witnesses.

"Well, Shue, we have found your wife's neck to have been broken," one doctor is reported to have exclaimed, according to a newspaper account. Another newspaper said that doctors found there was some residual bruising and finger marks to indicate she had been choked. One observer said Trout stopped whittling at the announcement and declared that no one could prove he had anything to do with it.

Another newspaper reported that "the neck was dislocated between the first and second vertebrae. The ligaments were torn and ruptured. The windpipe had been crushed at a point in front of the neck."

A Greenbrier newspaper wrote that "from one of the doctors we learn that the examination clearly disclosed the fact that Mrs. Shue's neck had been broken. The jury found in accordance with the facts above stated [and] charged Shue with murder."

Shue was arrested in late February 1897 but could not be arraigned until the next circuit court term in April. He was incarcerated in the old Lewisburg county jail and subsequently indicted by a Greenbrier County grand jury. His trial was set for the June term, 1897.

BUT HOW THEN does Mary Jane Heaster's supposed nighttime encounter with her daughter's ghost figure into Trout's arrest, indictment, and scheduled trial? Or does it at all?

That is an extraordinarily difficult question to answer because the *myth* that has grown up around "the wild rose of Greenbrier," as Zonie was called, and what actually happened have become so entangled that it's nearly impossible to separate out truth from fable. Much of the ghost story originates with Mrs. Heaster herself through conversations she had with neighbors and testimony at Trout Shue's trial. No one else could verify the spectral visits.

THE *LEGEND* OF Zona Shue's ghostly visit is that she first appeared to her mother about a week after her murder. Mrs. Heaster claimed to have been alerted to the possibility of foul play when she was given a sheet that had been placed on one side of Zona's head in the coffin. It looked clean, but smelled odd. When she washed it the sheet turned blood red, although other people saw it as pink. She said this "proved" that Zona had been murdered.

Simply put, Mrs. Heaster said Zona visited her over the course of four nights. The opening visit was short-lived; she vanished as her mother reached out to touch her. However, over the next three nights, Zona returned to Mrs. Heaster, each time giving new information and new clues about her death. Her neck had been "squeezed off at the first joint" by her husband. He grew furious when he discovered that she didn't have meat for supper.

Following the visits, Mrs. Heaster went to the Greenbrier County prosecuting attorney with the "information" Zona had given her, but her appeals were dismissed as the work of an emotionally distraught mother. She persisted in her efforts, however, and Zona's body was exhumed, the method of her death discovered, and her husband arrested.

Mrs. Heaster was even more specific about the circumstances of her daughter's visit during the testimony at her son-in-law's trial.

"(Zona) said she had plenty (of meat) and she said that she had butter and apple butter, apples, and named over two or three kinds of jellies, pears and cherries, and raspberry jelly, and she says she had plenty; and she says, don't you think that he was mad and just took down all my nice things and packed them away and just ruined them," Mrs. Heaster told the court. "And she told me where I could look down the back of Aunt Martha Jones', in the meadow, in a rocky place; that I could look in a cellar behind some loose plank and see. It was a square log house, and it was hewed up to the square, and she said for me to look right at the right-hand side of the door as you go in and at the right-hand corner as you go in. Well, I saw the place just exactly as she told me, and I saw blood right there where she told me; and she told me something about that meat every night she came, just as she did the first night. She came four times and four nights . . ."

Mrs. Heaster claimed never to have visited her daughter and son-in-law's home while they were married, only after she heard from her daughter's ghost. She visited the cabin and claimed she found the objects just as Zona had described them. The "blood" Mrs. Heaster reported seeing might have been at the place where Trout killed her, though there is little in the way of autopsy evidence to support the finding of any wounds that would have resulted in blood loss.

Mrs. Heaster denied under oath that she dreamed about Zona's return—"It was no dream, for I was as wide awake as I ever was," she insisted—and attributed the visitation to having prayed that her daughter would come back and tell her how Trout had murdered her.

"The Lord sent her to tell it. I was the only friend that she knew she could tell and put any confidence in. I was the nearest one to her. . . . They were not a dream. I don't dream when I am wide awake, to be sure; and I know I saw her right there with me."

Mrs. Heaster said Zona was no transparent wisp but was of flesh and blood. Neither did she shrink from the sight of her dead offspring.

"I got up on my elbows and reached out a little further, as I wanted to see if people came in their coffins, and I sat up . . . and it was light in the house. It was not a lamp light. I wanted to see if there was a coffin, but there was not. She was just like she was when she left this world. It was just after I went to bed, and I wanted her to come and talk to me, and she did. That was before the inquest and I told my neighbors. They said she was exactly as I told them she was."

Mrs. Heaster recognized her daughter's clothing, but Zona added a peculiar twist, so to speak:

"(She was wearing) the very dress that she was killed in, and when she went to leave me she turned her head completely around and looked at me like she wanted me to know all about it."

Zona allegedly told her mother how Trout came to kill her: "The first time she came, she seemed that she did not want to tell me as much about it as she did afterward. The last night she was there she told me that she did everything she could do, and I am satisfied that she did do all that, too," Mrs. Heaster said.

THE KNOWN *FACTS* about the death of Zona Shue and her husband's subsequent trial for her murder are something else indeed. The prosecution had a largely circumstantial case against Shue. There were no eyewitnesses. No evidence that directly placed Shue's strong hands around his wife's thin throat. No "smoking gun."

The doctors who performed the autopsy testified that she did not commit suicide, nor did she fall down the stairs. Her neck had been broken, but there were no outward injuries to indicate the fatal injury had resulted from the impact of such a plunge. Dr. Knapp clearly did not know what was ailing Zona in the month he saw her. He first put her death down as an "everlasting faint," which had no medical definition then or now. A week later he changed the death certificate to read "childbirth" as the cause of death.

The eleven-year-old who discovered the body, Andy Jones, was the closest to being a witness, yet even his memory and his testimony were inconsistent at best. In later years, he changed his story in each telling.

A newspaper recounted what Andy told the court:

"Shue went to the house of a Negro woman and asked the son (Andy Jones) of this woman to go to his house and hunt the eggs and then go to Mrs. Shue and see if she wanted to send to the store for anything. This boy went to the house of Shue, and after looking for eggs and finding none, he went to the house, knocked and received no response, opened the door and went in. He found the dead body of Mrs. Shue lying upon the floor. The body was lying stretched out perfectly straight with feet together, one hand by the side and the other lying across the body; the head was slightly inclined to one side. The Negro boy ran and told his mother that Mrs. Shue was dead."

Andy's mother gave some of the most damaging testimony. She said Shue had placed a large "collar" and "large veil" around his wife's neck when he took her upstairs to dress the body for burial. The implication was that he wished to hide her neck from public view.

Several witnesses talked about the general "floppiness" of her neck and the odd padding that had been placed on either side of her head, as if to keep it from rolling from side to side.

There might be another explanation for the wadding. Some speculated that if Zona had indeed died of childbirth, the still-born or premature baby might have been wrapped in swad-dling and placed beside her head. However, in all the secondhand reports of the autopsy nothing was mentioned of finding a baby's body in the coffin.

Other witnesses testified to Shue's general geniality in the days following his wife's death. He even boasted about how he'd planned all along to have seven wives.

Mary Robinson Heaster's testimony about the postmortem visit by her daughter provided dramatic evidence. Interest-ingly, the testimony was introduced by Trout Shue's defense attorney and not by the prosecutor. The speculation is that he wanted to show that she was mentally unhinged over the death of her daughter and that the jury should disregard *all* of her testimony.

Mrs. Heaster was a most persuasive witness. She provided many small details of what Zona had "said" in her visit and of what she was wearing, which matched other testimony of what she had on before her husband changed her clothes. Mrs. Heaster steadfastly denied making any of it up.

The judge instructed the jury to disregard the testimony about Zona's ghost, but it's doubtful they could have erased such powerful statements from the bereaved mother.

Zona Shue historian Katie Letcher Lyle has found that Mrs. Heaster could have learned most of the information about which she testified from people who had seen the body, knew the layout of the Shue house (Mrs. Heaster said she'd never been there), or otherwise had some intimate knowledge of the Shues' lives together. She testified in court that Zona told her specifically where her neck had been broken ("squeezed off at the first joint"), but that had been published earlier in the newspapers.

The defense did call Trout Shue to testify on his own behalf. He was by most accounts an engaging witness. Historian Lyle calls him "a remarkably attractive (man, with a) resonant voice, which he and his lawyers must have been aware of and probably banked on using."

That gambit may have backfired. He seems to have come across as something of a conceited braggart. The Greenbrier newspaper said: "His testimony, manner and so forth, made an unfavorable impression on the spectators."

He passionately denied having anything to do with his wife's death, said that he indeed "dearly loved" her, and asked the jury to look into his face to see that he was innocent.

The jury didn't believe him.

On July 8, 1897, Trout Shue was convicted of first degree murder with a sentence of life imprisonment at West Virginia State Penitentiary, Moundsville. The jury took just seventy minutes to decide on a verdict. Ten of the twelve men voted to hang Shue, but two others would not go along, perhaps because the evidence was entirely circumstantial.

But he very nearly ended up facing the gallows anyway. Three days after his sentence, on July 11, a mob formed with the intention of taking him from the jail and hanging him with a stout, new rope. However, authorities discovered the plot and thwarted the attempt. Eventually half a dozen men were identified as being participants and four were indicted.

Shue was transferred to the penitentiary on July 13, 1897.

The legend of Zona Shue's ghost got a significant enhancement when, on July 9, a newspaper in Pocahontas wrote this about Trout Shue's conviction:

Trout Shue, formerly of Droop Mountain, was found guilty of murder in the first degree, in Greenbrier court, the jury recommending a life sentence. The evidence was convincing that Shue had murdered his wife by breaking her neck, and the case presented this aspect, that the woman died of a broken neck, and that it was impossible for her to break it herself, and that no one could have done it except her husband. What was the closing scene of the woman's life will probably never be known, but the explanation of the "vision" of the woman's mother gives a very striking suggestion of the last quarrel which ended in the death of the woman. She said that her daughter appeared to her and said that on the last evening she had gotten a good supper except there was no meat on the table, and that her husband had become enraged on account of it. Shue is a bad man and he has no sympathy from the neighborhood in which he was raised.

Erasmus Stribbling Trout Shue never again set foot in Greenbrier County. He died in prison at about the age of forty, March 13, 1900. His remains were not claimed. What happened to them is not clear because prison records from that era have not been found. He may have been buried under a wooden tombstone at Tom's Run Cemetery or, as some claimed, his body was given to medical science.

THE GHOST OF Zona Shue, however, has never been fully explained. Did Mary Jane Robinson Heaster actually *see* her daughter on those nights, as the persistent belief would have it, or did she in her loathing of Trout Shue invent the entire story?

If one is doubtful of the ghost's authenticity, there are perhaps two explanations.

Historian Katie Lechter Lyle proposed one in her book, *The Man Who Wanted Seven Wives*. Lyle points to an odd concurrence in the pages of the *Greenbrier Independent* on January 28, 1897—the date Zona's death was reported on page three. On the front page of the same issue Lyle found a foreign news item in which a ghost returns to avenge its death.

The story was headlined "A Ghost Story" and read as follows:

J. Henneker Heaton tells in the London *Literary World* an interesting sequel to the most famous Australian ghost story, which came to his knowledge as one of the proprietors of the leading New South Wales weekly, *The Town and Country Journal*. One of the most famous murder cases in Australia was discovered by the ghost of the murdered man sitting on the rail of a dam (Australian for horse pond) into which his body had been thrown. Numberless people saw it, and the crime was duly brought home.

Years after, a dying man making his confession said that he invented the ghost. He witnessed the crime, but was threatened with death if he divulged it as he wished to, and the only way he saw out of the impasse was to affect to see the ghost where the body would be found. As soon as he started the story, such is the power of nervousness that numerous other people began to see it, until its fame reached such dimensions that a search was made and the body found, and the murderers brought to justice.

Lyle contends that Mrs. Heaster likely saw this story and, coupled with her grief, previous suspicions, and general hatred for Trout Shue (she called him "the devil"), concocted the midnight visits. Later she hoped to have other people swear they, too, were visited by Zona's ghost. That didn't happen. After the autopsy and after discussing Zona's final days on earth with her daughter's friends and neighbors, Mrs. Heaster was able to start adding detail upon detail so that by the time she was called as a witness months later her story came across as quite credible. She even produced the "red-stained" sheet as physical evidence.

"I believe Mary Jane Robinson Heaster lied outright . . ." Lyle writes, adding that she figured out a way to "prove" Trout Shue the murderer when she came upon the newspaper item from Australia.

But that may not have been the only "ghost story" of which Mrs. Heaster was aware.

Eleven years earlier, in November 1886, a rather remarkable incident was reported in Wheeling, West Virginia, a good distance of course from Greenbrier County, but a story nevertheless that had some striking similarities to what would take place years later.

This author discovered the story in the pages of the *Ottawa*

(Ontario) *Free Press* under the headline "Revealed by the Spirits: The Mystery of a Murder Solved by a Medium." The dateline is "Wheeling, W. Va., Nov. 24":

By a strange and what many people believe to be a supernatural revelation a murder committed five years ago has been exposed in this (Wheeling) city. A man who had a young son by a former marriage was left a widower a second time some five years ago. He had been married to his second wife about a year when she died; as is alleged, through breaking her neck by a fall down stairs. One of the dead woman's brothers, with the boy above alluded to, was recently passing along a street in this city when a man in front of them fell into a fit. The brother and boy stopped to watch the sight, and after the lapse of a moment or two the prostrate and writhing man on the pavement called out: "I was murdered! My husband shot me!"

The effect of this outcry upon the boy was remarkable. He turned pale and screamed out that it was true that his father did kill "mama," but if his father knew he had said so he would kill him.

In the excitement the man on the sidewalk recovered and attempted to slip away in the crowd, but when stopped denied that he had said anything, gave his name as Williams, and said he was a "medium." The boy, in answer to further enquiries, said his father and the dead woman frequently quarreled, and that his father shot her as she was going down stairs. Some of the relations of the family recalled that the woman's clothing was bloodstained when she was found at the foot of the stairs, and an investigation was determined upon. The remains were exhumed yesterday in the presence of a justice of the peace, when the breast bone was found to be perforated by a bullet, which was afterwards found in the coffin.

It is supposed that Williams became possessed of the secret in some way and took advantage of his alleged powers as a medium to make the matter public. The arrest of the alleged murderer will follow.

The coincidences are remarkable. A man on his second marriage. A quarrel. Death from an alleged "broken neck." The body found at the bottom of a staircase. A medium giving voice to the woman's alleged ghost contending that she was murdered. An exhumation and autopsy. And finally a presumed arrest, although that cannot be verified.

There is no evidence that Mrs. Heaster read of the Wheeling events, but neither is there incontestable evidence that she saw or heard about the Australian ghost story, although the latter is more likely, as it was carried on page one in a newspaper that she would have no doubt saved.

But perhaps, too, she remembered the Wheeling events from years before as well, and that she put together details of the Australian episode and the older Wheeling narrative to "create" her own ghost story.

The events are far distant and evidence is scant or nonexistent. The tale of Zona Heaster Shue has become embedded in West Virginia folk culture and will likely remain so despite any evidence to the contrary.

20

Kindred Spirits

Agatha, I came to visit you tonight.
    I wanted to share in the warm feelings that I think
you have for this place. Merry Christmas.

    —An anonymous person's comment in a guest
        book at the Karsten Inn

KURT MUELLNER WAS pleased that his plans to celebrate his mother's ninetieth birthday in January 2002 had gone off without a hitch. His son and daughter-in-law were going to attend, as were his cousin and her husband. His godson came up from

Chicago. The festivities were going to be held in the dining room at the historic Karsten Inn, in the Lake Michigan shoreline community of Kewaunee, Wisconsin.

Muellner, who operates a gallery and museum just down Ellis Street from the inn, is good friends with the inn's owners at the time, Ron and Roswitha Heuer.

He booked his out-of-town guests into three rooms on the second floor at the Karsten. The party was a grand success. Muellner bid his family good-bye and told them he'd meet them the next morning for breakfast at the inn.

He wasn't prepared for what they told him when he arrived the next day.

"My daughter-in-law came down first," Muellner says today. "She's quite outspoken and asked what the heck kind of place this hotel was? She said that about two o'clock in the morning she heard laughing and screaming and hollering going on outside her door and then it just disappeared. Then she heard somebody flushing toilets for the rest of the night."

Muellner's cousin came down next and complained about the same midnight upheavals. His godson chimed in a few minutes later with a nearly identical series of questions.

But Muellner knew none of that was possible—his relatives had been the *only* guests in the inn that night. It was impossible that they could have heard any sort of commotion being caused by somebody *living*.

WELCOME TO THE Karsten Inn, the spectral home of three mischievous ghosts and perhaps one of the most haunted hostelries in all of the Midwest.

Muellner knew the legends associated with the hotel, but never before had he or members of his family been affected by the haunting. He was suspicious enough to ask that Roswitha Heuer review the video surveillance tapes taken overnight on the second floor. She did. As they both suspected nothing showed up in the hallways.

According to the psychics who have visited the hotel, and many guests over the years, the hotel is the repository of at least three separate entities—an older man, who may be former owner William "Big Bill" Karsten, Senior, nicknamed thus for his three-hundred-pound-plus girth; a young child, possibly Karsten's beloved grandson, Billy; and a young woman, identified as a former hotel maid in the 1920s and 1930s, and Bill Senior's supposed lover.

Each member of this spirited trio has its own unique personality, according to those who have come upon them.

Bill Karsten's ghost is sometimes called the Old Sailor. He was a ship captain in his early years but the sobriquet may have more to do with the fact that his presence can be detected by a foul-smelling odor, an old salt who's been away from bathing facilities for too long. He is also prone to rearranging furniture, or playing tricks on maintenance staff.

The little boy Billy was Big Bill's grandson. He died of meningitis only a few weeks after his grandfather's death in 1940. He was five years old. Billy races through the hallways or may show up to have fun with other children staying in the hotel.

A front desk clerk says she's heard many stories from departing guests, especially those who stay along the second floor corridor.

"I've had (guests checking out) tell me that they've heard kids running up and down the hall around three in the morning. They get up to look out the door but nobody is there. Some have even heard kids playing with a ball because the bouncing is what woke them up, hearing the ball rolling and bouncing up and down the hall."

The maid is Agatha, although her given name is kept private as her descendants continue to live in the region. She worked at the hotel during the 1930s, living in a room on the third floor, directly above Big Bill's suite. Rumors of their affair circulated through the small city.

Countless guests in Agatha's old sleeping room, now renumbered 310, have reported eerie events during their stay.

Gallery owner Kurt Muellner had one of his few other direct encounters with the haunted side of the Karsten Inn inside Agatha's room.

"This would have been in July 2001," Muellner recalls. "I came in for coffee one morning and Roswitha told me a housekeeper had found the window open in 310. She couldn't close it. Now the maintenance guy back then was about six foot nine . . . he should have been a football player. Well, he'd gone up there and couldn't budge it."

Muellner was listening as hotel co-owner Roswitha Heuer told him what had happened. He scarcely believed what she was saying and thought it was "a bunch of baloney," in his words. Together Muellner and Roswitha climbed the staircase to the third floor.

"The hallways are hot in the summer because there's no air conditioning," Muellner says, "but when we got outside 310 I definitely felt a temperature drop. A big one. We unlocked the door and went in."

The window was open. Try as he might, Muellner could not budge it.

"It was like it was nailed open. So we left."

The next morning the maintenance man went back up to the room, but this time he carried a pry bar. He unlocked the door and walked in. The window was closed tight, yet nobody else that they knew of had been in the room since the previous morning.

THE KARSTEN INN is actually the second hotel on the corner of Ellis and Lake streets in Kewaunee, within eyesight of Lake Michigan. Charles Brandes built The Steamboat House in 1858 on land he bought from the government for $8.95. The hotel went through several owners and name changes until it was bought by "Big Bill" Karsten in 1911. Less than a year later, in February 1912, a fire outside the kitchen wall quickly engulfed the wood frame structure. All the guests and staff escaped, but the hotel was a total loss.

Karsten quickly rebuilt and opened a $55,000, fifty-two room, three-story brick building eight months later. A dining room seated ninety patrons at a time, and an elegant bar boasted a separate street entrance. Pictures taken of the original building show a broad porch running the length of the hotel which has been enclosed in a long, boxy entranceway. Though it has been extensively remodeled, that 1912 structure is the hotel that exists today.

Karsten retired in 1928 and sold the hotel to his son, Bill, Jr.

According to Kewaunee County historian Thomas Schuller, Big Bill was a larger-than-life character, and not only because of his rotund size.

A native of Germany, Karsten ran away to sea when just a

boy barely into his teens. He worked first as a cabin attendant and later as a crewman sailing to various ports around the world. He met and married Catherine Spearns in St. John's, Newfoundland, and together they immigrated to Milwaukee, Wisconsin. Karsten worked on Great Lakes ships, which often stopped at Kewaunee harbor, once one of the busiest ports on Wisconsin's shoreline.

Karsten eventually started in business. A beer company asked him to set up a distribution service in northeastern Wisconsin, and he decided that Kewaunee would suit his needs. He moved his family there in 1893 to pursue his career as a businessman and, later, an hotelier.

"He was not only a hotel keeper but the mayor of Kewaunee," Schuller said. "That kept him on the go, meeting new people who visited the city, and interviewing people who wanted to work at his hotel. This may be what led to the strained relationship between the mayor and his wife, or it could have been something else, but . . . Bill Karsten and his wife separated." She died in 1928 after several years of ill health, according to Schuller. Big Bill kept a suite of third-floor rooms at the hotel, although he had to move eventually to the second floor because his weight made it difficult for him to navigate the additional staircase. He died of a heart attack on January 4, 1940.

His grandson and namesake, Billy Karsten, was by all accounts nearly inseparable from his grandfather. The child tagged along as the old man lumbered through the hotel, checking on the employees even though he had passed on the ownership to his son. A few weeks after Big Bill's death, Billy contracted Haemophilus influenzae meningitis, a respiratory illness, and died at a Green Bay hospital.

It was also during that time that Agatha was hired as a maid. Her employment included her own room in a wing reserved for hotel staff.

"It didn't take long for stories to start circulating that Agatha and Big Bill Karsten were romantically involved," Schuller said. Agatha had been born and raised on a farm near Kewaunee. One of eight children, she was apparently raped by a drunken neighbor when she was twenty-one, and got pregnant. Her parents raised the child as their own, but money was scarce with eleven mouths to feed and Agatha went to work at the Karsten Hotel in 1925. She stayed until 1937. Citing her own ill health and that of her father, she moved to her brother's farm outside Kewaunee. She died in 1954.

Bill Karsten, Jr., operated the hotel until his own death from heart disease in 1964.

A series of owners then took over the hotel operations. They met with mixed financial success, but did discover some early indications that otherworldly denizens seemed to occupy at least a portion of the old hotel.

A remodeling in 1966 is generally thought to have triggered the first appearance of Agatha, according to writer Scottie Dayton who, along with Green Bay psychic Rita Ann Freeman, has documented many of the hotel's supernatural incidents.

Tradesmen felt sudden, bone-chilling drafts while working to remodel the third floor. They thought it was simply a product of spending the day in a drafty old building. But a few months later, the daughter of one of the new owners discovered there might be something more than drafts circulating through the rooms when she started decorating the lobby for Christmas. She'd hauled several boxes of decorations downstairs from storage shelves on the third floor until only one box remained. She went back up to bring it down. When she got there, the shelf was empty. As she turned to leave, she saw the box sitting on the floor next to the door. She grabbed it and rushed back downstairs "as fast as my legs could go."

New owners in the 1980s made additional changes to the hotel, including an extensive remodeling to the first and second floors. Again, workmen complained about the odd things they'd run into—tools would inexplicably vanish or they would find them moved, sudden cold drafts would drift by, doors might slam shut for no cause or, most upsetting of all, they claimed to hear the *sweep-sweep-sweep* of someone using a broom on the old wood floors.

Scottie Dayton said the housekeeping staff claimed to see apparitions and detected pungent smells. A kitchen worker polishing a mirror said he saw the pale reflection of a woman wearing an old-fashioned maid's uniform standing behind him.

A hotel manager in the late 1980s said someone pushed her

down the main staircase as she stood on the second floor landing.

On another occasion, a film crew from a Green Bay television station was scheduled to produce a Halloween special using the hotel as a backdrop—the owners had seen some opportunity for promoting the haunted aspects of the place. Before they arrived, the manager checked along the third floor, which was strewn with buckets to catch drips from the leaky roof. She said a weird feeling that upset her greatly came over her.

A cook at the time sometimes stayed the night if winter weather conditions prevented her from returning to her home outside town. Once she found hairpins strewn about in her room. They hadn't been there the night before, she said at the time.

BY 2001, GERMAN-BORN hotel professional Roswitha Heuer and several partners had acquired the hotel. Her husband, Ron Heuer, is a native of Kewaunee and a former executive with Universal Studios, Orlando.

They had met at a trade show in Germany, even though she was living near Miami and he was in Orlando, and ultimately married. He then took a job in California, while she commuted between her job in Florida and their California home. Ron later became involved in other businesses. In the 1990s, the couple decided to change their lifestyles and move back to Kewaunee. Ron Heuer owned acreage outside the small city, on which they decided to build a house.

Ron's brother passed away in 1995, and he and Roswitha were in Kewaunee for the funeral. They had dinner at the Karsten Inn, the only time he'd ever been in the hotel.

"When we came up here, I saw a for sale sign on the side of the hotel," dapper Ron Heuer remembers. "I said the place could be very pretty."

Roswitha, too, was taken with the beauty of the old hotel. "When I saw the lobby and how beautiful the rooms were, that did it. And when we came in a second time something just told me I had to have this," she adds.

Roswitha had been working in the hotel business in Boca Raton, Florida, before her marriage to Ron. She persuaded several investor partners that she'd worked with in Florida to look over the Kewaunee hotel as a possible investment. "They also fell in love with it," she says in her still-pronounced German accent. "But they sat in the lobby and wondered why no one was able to make the place work."

The Heuers opened the historic Karsten Inn in May 2001. Even with the tragedy of September 11, 2001, and the subsequent impact on travel, the Heuers managed to stay in business. Roswitha is the energetic, hands-on manager while Ron, with other business interests, assists in various capacities.

"I first heard the ghost stories from the real estate agent," Roswitha says. "I didn't believe them. I was raised in a way that what you don't see you don't believe. There's nothing like that out there. But when I signed the papers with the bank, they said to me, you're buying a place with a ghost. I said yeah, sure, that's a really cute story, but I'll believe it when I see it. Yet I was kind of intrigued by it all, but I didn't really believe in it."

It didn't take long for Roswitha to decide that *not* seeing can be believing.

"That first day I came in here . . . it was the seventh of May . . . I walked into the building and sat at the front desk. My brother-in-law had just left. I had closed everything up and was here all by myself. A big, cold rush of air went right through me. And I thought, well, that's kind of strange. I checked the air conditioning and the heater. The door hadn't opened. So I thought I was just imagining it."

But then her brother-in-law returned a couple of days later to help with some repairs and Roswitha wasn't so sure the previous incident had been all in her imagination.

"He'd come back to help me do some maintenance up in the rooms. He repaired something on a windowsill because he had pulled out the window, put it on the floor, and then had gone down to the basement. When he went back up to the room, the window was back in the wall. He came downstairs and asked if I had played a joke on him. I didn't know what he was talking about. He said he had pulled the window out and put it on the floor, but now it was back in. . . . He asked me if I'd been up there. I told him I didn't even know what room he was in. I had no idea what he was talking about."

A few days after that, his tool belt went missing from another room he was working on. Again, he thought perhaps Roswitha had something to do with it. And again, she had not. "That's when I thought this was all really too strange," she says.

Over the coming months and years, the Heuers would listen to all sorts of stories about their hotel and have enough personal experiences with unexplained events there to persuade them that there might be an existence beyond that which we can see, hear, feel, and touch.

She talked with psychics and ghost hunters, all of whom agreed that at least those three ghosts occupy the Karsten Inn.

"But they said they are good ghosts," Roswitha maintains. "They've been worried about this place because nobody had taken care of it, everybody tried to make it work and nobody has yet. So they're not bad entities. And besides . . . they're all German!"

THE HEUERS RESTORED the hotel to its turn-of-the-twentieth-century appearance with authentic Victorian furniture in the spacious lobby that also features a fireplace they keep lit on cool days. Elegant chandeliers cast a soft glow on the comfortable surroundings. Each of the twenty-three spotlessly clean rooms has a theme; fifteen are outfitted with Jacuzzi whirlpools. The restaurant specializes in German dishes, while the bar offers lighter fare.

The warm hospitality offered by the owners and staff and cozy ambiance of the rooms more than offset any concern visitors might have about additional ethereal guests they might encounter.

The hotel is popular with vacationers who want to explore the small communities that dot northeast Wisconsin's Lake Michigan shoreline.

And sometimes families discover their children have attracted the littlest Karsten ghost.

Typical, according to Roswitha, was the family staying at the hotel for the weekend. After they checked in, the couple's three-year-old girl wanted to leave the room to explore down the hallway. Her parents let her. After a short time she started banging on all the doors along the floor. Her mother came out to ask what she was doing.

"Looking for that little boy," she replied. She wanted to play with him. Her parents quietly explained that no other rooms had any little children.

Inexplicably, the family packed up and left in the middle of the night. As they were leaving, the little girl ran up to a photo hanging on a wall in the lobby.

"Mommy, that's the boy I was playing with," she cried.

The picture was of Bill Karsten, Jr., taken when he was a little boy. Though he died as an adult in 1964, there was a resemblance between him and his own son, Billy, the reputed child ghost there.

NOTHING EVIL OR dangerous has ever been attributed to the ghosts, according to the Heuers. They do seem intent, however, on reminding staff and guests of their continued interest in how the place operates.

"Last year we had a group of nuclear power people staying here," Roswitha says. A nuclear plant is located not too distant. "I was in Room 210 and complaining to myself that I was the only one working here that day. The restaurant and dining room were closed. And I was saying ah, damn, why can't the girls do a better job cleaning the rooms properly. I was going on and on. Then I suddenly heard what sounded to me like an old man wheezing and taking very deep, gurgled breaths."

Roswitha mumbled a quick "uh-oh" and quickly left the room, which is the same one in which Big Bill Karsten died at the age of seventy-eight, six decades earlier.

AGATHA STILL TAKES an interest in keeping the place orderly, according to Roswitha.

"I was dusting a room, under the bed, when I heard somebody moving stuff around in the bathroom. I looked but there was nobody in there, of course. I went back into the bedroom and it started up again. I got frightened and ran downstairs. I called my husband and told him he wouldn't believe what had just happened to me. He thought it had to have been somebody from next door. . . . I swear to God there was no one else there."

Agatha is also very protective. The Heuers once hired a hotel housekeeper who stayed for less than a week, claiming that in the middle of the night the door to the second floor fire escape flew open, followed by the door to her own room.

"I tried to convince her to stay, but she said, no, that she wanted to leave and go back to Florida," Roswitha says. So she did. Afterward, the Heuers say they discovered the woman had taken linens and other supplies from a storeroom. The supposition is that Agatha did not like her and took it upon herself to drive the woman away.

DIARIES ARE KEPT in each room. Guests are invited to note down their comments about their stay at the Karsten Inn. More often than not, however, the words speak more about encounters with the spirit world than comments about room cleanliness or restaurant cuisine:

Enjoyed our stay here. Didn't get much sleep—Agatha kept us up crying all night.

What an awesome place. Our stay was excellent. Only one little mishap. About twenty minutes after lights-out something (or someone) made a loud clash like an object falling on the floor. No one moved to investigate, a combination of being dog tired and somewhat spooked. In the morning, while we searched for the cause, we could not find anything out of place. Agatha's point was made— your presence was our pleasure.

I don't know whether Agatha was here or not, but a few weird things happened to us. The toilet flushed a few times by itself, and I thought someone was sitting on my legs. I thought it was (my husband) but his legs were on his own side of the bed. Very strange. But we will be back.

A Brown Deer, Wisconsin, writer, Cynthia Kalies, described an overnight stay on a bitterly cold night that convinced her that the stories about the Karsten were indeed accurate. She stayed on the hotel's third floor. She expected to find a warm and snug room, but instead discovered that the small space heater was barely keeping the chill off. This is her account:

"I stood by the heater wearing my coat for fifteen minutes waiting for the warmth, but I only felt drafty air movements. I checked out the bathroom, also cold. After a half hour of hoping for warmth, I went downstairs to talk with the barkeep; he told me that the space heater takes about fifteen minutes to warm the room and to turn it on maximum. I considered telling him it was already on max when I walked in, but he was busy, and what could he really do?

"Returning to my room, I felt determined to experience the warmth from at least the rushing waters of the Jacuzzi; I turned on the hot water, and pondered whether I should tell the front desk staff in the morning about the cold.

"After reading my book for a while, I called it a night. Only the bath nightlight was left on. It felt good to be under the warm covers. I was lost in thought when I heard someone walking loudly in the room above me. How rude, I thought. Then I remembered there was no room above me, I was on the top floor.

"I heard someone in my bathroom, and I was getting spooked. Suddenly I heard someone outside my door. Next, someone or something hit my door, and immediately the chair in my room was pushed aside, and I saw my suitcase on the chair flip up and over and drop on the floor.

"I jumped and yelled, breathing hard. I looked around the room, clearly seeing, even though it was night, but I did not get out of bed. Finally, I forced my eyes closed, determined to get some shut-eye.

"After a short time, I heard someone in the bathroom again. A burst of bravery, perhaps, but I quickly got up and marched over and flipped on the big light. Not a creature or a soul! I passed the sink mirror, but I could not look at it for fear of what I might see.

"Hurrying back to the security of bedcovers, I decided that whatever it was would not keep me from getting a decent night's sleep. But it wasn't over yet. I heard someone again upstairs (where there was no room), walking loudly.

"Finally, I dozed, and woke up the next morning to a cozy room with light streaming in through the windows. I turned on the TV, made coffee, and slowly got ready for my day. While drying my hair, all the electricity went off in my room, but not the built-in hair dryer. Surely it was a blown fuse, but the hair dryer should have also gone out. Maybe it was my companion from the night before hurrying me along so I would leave earlier."

ROSWITHA HEUER KEEPS a log of all the peculiar activities guests and employees report to her. Many are anecdotal, but they are numerous:

- A bell that had been installed to signal waitresses when an order was "up" was, in fact, never activated, yet it rang twice while Roswitha and a friend were standing within a few feet of the button that activated it.
- One employee is reluctant to use the basement laundry facilities when she is alone. She says there are "shadows" passing by her.
- Roswitha and the restaurant's chef sat at the front desk one afternoon. She thought he'd moved his hand because a shadow appeared to pass across his face. It happened a second time, and she asked him about it. He wondered if she asked because of the shadow he'd noticed going across them.
- A guest in Room 204 heard someone vacuuming the hallway floor at about 4 A.M. He told Roswitha that he was surprised hotel staff was working such early morning hours. She said they weren't.
- A state worker had just settled into her room for the night, flipped on the bed stand light, and had telephoned her husband. At that moment, a swirling mass of cold air swept through the room followed by a vaporous white cloud. The cloud flew over her bed and dissolved into the wall.

- A woman staying in a former maid's room jotted down a comment in the room diary and placed the fountain pen alongside it on the desk. She then went into the bathroom to shower. When she came out a few minutes later, the pen was lying several feet away from the table on the floor.
- Two overnight guests from Arizona found items in their room rearranged. "When we arose in the morning, a straw hat had moved to the bedpost and the water pitcher had moved near the sink. (My husband) swore he didn't move them."
- Two men staying in Room 310—Agatha's old room—were perplexed that the toilet kept flushing all night, even though one or the other got up several times to adjust it. A subsequent examination found nothing wrong with the toilet "flopper" or the plumbing connections.
- A visitor from Czechoslovakia staying in Room 312 was shaken when someone knocked on his door. A few seconds later it flew open. He jumped out of bed and looked up and down the hallway, but he was quite alone.
- A couple and their four-year-old boy planned to stay the night following their attendance at a wedding reception in the inn's dining room. They visited in the afternoon a few hours before the wedding but could not get their son to go upstairs to visit the room they'd be in that night. "He was hysterical," Roswitha remembers. Later that evening, as Roswitha sat in the bar visiting with a friend, she heard crying coming from the lobby. It was the same couple as she'd met that afternoon, only this time the mother was holding her son. He was crying at the top of his lungs. His father was trying to control him as well, but with as little success. "He said the child had gone to sleep downstairs so they'd taken him up to bed," Roswitha says. "But the minute they tried to put him down on the bed he was wide awake and screaming. He kept repeating 'go away,' 'go away,' and pushing away with his hands. That's what he was doing down in the lobby, too." Roswitha tried to calm him, but he kept looking past her, pushing away with his hands and saying 'go away.' They checked out of the hotel. When they came back a few days later to return a videotape they'd borrowed about the hotel, the child would not get

out of the car. The mother said the boy had never acted that way before in his life. It was almost as if the child was seeing something—and trying to get it to go away—that the adults could not.

- Another couple had a bit of a scarier encounter. Their boy also seemed to have encountered Billy as a willing playmate. The couple's boy ran out of the room several times because he wanted to "play" with the other child. Though his parents tried to dissuade him, he kept insisting that the other boy wanted him to play. Sometime that night the child's parents awoke when they heard the boy cry out. They found a teddy bear in his bed. The bear had been sitting on a shelf. But more disturbing was that an old hat pin was stuck in the bear. Apparently the pin had also stuck the boy in his foot. Neither parent had put the bear in the child's bed; the shelf on which it had rested was too high a reach for the boy.

- Roswitha often makes the morning coffee in a big, kitchen coffeemaker. In one instance, after she made the coffee and turned on the pot, she walked around the corner into the dining room. She then heard a *ka-ching* and rushed back in. The coffee filter was lying on the table, coffee grounds had spewed all over, but the pot still brewing. "It was a total mess," she recalls. Somehow she thinks the spindle holding the coffee basket and coffee grounds sprung out of the coffeemaker. The same peculiar mishap has befallen several other waitresses; in one instance the spindle holding the filter cup sprang out and landed halfway across the room from the coffeepot.

- Psychic Rita Ann Freeman told writer Scottie Dayton that the rank smell she detected in her second-floor room was being caused by old man Karsten. He didn't like her being in his old living room and that's how he was showing his disapproval.

Tammy is a Sunday desk clerk, waitress, and general all-around assistant. She is Roswitha's niece. The fleeting shadows elsewhere in the hotel find their way into the basement where the piles of daily laundry are washed and dried, as the day Tammy offered to help her foster sister do the wash.

"We'd waitressed all day," Tammy says, referring to the two of them. "When we got done there was still a lot of laundry to do. I asked her if she'd mind staying with me for a few hours and we'd get as much of it done as we could in that time. So we went downstairs and proceeded to do the laundry. We'd been discussing (some personal problems) and she started to cry. All of a sudden it appeared as if someone had closed the basement door. The room got real dark."

The door going downstairs had a large window in it, and the door had been open. The day was sunny. Tammy said it was as if someone had suddenly blocked the window and closed the door.

"We both simultaneously turned our heads to look at the door to see who had shut it, or how it got shut. But the door was still open. Neither had the sun been covered by clouds because it was still sunny. It was a beautiful day. We didn't say a word to each other, but we were both kind of scared. It was still dark in the room."

Tammy suggested they finish the load of wash they were working on and leave. Her foster sister agreed. The darkness lasted about three minutes or so, Tammy estimates.

"But then it was like the door reopened and the room lightened again. So we finished the laundry and went home."

The two later compared notes and agreed that what they had gone through seemed similar to what might have happened if someone moved in front of a window, like drawing a shade across the room.

PSYCHIC FREEMAN FOUND unambiguous indications of all three ghosts during her visit to the Karsten Inn.

On the second floor, little Billy ran up and "poked" her twice in the stomach, much as any child would do in trying to gain the attention of an adult. She didn't see him, but unmistakably felt the jabs.

Freeman also visited Agatha's old room—310—and found the ghost in a talkative mood. The ghost, Freeman told the Heuers, objected to the television in the room. Roswitha Heuer said it was the only one in the hotel they had trouble with—

when the set was turned on, the volume would be either turned too loud or nearly inaudible.

Room 310 is so charmingly decorated that it belies one's notion of a "haunted" room. The room features a modern queen-size bed surrounded by antique furnishings that would be familiar to Agatha. An old-fashioned washstand with a water pitcher and basin occupies one corner. Above it is a painting of a lovely Victorian woman with her hair piled high. She holds a flower in her hand. On another wall is draped a full-length, white lace dress. Neither one is attributed to Agatha, however. A more modern desk unit holds Agatha's offensive television set. The small bathroom features a white porcelain pedestal sink and a combination tub and shower.

Agatha insists on having the doors and windows open in her old room. Roswitha says she finds the door and window open in 310 "all the time" even though no one has been in the room. "I'll also shut the light off in 310 and close the door, and when I come back up the light is on and the door and window open," she says.

Staff members have seen the door to 312 swing open as they walk by. The same holds true for the fire escape door at the end of the hallway. Freeman says Agatha told her she used to walk around on a porch that formerly extended out from the fire door.

Freeman noted that Agatha's old room was very cool while the hallways were quite warm. She attributed it to the air conditioning unit, which she tried explaining to Agatha but without too much success. She didn't like it, Freeman said.

In addition to 310, other third floor rooms in which psychic phenomena have been reported include 305, 308, and 312. On the second floor, the rooms are 205 through 210.

Karsten Senior spent his final years lumbering through his second-floor suite, today's rooms 205–210, battling obesity, arthritis, and heart trouble. But hotel guests would usually find him in the lobby on most days, ensconced in his beloved club chair. His death at age seventy-eight did not come as a great surprise to most Kewauneeians, but the loss of his vast memory of history, still keen until his final days, was considered a great blow to the community.

THE KARSTEN INN has faced all manner of challenges and ownership changes over the past century. Yet in the face of all that, the hotel seems to rise Lazarus-like from what turns out to be its premature death. Whether it will continue to flourish through the twenty-first century remains to be seen. But one thing is certain . . . there are those who think that a ghost or three will continue to look after "their" hotel and do their best to protect it from harm.

It wasn't a frightening proposition to Roswitha Heuer.

"If you believe in God you shouldn't be afraid of ghosts."

THE KARSTEN INN is not the only haunted hotel in Wisconsin.

Milwaukee's historic Pfister Hotel has been noted for decades as the tramping ground for founder Charles Pfister's nightly strolls to ensure that his guests have a pleasant stay.

This Victorian "Grand Hotel of the West," as the Pfister was termed when it opened in 1893, was built at a cost of over one million dollars. It was described as one of the finest hotels between New York and the West Coast. Electricity, fireproofing, and thermostatic controls for every room were innovations at the time. An extensive remodeling in 1962 added a twenty-three-story tower and refurbished rooms.

The older, portly gentleman that visitors have spotted standing on the hotel's grand staircase is a mirror image of Charles Pfister's portrait in the lobby, witnesses say. The man has also been seen in the minstrel's gallery in the ballroom and checking out supplies in a ninth floor storage room.

THE WAITRESS AT the Boscobel Hotel had just finished making salads for a private dinner party when a sudden, cold current of air swept over her. From around the corner in the kitchen came the quick steps of someone walking away. But when she looked in the door no one was around. She reported the incident to the manager, who then realized he'd forgotten to turn on the kitchen deep fryers for those attending the dinner. He went in to switch them on, but was astonished to see that they were already heating. The switches were on. He checked with his son, at work in a different section of the restaurant, but he maintained that he'd had nothing to do with it.

Another visit from the ghost of Adam Bobel?

Best known today as the home of the Gideon Bible, the Boscobel Hotel dates to a few years after its founder, Adam Bobel, a Prussian emigrant, arrived in Boscobel in 1861. He served in the Union Army as a sutler, or government-approved vendor, selling supplies to soldiers at often inflated prices. Bobel and a partner built the two-story stone building in 1861 as a saloon and small hotel. A fire leveled it in 1881, but Bobel, by then the sole proprietor, rebuilt and opened the Central House in May 1881. He continued to operate it until his death in 1885.

The Gideons International Society had its beginnings in 1898 when two salesmen sharing a room at the Central House fell into a discussion about the lack of any organization that might provide "mutual help and recognition for Christian travelers." The two—John H. Nicholson and Samuel E. Hill—met again a year later and decided to act upon their earlier discussion. A subsequent organizational meeting in Janesville, Wisconsin, led to the formation of the Christian Commercial Travelers' Association of America, later the Gideons. They are best known today for placing Bibles in American hotel and motel rooms. Nicholson and Hill said the Boscobel Hotel was the organization's birth site.

Much of the original 1881 exterior remains in place, though the hotel has been closed in recent years.

But sometimes it was the chance to greet old Adam Bobel and his mysterious girlfriend that attracted visitors to the former Central House/Boscobel Hotel.

A former bartender says Bobel was sometimes joined by his old girlfriend on late night visits. A chef once saw a woman sporting a gay '90s bonnet stroll by the bar toward the dining room. He followed shortly thereafter to take her order, but the room was empty.

Bobel sometimes opened and closed doors—and even left tips on occasion for long-suffering waitresses. "I never worried when I was there. He never played malicious tricks," one former waitress said.

Overnight guests asked about the elderly man and woman they've seen strolling down the hall. They were surprised at the couple as they'd been told they were the only guests that night. When a picture of Adam Bobel was pointed out to them, they drew back startled. It was a picture of that "nice old man" they'd seen. Often they would *not* stay an additional night.

Sometimes it was only voices. Once half a dozen voices floated down a hallway where they were overheard by two women working there. They thought it odd that a group of people might be walking through the place. They checked throughout but found no one else there.

Adam Bobel seemed helpful, as well. A waitress was asked to retrieve a bottle of wine from a basement cooler. The particular bottle was under some newer vintages. But when she got downstairs she found the bottle propped on top of the wine rack. Someone trying to make her life easier, she thought.

But with less traffic through the building, Adam and his lady may now have decided to take up residence elsewhere.

THE OLD HOTEL has been around for nearly a century and a half. Through name changes, neglect, closings, disasters, and rebirths, this Brodhead, Wisconsin, landmark has survived it all.

Even the gentle lady ghost reputedly lurking within its walls is a survivor of sorts.

A vaporous woman drops in infrequently and instigates some unusual activities, according to reports by former owners and managers. She seems to be a protective spirit, interested mostly in seeing that the business continue in operation.

A woman who once owned the hotel told a reporter she'd had two encounters with the spirit of this woman who was supposedly killed in a 1905 fire at the place.

The first time came as she walked down the second floor hallway. Someone's hand touched her shoulder. It was a hand without a body, a hand that itself could not be seen.

The second occasion was a bit more real, if that's the correct term.

"I was working late one night in the dining room and saw a

figure pass down the hallway," she told a reporter. "But when I went out to see who it was, again, no one was there."

The ghost may be the daughter of the hotel builder, John Young. He put up what in more recent years was known as the Harris House back in 1868. But other records indicate that his daughter died at a fire in his home elsewhere. Whatever the case, there were those who thought the Harris House—no longer a hotel, but today a popular restaurant and bar under another name—had enough ghost stories associated with it to fill an entire night of Halloween thrills. Brodhead is in Green County, directly south of Madison, Wisconsin, a few miles from the Illinois state line.

That former owner, for instance, had several personal encounters with what she thinks was the resident ghost, and had heard many other tales from former employees. She talked about that ghost-sighting in an interview with a local reporter:

"I saw it moving past in a long dress . . . out of the corner of my eyes. And I was standing there by myself and it was still light out, and I called, 'Is anybody there?' "

That's not the first time the Harris lady was spotted.

"The previous owner's nephew said strange goings-on happened," the former owner asserted. "One night he was in the kitchen and he seen something in the corner of his eye, and he kind of ignored it. He went down in the basement and he saw a woman standing there, so he threw the bowl in the air and he ran out and locked up (because) he was working there late that night."

Another manager had a brief encounter with the phantom lady in an episode that may have included a timely warning. The manager had locked up and was counting the day's receipts. The money was to be put in an office safe in an upstairs office. As she reached to turn on the lights, she saw the form of a woman in a "high collar dress" with her hair tied up. The manager dropped the money and ran. When she went back later to retrieve it, she found a stranger passed out on the second floor. He'd broken in sometime earlier, and was unconscious from the effects of a drug overdose. She thought the ghost was trying to warn her to stay away, that the intruder meant to steal the money and then possibly do her harm.

A relative whose uncle bought the hotel in 1968 was a firm believer in the supernatural legacy of the Harris House, according to later reports. He was the same person who saw the woman standing in the basement.

His first in-person meeting with the ghost came some twelve years later as he prepared weekend salads very early one morning. Again, it occurred near the old dining room area.

"I had just finished the salads and was cleaning up," he told a reporter. "I stepped over to the dishwasher and opened it. As I did . . . I saw a figure in white standing in the doorway to the dining room. But when I looked directly at the door it was gone. . . ."

Two other episodes involved the ghost again becoming involved in money matters and the business-side of running the hotel.

He was adding up the day's earnings. He'd put his briefcase on a piano bench outside the office. He'd heard rustling from outside the door and found his briefcase lid closed. A few minutes later, after returning to the office, he again heard a noise and found his briefcase had been dumped upside down with its contents strewn about.

The owners were in negotiations to sell the place at the time, and he didn't think "the ghost was happy about us selling it." He added that once, when his uncle was talking about the sale with a visitor in the hotel bar, "several bottles suddenly came out of racks behind the bar and smashed on the floor."

A cook who had begun working at the Harris House would often regale listeners with her favorite ghostly incidents.

"Now this morning I came in to work and I was late," she told a reporter visiting the old hotel several years ago. "I am supposed to be here at five-thirty and I punched in at five fifty-seven. I went back into the dining room to get a chair . . . and there was nothing back there, of course. After I put the chair in the (kitchen) door, put the rolls in the oven, turned my grill on, I looked and there was two candles lit in the dining room. I would have seen that right away, because the door is right there. It was completely dark there."

She also thought the ghost was mighty handy in whipping

up desserts, based on an incident between a former owner and a new cook.

"She didn't know anything about making the pies. She talked to Mrs. Harris for a while, and then went back in the kitchen. . . . The pies were all made. There was a banana pie made, and Mrs. Harris had eaten the last banana. Mrs. Harris said, 'See I knew you could make them, but where did you get the bananas?' "

But the ghost in the former Brodhead hotel is a gentle soul whose comings and goings apparently never hurt anyone.

"Nobody has been injured, harmed, scared, or nothing," the former cook said. "This morning though, I didn't say nothing, I thought if she wants candles lit that's fine. I've been here at five-thirty and I'll see something and look up and say, 'If you want to help me I can use it.' "

And who among us would not agree that a little help with our daily chores would be a welcome relief—even if it was offered by a ghost?

SAMUEL BRADLEY TOOK six years to build the landmark Cobblestone Waystation Inn at East Troy, Wisconsin. Beginning in 1843—five years before Wisconsin became a state—Bradley dutifully hauled thousands of selected cobblestones he'd gathered from the glacial drift fields in southeastern Wisconsin and from along the shores of several area lakes. Once he had enough stones he started construction of his "monument," as he termed it, in 1846 on a corner lot of what is now South Church Street. When it was finished in 1849, his three-and-a-half-story Buena Vista House was a landmark hostelry in southeastern Wisconsin, noted for its unusual spring dance floor on the third floor.

A celebration of its opening boasted well-known personages from across the country. Abraham Lincoln allegedly stayed there during one of his infrequent forays to the state.

By 1852, the hotel's success enabled Samuel and his wife to pay off the mortgage years before it was due. Within a short time, they left East Troy telling friends and employees that they were going to England to visit Mrs. Bradley's relatives.

They never returned. From that day to this, no evidence has ever surfaced to indicate what happened to them.

However some believe they know exactly where Samuel Bradley is . . . still at the Cobblestone. Or at least his ghost, according to published reports.

The original building is still in excellent condition, a testament to Bradley's architectural and construction skills—he did both of those jobs himself. The hotel was abandoned for a while after the Bradleys' disappearance and then went through the hands of various owners. An interstate bus line once used it as their station in the community. But all during those years it served as a remarkably durable testimonial to one man's determination.

But as with all things, the passage of time and harsh weather took its toll on the Cobblestone. So it was that during its renovation in the 1990s, Cobblestone employees spoke of enough odd events to give them pause. And wonder if perhaps old Samuel Bradley had finally found his way back to East Troy.

A carpenter claimed that someone always seemed to be watching him as he worked. He'd often find his tape measure a yard or more away from where he'd put it down. And someone . . . or some thing . . . would turn low the clock radio volume, especially when music was playing. The clock was never tampered with, only the volume control.

A remodeling on the third floor included new curtains on the windows. Someone didn't like them. One day employees found them all on the floor. No one had been up there.

New pictures were hung throughout the second floor. A manager checking through the rooms found them all turned against the wall. She straightened them out, but a half hour later she again found them facing backward. Construction workers were outside on that day and only three employees were inside. All of them had been accounted for.

Then there is the rocking chair. Employees heard it on the third floor—a distinct *creak-creak-creak* on the ancient wood floors. They found it to be a problem, especially when the managers were finishing up their paperwork around ten o'clock at night. There was no rocking chair on the third floor.

A former manager called the phantom rocking chair "the most incredible noise you can hear."

NOT EVERYONE BELIEVES Samuel Bradley has returned as a ghost. A former twelve-year resident said she'd never seen or heard anything unusual, but she did recall that owners in the 1940s publicized a Cobblestone ghost on restaurant place-mats.

Perhaps that former manager had it right when she noted that in a building with as much history as the Cobblestone "there can't *not* be anything here. Something's got to be around."

CANADA

21

Wanderers

Whence and what art thou, execrable shape?

—John Milton, *Paradise Lost*

PUZZLING LIGHTS, GHOSTLY "wannabes," a departed husband who refused to stay away from his beloved wife, and poltergeists that flit about causing all sorts of disturbances are among those nomadic Canadian specters that materialized at the most inopportune of times, and with a suddenness that left more than a few perplexed witnesses.

The Lantern of Pale Moon

Chief Skeet of the Ojibwa nation was an old man of ninety years in 1936, living out his days in a Canadian hamlet at the northern tip of Lake Superior. He had seen the inexorable push of immigrant settlers across the north but had long ago adapted to the ways of the white man. He was one of a number of guides for General Garnet Wolseley's expedition from Ontario to Fort Garry, in August 1870, to put down the first Northwest rebellion.

As a respected elder, Chief Skeet was the keeper of the old stories told by his tribe and by other Native peoples of eastern and mid-Canada. One of those stories was the Cree nation tale of the lamp of the ghost woman, a flitting light seen on murky nights floating back and forth over Lake Winnipeg near Berens Island.

The Ojibwa chief related the story of how the ghost lamp came to be for anyone who would listen:

Pale Moon was a young Cree girl. She fell in love one summer with a Scottish trapper. Although his many trap lines ran through the upper reaches of Manitoba's lake country, he found many days to spend with his new love. The happy couple talked far into the night. He spoke of his young life in Scotland far across the Atlantic and she dreamed aloud of the many children they would have.

But a time came when the Scotsman's employer, the Northwest Fur Company, ordered him to report to their nearest trading post many miles distant on the southern shores of Lake Winnipeg. He promised to return in a single moon's time—one month. So Pale Moon waited.

And waited.

And when the waiting became unbearable and watching all day long in her village made her fearful that she would miss her lover should he return after nightfall, she took up a lantern each night at dusk and walked lightly to their secret meeting place on the lake's shore. She could more easily see his canoe should the moon be out and the sky clear.

Summer edged into fall. In time came the deep snow of winter to stay long into the new year. When at long last the snow melted and the swollen streams receded, spring tumbled back into a new summer. Still Pale Moon waited for the young trapper who never came.

Her Cree brethren tried valiantly to persuade her to give up her lonely vigil, but she refused. In time they accepted her decision, but were saddened that she had grown so pale and so thin. And on her face the laughter and smiles with which she once greeted everyone had vanished long ago into a weary countenance. Her faith in the Scotsman's promise was as unyielding as the granite boulder upon which she sat each night.

When a year and more had passed and Pale Moon still rejected her tribe's entreaties, they began to understand that her life, for good or for ill, would be forever bound to her vanished lover.

So it happened that on a November night a great early winter blizzard slashed across Lake Winnipeg, tearing apart the village teepees and frightening even the boldest of the men. Yet Pale Moon struck a flame, applied it to her lantern and set off in the blinding snow, just as she had done hundreds of nights before.

But this time, the thin, deerskin-clad girl did not return the next morning, nor on the mornings of the days and weeks and months that followed. A search through the deep snow by the Cree men proved futile. In time, the entire village moved to Shabandoway Lake in northwestern Ontario.

Two years passed before Chief Skeet came into the old Cree land leading a party of surveyors. Near the shore of Lake Winnipeg, at the hem of the forest, the party found the skeletal remains of a white man clad in furs. Near his outstretched arms lay the skeleton of a small woman clad in a deerskin dress. She held a lantern in her bony grip.

Neither Chief Skeet, nor the surveyors, nor anyone later could say how the couple perished—only that they had evidently died together.

That Lake Winnipeg coastline, nearly two hundred miles northwest of the city of Winnipeg, is still a forlorn and lonely place. The isolation gives rise to all sorts of notions, yet was there truth in Chief Skeet's memory of Pale Moon?

Native people say that the peculiar light floating back and forth just out of reach on the western shore is the lamp of Pale Moon searching for her Scotsman. Others claim it is a will o' the wisp come to claim another of the living. Still others dismiss the tale as myth and superstition.

The conclusive answer of course died with Chief Skeet decades ago. It is enough perhaps to know that those who knew him say that he was an honest man who always told the truth.

Unfortunate Eliza

Moncton, New Brunswick, today is a small, quiet city of some six thousand people on the southeastern tip of that Atlantic province, something less than twenty miles from Northumberland Strait across which lies Prince Edward Island. The city is easy to reach via high-speed interprovincial highways or by air at the Greater Moncton Airport. But in the late 1880s, Moncton was still isolated from the rest of Canada and dependent upon rail transportation for convenient connection with the rest of the nation.

Railroad tracks cut across the city at several locations, including Church Street. And that's where Eliza Bailey met her death and gave rise to one of the city's earliest ghost stories.

The month was November 1887. Miss Bailey was struck and killed by a train as she crossed the tracks. No one seemed to know how it was that she didn't see the oncoming locomotive.

Within weeks, railroad men began talking among themselves about a flitting female apparition they'd encounter at that same Church Street crossing. Some of the men and not a few townspeople descended on the offices of the local newspaper, *The Transcript*, asking about the truth behind the stories. The paper couldn't confirm the authenticity of the sightings, but they did recount two episodes related to them by witnesses.

At about two o'clock one morning, a west-bound special whistled through town, but as it approached the Church Street crossing, the engineer saw a woman walking deliberately down the tracks toward the approaching train. The engineer threw on the brakes, and got out with several crew members to look for the woman. They were unsuccessful, as was the newspaper in tracking down members of that particular train crew.

Another story held that on a different night a passenger train was stopped at the crossing when a woman some people recognized as Eliza Bailey, from the way she was dressed, climbed aboard one of the cars, strolled down the aisle and then exited, all without saying a word to anyone.

Horrific deaths at railroad crossings have led to countless ghost stories all across North America and beyond. Was there such a ghost in Moncton? Is she now gone? A century and more later it is nearly impossible to know, although the local *Transcript* newspaper seemed to think it unlikely in their comment on the ghost of Eliza Bailey: "A great many people talk so sincerely about the matter that they have evidently persuaded themselves the stories are true; but all efforts to trace them to a responsible authority have failed."

It

Was it someone playing a practical joke on naïve country people, as some folks thought, or was there really a distaff ghost aggravating the good people of the vanished community of Cowal, southwest of Hamilton, Ontario? Might there have been a connection between this ghost and the legendary burial place in that vicinity of the imposing Shawnee leader, Chief Tecumseh?

In that western Elgin County township of Cowal, near today's Cowal Road and Duff Line Road, a mysterious intruder leaving diminutive size-six footprints had residents agoggle. Even more amazing is that several people who chased after the interloper claimed it had the ability to jump fences at breathless speed.

Witnesses were unambiguous in describing the thing's appearance: Headless, though sporting a brown jacket with a hood. Around its lower half swirled a frilly white skirt; men's work boots completed the ensemble. Everyone agreed that based on the attire and its graceful sprint when anyone challenged it the thing was clearly female.

Was it a ghost?

The dozen or so Dunwich Township residents who confronted the compact apparition on its nightly rounds said it seemed to favor a remote area where legend had it the warrior chief Tecumseh had been buried.

Aligned with the British, Tecumseh led a confederation of Indians against the Americans during the War of 1812. He was killed on October 5, 1813, during the Battle of Thames in Upper Canada. Some accounts assert that Tecumseh died at the Battle of Moraviantown.

He was secretly buried by his comrades near the battlefield, though the exact location was never revealed by the Shawnee fighters or by his descendants. Some historians maintain that his body was disinterred and reburied elsewhere, possibly in Ohio or Oklahoma. Two other rumored locations of his grave are St. Anne's Island in the St. Clair River, at the head of Lake St. Clair; and Walpole Island, also on Lake St. Clair.

However, Tecumseh's great-grandson Ganwawpeaseka (Thomas Wildcat Alford) disputed those claims. He held the title of Custodian of the Tribal Records of the Absentee Shawnees. In a statement years after his ancestor's death, Ganwawpeaseka wrote:

"Some years after the burial of Tecumseh, a band of Shawnee returned to the scene to disinter the body of Tecumseh and bear it back to their Oklahoma reservation for a re-interment suitable for the greatest leader of their race. This party, selected because it knew the precise spot of interment along a small creek, found that the creek at flood times had washed away all evidence of the great warrior's last resting place. Rather than dig haphazardly in an effort to find the bones, the remains were left in place and the Shawnees still maintain their vigil at this spot with racial fidelity, in sorrow and silence."

Yet, a Shawnee tradition implies that Tecumseh may lie somewhere other than in southern Ontario: "No white man knows, or ever will know, where we took the body of our beloved Tecumseh and buried him. Tecumseh will come again."

Any connection between the purported Cowal ghost and a legendary secret Indian grave is anecdotal at best. Ghost or not, for a time the people in that rural hamlet had a real life mystery on their hands.

But not everyone was persuaded of its supernatural origins. Archie MacTavish snorted at the suggestion. He'd spent several nights tracking the elusive sprite, even though he'd made his mind up early on.

"I believe," he said, "it's someone not quite right in the head."

An Intimidating Presence

The ghost that farmers outside the community of Bruce, Alberta, encountered back in the summer of 1936 had the propensity to appear at inconvenient times and then to melt away into the countryside when anyone pursued it. Bruce is about seventy-five miles southeast of Edmonton.

The episode began in mid-August when a young man with a face one witness described as "several degrees paler than usual" scampered into the path of an oncoming car and leaped onto its running board. He screamed to the driver that a ghost was chasing him. The driver was so startled that he drove off the highway and into a ditch. Despite the young man's allegation, the driver saw nothing coming along in pursuit.

Once the word got out about the fellow's claims, farm families from miles around armed themselves with shotguns, thick clubs, and nasty-looking brushhooks. Only the brave or foolhardy were venturing out at night. Despite all that, there was no specific contact between the alleged ghost and its pursuers.

Was there a finale to this brief imbroglio? Apparently not. The ghost and its shenanigans dissolved into the eastern Alberta night air. A solution of sorts was offered. A conflict between neighbors of differing nationalities may have been at the heart of this ghost alert. One observer said it was "more of an attempt to intimidate than a practical joke."

Ghost Town

The old lady's death began it all. From all indications, it was a passing from natural causes but because she was a relative of the handful of people in the community, and since it was the first death in the First Nation reserve, people were understandably upset.

Nothing, however, prepared the authorities for what was to come next.

They had to evacuate the community's entire population of twenty persons because the woman's death caused everyone there to believe the reserve was haunted.

The place was Long Dog Reserve, Ontario, about four hundred thirty-five miles (seven hundred kilometers) northeast of Winnipeg. Established in the early 1990s, Long Dog was a barely noticeable pinprick on the Canadian map until media reports surfaced about the mass leaving.

An employee with the Wapekeka First Nation said the residents organized their own airlift a few days after the old woman's death. All of them claimed to have heard or seen evidence of the supernatural in their tiny district.

"I've heard the stories, too," the employee, Allan Brown, told reporters. "What they say is that they have seen figures, somebody walking around with a candle. And noises. They hear noises and all that."

Noises came from empty houses; shadows were glimpsed moving about in darkened rooms.

But Allan Brown thought the people had brought it on themselves, upset at the death of someone they were all related to. A sort of mass group hysteria.

"I can't say it's haunted," Brown said. "Sometimes when these things happen, people get imaginative."

Imagination or not, the evacuation of a community due to purported ghostly activity is one of the odder encounters with a belief in the supernatural.

Presentiments

Hussar, Alberta, is a tranquil community of a few hundred residents some sixty miles (one hundred kilometers) due east of Calgary. There are Lutheran Churches and a Masonic temple, a general store named Tom's, and new hockey and curling arenas. For entertainment residents can visit the Rod and Gun Club, or have fun at the Hussar Rodeo Daze and Duck Lake Daze, which is probably better than naming the latter celebration after another area body of water, Dead Horse Lake.

A sex scandal in the late 1990s involving teenage members of a local Hutterite colony attracted national and even international attention.

Ghosts would find it difficult to find a place to hide on the flat, windswept terrain that is eastern Alberta. And so many of the tales of the supernatural derive from the personal experiences of Albertans which may have occurred elsewhere.

Take Margaret C. Bell, for instance.

The late Hussar woman never saw a ghost, as far as it is known, nor did she have any *personal* encounter with haunted places, but the story she told in 1966 may have been far more powerful because it was integral to her very own family history. Where it took place was not important to Mrs. Bell. She simply called it *the unexplained* and left it at that:

"My story has to do with my (father's) grandparents. . . . In 1874, my grandfather had been ill for several months. Grandmother's children thought she needed a rest from nursing him; she went to stay a few days with her only daughter, and one of their sons stayed with grandfather.

"The morning of the third day there, in her dream she saw

her husband come to her. When she awoke she insisted on going back to him. She arrived in time to be with him for several days before his death, October 19, 1874. Grandmother was heartbroken because she had left him even for so short a time.

"She insisted upon staying on in their old home. A week later—in the early morning—in her dreams again her husband appeared to her, leading their only daughter by the hand as if she were a child. Grandmother awoke with a terrible foreboding concerning my aunt Laura. That day she was called to her death bed . . . Laura was aged thirty-four years.

"Things went on as usual for some time—then in 1875, one morning grandfather once again appeared to her in her dreams, this time leading one of their sons, Oren Birney, by the hand as if he were a child. Again grandmother was alarmed. She hastened to his home to find him very ill; and he, too, passed away a few weeks after grandfather's appearance to her.

"Grandmother lived on for fourteen years. She visited my parents, I recall. She was very tall, very stern of feature—and as a little girl, I was really afraid of her; but she was a real friend to my mother. In 1889, when visiting one of her sons, she told him one morning that his father had appeared to her in her dreams, had wandered around the room, and then had stood by her bed and looked at her.

"Grandmother told her son that her turn was next. She fell ill and died a few weeks after her dead husband's visit, as she had foretold."

MRS. BELL'S UNCLE told the story as something he could never fully explain or wholly understand. But Mrs. Bell's mother—the daughter of the clairvoyant grandmother—knew that her dear mother and father had loved each other so much in life that even in death they found a way to be together.

The Saskatoon Silhouette

James Johnson was killed in a most wicked manner. His end came at the sharp edge of a broadax. The vicious 1926 Saskatoon slaying, which a Regina newspaper termed "mysterious," may have been a not atypical case of violent death in sparsely settled western Canada, but an even more mystifying incident after the murder was anything but ordinary.

James Johnson's brother was one Henry Johnson, a shoe-maker living in Indian Head, Saskatchewan, about fifty miles east of Regina. Shortly after James's murder and funeral in Saskatoon, Henry received a memorial photograph of his brother's body in the open casket. The photograph appeared to have been taken by a commercial photographer. The coffin was centered in the middle of the photograph. Bouquets of flowers surrounded it. At the end of the casket, and thus directly above the dead man's head, was a big wreath of white flowers.

But it was an image inside that wreath that caught Henry Johnson's attention. One of the white flowers formed the per-fect silhouette of a woman's head as if on a cameo broach. The profile was distinct against the dark background of the coffin itself.

The oddity grew when Johnson rotated the picture to see if the cameo outline remained distinct. It did. As he turned the picture upside down, another outline took form. This one was of a man's head formed by the interior edges of the wreath it-self, again standing in stark relief to the coffin's dark top.

Johnson showed the photograph to several friends, who all confirmed that they saw the woman's head, and in some cases from as far away as eight to ten feet. Several noticed the man's head as well.

Said one observer: "Spooky, to say the least, is the verdict of those who profess to see something more than coincidence in the incident."

Rap Briefly

The poltergeist—or noisy ghost, to translate from the German—can take many forms. It might be associated with sudden, mys-terious fires; kitchen cabinetry doors coming unhinged; perfectly good furniture moving about the house of its own ac-cord; or, as in the case of the John McDonald farm, near Bal-doon, Ontario, flying hunks of timber, pots, pans, and rocks ricocheting inside and outside.

From nearly every corner of North America have come oddities that come to be classified as the work of poltergeists because no supernatural *entity* is alleged to have been caught sight of, nor can the activity be marked down as the work of human hands.

A puzzling series of raps, or tapping, is one of the most frequently occurring peculiarities attributed to the work of a poltergeist.

The famed mystery writer Mary Roberts Rinehart never did solve the haunting of a Washington, D.C., apartment she lived in that came replete with slamming doors, singular doorbells, and incessant, irritating rapping. The latter was especially annoying. It came from the far side of a closed door into her bedroom and from a bedroom headboard.

During the 1840s, Catherine and Margaretta Fox gave birth to the controversial idea of Spiritualism when both claimed that the dearly departed were communicating with them via a series of coded knocks. Though they later disavowed their ability to speak with the dead (they said they produced the knocks by cracking their finger joints), some followers believed they had been forced to distance themselves from the psychic world.

Kitchen dishes that continually rattled as if a perpetual earthquake were underneath, and a relentless tapping at their front door disturbed a family in Keswick, Ontario.

Perhaps the most infamous Canadian case of poltergeistic phenomena occurred at a small two-story cottage on Princess Street in Amherst, Nova Scotia. That's where Daniel Teed lived with his wife and children and his wife's two unmarried sisters, Esther and Jennie Cox. Sightseers, self-declared mediums, ministers of various religious persuasions, and opportunistic businessmen all trooped through the Teed homestead trying to figure out what was causing banging on the walls, invisible creepy crawly things under the bed quilts, flying furniture, and loud, orderly tapping that seemed to emanate from some intelligence beyond the human beings present. Esther Cox eventually went on the vaudeville circuit, where she purported to communicate with spirits who rapped back their answers. Esther was billed as The Girl With The Devils In Her.

(For stories about these cases, see the author's Haunted America *and* Historic Haunted America.*)*

A NUMBER OF other episodes of poltergeist rap have been widely reported in Canada, including these two oddities:

At London, Ontario, in early 1895, little Ada Ascott grew so nervous at being able to control the raps heard inside her bedroom wall that her family had to take her to a neighbor's home. They feared she would collapse under the strain. According to an account of the event, she no sooner entered the place than a company of invited guests, including newspaper reporters, heard loud scratchings on the neighbor family's wall. The group had followed along, curious to see if the girl could produce the manifestations away from her home and family.

The assembled curious threw out questions which the unseen respondent is said to have answered correctly with a code based on the number of raps. It had been similarly successful in little Ada's own home. London clerics denounced the event as a fake. The Ascott family asked several of them to investigate and there the matter must have rested.

THIRTY YEARS LATER and two thousand miles away, residents were atwitter in Edmonton's Bush Hill Park neighborhood when reports circulated about a strange rapping coming from an abandoned house.

The deteriorating pile reminded several observers of Pip's description of Miss Havisham's mansion in Charles Dickens's *Great Expectations*.

> Within a quarter of an hour we came to Miss Havisham's house, which was of old brick, and dismal, and had a great many iron bars to it. Some of the windows had been walled up; of those that remained, all the lower were rustily barred. There was a courtyard in front, and that was barred; so, we had to wait, after ringing the bell, until some one should come to open it.

There the similarities did not end. The Edmonton house had been owned by one Miss McCloy. She died without heirs in the summer of 1926. Like Miss Havisham, Miss McCloy was jilted on her wedding day, and perhaps, like Miss Havisham, forever after relived that bitter memory for all of her remaining days:

She was dressed in rich materials—satins, and lace, and silks—all of white. Her shoes were white. And she had a long white veil dependent from her hair, and she had bridal flowers in her hair, but her hair was white. Some bright jewels sparkled on her neck and on her hands, and some other jewels lay sparkling on the table . . . But, I saw that everything within my view which ought to be white, had been white long ago, and had lost its luster, and was faded and yellow. I saw that the bride within the bridal dress had withered like the dress, and like the flowers, and had no brightness left but the brightness of her sunken eyes.

Very little is known about Miss Havisham's Canadian counterpart. Contemporary accounts fail even to mention Miss McCloy's first name. What has been established is that Miss McCloy died of apparently natural causes in mid-1926 at her Bush Hill Park address. Her body, however, was not discovered until several weeks later. Police said there was no sign of foul play. She was a spinster. Authorities were unable to find any relatives and so her jewelry and small bank account—reported to be about a thousand dollars—were turned over to the city treasury. The coroner's office kept hold of the house keys.

Hers was a story as sad as that of Miss Havisham. Miss McCloy had been engaged to a young man. The couple carefully planned their wedding and the happy day arrived. With the new day also came a letter to the young bride-to-be from her groom-to-be. He had, he wrote to her, changed his mind and would not marry her. He was leaving immediately to travel overseas and would not see her again.

Miss McCloy was distraught at being abandoned, but her love for the nameless cad did not die.

The rose was his favorite bloom. That was the only flower she grew in the garden.

She did not take the scissors to his photograph as so many other abandoned lovers may have done. She kept it prominently displayed on her living room wall.

And incredibly the gossip was that her will deeded all her property to him, though that story cannot be verified. Following Miss McCloy's death, neighbors said that a stranger driving a car visited the house on at least one occasion.

However, most of what the Bush Hill Park community talked about was the faint rapping on Miss McCloy's living room wall. A gentle knock at the precise point where her vanished lover's photograph had once been placed.

EVEN TWO CONSTABLES weren't able to discover what was behind the mysterious rappings early one fall at the home of Edward Jowett in a suburban Toronto community known as East York.

The whole episode was nerve-wracking for Edward, his wife, and their children. At first they figured neighborhood children might be responsible since the knocks began at the front door. Polite, but insistent. No one was ever there. Then the raps migrated to other parts of the house—walls, ceilings, and once from beneath the dining room floor. They began at about midnight and might go on for minutes at a time. But it all was unpredictable. In time, not one member of the family was brave enough to get up and investigate the odd noises.

But then it all got to be too much and Edward telephoned police. Two constables answered the distress call. They agreed to secrete themselves inside the front door and wait . . . and wait . . . and wait.

They were not to be disappointed. The knockings came at midnight. Clear and distinct and just inches away from the constables' noses. The men pulled open the door. No one was outside. The knocking didn't return that night. Or ever again. Perhaps the sight alone of Canada's finest was enough to frighten away whoever—or whatever—was behind this brief but irritating affair.

22

Rarely Seen

> But if someone from the dead visits them, they will
> repent.
>
> —Luke, *16:30*

A DISPUTE OF sorts occasionally erupts in British Columbia
over the actual number of ghosts that can be accounted for in
that province. Some experts maintain that only a handful have
been sighted over the decades, while others equally vocal claim
that British Columbia is a veritable hotbed of supernatural activity.

Whatever the truth of the matter, some of the more interesting Canadian specters claim residency along the Pacific coast.

A Close Shave

There is, for example, the ghost that sat in a barber's chair and
wordlessly ordered up a shave and a haircut. The story, as told
by the late writer Waldo Kane of Vancouver, came from a
Cariboo Trail miner who claimed to have spoken to the recipi-
ent of the ghostly visit, a former American slave with the singular name of Moses, who worked as a barber more than a
century ago in the vanished community of Barkerville.

The town was formed when William "Billy" Barker struck
gold on Williams Creek. From 1862 to 1879, over 100,000
people traveled the Cariboo Wagon Road to converge on Barkerville in search of quick riches. At one time, the town was the
largest in Western Canada, and the largest west of Chicago and
north of San Francisco. It is now a British Columbia Provin-
cial Park catering to summer tourism events.

But when Moses was there, the town had already begun its decline. He decided to try out his fortunes for a time on the Coast, but met with little success. By and by, he set out to return to Barkerville with two traveling companions, both miners: an Irishman, John Barry; and an American, Morgan Blessing. Near the end of their journey, the men stopped for the night at a boarding house in Quesnel, about forty miles west of Barkerville.

As the men settled in for the night, Blessing drew a gold nugget from his backpack. He called it his "Guardian Angel." It had a general shape like an angel with outspread wings.

"This, gentlemen, will protect me from harm," Blessing said. "And if I desire it will provide me with passage back to the States."

But the next morning, the angel had vanished from his pack. He was much distressed.

There being little law in that region, Blessing announced the theft to those others boarding in the inn and asked them to search the premises. Suspicion fell on Moses because of his "suspicious" behavior and his difficulty in answering the accusatory questions. Though the nugget was not found in his belongings, Moses was tied up by Blessing and others and dragged from the boarding house. The landlord had stood by while his business was searched, but a hanging in his front yard was too much. He grabbed his shotgun and ran outside. He aimed it at the mob and ordered them to release Moses.

"You have no evidence, no nugget, nothing. You cannot hang a man without proof of his guilt," he yelled.

Blessing relented and ordered Moses to leave at once. Which he did.

The two other men left the roadhouse together the next day, but Blessing never reached Barkerville. Barry claimed that his traveling companion had returned to the Vancouver area, discouraged because Moses had gotten away with stealing his Guardian Angel nugget.

There were those, however, who suspected that Barry was the real culprit in this villainous theft. Yet nothing could be proven.

Until a ghost stepped forward to settle the matter.

That happened on a sultry, summer afternoon about a month after the theft of the Guardian Angel nugget and Moses's return to Barkerville. He was alone in his shop, leaning back in the single barber's chair, his feet propped up on the footrest. He'd been mulling over the mystery of Barry and Blessing and the strange disappearance of Morgan Blessing and of Barry's evasive answers in the matter. The outside door squeaked open on its old hinges. Moses swung around and got up to welcome the new customer.

But he wasn't prepared for what was coming through that door.

A tall man with wet and rotting clothes shuffled into the room. He stood silently looking down at Moses. His dark eyes were in stark contrast with his pallid complexion. The entire room suddenly stank of rotten vegetation and damp earth.

The stranger swayed as if he was about to fall. He grimaced in pain as he lifted his thin, right arm and placed his hand behind his head. Almost, Moses thought, as if he were trying to keep it on his shoulders. Moses grew uncomfortable at the man's bulging eyes glaring fixedly at him. They were dull, lifeless.

Beads of sweat formed on Moses's brow. He reached out to steady himself on the chair's armrest.

He knew who the man was.

Morgan Blessing.

Moses gulped and started to speak, but he couldn't say a word. It was as if his tongue had suddenly grown twice its size.

He also knew that this man standing before him was quite dead. Of that there was no doubt, even if he had never seen a ghost before in his life.

Yet strange as it may seem, Moses's professional acumen took hold and he made a slight bow to this dreaded thing.

"Before God, Mr. Blessing, is that you?" he asked in a voice so tremulous that at first he doubted it was coming from himself. "What can I do for you?"

Blessing—for that is most definitely who it was—made no reply, but he took a step nearer, his glazed eyes fixed intently on Moses.

Slowly and mechanically he leaned in toward Moses, removed his hand from the back of his head and ran it over his face, indicating that he wanted a shave. His beard was tangled and of several weeks' growth. His long hair was dirty and caked with mud.

Moses gestured toward the heavy wooden chair of the kind barbers used in that era.

Blessing shuffled forward, passing in front of the single shop window.

Moses could see right through him.

Could see so clearly, in fact, that the letters spelling out the barber's name on the window moved across the dead man's torso as he walked across the floor. He never took his eyes off Moses.

However, there was something else in the man's behavior, something that Moses's intuition told him was more complicated than just a simple case of Morgan Blessing's reanimated corpse come to seek some ghastly revenge.

So he talked.

"Mr. Blessing, I didn't steal your Guardian Angel. I'll swear to that, if that's what you've come back for."

Blessing made no reply.

Instead, he seated himself very slowly in the chair, but never taking his eyes off Moses, even when the barber turned his back to gather his scissors and razor. He could feel the dead man's gaze seeming to burn into his back like a red-hot branding iron.

Business was business. The ghastly customer had come in for a shave and a haircut, and so Moses placed a clean towel on the back rest and set about stropping the razor.

Yet Moses could not bring himself to start shaving the whiskers off a dead man, so he kept stropping and stropping the razor and wondering the entire time what he was going to do when at last the razor was more than sharp enough. His hand was trembling so that he thought for sure he'd cut the ghost's throat the minute he started to scrape away the stiff whiskers.

He didn't have to worry long, for suddenly Morgan Blessing was gone. He didn't get up, he just disappeared. The front door slammed closed. Moses quickly turned around and saw that he was alone in the shop. He ran to the street, but Blessing was nowhere in sight. He had vanished.

The towel Moses had put on the back of the chair was covered with a great red splotch of blood, and smelled like it had been shut up in a damp cellar. Even sending it to the laundry didn't rid it of its rank, clammy smell. He put it in the stove, but the red spot stayed in it even after the towel was all ashes.

WHAT WAS IT that Morgan Blessing wanted Moses to do, but failed to tell him? The old barber *knew* that John Barry had killed his partner, but his word against Barry's would not be good enough.

A few weeks later, it fell to one of Barkerville's infamous hurdy-gurdy girls to do in Barry. These were the loose women of the Gold Rush era who moved north to Canada following the California Gold Rush of 1849. The name derived from the barrel organ they danced to in saloons; although in the Cariboo they most often gyrated to a lively fiddle tune. Their arrival dates to about 1866 in Barkerville's Fashion Saloon and Martin's Saloon. Most returned to California by 1871 when the riches ran out, although many of them stayed to marry and take up the Western Canada pioneer life.

John Barry fell in love with one of the hurdies. For him, that was a fatal mistake. He gave her the Guardian Angel nugget, but he asked her to keep the gift a secret. She couldn't, of course, and began showing it to the other girls. Word quickly spread around Barkerville that she was sporting the by-now infamous Guardian Angel, and Barry was arrested on murder charges.

At the trial, the hurdy-gurdy girl was the primary witness against Barry. It was her testimony that put the Guardian Angel nugget in his original possession. But Moses also testified at Barry's trial about Morgan Blessing's spectral visit to his barber shop.

"Of course I knew Mr. Blessing was dead and I knew Barry had shot him in the head," Moses told the court. "And I knew Mr. Blessing wanted me to do somethin' 'bout it, but I didn't know what it was. The ghost hadn't said. And I was scared of Barry, too. That Irishman had the murderin' habit and I had no hankerin' to be his next victim."

Barry confessed and told them where Blessing's body could

be found, buried near a bush on the outskirts of town. It was enough for the jury. They found him guilty and sentenced him to be hanged, which he was a few weeks later.

Ghost on Air

The largest parish in the Diocese of British Columbia, including Vancouver Island and the islands in the Gulf of Georgia, is that of Christ Church Cathedral, Victoria. The cathedral was built in the Gothic style and is actually the third one to serve the diocese. The first, built in 1857, burned, and a second erected in 1872 to replace it soon proved inadequate for the congregation. The city's Law Courts now occupy the site of the earlier churches, across the street from the present cathedral.

Put up at a cost of over three million Canadian dollars in the late 1920s, it is one of Canada's largest churches, though a less grand cathedral than one might expect to find in Paris or London. But it does have unique configurations that make it a frequent destination for visitors. The pulpit was carved from the trunk of a five-century-old tree from Sussex, England. Twelve ancient stones formerly in the high altar screen in Canterbury Cathedral are placed near the altar in the church's Lady Chapel. The main tower spires reach over twelve stories high.

But few alive today remember that the cathedral's mortar was hardly dry before stories of unusual incidents circulated among the congregants, as well as an equally odd explanation of why they were occurring, according to this Canadian Press report at the time of the original construction:

> Ghosts have been known to inhabit old churches and terrify passersby with their unearthly noises, but the unexplained sounds that issue from this city's brand new cathedral are providing a different kind of mystery.
>
> The foundations of the new . . . Victoria cathedral have been barely laid, yet once in a while weird music is heard there.
>
> "It is really a most amazing phenomenon," states Rev. Cecil S. Quainton. "Sometimes it appears to be organ

music. At other times the sound is distinctly that of a piano and the other day I heard a human voice singing."

The dean is only one of many who have heard the mysterious cathedral music. Especially at night is the music audible. When it was first noticed people thought that a new organ was being tried out in the building, but enquiries elicited the information that no steps had been so far taken to equip the cathedral with an organ. In fact, the building will not be far enough advanced for such equipment for many months.

Close inspection failed to solve the mystery, but one theory that appears to have general acceptance is that the building has been acting as a reflector for a powerful radio set in the vicinity. It is also advanced that the copper roof of the cathedral may in some manner serve as a radio receiver.

Church visitors are encouraged to visit the shaded meditation gardens outside the church where they may relax and reflect in solitude, well away from the day's worries. And perhaps hear a stray, unaccounted for sound or two.

Old Siwash Hill

Farmer Frank Day trudged along Vancouver Island's old Comox-Courtenay Highway, his bag of groceries tucked securely under his arm. An old oil lantern swung from his wrist, illuminating the ground a few feet in front of him. He'd been shopping in town and was now heading home to his rural Courtenay farm with a few modest supplies. It was a still, dark Friday night in December 1940. If he'd stopped to think about it, though, Frank might have taken more careful notice of the date and then considered staying in town for the evening. The comfort of daylight can overcome the apprehension that might quite naturally set in when Friday the 13th is coming to a close . . . and the day has passed pleasantly.

Perhaps he had a fleeting notion of the date as he climbed Siwash Hill and passed the early Comox Indian burial site. Did his pace quicken? Did he glance nervously over his shoulder toward the sacred place? We don't know the answers to those questions, of course, but what we do know is that what he later said happened made up for all the bad luck that had *not* come his way that day.

At about the time he came abreast of the old cemetery, the faint glow from his lantern suddenly picked out the slender figure of a tall woman about twenty feet in front of him. She seemed to be swathed in some sort of a brown robe. Her arms were not evident; perhaps they were simply covered by the robe.

She vanished as suddenly as she had appeared.

Frank drew in a deep breath and carefully walked on. He hadn't gone but a few more feet when she was there again, but this time directly blocking his pathway, yet seemingly oblivious to his presence. She gazed away toward the sea some two hundred yards distant.

Frank pulled up short, fully expecting her to once again abruptly depart. She did not. Thus he was able to think about this most surprising visitor and scrutinize her more thoroughly than he might ever have wanted had he stopped to consider the circumstances.

There wasn't much that Frank Day knew about this particular neighborhood around Siwash Hill. He'd heard a rumor that a construction crew had unearthed a skeleton—thought to be that of a Comox Indian—and that its disjointed bones "caused quite a stir," as the newspapers reported it last year.

They'd said that a sailor by the name of J. Dalton, a leading stoker on one of the ships plying the Straits of Georgia, had a run-in with "something" one night on Siwash Hill as he was returning to his ship.

"I saw a thing about halfway up the hill," he told crewmates. "The thing made some mighty weird sounds and I took to my heels."

His mad dash reportedly ended when he went flying off the end of Comox Wharf.

A few motorists on the Hill told authorities they'd come upon a "dancing" apparition that seemed to flit in and out of their headlights before disappearing completely.

In both of these cases, the ghost was described in much the same way as Frank Day's.

Siwash Hill had the old Comox village boundary line running through it. Some five hundred yards from the top of it was the site of an old fort from which the Comox Indians defended their village in battle against the Queen Charlotte Islands Haida Band. But it was from the foot of the hill, in the burial ground of the Comox tribe on the side nearest to the water, that observers claimed the ghost first appeared, some said, to revisit the old settlement.

THAT CERTAINLY SEEMED to be the case for Frank Day as he carefully watched the weird figure in front of him. He noted with a certain amount of awe that at the points at which there should have been feet were just hazy smudges. Its feet didn't seem to touch the ground.

It didn't stand still. Slowly the entity turned toward Day, perhaps attracted by the oil lamp in his hand, which shook a bit. The light was steady enough, however, for him to see into the ghost's face. Where the eyes should have been were deep black holes.

"They were piercing holes that seemed to look through me," he later told a reporter. And it did seem to be a female. A mass of hair fell down about its shoulders, and seemed to be gently blowing in the sea breezes.

The ghost was startled by the headlights of an oncoming car. Frank turned to look down the hill, but when he glanced back the mysterious figure had gone.

Day later said he was at first certain that a friend was playing a trick on him, but when the ghost simply vanished he thought better of his first conclusion.

"I have always laughed at ghosts and things of that kind," he told the reporter. "But I was in my sober senses, and I have told you exactly what happened."

Old-timers in the region predicted the ghost would walk soon after the graveyard was disturbed by the construction crew. They were right. Motorists saw it, as did Dalton the sailor. Frank Day's personal confrontation came almost exactly a year to the date after the scattered bones of the skeleton had been uncovered.

23

The Unpleasant Dead

It is the same as the television, that Shaking Tent. If
you could witness it, you would really like it. You
would have a great time.

—Mary Madeline Nuna, *Innu Nation*

ACROSS THE NORTHERN reaches of Canada are isolated settlements that, despite the intrusion of satellite television and mobile phones, retain much of the rusticity of generations past. When the long hours of winter shroud these hamlets in vast, frozen darkness, the patient ghosts of an earlier, more dangerous time dance close by, and then stories are told of those shadowy beings and their puzzling practices.

From the Northwest Territories to Nunavut in the Far North and down into the Ontario subarctic wilderness, ghost stories have been a central part of the lore in those regions for centuries. Whether it's spirit forces shaking tents, strange bush men, a phantom riverboat, or frozen corpses, these northern Canadian accounts have a chill factor all their own.

The Shaking Tent

Despite Jesuit Father Paul LeJeune's best efforts the young Huron, Manitou-Chat-Che, did not take well to his newfound Christian faith. Within a few months of his conversion, Manitou-Chat-Che had reverted to his former native ways, a system of beliefs that Father LeJeune derided as devil worship. The Native man argued otherwise. His medicine man, his *pilotois*, was stronger than the Black Robe's god.

"Come with me and you will be convinced against your will of the feats of our medicine man," Manitou-Chat-Che offered.

"Do your worst," Father LeJeune challenged, adding that he was willing to wait as long as need be.

In a short time Manitou-Chat-Che came back to the priest and said all was in readiness. The priest would join a number of tribal members to watch and listen as the shaman summoned the spirits. Father LeJeune would then see what miracles the medicine man could achieve.

According to Father LeJeune's narrative of his experiences among the Huron People, *Relations*, published in 1634, and more modern scrutiny by Canadian ghost folklorist R. S. Lambert, this is what the Jesuit indicated that he witnessed:

"Toward nightfall, when I was resting, two or three young men erected a tent in the middle of our cabin. They stuck six poles deep in the ground in the form of a circle. To hold them in place they fastened to the top of these poles a large ring, which completely encircled them. This done, they enclosed the edifice with blankets, leaving the top of the tent open. It is all that a tall man can do to reach to the top of this round tower, capable of holding five or six men standing upright.

"When the tent had been erected, the fires of the cabin were entirely extinguished, and the brands thrown outside lest the flames frighten away the 'spirits' or *'Khichi-gouai'* who are to enter this tent. A young juggler (medicine man) slipped in from below, turning back for this purpose the covering which enveloped it; then replaced it when he had entered—for they must be very careful that there be no opening in this fine palace except from above. The juggler, having entered, began to moan softly, as if complaining. He shook the tent first without violence. Then, becoming animated little by little, he commenced to whistle in a hollow tone, as if it came from afar; then to talk as if in a bottle; to cry like the owls of these countries; then to howl and sing, constantly varying the tones; ending by these syllables—*'ho ho, hi, hi, gui, gui, nioue'*—and other similar sounds, disguising his voice so that it seemed to me I heard those puppets which showmen exhibit in France. At first he shook this edifice gently; but as he continued to become more animated, he fell into so violent an ecstasy that I thought he would break everything to pieces . . . I was astonished at a man having so much strength; for after he had once begun to shake it, he did not stop it until the consultation was over, which lasted about three hours."

Although he could hear all that was going on in the tent, Father LeJeune stayed on the outside. He was not impressed with what he termed the "performance" and made no attempt to hide his contempt. He chided the spirits for being "asleep" and begged the audience to make more noise. He laughed that the medicine man was going to hurt himself by shaking the tent too much.

Manitou-Chat-Che hissed back, "Be quiet, Black Robe! The soul of our medicine man has now left his body, and has risen up to the top of the wigwam. It is hovering there, to meet the spirits."

The medicine man's voice grew louder and stronger. Suddenly, a cry went up from the Natives gathered around the tent. They pointed toward the tent peak. In the cabin's darkness fiery sparks flew from the vent hole at the topmost point of the medicine man's tent. One of his assistants began a rhythmic beat on a small, hide-covered drum that smoothly escalated in tempo and intensity; several of the young men in the audience were moved to jump up and begin dancing around the tent.

The appearance of the sparks meant that the spirits had arrived and were now ready to answer questions posed to them.

In a high-pitched, hoarse voice Father LeJeune heard the medicine man ask about his own and his wife's health. Another voice answered that he would survive the winter, but that his young wife would die before the spring thaw.

Father LeJeune chuckled and called out to the medicine man:

"I could have said as much myself. Your poor wife looks half dead already. As for you, you look perfectly healthy and have a hearty appetite. I don't doubt that unless you have an accident, you will not only survive this winter, but next summer as well."

The next questions were the most important to the Huron people:

Would the winter be especially harsh? Would game be plentiful?

Again, but in a voice distinct from the earlier ones, the conjuror answered. He was evasive. He did not see deep winter snow, and the moose were at a considerable distance.

The priest again shook his head. The performer was too "politic" to be specific and say just *where* the moose—so necessary for the Huron's winter food supply—would be holed up. Why could the spirits not see clearly for surely they were all knowing?

With that all became quiet in the tent and in the cabin. The assembly was over. And before Father LeJeune could grab the medicine man to question him further, he had slipped out of the tent and stolen away.

THE SHAKING TENT ceremony has been described as at once the most famous of all Canadian ghost stories and in centuries past one of the most important yearly rituals in the Great Lakes and Subarctic Native communities.

Its purpose was multifold.

The medicine man answered questions about the future put to him by those watching the ceremony. Sometimes he might ask questions about his own future as well, the general health and well-being of the questioner and his distant relatives. The spirits would answer the questions, often in peculiar voices seemingly coming from a long distance as if through a length of pipe. At other times, he consulted a Mystical Turtle that usually lay on its back inside the tent, invisible to all save the mystic Native. He sent the turtle's spirit to distant regions to find answers to the most difficult questions.

Queries about the quality of the hunt and the location of caribou and deer were central to the ritual as tribal members prepared for the long white of winter.

The system for erecting the Shaking Tent varied only slightly in its details from tribe to tribe.

The medicine man, or *shaman* (sometimes identified as the *kakushapatak* or *pilotois*), and his assistants began with a conically shaped frame made from four to eight saplings created inside a larger tipi or a log cabin, as in the case of Father LeJeune. The greater the number of poles used to build the small tent, the stronger the medicine man's power. Once the framework was secured, usually with rawhide strips, the entire form was wrapped with bark, cloth, or most often caribou hide. The whole unit would be placed over fresh fir boughs. Sometimes rattles were prepared by inserting lead shot or pebbles into deer or caribou hooves that were then attached to the tent frame so that when the tent shook, the rattling would add to the tumult of the ceremony.

Once the "conjuring lodge," as it has been termed, was finished, and the *kakushapatak* had ducked inside, the tent began to shake ferociously and strange voices issued from within. The belief was that the powerful medicine man beckoned the ghosts to enter the lodge and that these spirits and not him were then responsible for making the tent shake. Sometimes the witnesses were treated to peculiar lights such as those bright sparks Father LeJeune reported seeing.

Unless someone had very strong magical powers, those gathered for the occasion could not enter and sit with the medicine man. The tent was built in this very specific manner so that its power was extraordinarily strong. Anyone who was weak of spirit or inexperienced in the ways of the *kakushapatak* could put himself in jeopardy by trying to enter the Shaking Tent.

CANADIAN ANTHROPOLOGIST A. Irving Hallowell interviewed many Natives about their belief in the Shaking Tent. One man who had witnessed the ceremony told him: "We cannot see them, but we understand that turtle rests at the bottom of the lodge, feet up, keeping it from sinking into the ground; that thunder is at the top, covering it like a bird; and that the other spirits are perched around the hoop that encircles the frame. They look like human beings about four inches tall, but have long ears, and squeaking voices like bats."

In the early twentieth century, some Inuit of Labrador and Quebec adopted terminology from parapsychology to describe the forces surrounding the Shaking Tent. An "electricity was in the air" after the tent was erected, they said, and inside the tent the medicine man used "telepathy" to communicate with the dead or with those at a distance.

The Shaking Tent was always a source of entertainment for the isolated Native people, Madeline Nuna said: "The Shaking Tent was really good to witness or be part of. . . . I certainly laughed because it was a great time. When they were singing they could be heard. Someone would sing inside the Shaking Tent sometimes." Even well into the twentieth century, when the Shaking Tent ceremony was going through its final decades, it took on some of the vestiges of what is now associated with radio and television entertainment. A young man from the Sheshatshiu Innu commented on the ritual in such a manner that today might be more associated with citizen's band radio or a kind of spiritualist cell phone. He noted that the medicine man's communication with relatives and friends living at a distance is ". . . very similar to a radio . . . if there were people in George River, or people in St. Augustin, and you wanted to communicate with them, then you could do the Shaking Tent."

NO ONE DOUBTED the efficacy of the medicine man or the validity of his predictions arising from his hours in the Shaking Tent. As early as 1609, French explorer Samuel de Champlain learned of the unyielding trust the Huron, Montagnais, and Algonquin people put into the ceremony. Once de Champlain was with these people when they went to battle against their ancient enemy, the Iroquois. He was confounded to discover the warriors did not post a nighttime sentry to guard against surprise attack. He learned this was not done because each evening a Shaking Tent was built and each camp's *pilotois* would then foretell the future. Once he did that, the camp was assured of a specific outcome, even if it meant a disastrous engagement with the enemy and the death of warriors. However, the medicine man was the one required to stay alert to any unexpected danger, though one would suspect this should have been a moot point. If he was correct in his earlier predictions he ought to have known all beforehand.

De Champlain was even more cynical about the true nature of the Shaking Tent ceremony than Father LeJeune. He said the medicine man alone shook the tent and the different voices were produced with some elementary knowledge of ventriloquism. As far as the type of sparks that Father LeJeune detailed some years later, de Champlain flatly denied ever seeing anything of the sort. He reportedly said of the medicine man's claim to supernatural powers that "these scoundrels deceive these poor people to get things from them."

It was left for Jesuit Father Paul LeJeune a quarter of a century later, however, to conduct the first significant study into the traditional Shaking Tent practices of the Native people. Though he was termed the first "psychic researcher" in Canada by researcher R. S. Lambert, Father LeJeune clearly brought a decidedly religious point of view to his investigation and writings.

The French-born son of Huguenot parents, Father LeJeune was an intelligent, well-educated young priest who arrived in Quebec in 1632. His assignment was to convert the Indians to Christianity, and more specifically to Catholicism, as head of the Jesuit Mission to the Huron. He soon discovered that the medicine men were at once respected and feared for their ability to communicate with the unseen supernatural forces they believed were abroad in the world. They would be his biggest foes; his solution was to closely learn their behaviors and observe their shamanistic practices so he could reveal their deceptions.

To accomplish those goals, he lived for many years in the same harsh wilderness conditions the Native people endured. He learned their languages and traditions in order to gain their trust, if not entirely their souls. He learned about the medicine man's background and how these individuals went about learning and practicing their craft.

Father LeJeune understood the supernatural basis for their religious practices because the same concept was at the heart of his religion as well, albeit within the Catholic doctrine. Thus, he was a constant critic of the medicine man, always pointing out flaws in his "performances" and deriding him as a "sorcerer" who practiced "devil worship."

Father LeJeune did not give up his investigation of the Shaking Tent after that first ceremony. He accompanied Manitou-Chat-Che to more rituals. The Indian told him that if he would enter the tent he would see for himself how his soul might rise out of his body and hover near the vent hole. The priest declined saying he feared that the medicine man would harm him because he feared being exposed as a fraud.

What Father LeJeune wanted more than anything else was to confront the medicine man face to face to ask him questions about his religion and his beliefs. At last, Father LeJeune cornered the shaman and demanded that he answer any questions put to him as he, the priest, would do if asked about Catholicism.

The medicine man agreed.

First, Father LeJeune wanted to know exactly what the spirits looked like. According to the priest's diaries and scholar R. S. Lambert, the Indian spoke only in parables.

"I will tell you a story, Black Robe," the unidentified medicine man began. "Once two Indians built two wigwams side by side to call the spirits to them. One of these Indians had treacherously killed three men with an axe, and the *khichi-gouai*—the spirits—were very angry with him. So they entered the wigwam, and put him to death. Afterwards, they crossed over into the wigwam of the other man and, thinking that he must be a friend of the first man, set about putting him to death, too. But this man had an axe with him and defended himself so well that he killed one of the *khichi-gouai*, and in this way it was found out how he was made. He was only as large as my fist, and his body was of stone and long at the end."

Father LeJeune snorted that the "spirit" was really a piece of stone.

The Indian patiently explained that this was not the case. "He was of flesh and blood for beside him lay the axe that had killed him, covered with blood."

When the priest wondered how such a thing could fly—for the medicine man affirmed that the spirit had neither wings nor feet—he was told that he did not understand the ways of the spirit.

"Of a truth this Black Robe has no sense," the medicine man said.

The priest then recalled the fiery sparks he saw near the top of the tent.

"They must have come from a pipe of tobacco," he challenged.

"I took no fire into the wigwam, Black Robe," the shaman replied. Nor could he have hidden anything on his person. "I was naked when I entered the wigwam," he said.

When Father LeJeune turned to the subject of the actual tent shaking, he was met by equally obscure replies, according to his account.

"How could one man do that unaided?" his opponent replied. "Did you not put your hand on the poles and try to do it for yourself? You found it solid as a rock. Later you saw it sway to and fro, and even bend down its top, though it was taller than a man. It shook so long and so violently that you must admit no human strength could cause this movement."

The priest allowed as much.

At this point in the argument, Manitou-Chat-Che apparently joined in the fray.

"Next time, Father Black Robe," he said, "you must crouch down on the ground outside the wigwam and look under the beaverskin robes. Then you will see the arms and legs of our medicine man sticking out under the bottom of the tent, at the very moment when the top is being violently shaken by a strong and violent wind. The breath of the approaching spirits."

The method by which the tent shook continued to perplex Father LeJeune. He witnessed the shaking on many occasions and it always occurred with such force and such a length of time that he found it difficult to imagine that a single man could keep up such a physically powerful act for hours upon end, as was sometimes the situation. The Indians' view was that the shaking came from the spirit wind entering the tent with such a force that the shaman had to leave or face being sucked into a chasm.

LEVITATION WAS ANOTHER achievement claimed by the medicine men during the Shaking Tent ritual.

Father LeJeune's Native contacts claimed to have seen the medicine man's garments tossed out of the tent and then he himself rise above the ground to nearly the vent hole. A soft "thud" suggested the medicine man had fallen back to earth. The most extraordinary description of this legendary ability came from a young Native Catholic convert who said he had personally seen a medicine man go into a trance, drop his caribou skin robe on the ground, rise, and then disappear into the air. He didn't return to the village for several days, and even then professed to have no memory of what had happened to him.

The priest cautiously noted in his *Relations* that he had not personally seen such acts of levitation, and maintained his disparaging attitude toward any such ability.

But while he doubted the shaman's abilities, Father LeJeune believed that on occasion it was possible for them to bring about real harm. This he attributed to an unwitting pact with Satan, not unlike those liaisons the Church accused various European and New World people of having with the devil. He wrote: "Not that the devil communicates with them as obviously as he does with the sorcerers and magicians of Europe; but we have no other name to give them, since they even do some of the acts of the genuine sorcerers—as, to kill one another by charms or wishes or imprecations, or by poisons which they concoct."

With such a strong belief in the power to communicate with distant peoples and affect future events, did the Native people try to use the force against the Jesuits or other white intruders? Father LeJeune cites no such case, but a few years after his death another priest, Father Lalemant, recalled such a case: "Father Pierre Pijart, having a dispute in the village of Saint Jean with an old magician of the country, this barbarian, having become angry, threatens him that we might surely make up our minds to die, and that already Echon (Father de Brebeuf) was stricken with disease. Father Pijart laughed at this old man—it not being three hours since he had left Father de Brebeuf at the house of St. Joseph in very good health. The magician answers him: 'Thou wilt see whether I am a liar. I have told thee enough.' In fact, Father Pijart, having returned the same day to St. Joseph, two good leagues distant, finds Father de Brebeuf attacked with a heavy fever, a pain in the stomach, and headache, and with all the symptoms of a severe illness; at the moment when the magician had spoken, no savage had been warned of it."

Coincidence or not, Father de Brebeuf recovered fully in a short time.

FIRE HANDLING WAS another practice observed by Father LeJeune and his fellow missionaries over the years. Another priest sent Father LeJeune a stone that he said had been carried red hot in the mouth of a medicine man. The stone had been softened to such a degree that a clear set of teeth marks was visible on it.

Unlike other ceremonies, Father LeJeune actually witnessed an "ordeal by fire" and wrote about it in his missionary testimony:

"A number of stones were brought, and to make them red-hot, a fire was prepared, hot enough to burn down the cabin. Twenty-four persons were chosen to sing and to perform all the ceremonies. . . . I was waiting all the time to see what they would do with these stones that they were heating, making red-hot with so much care. You may believe me—since I speak of a thing that I saw with my own eyes—they separated the brands, drew them (the stones) from the midst of the fire, and holding their hands behind their backs, took them between their teeth, carried them to the patient, and remained some time without loosening their hold, blowing upon them and growling in their ears.

"I am keeping one of the stones expressly to show you. . . . The stone is about the size of a goose egg. Yet I saw (a medicine man) put it in his mouth, so that there was more of it inside than out. He carried it some distance, and after that it was still so hot that when he threw it on the ground sparks of fire issued from it. . . .

"One of our Frenchmen had the curiosity to see if, in reality, all this was done without anyone being burnt. He spoke to this Indian who had filled his mouth with live coals. He had him open his mouth and found it unhurt and whole, without any appearance of having been burnt. And not only these persons, but also even the sick people were not burned. They let their bodies be rubbed with glowing cinders without showing any evidence of pain, and without their skin appearing in the least affected."

The Jesuits who ran the various Indian missions did not agree among themselves as to the soundness of the claims made by the tribes' medicine men. Father LeJeune appears to have been the stoutest debunker of the shamans' claims, as he noted in his derisiveness of the majority's claims to supernatural power. However, one of the men who followed him, Father de Brebeuf, was a bit more accepting of the possibility that the Indian spiritual leaders had powers that could not be explained rationally, although he attributed them to another equally spiritual concept, Satan, as he noted in his missionary accounts from 1637, and quoted by paranormal historian R. S. Lambert:

"That they have these gifts of God, no one in my opinion will venture to assert. But that all they do is the product of deception or imagination hardly accords either with the reputation they have acquired, or with the length of time they have practiced their profession. How comes it that their tricks have never been exposed through all these years, and that their trade has been so well rewarded—if they have never succeeded except through sheer imagination? There is, therefore, some ground for thinking that the Devil does sometimes lend them a helping hand, revealing himself to them for some temporal profit, as well as for their eternal damnation."

Father LeJeune's successor at the Huron Mission was one Father Paul Ragueneau. He, too, became intimately familiar with all the practices made by the medicine men—specifically their claims of clairvoyance—but was as harsh as his predecessor in judging their capabilities:

"I have seen some of them who claimed to have worked miracles, change a rod into a snake, and restore to life an animal that was dead. By dint of repeated assertions, some people came to believe them, and even declared that they had witnessed the phenomena. They have boasted in our presence of having performed these feats; but we have challenged these gentry and, in order to goad them on to greater activity and so to bring public confusion on themselves (for we were quite sure they would not live up to their claims), we have promised them great rewards, if they would perform their miracles before us. They have tried to evade the challenge without showing confusion; but their shameful retreat amounts to a serious admission that their game was really all trickery, and that they only appear convincing to those who accepted their false claims without examining them."

During the 1700s there were further accounts of the ceremony. One from Alexander Henry the Elder, in the years 1760–1776, recounted the time in 1764 when the Ojibwa were considering whether or not to accept an invitation from the

British to negotiate a peace treaty following their successful triumph over the French in Canada. Alexander Henry found himself isolated in Sault Ste. Marie with the Ojibwa. He urged them to accept the peace offer so that he might go with them.

The Ojibwa were suspicious. They wanted to consult the Shaking Tent before undertaking such a risky adventure.

A large wigwam was built, inside of which was a smaller, traditional Shaking Tent made from five poles ten feet in length and eight inches in diameter. A hoop held them together at the topmost point. Moose hide was hung over the timber frame. The ceremony began well after midnight that evening.

A nearly naked medicine man entered the tent, according to Alexander Henry:

"His head was scarcely inside when the edifice, massy as it has been described, began to shake; and the skins were no sooner let fall than the sounds of numerous voices were heard, and beneath them, some yelling, some barking like dogs, some howling like wolves; and in this horrible concert were mingled screams and sobs, as of despair, anguish, and the sharpest pain. Articulate speech was also uttered, as if from human lips, but in a tongue unknown to any of the audience."

Soon the Great Turtle appeared, the medicine man announced in his own language, and was prepared to answer any questions.

Much to the relief of the Ojibwa gathered for the ceremony, the Great Turtle answered a question about the intent of the British by saying that the peace gesture was not a trap and that the Indians would be welcomed with many gifts to take back to their village.

Although Henry suspected fraud on the part of the medicine man, as had other Westerners before him, he could not refrain from asking his own personal question: He wanted to know if he would ever return to France.

The reply in the same voice as the Great Turtle was in the affirmative: "Take courage, white man, no harm will come to you. In the end you will reach your friends and return in safety to your own country."

Famed Great Lakes English explorer Jonathan Carver wrote of meeting a large group of Cree on the shore of Lake Superior near Grand Portage, Minnesota. They had a large cache of furs to deal for food with European traders. Carver said the traders were late and the Indians running short of food. He, too, was anxious for their arrival so that he might travel back East with them. They built a Shaking Tent to find out when the Europeans would arrive.

Carver was invited to sit in on the ceremony but he initially declined. He dismissed the practice as so much fraud and superstition.

He was persuaded to attend when the Cree chief made it clear the ceremony was being held partly for his own benefit so that he, too, would know when he might be able to leave.

Carver acquiesced and was led the next day to a large wigwam. He sat on a deerskin with many other Cree.

He wrote of the experience:

"In the center I observed that there was a place of an oblong shape, which was composed of stakes stuck in the ground, with intervals between, so as to form a kind of chest or coffin, large enough to contain the body of a man. These were of a middle size, and planted at such a distance from each other that whatever lay within them was readily to be discerned. The tent was perfectly illuminated by a great number of splinters cut from the pine or birch trees, which the Indians held in their hands."

The medicine man wrapped himself in an elk skin, Carver said, so that he looked like an "Egyptian mummy." Only his head was visible. He was placed inside the tent by several of those gathered around. After mumbling and moaning for several minutes, he started to speak in a variety of Indian languages Carver did not understand—Ojibwa, Ottawa, Cree, he thought—gradually working into a frenzy of shouts and grunts. He grew quiet and at last shook off his elk skin cloak and stood up.

He spoke clearly:

"My brothers, the Great Spirit has deigned to hold a talk with his servant at my earnest request. He has not indeed told me when the persons we expect will be here; but tomorrow, soon after the sun has reached his highest point in the heavens, a canoe will arrive, and the people in that will inform us when the traders will come."

Carver doubted the medicine man but joined most of the Cree the next morning on the shoreline to see if the prediction would be fulfilled. At the hour appointed by the Great Spirit, a canoe came into sight. When they reached land, the Cree welcomed them and took them to the chief's tent and a traditional ceremony of welcome extended to all visitors, but which must have seemed tedious to Carver given the uncanny nature of the strangers' arrival.

At last they were asked if they knew anything of the white traders.

Yes, came the reply. They'd seen them two days earlier. Further, they said the men would arrive at the Cree camp on the next day.

And they did.

Carver's ability to accurately report his travels is often questioned, and justifiably so. However, he was steadfast in his assertion that nothing fraudulent occurred in the Cree medicine man's performance, or in his amazement at how the prediction came to pass, although attributing to himself an objectiveness New World historians came to question in other of his accounts.

"The circumstances of it, I own, are of a very extraordinary nature. However, as I can vouch for their being free from either exaggeration or misrepresentation, being myself a cool and dispassionate observer of them all, I thought it necessary to give them to the public, leaving them to draw from it what conclusions they please."

WHAT OF THE Shaking Tent in more recent times?

In 1860, the German anthropologist J. G. Kohl published his study of Great Lakes Native communities. *Kitchi-Gami: Wanderings Round Lake Superior* included an account from a white trader who was one of the rare witnesses to a Shaking Tent ceremony. He includes a detail not mentioned in earlier testimonies, according to folklorist R. S. Lambert, the presence of a hallucinogenic that could well have contributed to the medicine man's behavior.

According to the anonymous trader:

"Thirty years ago I was present at the incantation and performance of a *jossakid* (medicine man) in one of these lodges. I saw the man creep into the hut, which was about ten feet high, after swallowing a mysterious potion made from a root. He immediately began singing and beating the drum in his basketwork 'chimney.' The entire case began gradually trembling and shaking, and oscillating slowly amid great noise. The more the necromancer sang and drummed, the more violent the oscillations of the long case became. It bent backward and forward, up and down, like the mast of a vessel caught in a storm and tossed on the waves. I could not understand how a man inside could produce these movements, as we could not have caused them from the exterior. The drum ceased, and the *jossakid* yelled that the spirits were coming after him. We then heard through the noise and crackling and oscillations of the hut two voices speaking inside, one above, and the other below. The lower one asked questions, which the upper one answered. Both voices seemed entirely different, and I believed I could explain them by very clever ventriloquism. Some spiritualists among us, however, explained it through modern spiritualism, and asserted that the Indian *jossakids* had speaking media, in addition to those known to us, which tapped, wrote, and drew."

Kohl found that even if a medicine man had converted to Christianity, he rarely admitted to any deception on his part during the Shaking Tent ritual. Kohl detailed an experience from the same white man who once sat with a terminally ill Indian man who had been a shaman in his younger years. In this case, he continued to assert that the spirits alone caused any manifestations:

"I have become a Christian, I am old, I am sick, I cannot live much longer, and I can do no other than speak the truth. Believe me, I did not deceive you at that time. I did not move the lodge. It was shaken by the power of the spirits. I only repeated to you what the spirits said to me. I heard their voices. The top of the lodge was full of them, and before me the sky and wide lands lay expanded. I could see a great distance about me, and believed I could recognize the most distant objects."

No less an observer than Sir Cecil Denny came away mystified by his visit with a medicine man. It came about during Denny's early years as a member of the RCMP. He had camped near a Blackfoot settlement on the Red Deer River.

Denny with his interpreter walked over to the medicine man's tent—set some distance away from the others—late one night and later recorded his observations:

"We entered the lodge, which had only a small fire burning in the center. The medicine man was sitting wrapped in his buffalo robe at the head of the teepee, smoking one of their long medicine pipes. He paid no attention to us whatever. I therefore sat down near him, lighting my own pipe and, placing a present of two plugs of tobacco near him, proceeded to smoke quietly, without a sign of recognition being made by the Indian. Everything was very still in the lodge, while outside in the main camp drums could be heard beating in different parts, wherever dances were being held. We had sat this way for quite a time when I was startled by the sound of a bell ringing above me, over the top of the lodge. I could see nothing, and the Indian made no move. Presently the teepee itself began to rock, even lifting off the ground a foot or more behind me. When it is remembered that a large Indian tent consists of dozens of long poles crossed at the top, wide apart at the bottom, and covered with buffalo hides, it will seem that it is nearly impossible to lift one side—for no wind can blow them over. The rocking motion ceased after awhile, and I went outside the lodge to see if anyone had been playing tricks; but not a human being was in sight near us, the moon was clear, and you could see a long distance. On returning and resuming my seat after a short interval the tent began again to rock, and so violently that it would sometimes lift several feet on one side, so that you could plainly see outside. My interpreter was thoroughly frightened by this time, and I was not much better, but the Indian never stirred. However, we had seen enough, and left, returning to our camp thoroughly mystified."

Denny also wrote of seeing a medicine man dance inside a red hot copper kettle without getting his feet burned, and witnessing another securely bound with rope and then tossed into a Shaking Tent, the floor of which had been covered with upright thick, pointed sticks buried in the earth. He swiftly emerged without the ropes and without any wounds from the jagged sticks.

EVIDENCE SUGGESTS THAT the Shaking Tent tradition declined substantially in the twentieth century. The old ways were dying out, traditional religion was giving way to mainstream practices, and fewer Native people were living in isolated communities. Yet in the Far North and in the more inaccessible regions of the Canadian West one heard infrequent stories of Shaking Tent ceremonies well into recent times.

A Hudson's Bay Company representative in the Mackenzie River Basin wrote in his company's magazine about August, an elderly medicine man who allowed him and several other white men to witness such a ceremony in the late 1920s. Historian Lambert includes the account as a principal example of the continuation of this ancient ritual. It is an especially clear portrait of how the medicine man set up the ceremony:

"Before dusk two Indian lads went to the bush to get the necessary willow poles, which were driven fast into the ground and fastened with two willow hoops, one in the center, the other tapering the poles at the top. The poles were tested by nearly all present, and were found immovable. A can of shot was tied to the top of the poles, and the birch bark was then fastened on the outside to complete the construction. As it darkened and the moon came up, the Indians squatted in a circle around the wigwam at a distance of four or six feet from it. A small opening was made in the west for the Indian to crawl in, and closed immediately on his entrance. The wigwam commenced to shake as soon as the Indian disappeared, and the can of shot began to rattle. The Indians were awe-stricken while the medicine man commenced an eerie type of song. This lasted nearly half an hour; and he then commenced to talk, telling them in their native tongue that he had got in touch with the spirits and expected them at any time, although they were having a little difficulty to reach him. All the time the wigwam continued to shake. A small disturbance took place, and a strange voice was heard. The medicine man's voice could be heard at the base of the wigwam, while the strange voice came from the top. The voices were decidedly different. After having conversed with the strange voice for some time, August told the silent watchers that he could answer any of their questions, but they had first to place a plug of chewing tobacco under the teepee. He was soon showered with questions, many of them being of the type, 'How many fish will I gather in the morning?' And 'What luck will I have in trapping this year?' When the native questions became fewer, August said he would be glad to answer any question asked by the white on-lookers. At the suggestion of others, I asked: 'May we hold the wigwam while it is shaking?' A rapid talk by August commenced in the wigwam, and I could feel an unpleasantness among the Indians about me. Although I do not understand their language, I sensed something was wrong, and I was told that August had said that if the white people interfered with the motion of the wigwam, he would make such a big wind it would blow people and houses into the lake. One Indian, in a fit of excitement, called upon his people to 'clean it up' on the whites. I, having asked the question, immediately told the Indians that we did not wish to interfere if trouble might result. This passed over, and although the wigwam had not once stopped shaking, the medicine man decided to show more of his powers. He said he was going to call the spirit of a bear into the wigwam and show how he could kill it with his hands. When the bear spirit arrived in the wigwam, great excitement arose among the Indian onlookers. The fight began, and this was where I received my great surprise. The Indians seated around yelled to August *'an-buck'* (get stronger). The top of the wigwam bent until it nearly touched the ground during the fight. An Indian turned to me saying, 'Now do you believe it?' Naturally, I answered 'Yes,' there being about six hundred be-lievers there! Eventually, the bear spirit was killed, and August repeated the feat with the spirit of a lynx, which brought yells of excitement from the gathering. Daylight was breaking when August emerged from the wigwam with beads of perspiration covering his face. The bark was immediately removed from the wigwam, and we examined the poles and were surprised to find them as solid as they had been at first. I have been in-formed, although I have not witnessed it, that August can make a teepee shake by merely throwing his hat into it."

THE INNU MARY Madeline Nuna spoke in the early 1990s about her memories of the Shaking Tent, but couched them in terms of the ritual's value as entertainment for the isolated communities in which it was still practiced at midcentury.

Nuna told interviewers Peter Armitage and Pien Gregoire of the Innu Nation that when she moved to Sheshatshit, the shaman Uashau-nipan performed the Shaking Tent ceremony, only outside the community, in the countryside.

"We always went there when we went into the country," she said. "That's where he would perform the Shaking Tent ... when people would get there."

She likened the ceremony to television, perhaps in its ability to bring both news and information from long distances.

"Yes, I laughed because it was a great time. When they were singing they could be heard. [People] would sing inside the Shaking Tent sometimes. Like yourself," she said to the interviewer, "the way you are, you could be brought into the Shaking Tent. When someone is brought in there, they sound so close. . . . Like the late Mary told us once that our father was brought in there—we weren't there at the time. We went into a different area. The late Uashau-innu was the late Mary's father. She said that a Shaking Tent was being performed by her father. She told me that my father was brought in there—he sounded very clear [and close]. She said that he was singing. It's only his spirit which is brought in there, not all of his physical being. Only his spirit. You would hear him very clearly. It's like the way someone speaks to you. That's the way he sounds. It's very good fun. It's a great time. It's like a television. And when stories are being told, it would be like listening to a radio. For example, people speak there from inside, telling where the animals are. The things, which are being sought [for hunting]. For example, if you wanted to kill caribou, it would tell you exactly where the caribou [are]."

While in earlier centuries the Mystical Turtle might have been the shaman's oracle of choice, in Nuna's community the spirit was called Toadman and it was he who was the source of distant knowledge.

"He is brought into the Shaking Tent. He also sounds like an Innu when he speaks. . . . And you could speak to it if you wanted to. If you want to ask him for something or you want to find out about something, you would ask him and he would tell you."

She remembered that Toadman also spoke about himself.

"He said that he is handsome," Nuna said. "It is said that he is very good and looks like a white man. He is the one who took . . . an Innu woman a long time ago. It is said that he talks about his wife. It is said that he claims his wife will never die as long as he lives."

Like the Mystical Turtle, Toadman burrowed in the mud.

"It is said that he lives under the ground . . . where the Toadman lives. It must be the same as if he was living under the mud. It is said that he took the woman from the mud. She was an old man's daughter. He grabbed her from the mud when he took her. . . . She must have been picking bakeapples at the marshes. She was stuck in the mud. That's when he grabbed her feet or legs. It is said that she described his hand as being very pale."

Toadman lived everywhere, Nuna said, and could not be harmed. His hands were "like steel." He had very "strong hands."

A reflection of how the Toadman adapted to modern times arose with the Innu woman's story of several tough young men who had the impudence to mistreat a frog.

"I heard one time that over at the beach where the new houses are that the kids . . . maybe four, five, or six years ago . . . are always drinking beer. Those young men were playing with a frog. It is said that you cannot be disrespectful toward it. They were making it drink hard liquor. They must have been drinking hard liquor at the beach. And it is said that they heard someone. When this happened they ran away. They said that they heard someone singing at the time. This must have been Toadman, who they were playing with, whom they were disrespectful of. They said that he was singing and they ran away . . . it is not good to be disrespectful of it."

WHETHER WE ATTRIBUTE the Shaking Tent ritual "to hallucination, caused by autosuggestion," as one psychic researcher said was one possibility, or some other cause, there is little doubt that the medicine man *himself* believed in his power. Few, if any, observers of the ritual ever detected deliberate and outright fraud on his part.

When Richard S. Lambert surveyed the three-century history of the Shaking Tent, he found commonalities in a half dozen displays of the medicine man's "powers":

- The tent itself shakes either moderately or with a significant movement once the medicine man is inside, although some eyewitnesses claimed he often protruded from the tent or had his arms and legs extended in a way that would preclude physically moving the animal skin covering;
- Audience members often strapped the medicine man's arms and legs together so that he would seem to be unable to control the tent movements;
- A variety of different voices seemed to come from ground level and from the top of the tent; what Lambert called "the incantation," or weird chanting and howling calling upon the spirits to appear;
- The arrival of the spirits in the form of "fiery sparks" bursting through the tent's smoke hole; this was not reported in all cases, however;
- The use of "spirit interpreters," such as the Mystical Turtle or Toadman, to declare that the medicine man was ready to answer questions about the future, the prospects for a successful hunt, or more mundane inquiries about distant relatives and friends; and finally
- A healing function for the sick and injured that Lambert attributed to the power of suggestion or to hypnotism.

Lambert notes that anthropologist Irving Hallowell—who apparently witnessed several of these ceremonies himself—cited the possibility that, absent the investigator's unquestioning belief in purely supernatural forces, the medicine man manipulated the tent himself, perhaps unconsciously, and within "his personal inspiration and beliefs."

Hallowell found, for instance, that the traditional barrel shape of the tent made it not difficult for a single man to make it vibrate.

Given all of that, however, there is historian Lambert's reflection on how very difficult it must have been for one person to do all that was attributed to the traditional medicine man during the Shaking Tent ceremony:

". . . the operation . . . requires uncanny knack and almost incredible skill and vigour. Good performances last for several hours at a time, during which the Tent is scarcely ever still. At the same time, the medicine man must sing and talk continuously in several different voices. He must memorize his songs; have powers of dramatic representation (e.g. of fights with animal-spirits); prognosticate the future; answer questions; and carry on a smart repartee with his audience."

Perhaps then it is some combination of all of this, both the explainable and the unexplainable, at least in modern terms. That the medicine men were skilled magicians and probably ventriloquists is indisputable. Yet, as Lambert noted, there might have been something more.

"There can be no question," Lambert wrote, "but that his *skill* is supernormal, even if his *powers* are not."

Northern Shades

The swift-moving central Arctic storm plunged through the Nunavut hamlet of Spence Bay stranding for the night the dozen or so federal and territorial officials. Until the storm abated and they could fly out the next day, the men passed the time in various ways—a foursome got up a game of bridge, some others found comfortable chairs and read, while a few ended up in the living room of the Hudson's Bay Company's residence listening to tales of the region spun by famed storyteller Ernie Lyall.

Lyall was then a government official in Spence Bay after working thirty years with Hudson's Bay. He'd come to the Arctic in 1927.

On that night, however, he found a rapt audience for one of the favorite forms of storytelling in the regions where manufactured entertainment was still rare—ghost stories. And not just any story, but his account of how that very Hudson's Bay residence was haunted by the ghost of a murdered woman. He knew the story well. He was one of those who recovered her body.

Spence Bay—or Taloyoak—is on the southern edge of the Boothia Peninsula in Nunavut, nearly seven hundred and fifty air miles from Yellowknife. The name means "caribou blind" in Inuit. It's about as isolated a place as you'll find anywhere on earth. The community was formed after 1934 when the Hudson's Bay Company resettled Inuit there from as far away as Cape Dorset. Today it is best known for highly unusual arts and crafts, including hand carvings and Native woven goods dyed with colors derived from local plants and lichens.

But Ernie Lyall liked storytelling the best, he told a Canadian Press reporter, and knew intimately the details of that Hudson's Bay house's haunting.

The woman had been murdered in the middle of winter at an area called The Barrens, between old Fort Ross and Spence Bay. That's where Lyall and a friend found her.

The killers were never apprehended.

The two men packed the body back to the community but immediately hit a snag—the ground was frozen many, many feet deep and would remain so until the brief Arctic summer months away. It would be impossible to inter the body anytime soon. They needed a place inside a building where they could store the body; leaving it outside would subject it to the occasional predators such as wolves or bears. The Hudson's Bay residence was unfinished and thus unheated. Lyall put the woman's body in what would become the living room.

Eventually a memorial service was held and the woman was buried. That's when the troubles began, according to Lyall, who moved into the house when it was completed a few weeks after the funeral.

"We were just starting to sit down to dinner one evening when the outer door opened and we heard footsteps coming into the room, then a person cleared her throat," Lyall said. "We went to see who it was, but there was nobody there."

The repetitious footsteps and throat-clearing continued night after night. And always at dinner time. Lyall became so frustrated that one evening he hid under his desk near the door to try and catch the culprit. Nobody came and he went back to supper. Just as he sat down the door opened and closed.

"That went on every night for the rest of the winter," Lyall said.

The ghost continued to haunt the old Hudson's Bay Company dwelling for long after that.

THE STRANDED OFFICIALS were kept spellbound by Ernie Lyall's stories. He also told them of the mysterious ways of the Inuit medicine man, or shaman.

Lyall spoke of the time he and a companion holed up overnight in one of a group of igloos, or snowhouses, as they were traveling across the open tundra. Hunters build them as temporary shelters. In this igloo, however, the men found a young Inuit girl on the verge of death. A shaman was called by her parents to see if his magic might cure her.

Lyall remembered that night:

"The kid was lying on the one sleeping bench used by the whole family. A pane of clear ice in the side of the snowhouse let in the moonlight.

"When the shaman came in, the moon was shining right through this window and he called down his spirits. They were little dogs that I saw as clear as anything. They came in through that one window, ran down his arm, and jumped to the floor. There were about six or seven of them that circled around the bench where the child lay. Then they ran back up his arm and out the window."

The shaman left and the child fully recovered. Was it the shaman's magic, or the natural healing properties of a strong, young child? Ernie Lyall didn't say, but his listeners probably knew what his answer would be.

Nahkah

The fifty-one residents of Trout Lake, in the southwest corner of the Northwest Territories, easily counted their resident population. But for a period of time in the late 1960s and early 1970s, officials and residents there feared another *being* was lurking nearby, one who seemed to survive quite well away from civilization and on only that which the wilderness could provide.

Did this *thing*, called *Nahkah*, or bush man, by the Native People actually exist? Was it a phantom? Or was it the product of imaginations writ large in a community where the only way in was by bush plane, any other habitation was a hundred miles distant, and muskeg bogs covered the land in all directions?

Those who saw the blond-haired phantom swear he was real. He hid behind cover to spy on residents. One young girl and her brother encountered the Nahkah when they were out chopping wood.

"He was laid down on his face and we didn't see him at first," the girl told a reporter. "But he jumped up and we saw him. He was a big man with no beard. He shaves, I guess. And he was coming toward us, so we just ran away. He had a funny little dog with him."

A blond mystery man who shaves and travels with a small dog. Hardly seems to be the stuff of ghostly terror, but for those in Trout Lake it was a mystery they didn't enjoy.

Other descriptions had him definitely a white man, but wearing camouflage, military–type clothing, and carrying a rifle. Some thought he might be an American deserter from the Vietnam War. He'd been seen or heard over a period of some five years. Families sitting down to supper in their cabins might glimpse a face through a window and then discover footprints when they went outside to confront the stranger; rifle shots would be heard from the distant forest when all the villagers were accounted for; or dogs were set off barking after they saw someone running through the village.

The Royal Canadian Mounted Police were eventually called in when villager fishermen discovered their catches had been taken from their nets, and caribou and moose meat stolen from drying racks outside several houses.

The isolation of Trout Lake led to the most perplexing question of all: Where did this mystery man . . . if it was a man indeed . . . go in the winter? Signs of his presence were seen only in the spring, summer, and fall. Soon after the first snowfalls, he seemed to have vanished. But vanish to where? It's not as if he could steal away to his own snug harbor. Trout Lake is nearly six hundred miles northwest of Edmonton, Alberta. Great Slave Lake separates it from Yellowknife. The nearest other settlement is virtually impossible to reach on foot, so bush planes are the standard transportation in and out of the region. The thermometer tumbles to over sixty degrees below zero in the winter, and ice remains on the lake well into June.

One of those who personally encountered Nahkah was Chief Joseph Jumbo, who at age seventy-seven had seen much in his lifetime and dismissed those who thought the shadowy intruder was imaginary after he had his own encounter with the man.

"I was setting my nets in the mouth of the creek when this man began to whistle at me from the bushes along the bank," Jumbo told a reporter. "I told him I was chief here and if he would come out in the open we would be happy to give him anything he might need—food, clothing, or moccasins. But he would not come out at all and I began to get scared.

"We'd be perfectly happy to leave him alone if that was what he wanted, just so long as we knew who he was and what he was doing. Now we are worried for our kids; he might do something to them. He might grab a child or a young girl."

The villagers continued to watch . . . and wait.

What Cruises Lake Laberge?

There are strange things done in the midnight sun
By fine men who moil for gold;
The Arctic trails have their secret tales
That would make your blood run cold;
The Northern Lights have seen queer sights,
But the queerest they ever did see
Was that night on the marge of Lake Laberge
I cremated Sam McGee

—Robert W. Service, from *The Cremation of Sam McGee*

If the Seven Seas can have a phantom ship known by all as the Flying Dutchman, why not a river in North America with its own ghostly paddle wheel steamer? That is precisely the question one asks upon the discovery of such an inland vessel on the legendary Yukon River where it widens into Lake Laberge, a few miles north of Whitehorse, Yukon Territory. Perhaps the ghost steamer might even have been one of the "queer sights" under the "Northern Lights" that inspired

Robert Service in his classic Yukon poem, "The Cremation of Sam McGee."

The specter steamboat was seen on several occasions going up Lake Laberge toward the Yukon River, according to writer and historian Chappie Chapman.

"The paddle wheel is turning but it does not create a large wave astern as did the old steamers, but in its place it leaves a phosphorescent light after it has passed. On approaching the head of the lake it seems to skim over the sandbars without any trouble, but these bars would have stopped the steamers of days gone by," Chapman wrote.

The ship's name seemed to be written on the pilot house, but the twilight gloom in which the ship was always seen made it hard to decipher the letters. Even stranger is that a few passengers appeared to be huddled together on the upper deck, as if trying to stay warm in the freezing night air.

Chapman believed there were three "candidates" for the ghostly steamship, all of which sunk in Lake Laberge. Although the steamer *A. J. Goddard* was built in San Francisco, it was later taken apart and then transported to Lake Bennett where it was reassembled in 1899, the first paddle wheeler to arrive in Dawson. It ran aground at what came to be known as Goddard's Point, but at only fifteen tons it seemed to be too small to fit the description of the ghost boat.

Taylor and Drew Limited of Whitehorse built and owned a second boat, the paddle wheel steamer *Thistle*. It plied the Pelly and Teslin rivers for many years, supplying frontier outposts along the way. A wind storm sank it in Lake Laberge but, as Chapman noted, there is one very good reason that the *Thistle* is probably not the phantom:

"There was no loss of life (on the *Thistle*) except for a cow that was on the barge the *Thistle* was pushing. . . . As there does not appear to be a ghost cow on the ghost ship, it is hardly likely that our mystery ship is the *Thistle*."

The third ship—and the most likely candidate Chapman suggested—was the *Vidette*, at thirty-four tons certainly large enough to pass for the ghost steamer. It also has an intriguing history. Built at St. Michael in 1898, the vessel was originally called the *Mae West*, but was renamed the *Vidette* when the

Royal Northwest Mounted Police bought it to use as a patrol boat on the Yukon River during the Gold Stampede. The *Vidette* ended its career as a cargo ship on the Stewart River and other tributaries before sinking on Lake Laberge in 1917.

But one episode involving the *Vidette* might indicate a reason for ethereal passengers to mill about on the deck of the ghost ship.

"She was chartered by a man named Envoldsen to make a trip up the Pelly River to Hoole Canyon," Chapman wrote. "He sold tickets to a group of prospectors to go to Hoole Canyon, where he represented that there were many opportunities to stake rich claims. On their arrival at Hoole Canyon they found that due to the high rock walls of the canyon there was only room for one claim and that one was already staked and being worked. The stampeders on the *Vidette* were very angry and were threatening to hang Envoldsen, but he escaped into the bush. Several months later he made his way back to Dawson on foot."

Nothing is known of Envoldsen's eventual fate, but Chapman suggests that those figures sometimes glimpsed on the ship's deck might be the original ill-fated prospectors cheated by Envoldsen and still looking for their lucky strike.

While there have been no recent sightings of the *Vidette*, as far as anyone knows, it may still be plying those historic waters as the few residents along the shore keep a sharp lookout for a gloomy relic of the days when steam-driven paddle wheelers ruled the rivers of North America.

Stranger in the Hen House

Most of us in these early years of the twenty-first century feel far removed in time from the pioneer lifestyles of a century and more ago. Difficult tasks such as clearing the land, planting crops, and raising our own livestock—and all without modern machinery and while the family squeezed into a small log cabin—are as unfamiliar to us as the dark side of the moon. Yet it does seem that the memories of those times, as recollected by the men and women who lived them, remained sharp and focused many decades later.

Even in the most isolated surroundings baffling mysteries might have unfolded that remained forever unsolved and thus forever fixed in the minds of witnesses, as in the case of Iris Couster, of Craven, Saskatchewan, a hamlet northwest of Regina. In published remarks fifty-five years after the events took place, Mrs. Couster recalled a creepy few days during her childhood on a homestead near present-day Leedale, southwest of Edmonton, Alberta, near Gull Lake. As a child, she lived in a two-room cabin with her parents and her brother. As with most homesteaders, the family had to rely on its own quick wits and problem-solving abilities on a day-to-day basis. But sometimes even that wasn't enough. This is her story of a mysterious visitor who may . . . or may *not* have been of flesh and blood:

"It was in early June, 1907, and it had rained for several days. My brother and I were sitting by the window looking out, when we saw a man emerge from the tall timber nearby and pass within a rod (about sixteen and a half feet) of the window. He was tall and wearing a black felt hat. We called our mother and the three of us watched him as he walked down the pathway leading to the half-open door of the hen house and disappeared into the building. Our small dog had seen him and began to bark.

"We kept on watching to see him come out, as in those days homesteads were lonely places. After we had stood there for ten minutes or more, and saw no sign of the man coming out, my mother called to Dad, who was dozing on the bed, and told him that a man had gone into the hen house.

"Dad got up and walked to the hen house; no one was in there. There was only one door to the hen house and if the man had come out we would have seen him. Dad then looked to see if there were any tracks in the mud, but there were none. We all went out and looked for tracks, but couldn't see any. Dad accused the three of us of having too much imagination.

"A month later, in the early evening of a hot July day, Mother and I were standing at the cabin door when our attention was drawn by our small dog letting out a couple of loud barks. We looked, and there, coming through the tall timber, was this same man, who again walked within a rod of us and disappeared into the hen house as before. We were frightened as Dad was away and my younger brother had gone down to the end of the field to bring the cow home. The dog kept up a steady barking. We watched to see if the man came out, but there was no sign of him. Mother was worried because my brother had to pass by the side of the hen house on his way back with the cow.

"Shortly, I saw my brother coming, chasing the cow ahead of him, and he raced into the hen house before we had time to shout to him. The cow's watering pail was kept in the hen house. He came out again, quite unconcerned, and when we questioned him he was surprised, because he had seen no one.

"Several weeks later, a faraway neighbor was visiting us during the afternoon when the same thing happened again. The dog barked and we all were amazed to see the strange man appear, then vanish into the hen house. So we all put on brave fronts and walked down to the hen house. We glanced in every corner of the small structure, but there wasn't a sign of anyone!

"If it had been one person who had seen it, we could have put it down to a hallucination, but the first time there were three of us, the second time two of us, and the third time four of us, including an outsider.

"Mother told the story to different people later on, after we had left the homestead and settled in Saskatchewan, but each person had a different theory. One elderly lady who had lived near that part of the country at the turn of the century told us later that she had heard several men had been murdered there in the early days. Bones had been found on the Edward Dickson farm four miles away in 1904, but they were identified as Indian bones."

Neither Iris Couster nor her parents were ever able to unravel the mystery of the hen house intruder.

Selected Bibliography

BOOKS

Anaya, Rudolfo A. *Teaching From a Hispanic Perspective: A Handbook for Non-Hispanic Educators*. San Diego Office of Education, 1997.

Andrews, Clarence L. *The Story of Sitka*. Seattle: Lowman and Hanford, 1922.

Angell, Madeline. *Red Wing, Minnesota: Saga of a River Town*. Minneapolis: Dillon Press, 1977.

Arctander, John W. *The Lady in Blue: A Sitka Romance*. Seattle: Lowman and Hanford, 1911.

Armitage, Peter, and Gregoire Pien. "*Mary Madeline Nuna Talks About Shaking Tents and Anikunapeu (the Toadman)*. http://www.innu.ca/mmnuna.html, September 23, 1993.

Brimblecom, Deborah. *The Screeching Lady of Marblehead*. Beverly, Mass.: Wilkscraft, Inc., 1976.

Brown, Stephen D. *Haunted Houses of Harpers Ferry*. Harpers Ferry, West Virginia: The Little Brown House Publishing Co., 1976.

Coffin, Tristam Potter, and Hennig Cohen, eds. *The Parade of Heroes*. New York: Anchor Press/Doubleday Publishing Co., 1978.

Comstock, Jim, ed. *West Virginia Encyclopedia, Supplemental Series, vol. 16*. Richwood, West Virginia, 1974.

Dahlgren, Madeleine Vinton. *South Mountain Magic: A Narrative*. Boston: James R. Osgood and Company, 1882.

Dobie, J. Frank, ed. *Straight Texas*. Hatboro, Pennsylvania: Folklore Associates, Inc., 1966.

Drake, Samuel Adams. *A Book of New England Legends and Folklore*. Boston: Little, Brown, and Company, 1901. (Reissued by Singing Tree Press, Book Tower, Detroit, 1969.)

Dumschott, Fred W. *Washington College*. Chestertown, Maryland: Washington College, 1980.

Federal Writers Project. *Maryland: A Guide to the Old Line State*. New York: Oxford University Press, 1940.

Gallagher, Trish. *Ghosts and Haunted Houses of Maryland*. Centreville, Maryland: Tidewater Publishers, 1988.

Gibbs, James A. *Tillamook Light*. Portland: Binford and Mort, 1979.

Gorsuch, Robert Allan. *Folk Tradition in Kent County, Maryland*. Salisbury, Maryland: Shore Press, 1973.

Haining, Peter. *A Dictionary of Ghosts*. London: Robert Hale, Ltd., 1982.

Hamlin, Marie Caroline. *Legends of Le Detroit*. Detroit: Thorndike Nourse, 1884.

Handbook of Texas Online, s.v. "La Llorona." The University of Texas at Austin and the Texas State Historical Association. http://www.tsha.utexas.edu/handbook/online/articles/view/LL/lxl1.html.

Hayes, Joe. *La Llorona: The Weeping Woman*. El Paso, Texas: Cinco Puntos Press, 1987.

Helm, Mike. *Oregon's Ghosts and Monsters*. Eugene, Oregon: Rainy Day Press, 1983.

Hoxie, Frederick E., ed. *Encyclopedia of North American Indians*. New York: Houghton Mifflin, 2000.

Jones, Louis C. *Things That Go Bump in the Night*. Syracuse, N.Y.: Syracuse University Press, 1983.

King, Wendy A. *Clad in Uniform: Women Soldiers of the Civil War*. Collingswood, N.J.: C.W. Historicals, 1992.

Korson, George. *Coal Dust on the Fiddle: Songs and Stories of the Bituminous Industry*. Philadelphia: University of Pennsylvania Press, 1943.

Kushapatshikan: The Shaking Tent. http://www.innu.ca/shaking.html. Web site of the Innu Nation.

Lambert, R.S. *Exploring the Supernatural: The Weird in Canadian Folklore*. London: Arthur Barker, Ltd., 1955.

Landskroener, Marcia C., ed. *Washington: The College at Chester*. Chestertown, Maryland: Literary House Press at Washington College, 2000.

Lerner, Alan Jay. *The Street Where I Live*. New York: W.W. Norton, 1978.

Lyle, Katie Letcher. *The Man Who Wanted Seven Wives*. Chapel Hill, N.C.: Algonquin Books, 1986.

Miles, Dorothy. *The Wizard of Orne Hill and Other Tales of Old Marblehead*. Marblehead, Mass.: Privately published, 1985.

Norman, Michael, and Beth Scott. *Haunted America*. New York: Tor Books, 1994.

——————. *Haunted Heritage*. New York: Tor Books, 2002.

——————. *Historic Haunted America*. New York: Tor Books, 1995.

Rathbone, Alfred Day IV. *The Man With the Catgut Beard*. n.p., n.d.

Rhyne, Nancy. *Coastal Ghosts: Haunted Places from Wilmington, North Carolina, to Savannah, Georgia*. Wilmington, N.C.: East Woods Press, 1985.

Rinehart, Mary Roberts. *My Story*. New York: Farrar and Rinehart, 1931.

Roads, Jr., Samuel. *The History and Traditions of Marblehead*. Marblehead Mass.: Press of N. Allen Lindsey & Co., 1897.

Royal, Margaret, and Ian Girvan, eds. *Local Ghosts*. Bristol, England: Abson Books, 1976.

Scott, Beth, and Michael Norman. *Haunted Heartland*. New York: Warner Books, 1985.

Senate, Richard. *Ghosts of Ventura County*. Ventura, CA: Richard Senate, 1982.

Skinner, Charles M. *American Myths and Legends*. Philadelphia and London: J. B. Lippincott and Company, 1903.

Smith, Susy. *Ghosts Around the House*. New York: The World Publishing Co., 1970.

Thompson, Neil B. *Minnesota's State Capitol: The Art and Politics of a Public Building*. St. Paul: Minnesota Historical Society, 1974.

Tucker, Kathryn Windham. *Jeffrey, Ghost to Ghost*. n.p., n.d.

The Western Literature Association. *Literary History of the American West*. Fort Worth, Texas: Texas Christian University Press, 1987.

Whitaker, Terence. *Haunted England*. Chicago: Contemporary Books, 1987.

Young, Richard Alan, and Judy Dockery Young. *Ghost Stories from the American Southwest*. Little Rock: August House, 1991.

PERIODICALS

"A Capitol plan." Salisbury, Bill. *St. Paul (Minnesota) Pioneer Press*, January 1, 2004.

"A Ghostly Reminder of the Past: The Face-in-the-Door in Main Hall." Hackney, Dorothy. *The Alabamian*, University of Montevallo, October 29, 1993.

"A Haunting Picture?" Lyon, Ellen. *Hagerstown (Maryland) Herald Mail*, October 31, 1993.

"A Murder With a Real Ghost Story." Romine, Dannye. *The Philadelphia Inquirer*, May 14, 1986.

"A Spiritual Force or a Figment of Imagination." Tomaszewski, Dawn. *The Woods*, St. Mary-of-the-Woods College, March 7, 1974.

"A UVM Ghost Story." Citro, Joseph A. *Vermont Quarterly*, Fall 1997.

"An 'Odd Fish' Who Swam Against the Tide." Gilbert, Bil. *Smithsonian Magazine*, January 1999.

"Architect Cass Gilbert had a Capitol Idea." Millet, Larry. *St. Paul (Minnesota) Pioneer Press*, January 2, 2005.

"The Best Little Haunted Houses in Greater Cincinnati." Marsh, Betsa. *Cincinnati Enquirer Magazine*, October 31, 1982.

"Brindle Bull Branded Murder." Scobee, Barry. *The Cattleman*, March 1936.

"Bruce District Has Ghost Scare, Farmers Irked." n.a. *Edmonton (Ontario) Bulletin*, August 29, 1936.

"BSU Ghost Dinah Won't Communicate With Communicators." Hardin, Rosemary. *University News*, Boise State University, October 31, 1988.

"BSU Theatre Haunted by Distraught Ghost." Monroe, Julie. *The Idaho Statesman*, April 25, 1975.

"Bump in the Night at Texas Chancery." n.a. *Green Bay (Wisconsin) Compass*, October 29, 1983.

"Bumps in the Night." Covert, Colin. *Detroit Free Press*, October 26, 1980.

"Capitol Aura Phantasm or Fantasy of Weary Staff?" Dawson, Gary. *St. Paul (Minnesota) Pioneer Press*, September 25, 1991.

"Capitol Marks 100 Years." Ragsdale, Jim. *St. Paul (Minnesota) Pioneer Press*, January 2, 2005.

"Chamber Ghost Keeps Graveyard Shift Awake." Dumbell, Jim. *Raleigh (North Carolina) News and Observer*, August, 1980.

"Come Out and Help Me." Jarrell, Dwight. *Tacoma (Washington) News Tribune*, June 14, 1970.

"Cowal's 'It.' " n.a. *Regina (Saskatchewan) Leader Post*, February 5, 1946.

"Deneen Takes Hold, Begins the Cross-Examination of A.L. Luetgert." n.a. *Chicago Daily Tribune*, January 25, 1898.

"Does Ghost of Adam Bobel Haunt the Boscobel Hotel?" n.a. *Boscobel Dial*, October 29, 1987.

"Even John Barnard Believed the Story of the Screeching Woman," *Marblehead (Massachusetts) Register*, n.d., n.a.

"Faceless Nun Strikes Again." Stokes, Ashley. *The Woods*, St. Mary-of-the-Woods College, October 27, 2004.

"Fire Destroys Cottage in Ghost Neighborhood," n.a. *The Wilmington Advocate*, August 30, 1957.

"Four Months in a Haunted House." Jacobs, Harlan. *Harper's Magazine*, November 1934.

"Gently Rapping." *Calgary (Alberta) Herald*, February 11, 1895.

"George Gives Sorority a Spirited Outlook." Rutherford, Glenn. *Louisville Courier-Journal*, October 30, 1984.

"Gets Back Memory, Luetgert Quick Change on the Redirect Examination." *Chicago Daily Tribune*, January 26, 1898.

"The Ghost Has Her Day in Court." n.a. *Parade Magazine*, January 24, 1982.

"Ghost Legends Continue." Tan, James K.W. *The Alabamian*, University of Montevallo, October 25, 1984.

"The Ghost of Baranov Castle: Folklore or Fakelore." Pierce, Richard A. *Alaska* magazine, May 1970.

"The Ghost of Cline Avenue." George, Philip Brandt. *Indiana Folklore*, various issues.

"The Ghost of Florence Lee." n.a. *College Press Service*, May 13, 1993.

"The Ghost of Gallows Hill." Newber, J. Fred. *Scene Magazine*, February, 1986.

"The Ghost of Old Barkerville?" n.p., July 21, 1945.

"The Ghost of Seiter Hall." Rosdahl, Nils. *North Idaho Sunday*, October 26, 1986.

"The Ghost on The Campus." Swetnam, George. *Pittsburgh Press*, November 1, 1970.

"Ghost Paddle-wheeler Cruises Lake Laberge." Chapman, Chappie. *The Whitehorse (Yukon) Star*, January 6, 1984.

"Ghost Stories." Orton, Matthew. *Montevallo (Alabama) Today*, October 1991.

"Ghost Stories, a Ghoulish Gallery of Indianapolis Haunts." Bell, Steve. *Indianapolis Monthly*, October 1983.

"Ghost Stories Alive in Brodhead." Hirsch, Stephanie. *Monroe (Wisconsin) Evening Times*, August 29, 1989.

"Ghosts Haunt Mrs. Feldt." n.a. *The Regina (Saskatchewan) Standard*, January 6, 1898.

"Ghosts in Boise." n.a. *The Boise Weekly*, October 28, 1993.

"Ghosts in Tacoma? It's no Laughing Matter." Lane, Bob. *Tacoma (Washington) News Tribune*, February 18, 1979.

"Ghosts of Iowa." Lucht, Tracy. *Des Moines (Iowa) Register*, October 19, 1997.

"Ghosts of the Coastal Bend." Ammeson, Jane. *Texas Highways*, October 1983.

"Guilty: Adolph Luetgert Convicted of the Brutal Murder of His Wife Louise." n.a. *Chicago Daily Tribune*, February 10, 1898.

"Halloween Brings Memories of Ghosts." Tan, James K. W. *The Alabamian*, University of Montevallo, October 30, 1986.

"Has a Ghost Made a Haunt of House on 'Hanging Hill'?" Rogers, Dennis. *Wilmington (North Carolina) News and Observer*, n.d.

"The Haunted Inn." Dayton, Scottie. *Wisconsin Trails*, September/October, 2003.

"The Haunted Mirror." Wattam, Julia. *Fate Magazine*, March 1968, n.p.

"Haunting . . . Eerie Tale Inspires Transylvania Campus Ritual." Ward, Joe. *Louisville (Kentucky) Courier-Journal*, October 26, 1974.

"Headless Ghost of the Cape Fear Coast." Steelman, Ben. *Wilmington (North Carolina) Star News*, October 31, 2004.

"Headless Horsewoman Haunts HLMR Troops." Stewart, Ron, and Ric Young, *The Rustler*, King City, California, 1975.

"Historic Marblehead." n.a. *Lynn (Massachusetts) Item*, July 22, 1952.

"Hotel has Everything, Including Own Ghost." Starks, Norm. *Beloit (Wisconsin) Daily News*, July 12, 1989.

"Hotel Loses Its Haunt." Starks, Norm. *Janesville (Wisconsin) Gazette*, January 25, 1991.

"Hundreds Mill Around House in 'Ghost Hunt.'" Associated Press. August 18, 1957.

"Is TVI's JS Building a Haunted House?" McGahie, Amor. *TVI Times* (Albuquerque), October 29, 2002.

"Is Vincent Real? There's a Ghost of a Chance." Associated Press. *Louisville (Kentucky) Times*, November 29, 1980.

"Jilted Lover, Spy Part of Legend." McMahan, Liz. *Muskogee (Oklahoma) Daily Phoenix*, May 26, 1991.

"Johnson Found Not Guilty in Connection With Shooting Death in Seal Hall." n.a., *The Western Catalyst*, Macomb, Illinois, September 26, 1972.

"Jurors in Protest." n.a. *Chicago Daily Tribune*, January 29, 1898.

" 'La Llorana'—An Unfit Mother?" *Las Cruces (New Mexico) Sun-News*, October 30, 1983.

"The Legend of 'The Lady in Lace.' " n.a. *Monterey (California) Peninsula Review*, October 31–November 6, 1974.

"Legends From St. Mary-of-the-Woods College." Crawford, Michael L. *Indiana Folklore* 7, nos.1–2, 1974.

"Luetgert Denies It." *Chicago Daily Tribune*, January 23, 1898.

"Luetgert in Tears." *Chicago Daily Tribune*, January 22, 1898.

"The Man with the Catgut Beard." Rathbone IV, Alfred Day. *Country Life and Sportsman*, April 1938.

"Manslaughter Charged in Shooting." *Courier* News Staff. The. *Western Courier*, Macomb, Illinois, March, 7, 1972.

"Marmaracrian Sketch No. Three Written By Unknown Contributor: To Marblehead Weekly Register in 1831 Relates Legend of Screeching Woman." *Marblehead (Mass.) Register*, nd.

"Montevallo Ghost Stories: Halloween, Time for Ghostly Tales of School History." Maudlin, D. Scott. *The Alabamian*, University of Montevallo, October 25, 1995.

"Montevallo Ghosts Give Spirit to Campus." Stanley, Barbara. *The Alabamian*, University of Montevallo, October 20, 1988.

"A Moonlit Night." Tillotson, Jerry. *Wilmington (North Carolina) Star*, July 31, 1968.

"Moving Objects Spook Cobblestone Workers." Fornear, Margo. *East Troy (Wisconsin) News*, July 14, 1993.

"Mrs. Feldt is Angry." *Chicago Daily Tribune*, January 9, 1898.

"The Mysterious Priest." Harris, Stuart. *Birmingham (Alabama) News*, October 28, 1979.

"Nahkah Terrorizes Indians." Canadian Press. *Vancouver (British Columbia) Sun*, June 7, 1972.

"New Cathedral Already Boasts of Real Ghost." Canadian Press. *Edmonton (Alberta) Bulletin*, April 18, 1929.

"North to Freedom." Kinney, Terry. *Eau Claire (Wisconsin) Leader Telegram*, February 20, 2005.

"On a Clear Evening, Ghosts Walk." Stokes, Ted. *Oregon Journal*, July 1, 1969.

"The Past Still Lives." *The Copy*, n.a. Greater Baltimore Medical Center, October 1980.

"Personal and Otherwise." n.a. *Harper's Magazine*, January 1935.

"Photo of Johnson's Body in Casket, Shows Strange Faces Silhouetted Among Flowers." n.a. *Regina (Saskatchewan) Leader*, February 13, 1926.

"Revealed by the Spirits." n.a. *Ottawa (Ontario) Free Press*, November 24, 1886.

"Round Lake is Rich With Birds, If You Can Get Past the Ghosts," Yochem, Phyllis. *Corpus Christi Caller-Times*, January 14, 2003.

"Sanford Syse, U Speech Prof, Dies at Madison." *River Falls (Wisconsin) Journal*, December 6, 1973.

"Scans Letters to Mrs. Feldt." *Chicago Daily Tribune*, January 8, 1898.

"Scary Places II." Bell, Steve. *Indianapolis Monthly*, October 1984.

"The Screeching Woman." *The Boston Globe*, August 28, 1929.

"Sightings Cause Natives to Flee 'Haunted' Reserve." Canadian Press. November 2, 1995.

"So You Don't Believe in Ghosts?" Kelly, Bernard. *The Denver Post*, Oct. 28, 1963.

"Something Cold at the Foot of the Stairs." Dixon, S.C. *Emporia Journal*, n.d.

"South Mountain–Maryland Campaign." Burnham, Uberto A. *The National Tribune*, 1928.

"Spence Bay Good Ghost Story Spot." Canadian Press. *Lethbridge (Alberta) Herald*, February 5, 1972.

"The Spirit of Cameron Pass." *Canadian Statesman*, Bowmanville, Ontario, June 12, 1889.

"Stage Coach (sic) Inn: Grand Lady Lost." Smith, Wally. *Ventura County (California) Star-Free Press*, May 3, 1970.

"Stagecoach Inn in Conejo Becomes State Landmark." *Ventura County (California) Star-Free Press*, January 3, 1966.

"Stagecoach Inn Will Be Museum." *Ventura County (California) Star-Free Press*, August 11, 1971.

"The Staircase Ghost." Devon, Richard. *FATE Magazine*, n.d.

"State's Sleepy Hollows Rich with Legends of Ghosts." Porterfield, Mannix. *Sunday Gazette-Mail*, Wheeling, West Virginia, October 27, 1985.

"Strange Raps in Empty House." *Edmonton (Alberta) Bulletin*, July 28, 1928.

"Student Fatally Shot at Western." n.a. *The McDonough Times*, Macomb, Illinois, March 2, 1972.

"Study of Luetgert." n.a. *Chicago Daily Tribune*, January 31, 1898.

"Subal Spectre Jilted Again." n.a. *University News*, Boise State University, November 3, 1983.

"There's a Creak and a Clatter . . ." Erickson, Jim. *Tacoma (Washington) News Tribune*, October 31, 1981.

"Things That Go Bump in the Night." Miller, Steven G. *Surratt Courier*, November 1986, Surratt House and Tavern, Clinton, Maryland.

"Things That Go Bump in the Night: Frazier Haunted by Prankster." n.a. *Idaho State University Bengal*, October 31, 1986.

"This Grande Dame, at 100, Needs Minnesota's Help." Sturdevant, Lori. *Minneapolis (Minnesota) Star Tribune*, January 2, 2005.

"Tracking an Assassin." Mark, Sarah. *Washington Post*, Washington, D.C., April 14, 1995.

"Tradition or Apparition? Ghastly Rumors of Gates Hall Ghost still Haunting Panhandle University." Hamilton, Phillip L. *Austin (Texas) American Statesman* and The Associated Press, March 1993.

"Unexplained." Couster, Irish. *News of the North's Western Weekly Supplement*, Yellowknife, NWT, January 2, 1963.

"The Unexplained." Bell, Margaret C. *News of the North*, Yellowknife, Northwest Territories, Canada, June 29, 1966.

"Usual Hauntings." Wolfrom, Mindy. *North Idaho College Sentinel*, October 25, 2000.

"Visit From Beyond." Kalies, Cynthia. *Oconto Falls (Wisconsin) Times-Herald*, August 3–9, 2003.

"Weird Occurrences at Point Lookout." Norris, Joseph. *The Enterprise*, n.d., Lexington Park, Maryland.

"Who Could It Be, This Ghost of Capitol Past?" Dornfeld, Steven. *St. Paul (Minnesota) Pioneer Press*, October 17, 1991.

"Who's Afraid of Ghosts?" Coleman, Dorcas. *The Natural Resources*, Department of Natural Resources, Annapolis, Maryland, Fall 2001.

"With the Ghost Gone, Family Home is Silent." Robinette, Gale B. *Entertainment Puget Sound*, October 29, 1982.

"WIU Student Charged with Voluntary Manslaughter in Connection with Seale (sic) Hall Shooting Last Week." Neven, Bill. *The Western Catalyst*, Macomb, Illinois, March 7, 1972.

"Wraiths That Stalk Abroad on Both Sides of the Ocean." *The Philadelphia Press*, September 13, 1896.

"You Will Believe: Ghosts on Campus." Dowling, Katie. *The Elm*, Washington College, March 24, 1999.

UNPUBLISHED WORKS

Freymann, Sarah H. "Untitled Folklore Project." Unpublished manuscript, 1976, University of Vermont.

Gause, Lynne. "The Ghost of the Price-Jones-Gause House." Unpublished manuscript, n.d.

"Legend of Converse Hall, The." Unpublished manuscript, n.d., University of Vermont.

Millman, Lawrence. "An Icelandic Snake Story." Unpublished manuscript, 2000.

Neal, William Parker. "History of Emmanuel Chapel." Unpublished manuscript, Penn State University–Mont Alto, n.d.

"Screeching Woman of Oakum Bay, The." n.d, n.p.

WPA (Colorado) Writers Project Files, "Folklore, No. F-16, Superstitions; the Supernatural; Ghost Stories, 1936–1942."

WPA Historical Survey of The Monterey Peninsula, Project #4080, "Mystery of the White Horse and Rider at Carmel Mission." Personal interview with Antonio Machado, Carmel, California, November 12, 1936.

WEB SITES

Armitage, Peter, and Gregoire, Pien, *Mary Madeline Nuna Talks About Shaking Tents and Anikunapeu (the Toadman)*, http://www.innu.ca/mmnuna.html, September 23, 1993.

Buffalo, Paul. "Spiritual Doctoring, Tipi-Shaking and Bone-Swallowing Specialists." s.v. *When Everybody Called Me Gay-*

Bay-Bi-Nayss: "Forever-Flying-Bird: An Ethnographic Biography of Paul Peter Peter Buffalo." Interview with Tim Roufs. University of Minnesota. http://www.d.umn/cla/faculty/troufs/Buffalo/PB32.html.

Handbook of Texas Online, s.v. "La Llorona," http://www.tsha.utexas.edu/handbook/online/articles/view/LL/lxll.html.

Kushapatshikan: The Shaking Tent, http://www.innu.ca/shaking.html. Web site of the Innu Nation.

The Shaking Tent, s.v. "Orogenetics" http://www.desk.nl/~northam/oro/animist/hta.htm.

Teaching from a Hispanic Perspective, s.v. "La Llorona—A Hispanic Legend" http://literacynet.org/lp/hperspectives/llorona.html.

Willard Library, Evansville, Indiana "Ghost Cam," http://www.libraryghost.com.

Index of Place Names